BEYOND GOLD
AND DIAMONDS

SUNY series, Studies in the Long Nineteenth Century
—————————
Pamela K. Gilbert, editor

BEYOND GOLD AND DIAMONDS

Genre, the Authorial Informant, and the British South African Novel

MELISSA FREE

Cover illustration adapted from *The Story of "South Africa" Newspaper and Its Founder, Told by Others*, South Africa, 1903, opposite contents, *Internet Archive*, archive.org/details/storyofsouthafri00londuoft/page/n6/mode/1up. Cover design by Patrick W. Berry.

Published by State University of New York Press, Albany

© 2021 State University of New York

All rights reserved

Printed in the United States of America

No part of this book may be used or reproduced in any manner whatsoever without written permission. No part of this book may be stored in a retrieval system or transmitted in any form or by any means including electronic, electrostatic, magnetic tape, mechanical, photocopying, recording, or otherwise without the prior permission in writing of the publisher.

For information, contact State University of New York Press, Albany, NY
www.sunypress.edu

Library of Congress Cataloging-in-Publication Data

Name: Free, Melissa, author.
Title: Beyond gold and diamonds : genre, the authorial informant, and the British South African novel / Melissa Free, author.
Description: Albany : State University of New York Press, [2021] | Series: SUNY series, Studies in the Long Nineteenth Century | Includes bibliographical references and index.
Identifiers: ISBN 9781438481531 (hardcover : alk. paper) | ISBN 9781438481524 (pbk. : alk. paper) | ISBN 9781438481548 (ebook)
Further information is available at the Library of Congress.

10 9 8 7 6 5 4 3 2 1

For my parents, Gayle Covey and Steven Devico
6x

Contents

List of Illustrations   ix

Acknowledgments   xi

A Note on Terminology   xv

Introduction
A Single Frame: Southern Africa, Britain, and the Authorial Informant   1

Chapter 1
Preterdomesticity and the South African Farm: Women Old and New   19

Chapter 2
"It Is I Who Have the Power": The Female Colonial Romance   61

Chapter 3
Colony of Dreadful Delight: Gertrude Page and the Rhodesian Settler Romance   107

Chapter 4
"There Will Be No More Kings in Africa": Foreclosing Darkness in *Prester John*   135

Epilogue
Beyond the British South African Novel   155

Notes	173
Works Cited	237
Index	261

Illustrations

Map	From *A History of South Africa*, by Dorothea Fairbridge	xiv
I.1	*South Africa: A Weekly Journal for All Interested in South African Affairs*	2
1.1	Advertisement for one of the four film versions of *Jess* produced between 1905 and 1917	22
2.1	"The Zulu leapt into the air"	93
3.1	From Page to screen	108
3.2	Page in the company of Kipling and Haggard	109
3.3	Gertrude Page	112
3.4	Gertrude Page in modern attire	129

Acknowledgments

Joe Valente, Antoinette Burton, and Jed Esty have inspired every page of this manuscript. My gratitude at having been able to work with them is beyond measure.

Patrick W. Berry, Pat Kennedy, and Joe Corless have been consistent, generous, loving allies. They have championed my work and enhanced every aspect of my life. I aspire not only to think like them but also to be like them.

I am grateful for the time and insight of more readers than I can remember, but I will try. Friends, peers, and colleagues who have read and commented on multiple drafts of the manuscript include Peter Garrett, Terra Walston Joseph, Keguro Macharia, Danielle Kinsey (who came up with the title of chapter 3), Praseeda Gopinath, Don LePan, Elizabeth Horan, Dan Bivona, Ron Broglio, Tobias Harper, and Christine Holbo. Others who have read and advised me on some of the work include Jay Michael Lane, Rachel Ablow, Mike Goode, Supritha Raja, Coran Klaver, Ann Colley, Kevin Morrison, Libby Tucker Gould, Scott Henkel, Nicholas D. Nace, Juliet John, Isaac Joslin, Leila May, and Cannon Schmitt. Paul Cox, curator of the Woburn Sands Collection, shared with me what he knew of Gertrude Page.

Friends and family who have supported and encouraged me include Sho-Yin Chen-Berry, Emma Berry, Catherine Lidov, Jodi Marshall, Ellis Bacon Jr., Alex Crump, Amanda Roth Klaas, Katherine Piatti, Bob Swinford, Katrina Royce-Malmgren, Beppe Cuello, the Nieves family, Corrine Whitmore, Virginia Shirley, Deb Hibbard, Matt LaBarre, Marnie Jostes, Brad Irish, Marie Webb, Tracy Morehouse, Tara Ison, Matt Cordial, and the Night Squad, especially Margery Rose-Clapp, Melanie and Alice Spatgen, Lisa Chamberlain, Cheryl Gibson, Cynthia and Blueberry Lim, and Marc

Leichter. Cheryl Lawyer got me over the finish line when I hit the wall; she kept me sane and laughing these last long miles.

My sweet grandfather Perley Covey sent me a $100 a month to assist with living expenses when I started my doctoral program. He gave me what he called a fifty percent "raise" two years later. I miss him and wish that I could put this book in his hands. My little Uncle Danny and my grandmother Julia Covey are a part of all that I do. Dottie Buttler, Maureen and Bob Edelblut, and Geline Covey believed in me and told me so.

My mom, Gayle Covey, and my dad, Steven Devico, are in a class by themselves. My mom got me my first library card and ensured that I received the best education possible—at Caedmon, Chapin, Duke, North Carolina State University, and the University of Illinois at Urbana–Champaign. My dad put me first more times that I can count, and more, I am sure, than I will ever know. They were major donors not only to my education but also to my health and happiness.

Miss Judith Phelps made me want to be an English major. Professor George Williams made me accountable. And Carol Neely bought me time. Charlotte Brontë made me fall in love with words on a page, particularly those placed there in the nineteenth century. The work of Anne McClintock and Laura Chrisman set me on the path to this manuscript.

My four-leggeds—Pumpkin, Grimmy, Barack O'Bunny, Munchkin, Odie, and Opal—reminded me that what really matters is a warm place to sleep, a romp out of doors, and some occasional cuddles.

The project has received support from the English departments at the University of Illinois at Urbana-Champaign, Binghamton University, State University of New York, and Arizona State University; the Graduate College, the Illinois Program for Research in the Humanities, and the Unit for Criticism and Interpretive Theory, all at the University of Illinois; and State University of New York / United University Professions. It has also benefited from the anonymous readers and editorial team at State University of New York Press. The epilogue, in particular, has been substantially improved by the readers' suggestions.

This book would not be what it is without interlibrary loan. Those who work there are the unsung heroes of good research. I am grateful to the interlibrary loan departments at my home institutions, the University of Illinois, Binghamton University, and Arizona State University, as well as at other departments, where people whose names I will never know pulled, scanned, and packaged material.

Portions of the introduction and of chapters 1, 2, and 3 include revisions of material that was previously published as "British Women Wanted:

Gender, Genre, and South African Settlement," *The Oxford Handbook of Victorian Literary Culture*, ed. Juliet John, Oxford UP, 2016, 284–309. It is reproduced here by permission of Oxford University Press (global.oup.com/academic/product/the-oxford-handbook-of-victorian-literary-culture-9780199593736?cc=us&lang=en&). Chapter 2 also contains revisions of material that was previously published as "'It Is I Who Have the Power': Settling Women in Haggard's South African Imaginary," *Genre*, vol. 45, no. 3, Fall 2012, 359–93.

Beyond Gold and Diamonds, long in the writing, is even longer in the making. Its roots lie in my experience as a teenage backpacker, seated at a café in Greece with a young white South African woman. It was the tail end of apartheid, and when the waiter, whose ethnicity and nationality I do not know, discovered where my companion Helena was from, he refused to serve her, a gesture of disapproval for her country's racist policies. I can still picture her face, the pain at being held accountable for a system she abhorred vying with . . . gratitude? relief? approval? (there is no right word) . . . that the outside world was finally putting appropriate pressure on South Africa to end apartheid. Many years later, when I read Olive Schreiner's *The Story of an African Farm* for the first time, I was struck by how absolutely Lyndall saw herself as English, despite never having been to England. Though I would later learn that for most South Africans in the period English denoted British lineage, Lyndall's identification was more than a name; it was also a desire. I have often wondered how these two pieces fit together, or perhaps why it is that I hold them together in my mind. In my memory, a late twentieth-century young South African woman feels she cannot claim her own identity because it is linked to a system of oppression that she opposes. In Schreiner's novel, a late nineteenth-century young South African woman claims an identity not truly her own because it affords her privilege. For Helena and Lyndall, both white women of British descent, South Africa was the home that could never be home.

It is this paradox that *Beyond Gold and Diamonds* seeks to explore. It does so primarily through the authorial informant, who is herself always only partially at home, as she is also always partially in exile. Perhaps that is why generic innovation was so key to her: it was a means not only to negotiate sociopolitical challenges but also to explore new terrain in the hopes of someday locating herself. Schreiner, Haggard, Page, and Buchan—each has a foot in two worlds but is standing wholly in neither, which is precisely how we might describe British South African literature.

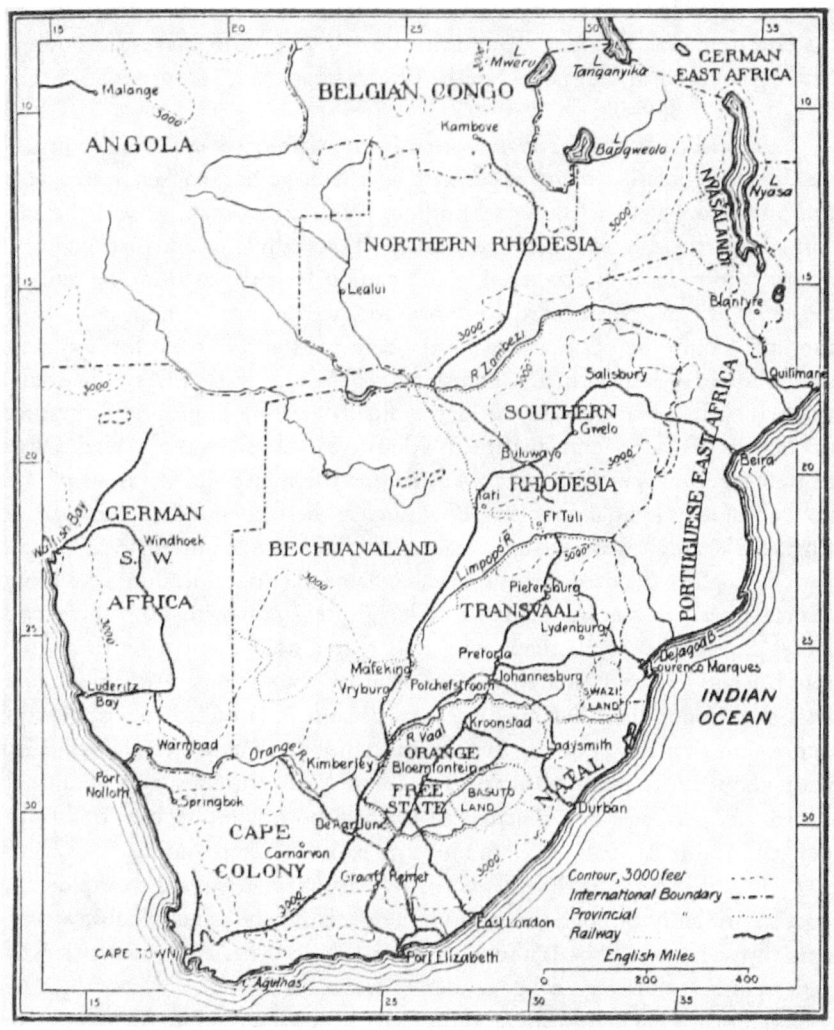

Map. Source: Dorothea Fairbridge, *A History of South Africa*, Oxford UP, 1918, page 269.

A Note on Terminology

Dutch/Boer/Afrikaner

The population of primarily Dutch, German, and French Huguenot descendants in southern Africa was known as Dutch or Boer, meaning farmer, until the end of the nineteenth century. From that point on, Afrikaner, meaning African, was its preferred term.

Dutch / the *taal* /Afrikaans

The Dutch originally spoken by colonists in southern Africa morphed over time through contact with other languages, both European and indigenous. Though the Boers called their language the *taal*, meaning language, the British most often referred to it as Dutch. By the turn of the twentieth century, the language was pretty close to modern Afrikaans, which was made an official language of South Africa in 1925.

Indigenous Proper Names

Consistency is impossible. Modern usage frequently differs from earlier usage, as in Ndebele/Matabele. Even within earlier usage, there is variation. For instance John Buchan employs Mosilikatse, while Sol T. Plaatje employs Mzilikazi, and still others employ Moselekatse. Some terms were not used by the very groups they were meant to denote, as with Hottentot (Khoikhoi) and Bushmen (San). I generally use the terminology of the author I am discussing, sometimes followed by the more contemporary name in parentheses. During the colonial period, whites in southern Africa used the term

Kaffir to denote Bantu peoples. By the turn of the twentieth century, they had begun using it to denote blacks more broadly. By the middle of the twentieth century, kaffir (most often in lower case) had become a strictly pejorative term.

South Africa / Southern Africa / South African

By South Africa the British of the period meant "the great cone of land projected southward between the Southern Atlantic and the Indian Ocean," with the Zambezi River serving as a rough northern limit.[1] I use southern Africa. Both South Africa and southern Africa generally denote indigenous land, the Dutch republics, and British territory, inclusive of Rhodesia, which became self-governing in 1923 after twice declining to join the Union of South Africa, formed in 1910. When referring specifically to the Union, I use South Africa. I employ South African rather than southern African as a possessive for both region and country (Union).

Introduction

A Single Frame:
Southern Africa, Britain, and the Authorial Informant

Shortly after her arrival in London in 1895, Poppy Destin, the heroine of Cynthia Stockley's 1910 novel, *Poppy: The Story of a South African Girl*, catches a glimpse of her former home, on a street corner outside a

> paper shop, which had many news-boards exposed, with the "sheets" hanging . . . from them. One yellow sheet stood out boldly with the words "*South Africa*" in black letters across it. A pang of joy shot through her. She could have fallen down before that . . . paper and kissed the magic words. The name of her own land![1]

Poppy and those like her, who were situated in the metropole but interested in southern Africa, would have had access to over half a dozen weeklies that focused specifically on the region.[2] The paper that catches Poppy's attention is most likely *South Africa: A Weekly Journal for All Interested in South African Affairs*. Begun in 1889 by Edward P. Mathers, Englishman, established journalist, book author, and Fellow of the Royal Geographical Society, *South Africa* had the "largest circulation of any South African newspaper."[3] Written for "all classes interested in and resident in South Africa," the paper had its headquarters in London and was shipped weekly to Cape Town for South African distribution.[4] Available by subscription, it was also "on sale at all bookstalls throughout the United Kingdom" and at "newsagents in all South African centres."[5]

Figure I.1. *South Africa: A Weekly Journal for All Interested in South African Affairs.* Source: *The Story of "South Africa" Newspaper and Its Founder, Told by Others,* South Africa, 1903, page 17, *Internet Archive,* archive.org/details/storyofsouthafri00londuoft/page/16.

On its front page, beneath the title that captured her eye, Poppy would have seen an impossible image: St. Paul's Cathedral and Table Mountain set against the same horizon, above which the rising sun cast its many rays.[6] In the inlet by the famous Cape landmark, Poppy would have spied two or three ships whose sails bore the names of South African resources: coal, feathers, copper, diamonds, wool, silver, and gold. Lower still, she might have noticed columns listing the names of southern Africa's several regions—Cape Colony, Transvaal, Natal, Orange Free State, and Rhodesia—and their most prominent cities. Finally, her gaze might have been drawn to the bottom of the masthead, where the key features of the journal were often listed in succession: commerce, finance, industries, mining, agriculture, politics, society, and exploration. Over the years this quarter-page header varied slightly: figures were added to or removed from the South African coastline, St. Paul's was flanked by smaller buildings or stood alone, the items emblazoned on the ships' sails changed and were rearranged, the names and numbers of the regions (whether British colonies or Dutch [Boer] republics) and cities altered, and the list of the journal's categories was sometimes omitted.[7] But in the early years of *South Africa*'s publication the overriding message was the same: the ships pictured crossing between southern Africa and Britain, captured in a single frame, carried not only colonial resources and metropolitan emigrants but also Britishness, in both directions.

Southern Africa's emergence from the sidelines to the foreground of imperial consciousness was at once a material and a discursive event. Though the region had been under British control since 1806 and the first major influx of British emigrants took place in 1820, it was not until the discovery of its vast mineral wealth decades later—diamonds in the 1860s and gold in the 1880s—that Britons really turned their attention there.[8] As investors, prospectors, and emigrants undertook the roughly three-week, six-thousand-mile journey from Southampton to Cape Town, the "most stagnant of colonial regions suddenly exploded into activity."[9] The white population swelled from approximately a quarter of a million in 1865, before the start of the mineral revolution, to 1.117 million in 1904.[10] Urban centers, the mining industry, the colonial administration, and the economy grew exponentially. As Britain's commitment to securing dominance throughout the region intensified, so, too, did tensions with both indigenous Africans and the (mostly) agrarian Boer population, whose (mostly) Dutch, German, and French ancestors preceded them there by well over a century.[11] The British fought the Anglo-Zulu War (1879), the First Anglo-Boer War (1880–1881), the First Matabele War (1893–1894), the Second Matabele War (1896–1897), and the Second Anglo-Boer War (1899–1902).[12] In the name of Queen Victoria, Cecil Rhodes's British South Africa Company seized most of Matabeleland and Mashonaland in the 1890s. The white population of Rhodesia—as the territory would be named in 1895—grew from less than two hundred in 1890 to nearly forty-eight thousand by 1930.[13] The British acquired the Transvaal (South African Republic) and Orange River Colony (Orange Free State) from the Boers in 1902. The Union of South Africa, which officially joined the Transvaal, Orange River, Cape, and Natal, was debated, enacted, and in 1910 finally formed. At the same time, a generation of fiction writers was creating a southern Africa of the imagination, a place in which, for the British, greater challenges yielded greater authority, not least for women.

The discursive production of British southern Africa was in large part the work of those whom I term *authorial informants*, British authors who spent significant time in the region and wrote about it as insiders. Claiming both an expertise predicated on and an identity enhanced by South African Britishness, these writers include H. Rider Haggard, southern Africa's most popular novelist; Gertrude Page, Rhodesia's first famous novelist; and John Buchan, whose best known protagonist spent three decades in southern Africa. For these best-selling writers, living in southern Africa was authorizing: British identity, they suggested, was more authentic, because more comprehensive, when informed by colonial experience. It was also generative: using generic innovation to contend with such sociopolitical issues as female authority, Boer political power, African nationalism, and European ambition, Haggard, Page, and Buchan introduced, respectively, the female colonial romance, the Rhodesian settler romance, and the modern spy thriller. Southern Africa's first famous novelist was not an authorial informant, but the colonial-born Olive Schreiner. Like Haggard, Page, and Buchan, Schreiner spent time in both southern Africa and Britain, was viewed by metropolitans as an expert on the former, and used generic innovation to explore sociopolitical issues. For this self-described "English South African," southern Africa's promise fell short, but her frustration nonetheless engendered the New Woman novel.[14] Tracing the ways in which genre enabled each of these authors to negotiate cultural and political concerns through a distinctly British South African lens, *Beyond Gold and Diamonds* functions as a literary history in a double sense: it reads British South African literature as a field, one that overlaps with but exists apart from both a national South African literary tradition and a tradition of South African literature in English, and it demonstrates how southern Africa shaped British literature.

As constructed by authorial informants, southern Africa has little in common with either the "undiscovered" Africa of the early and mid-Victorian imagination or the Belgian Congo of Joseph Conrad's *Heart of Darkness* (1899/1901), the default text of Victorian, modernist, and postcolonial studies for interpreting British perceptions of Africa in this period. Self-styled experts, authorial informants characterize southern Africa not by darkness but by light, not by regression but by progression, not by danger but by opportunity, not by indigeneity but by Britishness. Frequently referred to as a "white man's country" and considered not only geographically and "environmentally" but also essentially "separate from the Dark Continent," southern Africa, as the British saw it, was "suited to the white man's occupation the further . . . south" one went.[15] Resplendent with the dazzle of the Victoria Falls, the sparkle of Kimberley diamonds, the gleam of Transvaal gold, the coruscation of captured sunlight reflecting from mirrors held by Cape colonists along the shore as they welcomed new arrivals, by the 1880s Africa's "southernmost sixth" was no longer a shadow at the edge of the map; by the end of the century "every London shopboy" was familiar with its landscape.[16]

Perhaps the most significant distinction between "darkest Africa" and discursive southern Africa is the way in which each interacts with Britishness.[17] In *Heart of Darkness* the best an Englishman can do is not regress. Conrad's story famously depicts the subsumption of Western values by African primitivity leading ultimately to the consumption of the metropolitan himself. Marlow succeeds by managing not to descend, unlike Kurtz, into the "black and incomprehensible frenzy" along whose edge he rides.[18] The impotent witness of good conscience, he maintains his "original" identity in the face of the rapacious imperialist and the primitive "native."[19] The triangulation in southern Africa is different. There, the Boers, an independent largely European-descended population, are cast as regressive, as evinced by their rejection of capitalism, disregard for education, dislike of the British, "heartlessness" toward the indigenous, and nomadic pastoralism; the indigenous Africans as absent, unthreatening, or conquerable; and the British as self-actualizing.[20]

Nonetheless, the literature of southern Africa's authorial informants lacks the "paradise complex" that is the hallmark of "booster literature," a tendentious genre written to encourage colonial emigration.[21] Exploring shifts in gender dynamics, African politics, and both metro-colonial and Anglo-European relations through generic innovation, southern Africa's authorial informants imaginatively redirect potentially threatening authority toward imperial ends. Schreiner also engages in generic play, but with different motives and toward different ends; grappling with her ambivalent subject position as a South African–born white woman, she challenges the notion that meaningful authority is available to British colonial women.[22] The concerns of these writers yield new generic forms that circulate in colony and metropole alike, anticipating and influencing developments in British literature more broadly.

The Authorial Informant

The authorial informant—and Schreiner's authority—is enabled by the late nineteenth-century convergence of a number of factors that can be loosely grouped as: a) the rise of "the cult of the specialist or the 'expert'" and "the cult of personality"; b) the "the new literacy of the lower classes," the growing power of the popular press, and "the easy transactions between fiction-writing and popular journalism"; and c) the increase in both "the visibility within popular culture of the imperial project" and the value placed on colonial experience.[23] So while Dickens was a famous author known *to write about* social issues, Haggard was a famous author known *to be an expert* on southern Africa. While divisions between fiction and nonfiction had never been hard and fast, a broader readership eager to consume accessible and often sensational journalism made those lines even finer and looser. While Britain's imperial enterprise had long been intrinsic to British identity, its increasingly self-conscious addition of territory—manifest most ostensibly in the "scramble for Africa"—meant that Britons could no longer claim that their empire had been acquired "in a fit of absence of mind."[24] While colonists had historically been viewed as "offshoots of the national centre," this was decreasingly the case as the century waned.[25] And while so often in the literature of the authorial informant "an English colonist is an Englishman [or -woman] improved," the authorial informant him- or herself was even more so.[26]

The concept of the authorial informant plays with that of the "native informant," introduced by Gayatri Chakravorty Spivak. The latter refers to a colonized subject who provides insight to the colonizer about his "and occasionally" her native culture, and though he or she usually accrues certain privileges in doing so, the native informant is always subordinate to the colonizer.[27] At the same time, the native informant communicates the colonizer's values to the colonized. He or she is thus a kind of middleman or -woman. So, too, is the authorial informant. But while both the authorial informant and the native informant claim an expanded identity, the latter occupies only one imperial subject position—that of the colonized—while the former occupies two—that of both colonial and colonizer.[28] This position is illustrated by a recruitment speech Haggard delivered in 1914 in his hometown of Ditchingham, Norfolk just after the outbreak of World War I. "The England you know," he told his listeners, "is not all England. There are many Englands beyond the seas, and it so happens that I am able to bring you a message from some of them." His "Call to Arms" to defend not one but "many Englands" hinges on his authority to speak not only to but also for and about the British.[29] As a metropolitan, Haggard addressed locals as one of their own, in the very county in which he was born. As a former resident of southern Africa, he also represented colonials, particularly South Africans, as a colonial advocate. Asserting less a dual than an enhanced British identity, Haggard averred a greater knowledge of Britain than both those to and those for whom he delivered his "message."

The expertise of authorial informants was assumed by as well as attributed to them. Unsolicited and by invitation alike, they expressed their views on strategies, circumstances, and events in, about, and affecting southern Africa—in speeches, essays, letters to the editor, interviews, and columns, and even as political candidates.[30] As Paula M. Krebs has argued in her study of public discourse during the Second Anglo-Boer War, "literary figures who were . . . directly addressing empire in their fiction were called upon to address imperial questions in the press as well."[31] This is as true of Haggard, who was approached by both the *Times* and the *Daily Express* to write about the war, as it is of the South African–born Schreiner.[32] Their experience was not only more extensive than that of someone who, after a "flying visit" to a colony, would "go home and write special articles and things as connoisseurs," which are essentially "superficial," it was also less general and more sustained than that of someone like Anthony Trollope, who made lengthy visits to, then wrote entire books about colonial regions, including southern Africa.[33] Where Trollope's writing belies any colonial affiliation, one sees, at times even feels, in the writing of southern Africa's authorial informants that the region is a part of them.[34]

The translocal, another term deployed in postcolonial studies, further helps to elucidate the authorial informant. As theorized by Tony Ballantyne and Antoinette Burton, the translocal suggests movement, exchange, and transformation across the "webs of empire."[35] If a contact zone is a place or space, transculturation a process, and hybridity a result, the translocal, necessarily kinetic, is all three at once.[36] Applied to the authors and texts that are the subject of this study, the translocal provides a framework for reading beyond the bounds of national histories—British, South African, and Rhodesian—in order to examine the interdependence of national and imperial cultural formations.[37] Not only did Schreiner, Haggard, Page, and Buchan spend significant time in both southern Africa and Britain, at various points each thought the former might be or become his or her permanent home.

When not in southern Africa, these writers occupied a position we might call *colonial exile*. Whether colonial born, like Schreiner, or colonial adjacent, like Haggard, Page, and Buchan, whose extended time in the region compelled their identification with it, the colonial exile is incomplete when elsewhere, even as he or she has been enhanced by colonial experience. Often, the colonial exile speaks or writes, like Page, of "yearning" to return.[38] "Whoever has once drunk Vaal [River] water, says the proverb, will always return," writes Buchan in his autobiography. "Who wears *veld-schoens* [leather sandals] will return to the veld," claims the narrator of Stockley's *Wild Honey* (1914). "Once the Golden Land gets its grip on the heart-strings, there is no settling down happily" in England, notes an anonymous writer in *South Africa*.[39] Lilias Rider Haggard wrote of her father: "For Africa he was always homesick." Allan Quatermain, his most famous character, describes the feeling as "a great craving." Haggard himself ascribed the very existence of his African fiction to this "longing," for it was when "the 'pull' of Africa got hold of me, [that] I began to write." He returned briefly just twice, and though he professed, "I should like to end my days in Africa," he did not.[40] Neither did Buchan, who died in Canada while serving as its first governor general, a position he had hoped to hold in South Africa.[41] Both Schreiner and Page died and were buried in southern Africa. But all of these writers carried the region with them, as their writing so clearly bears out.

Why British South African Literature?

Recent historiography has "raise[d] the profile of the specific form of imperialism known as settler colonialism."[42] This includes John Darwin's *The Empire Project: The Rise and Fall of the British World-System, 1830–1970* (2009), which conveys the "inter-dependence" of empire's constituent parts and locations, particularly in terms of economics, and James Belich's *Replenishing the Earth: The Settler Revolution and the Rise of the Anglo-World, 1783–1939* (2009), which describes the "the nineteenth-century long-range mass transfer of goods and people[,] . . . money, information, and technical knowledge" as a "revolution."[43] Thoroughly researched and vast in scope, both are, nonetheless, exceedingly thin on culture. The new imperial history has drawn attention to the mutually constitutive nature of colony and metropole, the imbrication of the cultural and the political, and the webs of communication and exchange that crisscrossed the empire.[44] Until fairly recently, however, it has had little say about settler colonialism, as distinct from incipient nationalism.[45] Two exemplary collections that are rich in cultural analysis, interdisciplinary in methodology, and attentive to both gender and race are Philippa Levine's *Gender and Empire* (2004) and Annie E. Coombes's *Rethinking Settler Colonialism: History and Memory in Australia, Canada, Aotearoa New Zealand, and South Africa* (2006).[46] Surprisingly little space, however, is given in either to colonial southern Africa.

Literary scholarship that offers close readings of colonial discourse while attending to the networks of empire has tended to treat India, a colony of occupation, "as the definitive site of British imperial culture," and to privilege the metropolitan writer.[47] Literary critical examination of settler colonialism is at last, however, on the rise. Jude Piesse's *British Settler Emigration in Print, 1832–1877* (2016), a study of the ways that both "mainstream" and "feminist and radical" metropolitan periodicals depicted settler emigration in the early and mid-Victorian period, is a welcome contribution; it should be noted, however, that it "sets out to tell the story of [early-mid Victorian] settler emigration history from a metropolitan, British point of view."⁴⁸ Focusing on almost precisely the same period, Jason R. Rudy mines colonial archives in *Imagined Homelands: British Poetry in the Colonies* (2017). Though an important book, it gives more attention to "the transportation and adaptation of British culture" than to "the emergence of new traditions" or, correlatively, colonial influence on metropolitan literature.⁴⁹ "Highlighting settler colonialism's neglected cultural significance," Tamara S. Wagner has done a great deal to develop settler colonial studies. Her edited collection *Victorian Settler Narratives: Emigrants, Cosmopolitans and Returnees in Nineteenth-Century Literature* (2011) does some important feminist recovery work, though its attention to both race and southern Africa is negligible. *Domestic Fiction in Colonial Australia and New Zealand* (2015), which Wagner also edited, and *Victorian Narratives of Failed Emigration: Settlers, Returnees, and Nineteenth-Century Literature in English* (2016), her recent monograph, continue to expand the field in their discussion of colonial as well as metropolitan writers, but they, too, sideline southern Africa.⁵⁰ If Wagner's primary interest is the Antipodes, she is not alone; scholarship on settler colonial discourse in recent years has favored this region.⁵¹ Two decades ago, Laura Chrisman observed that "South Africa . . . occupies a marginalized place in cultural studies of British imperialism."⁵² Unfortunately, this remains the case.

Between the formation of the Union and the first democratic elections in 1994, monographs on South African literature generally focused on either "white writing," writing by Afrikaners (whether in Afrikaans or English) or by South Africans of British descent; "black writing," writing by indigenous Africans; or the writing of a single indigenous ethnic group.⁵³ Manfred Nathan's *South African Literature: A General Survey* (1925), which discusses both Afrikaans and English literature, was the first of its kind. He "regard[s] as South African literature that which is *in or of South Africa*."⁵⁴ This includes not only those "born in South Africa [or] who have spent all or most of their lives there" but also "those writers who have resided in South Africa for a period sufficiently long to enable them to be regarded as speaking with authority on South African affairs, or to have assimilated the local atmosphere sufficiently for the purpose of describing South African life at firsthand, and with more less of fidelity [*sic*]."⁵⁵ Though Nathan includes Schreiner, Haggard, and Page, he mentions Buchan only briefly, for, as he sees it, Buchan "more properly belongs to English literature."⁵⁶ Stephen Gray's *Southern African Literature: An Introduction* (1979), which David Attwell describes as "the first systematic introduction to the field," almost exclusively surveys writing in English, including "black English."⁵⁷

Schreiner, of course, makes the cut, as do Haggard and Buchan, while Page does not. In *White Writing: On the Culture of Letters in South Africa* (1988), which centers on the pastoral, J. M. Coetzee looks primarily at literature in English, including "the great antipastoral writer" Schreiner—to whom "the Cape Colony, and perhaps all colonies, are . . . anti-Gardens, dystopias"— though he devotes one chapter to Afrikaans writer C. M. van den Heever.[58] Malvern van Wyk Smith's *Grounds of Contest: A Survey of South African English Literature* (1990) includes Schreiner, excludes Afrikaans writers, and, like Coetzee, leaves Haggard and Buchan to the British.

Since the end of apartheid, South African literary historiography has been more expansive. Its historical sweep is greater; it is more ethnically and also often more linguistically diverse. Though mostly "written in English for a wide international readership," it seeks to be multilingual in other ways.[59] It might discuss texts originally written in any South African language from Afrikaans to Zulu. Among its subjects might be orature, from praise poems to songs, in any of southern Africa's many indigenous languages. It might quote passages in the language in which they were originally written or spoken. And it might attend to "translingual writing": "writing done by authors who work in more than one language and whose writing is generally informed by knowledge of several languages."[60] In *Southern African Literatures* (1996), Michael Chapman examines literature from South Africa as well as the countries that it borders.[61] At times, postapartheid scholarship puts forth a national "developmental narrative," which moves through colonialism, apartheid, and resistance to arrive at a universally democratic present. Christopher Heywood's *A History of South African Literature* (2004), for instance, is divided into two parts: "Part I: Towards Sharpeville" and "Part II: Transformation."[62]

Astoundingly, there is no overview of or substantial critical work on British South African literature.[63] I would define this as literature written about southern Africa by British emigrants, their descendants, or Britons who spent time in the region between the turn of the nineteenth century and the early 1920s. This period begins with Britain's acquisition of the Cape and ends around the time of the Balfour Declaration of 1926, which established South African autonomy in foreign affairs. Two years earlier, Barry Hertzog had become South Africa's first National Party prime minister; in keeping with his party, he supported South African autonomy, Afrikaner interests, and white supremacy. Two years before that, Rhodesia had declined to join the Union of South Africa for the second time (the first preceded its inception), making it quite clear that it was forging its own path. Given that there was scant fiction—less than twenty novels by one account—and not much more poetry written in or about the region until the 1880s, the bulk of British South African literature appeared in the two decades before and after the First Anglo-Boer War.[64] If not the "pivot of the Empire" that W. T. Stead claimed it was in his review of Schreiner's *The Story of an African Farm* (1893), southern Africa was nonetheless a central concern of a number of important writers.[65]

Schreiner, Haggard, Page, and Buchan were the most popular, outspoken, and influential British South African writers. Prime Minister William Gladstone sent Schreiner his congratulations on the success of *The Story of an African Farm*. A thirteen-year-old Winston Churchill wrote Haggard a letter praising *Allan Quatermain* (1887). A British member of parliament recommended Page's writing to King George V. At least three prime ministers—Arthur Balfour, Stanley Baldwin, and Clement Atlee—read Buchan.[66] They shaped the literature that followed them, from the New Woman novel to the empire romance, from the adventure novel to the spy thriller. Other British South African writers include Arthur Conan Doyle and Rudyard Kipling, both of whom spent time in southern Africa during the Second Anglo-Boer War. I would only cautiously describe them as South African authorial informants, however, since their time there shaped neither them nor their fiction to the degree that it did the authors and novels that are the subject of this study.

Doyle, who spent six months in southern Africa in 1900 with the volunteer medical corps, wrote two widely read works of nonfiction about the war: the four-volume *The Great Boer War* (1900) and the much shorter *The War in South Africa: Its Cause and Conduct* (1902). Already famous as the author of numerous Sherlock Holmes stories, he used his platform to justify and chronicle the war in the first publication and to defend Britain's role and policies—including its administration of concentration camps—in the war in the second.[67] The only fiction Doyle set in southern Africa was "The Mystery of Sasassa Valley: A South African Story" (1879), an adventure about the unearthing of a diamond, whose glint had long been mistaken for the "glowing eyes" of a "frightful fiend" (148). His first published story, it was written years before he visited the region.[68]

Kipling, who spent far more time than Doyle in southern Africa—a short visit there in 1891, a four-month stay in 1898, and annual three-month visits with his family from 1900 to 1908—wrote both fiction and nonfiction about, set in, or clearly inspired by the region. Specifically, he wrote two children's parables, included in *Just So Stories for Little Children*

(1902); a handful of fables and maxims for the troops, published in *The Friend* (1900), a newspaper distributed by the British after their seizure of Bloemfontein, the Orange Free State capital; two tracts for the Imperial South African Association, a metropolitan organization whose stated aim was "to uphold British supremacy and to promote the interests of British subjects in South Africa"; a number of articles for British newspapers; just over two dozen poems, many of which were collected in 1903's *The Five Nations*; and eight short stories, several of which appeared in 1904's *Traffics and Discoveries*.[69] His first South African piece was the wildly popular poem "The Absent-Minded Beggar" (1899), which, though not quite up to his (own) standard of writing—"I would shoot the man who wrote it if it would not be suicide," Kipling quipped—helped to raise a quarter of a million pounds for the dependents of Britons fighting in the war.[70] Set to music by Arthur Sullivan, sung in West End theaters, East End music halls, and beside barrel-organs throughout Britain, "reproduced on scarves, handkerchiefs, matchboxes, caps, vases, and biscuit-barrels," the song was so widely disseminated that "there could scarcely have been anyone who did not know at least its refrain."[71] Given the poem's success and Kipling's long-standing reputation as India's foremost authorial informant, much was expected of the "most important spokesperson for empire at the turn of the century."[72] "The Absent-Minded Beggar" aside, Kipling's South African writing was, nonetheless, neither popular nor well received. Though several of his short stories are productively informed by a precarious tension between loyalty to empire and loyalty to race as he wrestled with the implications of arming people of color, his most powerful work—including *Kim* (1901), published and partially written during the war—remains that which he set in India.[73]

Schreiner, Haggard, Page, and Buchan have not generally been read as British South African writers. Schreiner, claimed by both South African and British literary canons, is often viewed as more cosmopolitan than colonial, despite the fact that she wrote her most important novel long before she left southern Africa. Haggard is usually considered a British writer, though he is reluctantly included in a number of South African surveys.[74] Buchan is almost exclusively read as British. Page fell by the wayside as Rhodesia increasingly became a distinct cultural entity.[75] When their work is read as part of a British literary tradition or "post-colonial critical canon"—as colonial discourse—its South African-ness is often neglected. As Chrisman notes, British and American scholars have shown a "preference for a version of Haggard and Schreiner as general Africanists."[76] And despite its exploration of emergent black nationalism, Buchan's *Prester John* (1910) has received surprisingly little attention, as has the South African background of his most popular character, Richard Hannay.

Beyond Gold and Diamonds argues that these writers can be read productively as British South African. It considers the reasons for the emergence of the New Woman novel in what many, like Stead, viewed as the most unlikely of places.[77] It puts the first New Woman novelist directly in conversation with the Victorian period's most famous romance writer, offering new ways of interpreting both, particularly in terms of colonial subjectivity and gender. Bringing critically overlooked texts to light, it insists that, contrary to conventional wisdom, the male imperial romance was not Haggard's most interesting literary contribution. It unearths Page, making connections between her work and that of both Schreiner and Doris Lessing. In doing so, it draws a line from southern Africa's first famous novelist through Rhodesia's first famous novelist to Rhodesia's most famous novelist. And it identifies the concerns that compelled Buchan to bring down the curtain on the imperial romance, only to transport a character seemingly plucked straight from the genre to the metropole now in need of his strengths. Though the study is representative rather than comprehensive, it demonstrates that reading British South African literature as a field brings its significance to British literature—meaning also southern Africa's significance to British literature—into view.

The Fiction of Race

For all its variation, British South African fiction, like much colonial discourse, is remarkably consistent in the limited ways it depicts the indigenous. Despite their actual numeric majority in southern Africa, they are often all but absent. Despite the reality of their presence as laborers, in towns, on farms, and in mines, they remain exotic. Despite the fact of consistent, persistent European aggression into the interior, it is they who are malign. Southern Africa's population looked nothing like its representation in British South African fiction—that is, almost entirely white. Figures vary, but indigenous Africans outnumbered those of European descent by roughly ten to one before the start of the mineral revolution and six to one at century's end. There was variation within the colonies; the ratio in Rhodesia, for instance, was around thirty to one in 1898.[78] In the first Union census, taken in 1911, the population was around twelve million. Four million blacks comprised sixty-seven percent of this total, 1.3 million whites twenty-one percent, 500,000 "Coloureds" nine percent, and 200,000 Indians three percent.[79]

Asians had been coming to southern Africa almost as long as Europeans. The Dutch brought over approximately sixteen thousand Indians as slaves. Between 1860 and 1911, more than 150,000 Indians came as indentured laborers, many to work on Natal's sugar plantations, while some came independently to trade.[80] When a labor shortage arose following the Second Anglo-Boer War, thousands of Chinese came over as indentured laborers—roughly sixty-four thousand between 1904 and 1910—to work on the Transvaal gold fields.[81] Yet Indians and Chinese are nowhere to be seen in the fiction.

Those of mixed race appear only occasionally, despite the fact that Africans and Europeans had intermixed since the latter first arrived in southern Africa. Though the Boers were primarily descended from Dutch, German, and French Huguenot emigrants, some were also descended from indigenous communities. The Griqua, the majority of whom lived near the Transvaal at the start of the mineral revolution, were a culturally distinct group of people with mostly Dutch and Khoikhoi ancestry. The large "Cape Coloured" population was comprised of Khoikhoi, former slaves, and many of mixed race.[82] And of course indeterminate numbers of mixed-race people lived and passed as members of the community or ethnicity into which they were born, which was generally the distaff side. This fact and apartheid have meant that until the last thirty years, stark divisions remained when it came to the classification of literature.

The few mixed-race characters one does find in British South African fiction are almost always among those "call[ed] . . . mean white[s]."[83] Greedy, cowardly, and duplicitous, mean whites are loyal to none but themselves. They have little if any regard for "European" values, and their sustained engagement with indigenous Africans has had an unwholesome effect on them. Their vice, which often includes miscegenation, is written on their flesh. This includes Haggard's Swart Piet, a Boer villain in *Swallow* (1898), whose "dark face and savage temper had earned him the name of 'the little Kaffir.'" "Born of white blood and black, [he] is false to both and a disgrace to both."[84] It also includes Buchan's Henriques, a double-dealing Portuguese with "mean eyes and [a] cruel mouth," "whose skin spoke of the tar-brush."[85] As the white narrator of *Prester John* views Henriques, he is "a traitor to the white man's cause . . . whose name is a byword among honest men." In the eyes of Henriques's black ally, he is a "Kaffir . . . in everything but Kaffir virtues."[86] White men of low character, "who took to the wilderness as a last resource, [could also] by degrees s[i]nk to the level of the savages among whom they lived." Ishmael, for example, in Haggard's *The Ghost Kings*

(1908), who "chose to come and live in a place where there [were] no laws or civilisation," dresses in animal skins and resides in a kraal (homestead) with his African wives and their children.[87] Such characters quite often go mad, consumed by ungoverned passion. The degraded state of these white men, the paucity of mixed-race characters, and the reprehensibility of those who do make it onto the page are part of what Jennifer DeVere Brody describes as the "convoluted construction[] of pure whiteness and pure blackness in Victorian culture."[88] This construction was especially torturous in a South African context, where the reality of hybridity daily stared one in the face. Constructing their "purity" in contradistinction to Boers and other whites, the British claimed, through moral and genetic superiority, the greatest fitness to rule.

As I discuss in chapters 1 and 3, respectively, African erasure is most notable in Schreiner's earliest novel, *The Story of an African Farm*, and throughout Page's work. Of "the occlusion of black labour" in the South African pastoral, Coetzee has written: "If the work of hands on a particular patch of earth is what inscribes it as the property of its occupiers by right, then the hands of black serfs doing the work had better not be seen."[89] Black Africans hover around the edges of *The Story of an African Farm* as servants, laborers, and the long-dead creators of cave paintings, but they play no role in the lives of the story's white characters. Schreiner would eventually recognize this discursive violence and come to champion African rights, but she is an exception. On the rare occasions the indigenous are mentioned in Page's writing, they are dirty, lazy, and intractable servants—little more than one of many obstacles on the path to colonial maturity for the new female emigrant.

Haggard and Buchan exploit black Africans romantically. At times Haggard casts them as brutal and unrestrained; at other times he makes them more nuanced characters. Even when he renders them sympathetic, they are also exotic. As I argue in chapter 2, the colonial woman's ability in the female colonial romance to negotiate with African leaders is a sign of her fitness for the work of settlement, while alliances with indigenous women enhance her strength. Though these leaders are not always malevolent and these allies are always benevolent, both are props in a largely British drama, or at least one in which British interests and characters prevail. That said, Haggard did write an entire novel populated almost entirely by indigenous Africans, *Nada the Lily* (1892), mentioned here in the epilogue. As we see in chapter 4, Buchan's *Prester John* is preoccupied with the growing presence of African nationalism. The young narrator's "admiration" for the novel's vigorous and charismatic black leader is matched only by his certainty that he must not triumph, lest he "wipe out the civilization of a thousand years, and turn us all into savages."[90] For besides the eponymous African, an exceptional man, and a "well trained" female servant, the Africans in the text are a largely undistinguished mass of followers, filled with "the fury of conquest, and all the aboriginal passions."[91] For the most part, British South Africans took pains in their writing to deny such fury and passion in themselves, even as they consumed the guts of the earth with the labor of Africans they treated as disposable bodies.

Overview

Following Edward Said, *Beyond Gold and Diamonds* takes as its subject the discursive representation of empire.[92] Specifically, it examines the South African writing of British writers with translocal identities and interests. Chapter 1, "Preterdomesticity and the South African Farm: Women Old and New," offers a radical reinterpretation of Schreiner and Haggard, associated respectively with the New Woman novel and the male imperial romance. Though *The Story of an African Farm* in many ways enabled Haggard's female colonial romances (the subject of chapter 2) and Page's Rhodesian settler romances (the subject of chapter 3), it differs significantly from them in its denial of the fantasy of female empowerment in southern Africa. Its heroine's failure to achieve what Haggard's and Page's heroines attain is a reflection of Schreiner's feminist integrity; at the same time, it is a mark of her inability to think beyond the frame of the domestic novel it implicitly critiques, or to consider the value of either cross-cultural or female-female alliances. Reading Schreiner's Lyndall against the eponymous heroine of Haggard's *Jess* (1887), chapter 1 demonstrates the limits of intellectual feminism manifest in Schreiner's novel and the surprisingly feminist implications of Haggard's. A realist novel that depicts both war and romantic love, *Jess* is a tale of action but is not adventure fiction per se. To the degree that it is a "romance," then, it is only so in the modern sense of foregrounding romantic love—like Page's settler romances—not in the contemporaneous sense of depicting the strange or fantastic—like Haggard's male imperial and female colonial romances. Set during the First Anglo-Boer War, *Jess* attempts to resolve the colonial problem that caused Haggard to "abandon"—as he put it—his South African life: Britain's 1881 surrender of the Transvaal to the Boers at the war's end. "Deserted," like the colony, by the mother country, farm and family are successfully recovered by Jess, whose courage is contrasted with the weakness of imperial policy in southern Africa.[93] Conflating domestic and military stakes, Haggard stages victory on a small scale through the heroics of a woman who achieves what the empire will not.

Chapter 2, "'It Is I Who Have the Power': The Female Colonial Romance," argues that Haggard's female-centered colonial romances *Benita* (1906) and *The Ghost Kings* attempt both to manage the problem, as he saw it, of growing twentieth-century British feminism and to serve the goal of anglicizing southern Africa. But even as Haggard fictively reroutes feminist focus from domestic politics to imperial consolidation, his settler heroines transcend their ostensible function, manifesting an authority whose implications reach beyond the page. While British women in the colonies were generally portrayed recreating British domesticity and its adjacent values,[94] Haggard's colonial heroines display characteristics more often associated with male adventurers. Using courage, confidence, and savvy, they defend themselves and their loved ones against ill-intentioned white men as well as negotiate with indigenous leaders and soldiers in indigenous space. Forming alliances with other women, they also engage in what I term *mystical feminism*. Enabled through cross-cultural—and sometimes cross-racial—female-female bonds, mystical feminism entails the use of extrasensory powers for self-preservation or benevolent ends, enhancing the heroine's power and authority among whites and the indigenous alike. A conservative gesture with inadvertently feminist implications, Haggard's reinvention of the British woman as the British South African woman turns fear (of the modern woman) into strength (of the empire), while also extending female influence.

Chapter 3, "Colony of Dreadful Delight: Gertrude Page and the Rhodesian Settler Romance," explores the ways in which Page, an English emigrant to Rhodesia, posits Rhodesian domesticity as an emancipatory modernity for British women. Encouraging female emigration to Rhodesia as a means of bolstering the empire and liberating the self, Page envisions imperial subject positions for white women beyond those of mother, missionary, and martyr. Influenced by the New Woman novel that flourished in the 1890s and anticipating the empire romance that took off after World War I, her Rhodesian novels depict female emigrants achieving authority through colonial trial, frequently with the help of a more seasoned colonial woman.[95] Titillating her readers with the prospect of illicit gratification, Page suggests that sexual temptation is one of the many challenges-cum-pleasures that Rhodesian women face. If courage is often required to resist it, it is also sometimes required to give in; for not only do women have a right to their desire in this land of "freedom from narrow conventionalities," they also have a right to their satisfaction. A writer of fiction and nonfiction alike, Page both illustrates and models the transformation into colonial maturity that is available to women who learn to navigate this new terrain.[96]

Chapter 4, "'There Will Be No More Kings in Africa': Foreclosing Darkness in *Prester John*," claims that Buchan's novel, influenced by his administrative experience in southern Africa during and immediately following the Second Anglo-Boer War, bridges the gap between the imperial romance and the spy thriller at the moment of South Africa's union. Demonstrating the implausibility of southern Africa as a site of mystery, depicting the demise of indigenous autonomy, and asserting the inevitability of British supremacy, *Prester John* eliminates any residue of exoticism, squelches indigenous militarism, and minimizes the presence of the (recently reenfranchised and politically ascendant) Boer populace. Ignoring Afrikaner nationalism and representing African nationalism as a final failed bid to reclaim what had long since ceased to belong to the indigenous, the novel imagines the anglicization of southern Africa as a fait accompli. At the same time, it anticipates the political turn from colony to (European) continent and the literary turn from adventure novel to spy thriller that would coincide with World War I.

The epilogue, "Beyond the British South African Novel," illustrates movement in two different directions, one beyond South Africa and one beyond Britain. In its analysis of what is often referred to as the Hannay quartet (1915–1924), it demonstrates that South African Britishness, as Buchan conceived it, defends a Britain both materially and ideologically besieged.[97] At the precise moment when Britain, having consolidated its empire, turned its attention to Europe, Buchan turned his attention there as well. Abandoning the imperial romance for the spy thriller, he introduced the character of Hannay, whose South African–honed skill set protects Britain from radical and foreign influences on the eve of, during, and in the aftermath of World War I. A colonial past thus prevents a continental future from consuming a vulnerable metropole, evincing the importance of southern Africa to British integrity. In its analysis of Sol T. Plaatje's *Mhudi* (1930), the epilogue demonstrates the influence of orality and the British South African novel alike on the first novel in English by a black South African. Combining traditional African storytelling techniques and the generic innovations of the female colonial romance specifically, Plaatje lays claim to black African belonging in South Africa's past, present, and future.

Chapter 1

Preterdomesticity and the South African Farm

Women Old and New

The arrival of Olive Schreiner and H. Rider Haggard on Britain's literary scene coincided with southern Africa's rise in imperial consciousness. Most literate Britons would have known about the (1867) discovery of diamonds near the Vaal River, which marked the start of the mineral revolution; Britain's (1877) annexation of the Transvaal (South African Republic) from the Boers; the Anglo-Zulu War (1879); the First Anglo-Boer War (1880–1881), and the resultant reinstatement of the South African Republic (1881); and they would soon learn about the (1886) discovery of gold on the Witwatersrand and subsequent gold rush.[1] *The Story of an African Farm* (1883), the first internationally successful South African novel (a novel that "every one has read," remarked W. T. Stead in 1894) addressed almost none of these events, though it "set [the 'Karoo'] on a pinnacle of fame" and made the South African–born Schreiner the empire's first colonial literary celebrity.[2] Set on a rural Cape farm in the late 1850s and 1860s, *African Farm* is in many ways a domestic tale gone awry. It has long been recognized as the first New Woman novel, while its heroine Lyndall has been called "the first wholly serious feminist heroine in the English novel."[3] Haggard's success came only with the publication of his third novel (and fourth book), *King Solomon's Mines* (1885), about which the journal *South Africa: A Weekly Journal for All Interested in South African Affairs* asked rhetorically in its inaugural issue (1889): "Is there anyone who has not read this book?"[4] A "history of wild adventure" set in unexplored southern Africa, *King Solomon's Mines* was the type of tale that Schreiner, in her preface to *African Farm*, derided for lacking "contact with any fact."[5] *She* (1887), *Jess* (1887), and *Allan Quatermain* (1887), three more South (or in the case of *She*, central) African novels followed in rapid succession, establishing Haggard, a British-born son of privilege who had spent half a dozen years in southern Africa, as an expert on the region and the first major metropolitan author affiliated with it. Nothing he later wrote would surpass the popularity of these four works, of which all but *Jess* are imperial romances.[6] Set in the Transvaal during the First Anglo-Boer War, *Jess* is a realist novel containing elements of adventure. It entwines the political, the martial, and the domestic through its modern settler heroine. In its own right, the novel illustrates the complexity of the colonial-metropolitan relationship and British identity. Read against *African Farm*, *Jess* illustrates the generic and feminist boundaries of Schreiner's novel while opening up generic and feminist possibilities of its own.[7]

Though few critics have invoked the two novels together—due largely to Haggard's posthumous reification as the quintessential "imperialist romancer[]" and the correlative turn away from the historically specific *Jess*—there are a number of reasons for doing so.[8] *African Farm* and *Jess* were published four years apart, during which time the two authors met as well as read one another's work.[9] Two decades later southern Africa's principal authorial informants were still "the only two writers of South African fiction [to] have achieved world-wide celebrity."[10] They both tell the story of orphaned English—as South Africans of British descent were known—relatives and age-mates, one submissive, one independent, on a remote South African farm. Most importantly, and in unexpected ways that I will demonstrate, they cast one another's generic and political functions and limitations in sharp relief. My intention, however, is neither to undercut the value of Schreiner's feminism, which is everywhere apparent in her writing, nor to act as an apologist for Haggard's misogyny, which proclaims itself elsewhere.[11] It is, rather, to address a series of questions that a comparison enables, questions that have not previously been asked or satisfactorily answered: Why might the first "Modern Woman Novel" have emerged when and where it did?[12] In what ways and why was it also traditional? What do we lose in confining our reading of Haggard to the imperial romance? And why was he compelled and able to execute a realist novel with such surprisingly feminist implications?

As a starting point, consider the primary issues the novels confront, their means of doing so, and the results. Both novels, which explore the gender dynamics of colonial subjectivity, signal a crisis of identity in their authors, a colonial female who expects authority but is constrained by social politics and a colonial male who expects loyalty but is constrained by imperial governance. Both novels, which attempt to resolve their crisis through the figure of a colonial woman, challenge generic conventions. *African Farm* does so by thwarting the premise and outcome of the domestic novel, and *Jess* by combining elements of domestic and adventure fiction. Both novels imagine new spaces for colonial women beyond the matrimonial and the maternal. *African Farm*, however, ultimately fails to liberate its largely static feminist heroine or to move beyond the domestic frame it implicitly critiques, while *Jess* vindicates the colony through the actions of a heroine who lacks a feminist consciousness yet advances the female adventure tale. In short, both novels are political, preterdomestic, and ultimately predictive.

A feminist critique of female oppression in British southern Africa, *The Story of an African Farm* is the prototype of the New Woman novel, more than a hundred of which would be published by century's end.[13] Written, as Schreiner put it, in the hope that someone "struggling with . . . the narrowness and iron pressure of their surroundings . . . might read it and feel less alone," it focuses on two female cousins, Lyndall and Em, their life under the rule of the latter's Boer stepmother, and their quest for fulfillment, the former through independence and the latter through traditional domesticity (*Letters* 210). A psychological portrait of subjectivity, *African Farm* has been credited with anticipating modernist experiments in interiority.[14] Marking an end as much as a beginning, the novel registers the incipient demise of the domestic novel as well as its long-standing authority. Where the domestic novel "chronicle[s] a process of domestication, whose ultimate success . . . is signaled by [its] heroine's marriage to a suitably upstanding man," *African Farm* chronicles its heroine's rejection of domesticity and its chief marker of success.[15] Where the domestic novel "unfold[s] the operations of human desire as if they were independent of political history," *African Farm* explicitly refuses this distinction.[16] Its heroine's declension of marriage hinges precisely on the loss of freedom it would entail; it is authority, not status, for which she longs.[17] Where the domestic novel conveys "a feeling of hominess" and connection, *African Farm* is pervaded by a sense of "hostil[ity]" and isolation.[18] The novel, thus, not only announces the New Woman's birth and emergent self-consciousness, it also critiques the genre to which her predecessor, the angel in the house, had long been confined.

An imperialist critique of Britain's unwillingness to defend its South African colonials, *Jess* is Haggard's only South African realist novel. Multiple editions, adaptations for stage and screen, a fictional parody, frequent mention in advertisements for Haggard's other works, and laudatory references in both the metropolitan and South African press attest to its decades-long

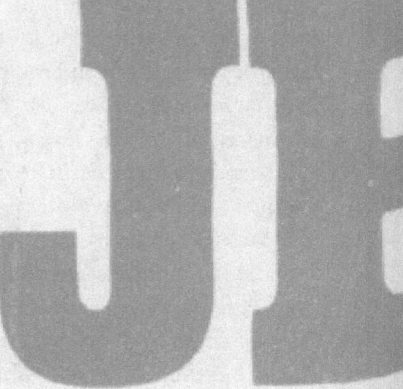

Figure 1.1. Advertisement for one of the four film versions of *Jess* produced between 1905 and 1917. Source: "Jess: A Tale of the South African War, by Rider Haggard," advertisement for *Jess*, directed by George O. Nichols, Thanhouser Production, 1912,

Supplement to The Bioscope, November 14, 1912. xxi.

John Neil and Jess in the torrent.

ean War, by

...AGGARD

...O MASTERS.

Length 3,000 ft.

THE WOMAN IN WHITE,

...ASED JANUARY 22nd. By WILKIE COLLINS. Length 2,000 ft.

cannot afford to miss ! ! !

...AN STOCK.

...PORT CO., LTD.,

STREET, LONDON, W. Telephone—Gerrard 8080.

renown.[19] "A living record of our shame in South Africa," as Haggard put it, "written by one by whom it was endured," it focuses on sisters Jess and Bessie, their life with their uncle in the Boer-majority Transvaal in the leadup to and during the First Anglo-Boer War, and their commitment to family, particularly that of Jess, who sacrifices both love and life for her more traditional sister (*Days* 1: 265). A portrait of female heroism in wartime, *Jess* makes the distinctly modern move of unloosing the heroine from the limits of conventional domesticity, pitting her against one of the leaders of the Boer rebellion in her efforts to protect the family "abandon[ed]" by the metropole. Contrasting courageous female action with an "emasculated" imperial policy, *Jess* collapses the domestic and the martial, inadvertently producing feminist effects.[20] The novel, then, both announces the modern female adventure heroine and forecasts the female colonial romance, the subject of chapter 2.[21]

Written when Schreiner was a colonial governess in her late teens, *African Farm* enabled its author to confront the trauma of growing into South African white womanhood: a position of weakness, relative to white men, if also one of power, relative to children and nonwhites. Despite her childhood fantasies of vindication, its protagonist Lyndall is as powerless as an adult as she was as a child; manipulation and refusal remain her primary defenses against the desires of others. And though she eschews traditional domesticity, she fails to pursue a sustaining alternative; similarly, the text, which rejects the tenets of the domestic novel, employs, even as it distorts, many of its conventions.

Written less than five years after Britain's loss of the First Anglo-Boer War, *Jess* enabled Haggard to confront the trauma that drove him to leave southern Africa: Britain's surrender of the Transvaal.[22] The British South African that Haggard once was, Jess represents the ambivalence of this colonial position, one that Haggard himself could not endure, either as a British-identified citizen in an Afrikaner republic or as a proud British subject humbled by imperial surrender. Recuperating farm and family, both "deserted," like the Transvaal, by Britain, Jess is at once that which protects and that which is in need of protection, both the power that Britain failed to supply and the territory to which it failed to supply it (*J* 266). Through Jess's heroics, Haggard not only enacts a fantasy of recovery, he also redresses his shame by shaming the mother country for its failure of commitment. Jess's successful defense of a besieged domesticity contrasts sharply with Lyndall's aimless flight from an internally crumbling one. And though both text and protagonist shore up colonial domesticity, *Jess* celebrates the traditionally masculine acts of its heroine.

Both novels challenge the fantasy of colonial freedom through the depiction of thwarted promise. For Schreiner, blame rests implicitly with both metropole and colony, between whose gender politics she makes no distinction (they are British broadly rather than South African specifically). For Haggard, blame rests exclusively with the metropole, whose vacillating imperial policy he contrasts with colonial resolution. If for Schreiner the question is "How can South African white women flourish given (British) social restrictions?," for Haggard, the question is "How can South African colonials flourish given (British) imperial policy?" Through its portrayal of a heroine's confinement, *African Farm* critiques social conservatism. Through its portrayal of a heroine's self-determination, *Jess* critiques imperial retrenchment. The social standards that make Lyndall's position so dire fall away in Haggard's rendering of the extremity of war, in which necessity trumps convention. More steadfast, committed, and capable than the imperial government, Jess steps up because it did not. That her gender makes her an unlikely avenger makes Haggard's pointed rebuke that much more incisive. Given the ideological variance of the two novels, it is ironic that Jess manifests a potency of which Lyndall only dreams, for though a feminist rebellion against the angel in the house and the domestic novel, *African Farm* remains tied to both, while *Jess*, though unconcerned with women's rights, expands the possibilities of colonial womanhood through generic hybridity that hinges on female agency.

South African Ties

In an 1894 article in the *Review of Reviews*, W. T. Stead identified *African Farm* as "the forerunner of all the novels of the Modern Woman. . . . Written by a woman about a woman from the standpoint of Woman." Such novels recognized that women were at a disadvantage in society, as well as suggested that women desired more out of life than marriage and family and that they disdained "loveless marriage and . . . enforced maternity."[23] The same year, Sarah Grand coined the term "New Woman" to denote women—fictional and otherwise—with views similar to those expressed by the Modern Woman novel as Stead described it.[24] The New Woman novel, as the burgeoning genre became known, included not only those of the type outlined by Stead, but also those that explored while ultimately rejecting the progressive ideas of the New Woman.

Though the New Woman novel was primarily a metropolitan phenomenon, its birthplace was southern Africa. As Stead himself noted, "the Cape has indeed done yeoman's service to the English-speaking world. To that pivot of the Empire we owe our most pronounced type . . . of the Emancipated Woman."[25] It was here that a young, observant Olive Schreiner registered, recorded, and resisted gender inequality as she grew from a girl into a woman. Surrounded by the rhetoric of promise—as diamonds were discovered, gold mines were dug, railways laid, and people poured in from across the empire—Schreiner came to recognize that such promise was gendered, with scant options available to women. She watched her mother, a gifted linguist and artist born Rebecca Lyndall, spend her life caring for her children—twelve in total, five of whom died before the age of six—as she moved first to and then across southern Africa, with the shifting moods and fortunes of her husband. At the diamond fields, Olive and her sister Ettie cooked, cleaned, and cared for their brother Theo, while he mined his claims in pursuit of wealth. And while she read avidly—Shakespeare, Montaigne, Gibbon, Coleridge, Shelley, Emerson, Carlyle, Tennyson, Dickens, Darwin, Spencer, and Mill, among others—the only formal education she received (prior to a short stint in nursing school) was a few years under the instruction of Theo, headmaster of a public school.[26] Lyndall, like Schreiner, was an isolated, knowledge-hungry, philosophical child. "When people say it is unnatural for people placed as [she was] to have such thoughts and feelings," wrote Schreiner in a letter to her close friend Havelock Ellis, a prominent sexologist and one of a number of progressive intellectuals with whom she spent time in England, "I laugh to myself. It isn't that one can't teach oneself everything, one can, but it's [at] such a fearful cost of strength" (*Letters* 47). Author and heroine alike yearned for the "freedom and independence" their learning taught them to value, not least as a way out of "dependence" on men (63). Only Schreiner, however, attained them. As she well knew, her professional income and modern marriage—to a freethinker who encouraged her writing and hyphenated his surname with hers—made her an exception among women. More commonly, "our unused emotional and intellectual energy [lies] unused [*sic*] within us" and women fail to attain the "freedom, freedom, freedom, that is the first great want of humanity."[27] These are the brutal truths that Lyndall's fictional death writes large.

From an early age, Schreiner, like Lyndall, refused to "go with the drove" (*SAF* 189). Though reared by a missionary father, she "began to be a free-thinker" at the age of ten (*Letters* 45). Giving expression to her doubts about Christianity cost her both personally and professionally. For instance, she lost an important friendship and the approval of at least two siblings; and since "she resolutely refused to teach religion," she found her wages as a governess substantially reduced.[28] Christened Olive Emilie Albertina Schreiner—a name that denoted three of her brothers who died in infancy—and "known variously as Emilie, Emmie, Empie, Em, or Milly," Olive declined these monikers in her mid-teens, requesting instead that her family call her Olive, which they seem to have done.[29] Carving out her own path—and defying expectations—Schreiner planned to be financially independent: "I made up my mind when I was quite a little child that as soon as I was able I would support myself, for I see no reason why a woman should be dependent on her friends [including family] any more than a man should" (*Letters* 15).[30] At fifteen, she became a governess, a position she would hold with several, mostly Boer, families for the better part of the next ten years. During this time, she not only saved up the cost of a passage to Britain, where, undeterred by the paucity of female doctors, she planned to attend medical school, she also carved out time, often at the sacrifice of sleep, to draft *African Farm*, as well as parts of *Undine* (1929) and *From Man to Man; or Perhaps Only* . . . (1926), the last two of which were published posthumously (the latter, as an incomplete text) (*Letters* 26, 109). After a brief broken engagement when she was seventeen, Schreiner formed the radical position that marriage was *not* the only course a woman might take. "No one will ever absorb me and make me lose myself utterly," she wrote, "and *unless someone did I should never marry*. In fact I am married now, to my books!" (*Letters* 22; my emphasis).[31] In 1881, just shy of her twenty-sixth birthday, she set sail for Britain, where she briefly studied nursing—medical school having proven too expensive—at the Royal Infirmary of Edinburgh (*Letters* 26). Finding herself too ill to continue her studies there (on her health issues, see the next paragraph), she almost immediately left for London, where she soon sought a publisher.[32] After *African Farm* was accepted by Chapman and Hall in mid-1882, the characteristically confident Schreiner withstood the publishing company's pressure to revise the text so that Lyndall would marry the father of her child—lest, Frederic Chapman worried, "the British public . . . think it wicked"[33]—as she would later "insist[]" that they publish it cheaply to make it accessible to the working class (*Letters* 209, see also 210).

Despite the limitations imposed on her by an empire that touted freedom but withheld it from women, Schreiner successfully carved out an unconventional life for herself. "Rejecting the powerlessness of the traditional female role," as her biographers First and Scott note, she aspired to and ultimately "adopted a man's pursuits: economic independence, creative work, freedom to travel, and a measure of sexual autonomy."[34] From her mid-teens onward, however, she was plagued with headaches, asthma, and chest pains, which, it has been speculated, may have been caused by her ongoing struggle against convention.[35] Of course, the dangers of retroactive diagnosis—made by humanists no less—are obvious, but if it is inadvisable to presume a link between Schreiner's physical ailments and the constant expenditure of energy required to overcome social limitations, it is certainly reasonable to point out that that link exists in Schreiner's fiction, in which the majority of her (largely unconventional) heroines die of (generally unspecified) disease. Most obviously, there is Lyndall, whose death, according to Schreiner's friend, the poet Arthur Symons, was "*not* a 'retribution' "—punishment for refusing to marry the father of her child; rather, it was the result of "struggle."[36]

While Symons describes the struggle as that "of helpless human nature against the great forces of the universe," in *African Farm*, as in *Undine* and *From Man to Man*, the heroine's struggle is much more specific: coming to terms with the discrepancy between the rhetoric of promise pervading British southern Africa and the reality of womanhood.[37] Each novel begins with the childhood of one or more South African girls, two of whom (Lyndall and Rebekah [*From Man to Man*]) are named after Olive's mother and one (Em) is named after herself, and tells the story of her/their grappling with the disappointments of womanhood. "When I am grown up, . . . there will be nothing I do not know," Lyndall imagines (*SAF* 46). "We will not be children always; we shall have the power too, some day," she further asserts (127). Undine similarly "dream[s] of the glorious time when she would be a woman and would know everything and . . . would be free."[38] Knowledge, however, brings them neither power nor freedom, and they soon learn that womanhood means suffering, as Schreiner suggested in her original dedication for *From Man to Man*, in which she wrote of her infant daughter, who lived for only sixteen hours, "*She never lived to shed a woman's tears.*"[39] This is true of all of Schreiner's heroines, whether, like Lyndall and Undine, they transgress social expectations or, like Em, they do not. The sexual double standard, marriage inequality, and the lack of educational and employment opportunities, which serve as impediments to (financial) independence, are inescapable "facts" for any British girl who grows to womanhood, "facts" that Schreiner lays bare. Eschewing the "brilliant" colors of the fantasists who portray "far-off lands" rife with adventure, Schreiner, as she notes in her preface to *African Farm*, paints "what lies before" her, using only "the grey pigments" at hand. One man's imagined world of possibility is another woman's reality of circumscription.[40]

Born in "the land of dust and diamonds," Schreiner saw that dust not diamonds was a woman's lot. And while this was not strictly a colonial phenomenon, the contrast between the rhetoric of promise and the actuality of restriction was starker in the booming southern Africa of Schreiner's era, where a relative degree of gender flexibility enabled English girls to envision bright futures that the persistence of social conventions would nonetheless thwart.[41] "Mirage," one of Schreiner's working titles for *African Farm*, and the epigraph that she considered along with it, "life is a series of abortions," capture the particularly gendered disappointment that she is at pains, not only in that novel but also in *Undine* and *From Man to Man*, to convey.[42] In contrast to Haggard as well as to Gertrude Page and John Buchan, South African–born Schreiner refutes the fantasy of colonial liberation so prevalent in British South African discourse from the discovery of southern Africa's mineral wealth through the decade following the (1910) formation of the Union of South Africa.

For Haggard, southern Africa was a place where someone like himself, the undistinguished youngest son of a British squire, could become a self-reliant man, which for him translated to working as an administrator, buying property, and establishing a literary reputation.[43] Indeed, as an anonymous critic wrote in 1887, his "literary shadow . . . is an African one, acquired by actual travel under the sun of Africa, and it sticks to him."[44] His African experience had begun twelve years earlier when, with his family's influence, the nineteen-year-old obtained a position as a secretary to Henry Bulwer, Governor of Natal. Quickly climbing "the colonial ladder," he accompanied Theophilus Shepstone, Special Commissioner to the Transvaal, in 1877 "on his special mission" to the Boer polity, which resulted in its annexation (*Days* 1: 102, 62). The two chief factors that the British proffered for the appropriation of an area that was, as one popular guide book noted, "nearly the size of Great Britain and Ireland" were the bankruptcy of its government and the threat of its attack by the Zulus, both of which certainly made the Transvaal's majority Boer populace less resistant than it would otherwise have been (some Boers even welcomed British protection).[45] But of course the act was primarily one of self-interest, for a Zulu takeover of the Transvaal would have increased African power in the region, while continued Boer control might have resulted in the establishment of a railway line from the Transvaal to the coast that bypassed British territory—and tariffs—and thus strengthened Boer power, politically and economically. Further, the diamond fields bordered the Transvaal, and there seemed every possibility that either diamonds or gold would be discovered in the Transvaal itself, as was indeed the case.[46] When the proclamation of the annexation was read aloud, Haggard was not merely present, he "finished the business" for the much more senior man who "grew nervous in reading it."[47] And when the British flag was first raised publicly in the Transvaal, Haggard also did the honors. It was a story he told many times, initially to his mother, to whom he wrote: "It will be some years before people at home realize how great an act it [the annexation] has been, an act without parallel. I am very proud of having been connected with it. Twenty years hence, it will be a great thing to have hoisted the Union Jack over the Transvaal for the first time."[48]

After the annexation, Haggard imagined various futures for himself, all colonial. "The probabilities are," he wrote to his father, "that I shall stay in this country for many years" (102). Shortly after his twenty-first birthday, he was appointed Master and Registrar of the High Court of the Transvaal, in which position he traveled extensively throughout the region, collecting notes that he eventually used to create "scenes and characters" in *Jess*.[49] During this period, he and a friend built and lived in "The Palatial," the Pretoria home that served as the model for the cottage of the same name and location in *Jess* (*Days* 1: 116). More than twenty years after its publication, a journalist noted that it "is the only South African novel so far as I know that has conferred upon any place of habitation some species of literary individuality. There stands to this day on the outskirts of Pretoria a house half-hidden by immense blue-gums, which is pointed out to visitors as 'Jess's cottage.'"[50] The three-thousand-acre farm that Haggard purchased with another friend in 1879, when he left the colonial service to farm ostriches, likewise appears in *Jess*—as the Croft family farm—though there it is double the acreage and located in the Transvaal, while the original was just across the border in Natal (*Days* 1: 195, 180). After marrying on an 1880 visit to England, Haggard returned, with his new wife, in December of that year to find "the Transvaal in open rebellion" (175). Their arrival thus coincided with the start of the First Anglo-Boer War, which ended just fourteen weeks later with the signing of a treaty in Haggard's own farmhouse.[51] It was an excruciating conclusion to an acquisition in which he had played such a symbolic role.

As Haggard saw it, Britain's surrender, which meant the Transvaal's retrocession and thus the reinstatement of the South African Republic, weakened Britain's position not only in southern Africa but also globally, by signaling a lack of support for its own loyal colonists, like himself. "Pain[ed]" by "this great betrayal, the bitterness of which no lapse of time ever can solace or even alleviate," Haggard "suffered the highest sort of shame, shame for my country" (*Days* 1: 265, 194, 201).[52] If he had been doubly stung—betrayed as a colonist, shamed as a native-born Englishman—so, too, he felt, had southern Africa, a victim of the Boers and the British alike. "Believing that soon or late the British power was doomed to failure and probably to extinction there," Haggard returned with his family to England.[53] He had been a resident of southern Africa for only six years and would not return for more than thirty, then briefly and only twice: in 1914 as a British royal commissioner and in 1916 as a representative of the Royal Colonial Institute. For the remainder of his life, however, he would use southern Africa as a setting in his fiction and embrace his reputation as a South African expert. Indeed, his 1881 retreat was merely physical, for the "betrayal" that caused him to leave southern Africa also impelled him to build his identity on its foundations (*Days* 1: 265), at once to "abandon[]" and to internalize his colonial subjectivity.[54]

"Downing-street and the power behind it took [the war] lying down, for I fancy that had the matter been left in the hands of the English colonists," claimed Haggard, "there would have been a different tale to tell."[55] It is, in a way, this tale that *Jess* tells. For while it does not revise history—Britain still surrenders instead of sending the reinforcements needed to defeat the Boers—it does tell the story of triumph on a small scale: the qualified triumph of the fictional family to whom Haggard bequeathed his South African farm. The novel's central, impassioned drama—Frank Muller, a Boer leader, versus the Crofts, an English colonial family—plays out as a version of the war in miniature. Knitting together the personal and the political, it suggests that British South Africans, "we far away people [who] are only the counters with which they play their game," are more committed to empire than those who determine their fate; and while it clearly takes aim at Gladstone and his Liberal administration, it nonetheless suggests that British policy in southern Africa (and toward the Boers in particular) had long been inconsistent (*J* 59). Making an implicit comparison between the weakness of an inconstant imperial policy and the focused determination of a South African frontierswoman, *Jess* contemns the former while extolling the latter. For if, as Haggard depicts it, "the British lion was a humble animal in those days[,] its tail . . . tucked very tightly between its legs," the British colonial is vigorous and undaunted (*Days* 1: 184). At twenty-three, the novel's eponymous heroine has spent just over half her life in the Transvaal (and the rest in England), with her slightly younger sister, Bessie, and their uncle, Silas Croft, a seventy-year-old farmer who migrated to southern Africa from England as a young man in 1830. Though a love triangle exists between Jess, Bessie, and John Niel, a thirty-four-year-old retired English army captain new to the colony, and another between Bessie, John, and Muller, the "Anglo-Boer" villain (whose father is Boer and mother is English), *Jess* is as much a war story as it is a love story (*J* 93). Metro-colonial rather than gender politics drive the novel, yet it not only develops the figure of the independent settler heroine, foreground by Schreiner, it also transcends the domestic parameters in which *African Farm*, despite its feminist politics, remains trapped.

Pairing I: Cousins

The Story of an African Farm announces the New Woman's birth and emergent self-consciousness through the figure of Lyndall, who conceives of herself and her desires in political terms and aspires to become, but is unable finally to operate as, a self-sustaining agent outside the home. Though she is undoubtedly a feminist heroine, she is nonetheless introduced to readers, like the heroine of so many domestic novels, through her physical attributes. An "elfin-like beauty," she is the classic picture of Victorian femininity: her figure is "slight," her hands "tiny," her arms "dainty," her feet "small," her features "delicate," her chin "dimple[d]," her mouth "little," and her eyes "large" (*SAF* 36, 281, 242, 187, 266, 46, 188, 126, 242). Beautiful and self-assured, "she is like a little queen: her shoulders are so upright, and her head looks as though it ought to have a little crown upon it" (181). "It isn't any one's [*sic*] fault that they love you," her cousin Em insists, "they can't help it" (233). A pill for some, "the strong note of independence struck by [the novel's] heroine, a girl who possesses that strange magnetism for men of all sorts and conditions," was nonetheless more easily swallowed, wrapped in such a conventionally attractive package.[56]

Despite Lyndall's good looks and charm, it is not she but her cousin Em who represents the Victorian "'angel in the house,' [a] woman who only aspires to join all the others in their destiny of wives and mothers." Literalizing the opposition between colonial innovation and colonial replication, the pairing positively affirms the exceptionality of the novel's central heroine—"the extraordinary woman," as Edward Aveling described Lyndall in his 1883 review—while upholding the values of "the ordinary woman," Em.[57] "A premature little old woman" while still in her teens (*SAF* 155),

Em is "in effect domesticated from the start."[58] Naïve yet capable, deferential yet protective, she is like "the accompaniment of a song. She fills up the gaps in other people's lives" (231). Accepting a proposal of marriage from Gregory Rose, Em declares, " 'I will do everything you tell me'. . . . What else could she say? Her idea of love was only service" (180). Collecting the accouterments of wifeliness, she moons over the linens, aprons, quilts, and embroidery she has stored, packing and repacking them while contentedly imagining the married life ahead of her: "Every day when Gregory came home, tired from his work, he would look about and say, 'Where is my wife? Has no one seen my wife? Wife, some coffee!' and she would give him some" (182). For Em, a model of "uncomplaining womanhood," servitude is a woman's natural role and leadership a man's.[59] Consequently, when Gregory, dejected by Lyndall's departure, ceases to instruct (or criticize) Em, she "wishes that he would still sometimes talk of the strength and master-right of man" (*SAF* 245). Preoccupied with Lyndall while engaged to Em, Gregory complains to his sister of Lyndall's pride, unconventionality, intractability, and "unwomanl[iness]" (205). "I pity the man who marries *her*; I wouldn't be him for *anything*. . . . Now Em—I'm very fond of her . . . —but if I tell her to put on a certain dress, that dress she puts on; and if I tell her to sit on a certain seat, on that seat she sits; and if I tell her not to speak to a certain individual, she does not speak to them" (206–07). Though his fiancée is everything that Gregory claims he wants a woman to be, the "but" that precedes his description is an indication of his true preference; for, as he soon realizes, he would rather "serve" Lyndall than "rule" Em (232, 245). True to form, Em willingly steps aside, making way for Gregory's betrothal to Lyndall, just as, after her cousin's death, she willingly takes him back.

Em's pliability and subservience contrast sharply with Lyndall's independence and assertiveness, qualities that intimidate the farm's two tyrannical rulers, Tant' (Aunt) Sannie, their Boer guardian, and Bonaparte Blenkins, the opportunistic Irishman who connives his way from schoolteacher to overseer. When Bonaparte is angry with Lyndall, he demands Em's expiation, just as Tant' Sannie, who "had struck Lyndall once years before, and had never done it again," thrashes Em when Lyndall defies her (91). "Lay[ing] her small fingers on the Boer-woman's arm," Lyndall secures her cousin's release, though "with the exertion of half its strength Tant' Sannie might have flung the girl back upon the stones. It [is] not the power of the slight fingers," but the look in her "clear eyes" that stays Tant' Sannie's hand (91). When Lyndall subsequently commands Bonaparte, who is in league with Tant' Sannie, with the single word, "Move!" he, "Bonaparte the invincible, . . . moved to give her place" (91). After Bonaparte beats Waldo Farber, the son of the caretaker whom Bonaparte supersedes, and locks him in the fuel-house overnight, Em " 'beg[s] Bonaparte to let him out, and he won't.' 'The more you beg the more he will not,' " explains Lyndall, promptly removing the key from its place, as Bonaparte and Tant' Sannie, cowed by the child, look on without interfering (126).

But there are limitations to Lyndall's authority, as she learns in her years on the farm and at the boarding school to which she successfully convinces the frugal, controlling, and conservative Tant' Sannie to send her. As a young child, Lyndall equates effort with success. When Em asks her why she succeeds at threading beads while she herself fails, Lyndall responds, simply, "I try. . . . That is why" (38). "She *always* does what she says," claims the former of her cousin, whose admiration for Napoleon, "the greatest man in the world," hinges on his determined acquisition of power (76, 47). "He was not born great, he was common as we are," says the poor, orphaned, rural, largely uneducated Lyndall, "yet he was master of the world at last. Once he was only a little child, then he was a lieutenant, then he was a general, then he was an emperor. When he said a thing to himself he never forgot it. He waited, and waited, and waited, and it came at last" (47). Lyndall bites her lip, grinds her teeth, clasps her hands, and takes what small actions she can as she awaits the adulthood that she thinks will bring her power (93, 92, 126). But authority never comes. Four years at boarding school fail to empower her in the ways she had hoped, though it does teach her that her gender is the principal cause of her disempowerment. "If Napoleon had been born a woman," she remarks on her return, "he would have risen; but the world would not have heard of him as it hears of him now," for he could only have "rule[d] in the dark, covertly, and by stealth, through . . . men" (192). It is a great disappointment for the woman who as a child had remarked that Napoleon's happiness was inconsequential: "he had what he said he would have, and that is better than being happy" (48).

Pairing II: Sisters

The contrast between Lyndall and Em (*African Farm*) is sharper than that between Jess and Bessie (*Jess*), both because Lyndall is more radical than Jess and because Em is more conventional than Bessie. While Lyndall consciously opposes a social system that oppresses (white) women at all times,

Jess, more narrowly and only implicitly, opposes social mores that would impede her own actions in wartime, on the basis of gender. And if Em "resembles a female from an earlier moment in the history of fiction,"[60] Bessie modifies without truly replicating that fictional female. In contrast to her adventure-seeking cousin, Lyndall—who says of herself, "I like to experience, I like to try"—Em is compelled to do no more than work, tend, and nurture—to meet gendered expectations (*SAF* 238). *Both* Jess and Bessie, however, display physical stamina and rugged courage, qualities not often associated with domestic heroines, though ones that Haggard suggests, in *Jess* as in the female colonial romance (see chapter 2), are compatible with colonial rurality and its associated challenges. Nonetheless, there are notable differences between the sisters, marking them as unconventional and traditional, respectively. While Jess is "not . . . good-looking," Bessie is "charming to look on" (*J* 178, 67).[61] While Jess is "deep[-]nature[d]," Bessie is "nature[-]made to love and be loved as maid and wife and mother" (52, 127). While Jess is "remarkable" and "interesting," Bessie is "sweet" and "simple-natured" (10, 67, 128, 257). While Jess is "peculiar" and "passionate," Bessie is "happy [and] plain-sailing" (98, 340, 31).

If Jess is "a feminine enigma," Bessie is easily identifiable as the domestic heroine, whose "housewifely" attributes are complemented by colonial vigor, a potent combination evinced by many of Haggard's (white) South African heroines (45, 13), as I discuss further in the next chapter. Well acclimated to farm life in the Transvaal, Bessie is a "daughter of the wilderness" (6). Readers first encounter her bravely hurling herself at a refractory ostrich that is attempting to kill John Niel.[62] "Moves like a springbuck," explains her uncle to the newcomer, "and what an eye and form! Work, too—she'll do as much work as three" (*J* 14). Though "weaker than [Jess], and less suited to bear pain," she "decline[s]" to "fly for [her] life into Natal," instead valiantly remaining by her uncle's side on his farm during the war (63, 237). She goes as far as to "throw her arms about his body to protect him" while he is being kicked by a "mass of Boers" (265). "As healthy, graceful, and generally satisfactory a young woman as a man could wish to see," Bessie "remind[s] [Niel] of a rich rosebud bursting into bloom" (14, 110). How long, he wonders, will "it . . . be possible to live in the same house with her without falling under the spell of her charm and beauty" (24). Not long, as it turns out, for though "not violently in love with her," he all too hastily proposes (100). At first, Bessie modestly demurs: "I'm not fit to marry a man like you. . . . I am nothing but an ignorant, half-educated farmer girl"—who is adept at Zulu, Dutch (the *taal*), and English, as well as South African farming techniques—"with nothing to recommend me, and no fortune except my looks" (109). To illustrate her inadequacy, she compares herself to her sister: "If it had been Jess now, it would have been different, for she has more brains in her little finger than I have in my whole body" (109).[63] More than once, Niel also reflects on the "strange contrast [between] the two" (24). For instance, he thinks: "Bessie was, no doubt, delightful and [pretty], but she had not got her sister's brains and originality" (67). More metaphorically, he judges, "the one is all flower and the other is all root" (161). Like Schreiner's Gregory, who is at first smitten with Em, Niel is initially drawn to the domestically inclined Bessie, but Jess's "intellect and originality . . . interested him intensely," and so, like Gregory, his attraction to the flower gives way before his passion for the root (67). In southern Africa, it would seem, Victorian femininity is no match for what one early twentieth-century critic described as the "mental masculinity so often displayed in [white] women" there.[64]

Bessie understands the distinction between herself and her sister: "I represent labor and Jess represents intellect. . . . [S]he got all the brains" (*J* 24). Indeed, it is through her mental acuity that "clever" Jess is first introduced (7). "Just like ten women rolled into one so far as her mind goes," observes another woman (168). But Jess is not merely intelligent, she is also "well-informed" and engaged, qualities that facilitate her heroism (31). An avid reader of "the standard authors," she writes poetry, collects literature, and speaks to Niel (before their occupancy of "The Palatial" during the siege of Pretoria) mostly "about books, or England, or some intellectual question" (12, 158, 32). "She ought to . . . write books and become a famous woman," notes her sister (24). A regular follower of "the home papers," she reads "the political articles in the *Saturday Review* aloud to" her uncle, a task for which she is better suited than Bessie, whose "mind was not quite in tune with the profundities of that learned journal" (58, 97). Speculating on the outcome of the war before it has even begun, Jess is the only one of the novel's English characters to accurately predict its outcome. Echoing Haggard's conservatism—and reflecting his hindsight—Jess notes: "The other people [Liberals] are in power now in England, and one does not know what they may do. . . . They might give us up to the Boers" (59). Where Lyndall's interest in politics is *limited* to the Woman Question, Jess's interest seemingly *excludes* it, and neither shows any concern for the position of indigenous Africans. Though Haggard (through his narrator and other characters) makes much of Jess's intelligence while Schreiner leaves Lyndall's to speak for itself, Lyndall is the intellectual feminist of the two; and in the end it is not so much Jess's mental prowess that makes her remarkable as her resolve and fortitude.

Theory over Practice: Lyndall

Boarding school provides Lyndall not, as she had hoped, with knowledge that will improve her condition, but with the knowledge that no knowledge can.[65] "I once heard an old man say," she tells Waldo, "that he never saw intellect help a woman so much as a pretty ankle; and it was the truth" (*SAF* 188). Anticipating elements of third-wave feminism, she has come to recognize social construction as the primary force behind women's inequality. Women, in short, are "crushed" into a handful of limited roles (185). Though "we all enter the world little plastic beings, [largely] blank[,] the world tells us what we are to be, and shapes us by the ends it sets before us. To [the male] it says—*Work!* And to [the female] it says—*Seem!*" (188). "We were equals when we [were] new-born babes," but from the time "we are tiny things in shoes and socks," boys and girls are treated differently (190, 189). Boys are permitted "their happy play" out of doors, while girls are made to stay inside, lest they "spoil" their fair "complexion[s]" and "white frocks" (189). Boys are given a decent education, while girls are sent to "finishing schools," where they are instructed in domestic tasks, like sewing and decorating (185). "I have seen some souls so compressed [there] that they would have fitted into a small thimble"—a crisp domestic image, reinforced by Waldo's gift of a thimble to Em—"and found room to move" (185). Through both formal and informal education, Lyndall concludes, "*the world* makes men and women" (188; my emphasis). Strength, knowledge, and labor, advantageous to men in "gain[ing] all that [the] human heart desires," are useless to women, who, confined to the domestic, are taught to "fit our sphere as a Chinese woman's foot fits her shoe, exactly, as though God had made both—*and yet He knows nothing of either*" (188, 189; my emphasis). Society, not nature (or divinity), "shape[s] us to our cursed end" so successfully that the "grown women" who as little girls yearned to join their brothers in "a more healthy life" have generally given up both "longing" and "striving" and learned instead to "march with [their] regiment" (189).

By the time that Lyndall returns from boarding school, "the position of women . . . is the only thing about which [she] think[s] much or feel[s] much" (187). She speaks on the subject primarily to Waldo but also briefly to her lover, RR, and to Em. Her arguments read like a roster of those articulated by the metropolitan New Woman the following decade: female education "cultivate[s]" "imbecility and weakness"; female intelligence is undervalued and underutilized; women, employed only as "ill-paid drudges," lack opportunities to do interesting work; women are judged by their appearance, but even beauty is a curse; marriage is for women a kind of slavery, though "old maidenhood[,] . . . a name that in itself signifies defeat," has scant advantages; and, denied the freedom of boys and men, women have few substantive choices in life (185, 190, 194).

Cogent, eloquent, and prescient though her expatiations are, they are not supported by a plan of action to implement change. She recognizes that society not ability hampers the female sex, predicts that society will eventually change, and aches to live in "the future," when "perhaps, to be born a woman will not be to be born branded," but she does nothing to bring that future about (188). If she desires a "time . . . when each woman's life is filled with earnest, independent labour," why, Waldo reasonably asks, "do you not try to bring that time? . . . When you speak, I believe all you say; other people would listen to you also" (195). Notwithstanding this encouragement, Lyndall does not lead, organize, or even participate in a group. She forms bonds with no women, white or of color. The Boers are "low," the boarding school matrons are "cackling old women," and her classmates are "suffocating" "things" (205, 186). Despite her use of the word "branded" to describe the plight of women, she speaks implicitly only of white women, utterly failing to make any connection between gendered and racial subjugation, or to form alliances with any of the African women for whom the farm is also home (188). As First and Scott note, "the imperative to self-reliance haunts her to the end of her life."[66]

Deeply entitled and filled with contradictory impulses, Lyndall does little for herself and less for others. She does not work as hard as Em. She does not try to make the most of her education. She does not hesitate to appropriate her cousin's fiancé. She does not consider joining Waldo in search of employment beyond the farm. She is attracted to the arts but "fail[s] to establish any calling or vocation." She uses both Gregory and RR, who surely has at least some claim on the child she prevents him from seeing. Sustained by RR's money, nursed by Gregory's hands, and most comfortable in the role of "queen," Lyndall does not offer significant assistance to anyone (*SAF* 181).[67] She desires "the knowledge and power of the male" but also "yearn[s] for the signifiers of femininity"[68]—"real diamonds," for instance, "pure, white silk, and little rosebuds" (*SAF* 45, 46). She does not want to marry—to be "h[e]ld . . . fast" (236), "to [be] master[ed]" (238)—but she can conceive of loving so "that to lie under the foot of the thing [she] loved would be more heaven than to lie in the breast of another" (232).⁶⁹

As Lyndall advances in the pregnancy that is more swan song than gestation period, she begins to connect her failure to thrive to defects in herself. "I will do nothing good for myself, nothing for the world, till someone wakes me," she tells Waldo. "I am swathed, shut up in self; till I have been delivered I will deliver no one" (*SAF* 196). On the night before her final departure from the farm, she goes to the graveside of Otto Farber, the farm's longtime caretaker and a surrogate father to her and Em. As she says goodbye, she laments not his passing but herself: "I am so weary of myself! It is eating my soul to its core—self, self, self! I cannot bear this life! I cannot breathe, I cannot live! Will nothing free me from myself?" (241) Gazing into a mirror back in her room, she again reflects: "We are all alone, you and I . . . ; no one helps us, no one understands us; but we will help ourselves" (242). Moved by self-pity to affirm her independence, Lyndall demonstrates absolutely no regard for the support she has received: from her cousin, who sacrificed her lover for her; from Tant' Sannie, who permitted her the education denied to Em; from Waldo, who left his beloved dog behind to care for her; even from RR, whose money put food in her mouth and a roof over her head. Lyndall's final breath is drawn in the sight of her own reflection as a disguised Gregory, unacknowledged and unappreciated, drives her home.

From one vantage point, Lyndall's sense of entitlement is an affirmation of the inherent equality of women, the fulcrum of her refusal to compromise; from another, it reflects both her limited perspective, her belief in the inherent superiority of whites in general and the English in particular, and her self-involvement. Social restrictions, though the primary, are thus not the only cause of her failure to establish a viable path for herself, to grow into the woman she desires to become; her own imperiousness, narrow scope, and self-absorption are contributing factors as well. So while Lyndall's failure to thrive legitimates the necessity of feminist rebellion, it also reflects the youthful, privileged, colonial, British female subject's inability to think beyond herself. One wonders if this inability is only Lyndall's, or whether it was Schreiner's as well; for not only does Schreiner treat the novel's black characters as little more than "reflector figures," she also gives no sign of recognizing that their plight resonates with that of white women.⁷⁰

Only later in life would Schreiner come to recognize and object to racial inequality, as she had long objected to gender inequality. In her fiction, this is most notable in *Trooper Peter Halket of Mashonaland* (1897), a semi-religious, allegorical, anti-imperialist novella in which the protagonist, a soldier in Cecil Rhodes's British South Africa Company (BSAC), eventually recognizes and rejects his former racism at the cost of his life.[71] It is also apparent in *From Man to Man*, in which the heroine reflects on her former racism, much like Schreiner herself, who attributed the change in her "feeling towards the native races [to] increased knowledge."[72] Schreiner also registered her opposition to racial injustice by "resigning from the South African Women's Enfranchisement League when its definition of the voting qualification was changed so as to exclude black women."[73] And in her 1908 article "The Native Question," she expressed her "oppos[ition] [to] a Union of South African states because of the colour bar in the proposed constitution." "In the end the subjected people write their features on the face of the conquerors," she wrote, for "the continual association with human creatures who are not free, will ultimately take from us our strength and our own freedom; and men will see in our faces the reflection of that on which we are always treading and looking down."[74]

Practice over Theory: Jess

Entirely silent on matters of female education, marriage, work, sexuality, and maternity, Jess makes no *arguments* in favor of social change. Her heroic and sexual *actions* break with gendered expectations, but they do not, unlike those of the New Woman, disrupt the social order.[75] On the contrary, in killing Muller—her most aggressive, least "feminine" act—Jess protects her sister's virtue and preserves the English family that the Boer leader, by murdering Bessie's fiancé, imprisoning their uncle, and forcing Bessie to marry him, sought to break apart.[76] Unlike the New Woman, who "refuses to be assimilated into the iconography of Victorian 'Womanhood,'" Jess, in her willingness both to surrender her beloved *to* and to kill *for* her sister, is an exemplar of feminine self-sacrifice.[77] Even her physical intimacy with Niel (who is engaged to her sister) does not mark her as transgressive. Depicted as an act of solemnity in the (erroneous, as is turns out) certitude of impending death, it is justified by a narrator who urges readers to condemn neither Jess nor "her lover" (*J* 301).

Referred to by four characters and the narrator a total of six times as "odd," a word that would come to be associated with the New Woman in the subsequent decade, Jess suggests this figure in limited ways.[78] For example, while she sees her own keen intelligence as more "curse" than "blessing," the burden stems from the exceptionality of her perspicacity—"lifting her above the level of her sex and shutting her off as by iron doors from the comprehension of those around her"—rather than from any social limitation (*J* 32). Lyndall, on the other hand, places the blame squarely on society. "What would knowledge help me?" she asks sardonically. "The less a woman has in her head the lighter she is for climbing" (*SAF* 189). The superiority of Jess's intellect to that of the man she loves, "a decidedly intellectual man . . . in [whom] Jess found a mind which, though of an inferior stamp, was more or less kindred to her own," distinguishes her from the Victorian angel, but her dream of service to him does not (*J* 126, 32).[79] For though it is spiritual partnership, rather "the idea of marriage, and that change of status which [most women] consider desirable" that appeals to Jess, she nonetheless yearns "to lay down her life, as it were, in the life of another" (32). After all, the narrator confidently asserts, "the prouder the woman the more delight does she extract from her self-abasement before her idol" (158).[80] Jess imagines something of a New Woman's future for herself, but only after "she had put herself out of the reach of passion" (150). Confident that "if she willed it, she could gain [Niel's] heart and hold it against all the world," she leaves her uncle's farm to encourage a relationship between Niel and Bessie (49).[81] Having learned of their engagement, she reflects on her own future:

> What was she to do with herself? Marry somebody and busy herself with rearing a pack of children? It would be a physical impossibility to her. No, she would go away to Europe and mix in the great stream of life and struggle with it, and see if she could win a place for herself among the people of her day. She had it in her, she knew that. (150)

For Jess, then, marriage is not the only acceptable path for a woman—independence being preferable to a union without "passion"—but it nonetheless remains the aspirational ideal, as much for women as for men. The gender politics of marriage go unremarked, both by Jess and the novel that bears her name.

She is nonetheless bold, self-reliant, and resourceful, qualities more often found in male than in female protagonists of the era. Having traveled two hundred miles from the family farm to Pretoria, Jess may be trapped on the outskirts of the now besieged city at the "outbreak of hostilities," but she is no damsel in distress (147). When Niel arrives to rescue her, she declares as much, condemning his folly and asserting her independence: "Why have you come? Why did you leave Bessie and my uncle? . . . You must have been mad! How could you expect to get back? We shall both be shut up here together now"—as indeed they are (152). Unlike Niel, who can "enroll himself in the corps of mounted volunteers," Jess cannot directly participate in the war effort (156).[82] Niel's contributions, however, like those of all the novel's Englishmen, are negligible. Given that the skirmishes in which he participates, like the major battles taking place farther afield, "were not, on the whole, creditable to our arms, perhaps the less said about them the better," opines the narrator (159). On one such excursion, Niel "was slightly wounded by a bullet which passed between his saddle and his thigh," summing up, in effect, Haggard's estimation of imperial (in)efficacy during the war (162). Niel's wound—like the war itself—turns out to be more serious than at first expected, since the walls around the (presumably femoral) artery, though only grazed, twice give way, causing major blood loss and requiring surgery. Without the attention of Jess, who fetches the doctor in the first instance, reduces blood loss in the second, and then vigilantly nurses Niel for three days, during which time "he lay in a dangerous state, . . . having so little blood left in his veins," he would surely have died (172).

Having saved the life of the man who came to rescue her, Jess next manages their escape, for while Niel optimistically awaits relief, Jess astutely takes matters into her own hands. In his failure of insight, Niel is like the rest of "these foolish people in Pretoria," as the narrator describes them, who "labored under a firm belief that one fine morning they would be gratified with a vision of the light dancing down a long line of British bayonets, and of Boers evaporating in every direction like storm clouds before the sun" (179). Jess, however, knows better. "Beginning to lose faith in relieving columns that never came," she concludes, "if we don't help ourselves, . . . we may stop here till we are starved out" (179). Unwilling to sit by and let that happen, she deftly negotiates with an old Boer farmer, whom she knows to be in debt to her uncle, for their pass to travel home.

While Jess, unlike Lyndall, may have nothing *to say* about sexual freedom, it is clear that she, too, sees intimacy as a personal expression that need not have procreative aims. Following the shock of the (false) report of Niel's death and his subsequent reappearance, Jess "for the first time, where her love was concerned, . . . put out all her strength," so that, as she gazes at him, "the smouldering embers broke into flame, and he knew that he loved this woman as he had never loved any living creature before"

(166). In light of Niel's engagement to Bessie, however, they "renounce" their mutual admission, until what they think is the last night of their lives (174). Though they have survived an assassination attempt (instigated by Muller), they nonetheless find themselves trapped "in [a] sinking waggon [*sic*] on the waters of the flooded Vaal" (*Days* 2: 207). At this point, they not only "exchange[] their undying troth," they also implicitly—or at least, symbolically—consummate it (*J* 289). As the wagon "swung . . . to and fro . . . in the rush of [the] swollen river," "the carcasses of the[ir] horses, r[i]s[ing] and f[a]ll[ing]" beside them, the corpse of their Zulu driver "stiffening" beneath them, moonbeams "quivering" on the "surface" of the water around them (230), Jess and Niel, no "longer capable of reason" (231), experience "the fullest and acutest joy that life has to offer" (230). On their solitary "bridge of passion made perfect and sanctified by its approaching earthly end," even "Bessie was forgotten, all things were forgotten in that consuming fire" (230). Of their feelings, words, and actions, the latter alluded to both directly—Niel "pressed his lips against hers and kissed her again and again" (230)—and indirectly—"r[i]s[ing] and f[a]ll[ing]," "stiffening," "quivering," "bridge of passion," "consuming fire," and so on—the narrator encourages readers to withhold censure:

> Let those who would blame them pause awhile. Why not? They had kept the faith. They had denied themselves and run straightly down the path of duty. But the compacts of life end with life. No man may bargain for the beyond. Even the marriage service shrinks from it. . . . [W]hy should they not take their happiness . . . ? (230–31)

Singled out by Haggard as one of his favorite passages[83] and celebrated by a narrator who describes it in matrimonial terms, this "wild . . . love scene" clearly marks Jess as unconventional (*J* 230). In her challenge to established morality, Jess, like Lyndall, augurs the New Woman heroine who would become a fixture of 1890s fiction.

Genre and Colonial Domesticity I: Invention and Retention

In his 1883 review of *African Farm* for the radical journal *Progress: A Monthly Magazine of Advanced Thought*, Aveling wrote that while he liked the novel, it was "pathetic . . . that this Lyndall of indomitable will, of unflinching courage, beautiful, able, fascinating, . . . does little or nothing." More recent critics have made similar points. "Lyndall resigns herself to failure," writes Ann Ardis. "She claims a voice—and then relinquishes it." According to First and Scott, Lyndall "presents herself as being able to *see* the good and the beautiful and to have no strength to *live* it. . . . She is capable only of perception of an alternative, not of bringing it about."[84] In the preceding quotations, Aveling praises Lyndall's character, Ardis her voice, and First and Scott her vision, the standout features of a novel valued largely for its progressive, anticipatory gender politics; but in tones of disappointment they also remark Lyndall's inaction, which they all seem to suggest mars the novel.

Lyndall's failure to implement her vision, to free even herself from confinement, reflects both the social restrictions and personal limitations that have already been discussed as well as a surprising degree of generic resilience. If Lyndall is trapped, so, too, is *African Farm*, by the parameters of the domestic novel beyond which it pushes but to which it ultimately returns. While Schreiner may have introduced British literature's first truly feminist heroine, giving rise to a genre, the subject of women's place in society was itself not new to fiction. Counterintuitively, perhaps, "the urgency of the woman question [is] possibly the most salient generic trait" of the domestic novel that preceded it.[85] But where the domestic novel centers on home, the New Woman novel charts a woman's steps beyond it. Where the domestic novel apotheosizes the angel in the house even as it also sometimes raises questions about the circumscription of her role, the New Woman novel "ruthlessly hack[s] away the foundations of an idealized femininity." And where the domestic novel frequently inflicts "approved moral retribution" on a woman whose sexual behavior veers in any way from the well-trodden path of heterosexual courtship and monogamous marriage, the New Woman novel might allow such behavior to go unpunished; it might even celebrate it.[86] *African Farm* falls somewhere between the two genres.[87] Struggling to imagine an affirming realm for women beyond domestic space, it poses the possibility of roles other than angel and outcast; and while it does not reward the angel, neither does it allow the New Woman to endure. Lyndall's ideas and desires make her a New Woman, but her "feminist rhetoric is at odds with the novel's plot," one that does not celebrate but nonetheless centers on domestic space, family, and courtship.[88]

The farmstead, for instance, is the axis of Schreiner's novel, but no one there is truly secure. In contrast to the ambient "hominess" of the domestic novel, estrangement pervades the farm.[89] After eleven years of loyal service,

Otto is undermined by the scheming Bonaparte and abruptly expelled. He takes almost nothing with him, because, as he puts it, "nothing is mine" (*SAF* 94). The African herder, unjustly accused of theft, is also, along with his family, forced off the land. Though Tant' Sannie manages the estate, her claim is both impermanent and conditional, for according to the terms of her late husband's will, it becomes Em's on her seventeenth birthday, and should Tant' Sannie marry before Em turns sixteen, she would forfeit the sheep that he left her. Though Em is the rightful owner of her father's books and mother's clothes, Tant' Sannie gives her access to neither. And though both she and her cousin reside under the same roof as her stepmother, "the house where Tant' Sannie lived and ruled was a place to sleep in, to eat in, not to be happy in" (54). They find happiness only in Otto's modest cabin, "the one home the girls had known for many a year," until Bonaparte takes it over (54). For the children, Lyndall, Em, and Waldo, "the farm is [a place] of walls, gates, [and] locked doors," which function to keep them both out and in.[90] Treated as interlopers, they are shut out of some spaces and confined to others when they dare to transgress.

If the children are not wholly welcome inhabitants of, neither are they part of social networks within or beyond the farm, since the "family-systems [and] town-systems" that support, even if they also challenge, the protagonists of the domestic novel are absent or extraneous in *African Farm*.[91] Em and Lyndall have no relatives but one another (and Tant' Sannie, by marriage), and Waldo has only his father. The remote farm almost never has visitors, no close neighbors are mentioned, the nearest town can only be reached by conveyance, and the most proximate mill is "some days" journey (*SAF* 85). Though Africans work and live on the farm—we hear of them churning butter, milking cows, herding cattle, cooking, cleaning, translating, even laughing, playing, and praying—they are nameless and almost entirely speechless.[92] Their communities are nearly as foreign to the children as the Boer community; and if Schreiner is indifferent to Africans, she is unsympathetic to Boers in this earliest novel. The former are widely diffuse and only marginally present through Tant' Sannie's suitor (and later husband), Little Piet Vander Walt, their "Boer-Wedding" (the title of part 2, chapter 6), and Sannie's niece Trana.[93]

For Schreiner's white protagonists, the land itself is no more nourishing than the homestead built upon or the communities within and around it. Settled by an Englishman, run by a Boer, managed by a German and later an Irishman, bequeathed to an English South African, and worked largely by Africans, the African farm in some sense remains staunchly African.

Put another way, the (African) land never wholly yields, either materially or metaphorically, to the hands of (European) interlopers. The sheep are "sluggish," "the land is dry and unforgiving, the livestock bare-ribbed, and the crops scant."[94] But if the farm is unproductive, so, too, are its white inhabitants, who largely fail to thrive, reproduce, or even survive, for neither the farm nor the settlers who occupy it are "integrated with the land." Both thus seem detached from or "outside history."[95] Of course, it is not that the land has no history, but that it cannot (like the subaltern) be heard or read properly. The whites cannot interpret the Bushmen paintings or understand the languages of Africans any more than they can build a future there for themselves.[96] "Schreiner's novel," writes Jed Esty, "emphasizes the futurelessness of life eked out on the edge of the veldt." The failure of both farm and protagonists to thrive, he further claims, "literalizes the pervasive political and economic fact [that] the colonies do not—cannot—come of age under the rule of empire."[97] Noted by Jean Marquard, J. M. Coetzee, and Stephen Gray as characteristic of white South African writing generally (and of Schreiner's novel in particular), white settlers' "estrangement, alienation, [and] displacement" express "the protagonist's [or protagonists'] insecurity" about and sometimes also the author's critique of colonial possession.[98]

The settlers' alienation from the unproductive farm is in some sense paralleled by readers' experience of a farm about which key details are withheld, name and location chief among them. Though Schreiner called the farm, and the novel itself, "Thorn Kloof" early on, she struck the name entirely from the published version; the farm that readers encounter is never named.[99] The novel opens with a reference to the "African moon," but South Africa is not named in the body of the text (*SAF* 35).[100] Readers somewhat familiar with southern Africa might (have) deduce(d), through a few suggestive details, that the novel is set in the Cape Colony, but Africa "remain[s] a gauzy backdrop."[101] No mention is made of topical controversies, events, or affairs (beyond two passing references to the diamond mines), including the state of relations between African groups, settlers and Africans, British and Boers, southern Africa's colonies, or colony and metropole. Of course, interactions between indigenous peoples and settlers, as well as between Boers and British, do occur in the text, but for the most part they lack social and historical context.[102] To some extent, then, the farm is both dehistoricized and "deterritorialized," prompting Aveling to remark that the novel records "events [that] might, with but slight modification, be recorded of an Indian bungalow or an English homestead."[103]

Having established the keynote of disharmony between home and inhabitant in *African Farm*, I now return directly to the question of its relationship to the domestic novel. Comparing the "Old World farming"—or provincial—novel to Schreiner's novel, Coetzee writes: "Whereas in the Old World model the farm is *naturalized* by being integrated with the land, and in turn historicizes the land by making the land a page on which the generations write their story, Schreiner's farm is an unnatural and arbitrary imposition on a doggedly ahistorical landscape."[104] What holds true for the "Old World" provincial novel, as Coetzee describes it, holds true for the "Old World" domestic novel as well. That is, it generally centers on an individual or a family who not only occupies but also *belongs* in and to a localized, concretized place (as it has at least as far back as Jane Austen)—be it farm, estate, village, or, less often, urban community—through which the family story can be told, which is to say history written.[105] Making the farm the story's core, while denying it specificity (in name and place), estranging the central characters from it, and significantly decontextualizing the land on which it sits, Schreiner draws attention to the lack of a cohesive family narrative in her broadly (African) but pointedly (the story) named *The Story of an African Farm*. In doing so, she grounds the novel in the domestic tradition, while upending many of the genre's central characteristics. Schreiner creates, we might say, a palimpsest, but she does not turn a new leaf; for unlike the many New Woman novels that would follow in its wake, *African Farm* fails to imagine a place for women beyond home, school, and sickroom. No details, for instance, are provided of Lyndall's initial meeting with RR, their courtship, or their first parting, and there is only the briefest allusion to a sexual encounter between them.[106] Of their travels together, readers hear little more—and then only at a remove.[107] As Laurence Lerner notes, with apparent dissatisfaction, "the author seems compelled to keep Lyndall offstage at all the important moments."[108] Such narrative decisions may reflect the limit of young Schreiner's imagination, though given her frequent emphasis on future possibilities for women, they more likely reflect her reluctance fully to explore the pain of her own corresponding moments of disappointment, her own increasing awareness of the circumscription of adult womanhood.[109] Certainly, they connect the novel to the tradition of domestic fiction, for inasmuch as Lyndall is dissatisfied with the constraints of domesticity, her story is almost exclusively limited to domestic space.

In contrast to the domestic novel's celebration of domestic values, rituals, and qualities, above all through the angel who embodies them, *African Farm* "pathologizes the domestic domain" and celebrates the heroine who seeks to escape it.[110] Not only, as we have seen, is home an unwelcoming place in Schreiner's novel but its "mother" and "fathers" are figures of excess and lack. Demanding, foul-mouthed, coarse, selfish, lazy, ungenerous, and unsympathetic, Tant' Sannie is anything but a model of domesticity, despite her position as the farm's head of "household" (*SAF* 82).[111] Though Em's father married her "when he was dying" in the hope that she would take better care of the girls "than an English-woman," he has obviously misjudged her (45). She offers the girls neither kindness nor affection and, stinting both books and schoolmaster, denies Em the formal education her father had hoped she would provide. Anticipating a betrothal on the basis of a most unromantic dream about "killing" a red-eyed "beast," Tant' Sannie holds an upsitting (201). This Boer tradition, in which a couple sits alone together through a single night, contrasts sharply with the slowly unfolding courtship depicted in the domestic novel. If, as Tant' Sannie describes him, her nineteen-year-old suitor, Little Piet, is a "stupid thing [who] doesn't know how to talk love-talk," she is not much better (204). Cancer, toothache, convulsions, "croup, measles, jaundice, dropsy," and death are among the subjects she introduces during their awkward night together. Urging her own suit, Tant' Sannie roughly proposes and is accepted "in a tone of hopeless resignation" by the young widower whose "pa" has urged him to wed "before the shearing-time" (202, 204). Returning to the farm that now belongs to Em, Tant' Sannie praises marriage and motherhood to the stepdaughter she mistreated, while her "mild young husband . . . nurs[es] the[ir] baby—a pudding-faced, weak-eyed child," whom she refers to as "it" (293). "If a woman's got a baby and a husband she's got the best things the Lord can give her. . . . As for a husband, it's very much the same who one has. . . . A man's a man you know" (293). Tant' Sannie's version of domestic bliss—an easily dominated husband, one as good as another, a sickly baby, in her husband's arms, and a home to which, due to her increasing weight, she will soon be bound—is as much a parody of the traditional ending of the domestic novel as her brief courtship is an inversion of its romance plot.[112]

If Tant' Sannie is a "monstrous mother," Em's (long deceased) father, Otto, and Bonaparte are all in their own ways faulty fathers.[113] Though Em's father carefully protected the children in his will, his decision to marry Tant' Sannie for their sake leaves them in uncaring hands. Otto, the girls' surrogate father, is "benevolent," patient, and nurturing, but he is also naïve; and in his "inability to distinguish good from bad and true from false, [he] leaves the children . . . vulnerable."[114] Both men are well intentioned, but show poor character judgment—regarding Tant' Sannie and Bonaparte, respectively—that redounds negatively to the three children. Merciless and scheming, Bonaparte is an impediment rather than an asset to their development. Though "installed as schoolmaster," he has nothing at all to teach the girls, as Lyndall quickly confirms when the Irishman identifies Copernicus as "one of the Emperors of Rome" (*SAF* 82, 76). In an act of treachery that directly results in the termination of Otto's employment and indirectly in the cessation of his heart, he deprives Waldo of his father. Claiming to "stand" in his father's "place," he then mocks Waldo's grief, destroys his sheep-shearing machine, trips him into a pigsty, beats him to within an inch of his life, and locks him in "solitary confinement," all while reveling in the boy's misery (122, 123). Several critics have described Bonaparte as Dickensian in his heartlessness,[115] and Schreiner herself noted that while she drew him "closely after life," she did so "in hard straight lines without shading" (*Letters* 35).

But if Bonaparte invokes tragedy in his excessive cruelty, he also invokes comedy in his unrelenting self-interest, as we see in his ridiculous efforts to secure wealth through women. Claiming first to be married to get into Tant' Sannie's good graces—"Dutch people do not like those who are not married," warns Otto—then later to be heartbroken at the news of his (fabricated) wife's passing, to elicit sympathy and make himself appear marriageable, Bonaparte flatters Tant' Sannie by degrees. He knows that the widow has possession of the farm for a few more years as well as "sheep and . . . money in the bank" (*SAF* 53, 200). When Trana comes to stay with her aunt, Bonaparte turns his attention to this taciturn, "lumpish," finger-sucking fifteen-year-old, whose "father's got two thousand pounds . . . and a farm, and five thousand sheep, and . . . many goats and horses" (117, 116). Wooing her with sighs and bumps ("Aunt, why does the Englishman always knock against a person when he passes them?"), whose meaning neither she nor her aunt correctly deciphers, Bonaparte makes his final move in a florid outpouring of affection and gesticulations that Trana, "who understood not one word of English," misinterprets as a sign of stomachache (118, 129). His suit is "abruptly terminated" when a furious Tant' Sannie, spying from the loft above, douses him in "a stream of cold pickle-water, heavy with [sheep] ribs and shoulders," which sends him permanently fleeing the farm (130).

Bonaparte's ridiculous pursuit of the two Boer women makes up only two of several dubious courtship plots in a novel that critiques the ritual. Others include the already mentioned courtship of Tant' Sannie and Little Piet, Gregory's quest after first Em and then Lyndall, and Lyndall's romance with RR. From the outset, when readers meet Gregory lovelorn and sighing, he is coded feminine, if not suggesting his unfitness as a suitor, certainly setting him apart from the traditional suitor of the domestic novel. Gregory's surname is "Rose," he takes after his mother, is closest to his sister, possesses a "fine nature" that irks his father, uses pink stationary, is "scrupulously neat and clean," and moons over his romantic interests, showing little restraint (a manly quality, by Victorian standards) in love (176, 174).[116] In Lyndall's estimation, he is "a true woman—one born for the sphere that some women have to fill without being born for it. How happy he would be sewing frills into his little girls' frocks, and how pretty he would look sitting in a parlour" (197). Ironically, he is never stronger and more heroic than when in women's clothes, which he dons, posing as a nurse (one of the few professional positions then available to women), to gain access to the dying Lyndall. Gregory's passion for Lyndall, whose "indifference" attracts him, proves greater than his passion for Em, whose compliance ultimately bores him (238). Nonetheless, he felt strongly enough about Em before his initial proposal to claim: "If she refuses me, I shall go and kill myself. . . . It is a choice between death and madness" (176). Hyperbolic though this particular declaration may be, "the avidity with which Gregory pursues Em and then Lyndall" is one of the many ways in which the novel "satirize[s] heterosexual courtship."[117]

As Lyndall is herself aware, neither Gregory nor RR would make her a suitable partner, for while marriage to the former, whom she does not desire but can control, would be strictly a matter of convenience, marriage to the latter, whom she desires but does not trust, would rob her of her independence. If RR is in some ways the classic romantic suitor, a "tall blue-eyed Englishman," "an officer, perhaps," wealthy, confident, and worldly, he is also possessive, patronizing, and snide (*SAF* 265, 266). If we are to take Lyndall's reading of him as accurate—and her judgment of character is generally correct—he loves her because he "cannot bear to be resisted and want[s] to master" her (238). If the pregnant Lyndall had snatched at his implied willingness to legalize their union, he would, she predicts, have abandoned her: "Your man's love is a child's love for butterflies. You follow till you have the thing, and then break it" (238). He does not gainsay her assessments. Lyndall's attraction to him is based on his strength and her fear of him, which inspire both "love" and "hate"; but as she knows that before long she would "come to [her] senses" and see that he is like "any other man," that he fails to touch the "higher part" of her "nature," and that he would soon grow tired of her, she declines to marry him (236, 237). Lyndall is not opposed to marriage per se, but she "cannot be bound to one whom [she] love[s] as [she] love[s]" him, someone whom she desires, yet who "call[s] into activity [only] one part of [her] nature"—the physical side—and who "would hold [her] fast" and curtail her freedom (279, 237, 236).[118] While the novel does not, then, celebrate Lyndall's relationship with RR, it does suggest the validity of female sexual desire outside of marriage. The heroine's proud assertion, "I am not in so great a hurry to put my neck beneath a man's foot; and I do not so greatly admire the crying of babies," offers a clear break with the domestic novel, but it is her decision not to place security or respectability (which marriage to either Gregory or RR would provide) over her desire (to be with yet not "tied" to RR) that makes the novel truly transgressive (184, 239).

A significant enough number of the first edition's readers "fancied" that "Waldo's Stranger" and "Lyndall's Stranger" (both title chapters as well as unnamed characters) were one and the same for Schreiner to feel that "a word of explanation was necessary" in the form of a preface (29). Their erroneous suspicion, she speculated, was perhaps due to "a feeling" that the former, a gentleman traveler who shared a single conversation with Waldo one "drowsy afternoon," "*should* return later on as husband or lover, to fill some more important part than that of the mere stimulator of thought" (156, 29; my emphasis). This expectation, in turn, she implied, has two causes: valuing marriage over intellect, and the primacy of the realist novel, which, in its tightly constructed plot structure, does not accurately reflect "the life we all lead" (29). But of course the two causes are directly related through the domestic novel specifically, which, often focusing myopically on heterosexual romance, contributes to the "feeling" that marriage is the fulfillment not only of plot but of "real life" as well. "By *not* reappearing as Lyndall's stranger, Waldo's stranger fails to complete the romance or marriage plot," and in so doing both thwarts the expectations of readers well versed in the domestic novel, which so often "conclude[s] with chastened brides hoping to find happiness in domesticity," and calls into question the values that undergird those expectations.[119]

The end of the novel finds Lyndall dead and Em once again engaged to Gregory, but if Lyndall's death is not a "retribution" for her declension of marriage, disinterest in motherhood, or "erotic ambition," neither is Em's betrothal a reward for her angelic attributes and aspirations.[120] While I have earlier suggested that Lyndall's death is the materialization of the difficulty of realizing female autonomy, it nonetheless links the novel to the domestic tradition. Formerly "the strident, confident intellectual," Lyndall ends her days docile, humble, and "melancholic." "Go[ing] into a decline" after mourning her child in the rain, she dies, as Lerner incisively puts it, a "most unfeminist" death. The New Woman novel thus ends tragically as the

"'Victorian sentimental,'" with the feminist heroine recast as the martyred mother.[121] And while Em remains the angel in the house, "Schreiner refuses to bestow a happy end even on [her] romance."[122] If Lyndall's death signifies the enormity of the obstacles standing in the way of a woman's acquisition of independence, the unlikeliness of Em's contentment casts doubt on a woman's satisfaction with the most traditional of paths. For not only would it seem that Gregory proposes to her the second time not for love of her but for love of Lyndall, who has ordained their marriage in an unsigned four-word letter—"You must marry Em"—that he carries in a black bag hung from his neck and pressed against his heart, but a "resigned[]" Em seems herself to suspect that disappointment awaits her (*SAF* 294, 296). She tells Tant' Sannie, with "a little shade of weariness in her voice," that "perhaps [marriage] might not suit all people, at all times, as well as it suits you" (293). Implicitly, if unconsciously, comparing her betrothal to her mother's "work-box full of coloured reels" for which she yearned as a child, only to receive it once "all the cottons [had been] taken out," she asks Waldo: "Why is it always so [that] we long for things, and long for them, and pray for them," but when they come "at last, [it is] too late, . . . all the sweetness is taken out of them[?]" (296). And when Em tells Waldo that her wedding is just three weeks away, "he did not congratulate her; perhaps he thought of the empty box, but he kissed her forehead gravely" (297). If Em's heavy heart, "the maternal legacy" of a sewing box stripped bare, and Waldo's clearly implied doubts about the success of Em's union with Gregory augur an unhappy marriage, the presence of Tant' Sannie's Boer baby and a crawling, laughing indigenous child suggest it may be a barren one; for while the domestic novel frequently concludes with the birth of an English heir, *African Farm* draws attention to the absence of the next generation's English *Rose*.[123]

The heroine's unorthodox views, the farm's inhospitality, the obviously flawed parents, and the shadow cast on romance all confound an affirming view of traditional domesticity. Yet while Schreiner is unwilling to celebrate domestic space, family, or courtship, she nonetheless makes them the focal points of her novel, chafing against but unable wholly to resist the seeming "inevitability of the marriage plot."[124] Unlike many New Woman novels of the 1890s, she fails to provide, perhaps because she cannot yet imagine, "a model of how female independence can be accomplished."[125] Though a feminist critique of sexual and social mores that gave birth to a genre, *African Farm* is ultimately entrenched in the generic frame of the domestic novel it obliquely critiques. Schreiner may have yearned for the independence that echoed rhetorically throughout white southern Africa, but faced with the stark reality of adult womanhood, she recognized its contingency in regard to gender, though not yet race. Marking an end as much as a beginning, *African Farm* registers the incipient demise of the domestic novel as well as its long-standing authority. Like Lyndall, it imagines a different future that it cannot quite reach.

Genre and Colonial Domesticity II: Expansion and Preservation

" 'Jess' is, par excellence, the romance of a woman," wrote an anonymous reviewer in the widely circulated *Athenaeum*, the year the novel was published. "It is the study of a strange and fascinating being, a story of noble love and devotion, not shrinking from crime and daring to face death. We . . . profess ourselves to be the slaves of the altogether human Jess, to our mind Mr. Haggard's most charming creation."[126] James Smith, editor of the *Cape Argus* and chair of the Anglo-African Writers' Club, a group composed "chiefly [of] men connected with the African press in London," put it much more simply when he introduced Haggard as the organization's first president: "We have fallen in love with Jess."[127] Less in spite than because of her defining action—her murder of Muller—the novel's heroine, like the novel itself, was long an object of admiration.[128] Four years before the publication of Thomas Hardy's *Tess of the D'Urbervilles* provoked such ire for its frank portrayal of female sexuality and violence, *Jess* seems not to have ruffled any feathers.[129] Of course, notwithstanding her romantic liaison with Niel, Jess does not, unlike Tess, live "in sin." But if Jess is not truly a "fallen woman," she is certainly a murderess. Her crime, however, is ultimately a crime of defense—of family and home—rather than a crime of passion. In committing it, she symbolically recuperates the loss of a war in which the British, despite their greater numbers, arms, and wealth, quickly surrendered to the Boers. If the novel's "background . . . is the shame and dishonour of England," its promise is the redemption that Jess represents.[130]

While Lyndall's failure to act frustrated Victorian readers, Jess's willingness to do so impressed them. But if Jess, like Lyndall, is no angel in the house, neither is she a New Woman. An *angel on the frontier*, we might call her, a colonial woman who, acting in the service of both family and empire, fights to preserve a colonial domesticity that enables greater freedom for women, though it also demands greater sacrifice. Drawing from both domestic fiction and adventure fiction, *Jess* is a kind of generic hybrid: home, family, and courtship figure prominently in the novel, but it is also a tale of female heroism in wartime. In Jess's martial actions, the text not only breaks with the domestic novel, it also evinces the capacity of colonial women to effect political change, even when not politically driven.

For while Jess murders Muller for the sake of her family, her action may well protect the whole of British southern Africa. Arrogant, truculent, and intimidating, Muller is among the most powerful men in the Transvaal. He aspires to usurp Paul Kruger and take over the presidency of the South African Republic, then to "push the Englishmen back into the sea, make a clean sweep of the natives, only keeping enough for servants, and [to rule over] a United Dutch South Africa" (*J* 113).[131] Unlike the other Boers in the novel, who are motivated to rebel by "Patriotism! Independence! Taxes!," Muller is driven by "ambition and revenge"—not simply against the British but also, more personally, against Bessie, who declines his marriage proposal; Uncle Silas, who refuses to encourage his suit; and John Niel, "his successful rival" (112, 121). Boasts Muller: "If I throw in my weight against rebellion there will be no rebellion; if I urge it there will be, and if Om [Uncle] Silas will not give me Bessie, and Bessie will not marry me, I will urge it, even if it plunge the whole country in war" (112). Silas does not, Bessie will not, and Muller thus "g[i]ve[s] the casting vote for [the rebellion] that [he] might win" the object of his "furious passion" (275, 257). "Overpowered" by "the strength of his jealous desire" and determined to "kiss [Bessie] over [Niel's] dead body," he arranges for the latter to be murdered (121, 94). When Bessie still refuses to "yield"—a command he puts to her four times—Muller threatens to have her uncle executed on trumped-up charges of treason, unless she "consent[s] to marry" him; and though she is sure "it will kill" her, she ultimately agrees (310, 307, 311). The "courtship of blood" that Muller sets in motion is brought to an end not by his marriage, however, but by his death (193).

Playing the roles of judge, warrior, and executioner, Jess thwarts Muller's personal and political ambitions as she defends the family that England forsook. Returning to the farm just one day after Britain's surrender, she finds the farmhouse burned to the ground, her uncle convicted of treason, and her sister blackmailed by Muller into accepting his proposal. "To attempt to portray the fury, the indignation, and the thirst to be avenged upon the fiend who had attempted to murder her and her lover, and had bought her dear sister's honor at the price of her innocent old uncle's life," the narrator tells readers, "would be impossible" (311). Though at first "mad with what she had seen and heard," Jess tempers her feelings and determines quite coolly that "death, and death alone, would stop" Muller (313). Trying him in an imaginary court, as he had tried her uncle by a bogus court martial, Jess thus "arraigned the powerful leader of men before the tribunal of her conscience, and without pity, if without wrath, passed upon him a sentence of extinction. But who was to be the executioner?" (313–14).

For this, she turns to "the Hottentot [Khoikhoi] Jantjé," the Croft family servant who witnessed the death of his parents and uncle at the hands of Muller twenty years earlier (37). The multiply notched stick that Jantjé carries everywhere with him is a record of the many cruelties Muller has inflicted on him, his family, and the Crofts; and though Muller refuses to acknowledge the "dark deed of blood" that hangs between them, Jantjé knows that retribution will come (83). After Niel heroically comes to blows with Muller in defense of Jantjé, the latter tells him that Muller's (English) mother, learning of the murders, predicted "that a curse would fall on [her family] and they would all die in blood," as, with the exception of Muller, they all have (81).[132] Jantjé thus alerts readers both to Muller's long history of violence and to the likelihood of his impending demise. Further, as the ongoing victim of Muller's physical and verbal abuse, the loyal Jantjé reinforces nineteenth-century Britons' belief in their superior treatment of the indigenous and in indigenous preference for British rule over that of the Boers.[133] But where Jantjé, inclined to alcohol, cowardice, and indecision, is the "very epitome of impotent, overmastering passion," Jess is focused, courageous, and controlled (28). Determined that "Jantjé should do the deed," Jess reminds him of Muller's many sins, indicates the necessity of his death, and evokes the memory of Mrs. Muller's prophecy (314). "He will die in blood," Jess tells him, "and he shall die to-night, and *you* shall kill him, Jantjé. . . . I will tell you how" (316). Though she "stir[s] up . . . Jantjé to the boiling-point of vengeance," even challenging him, when he wavers, to "be a man," he is unable finally to go through with the act (317, 320). "A strong woman [with] a will of iron," Jess therefore decides to "kill him *like a man*" herself (300, 321; my emphasis). Using Jantjé's "very heavy," "foot long," Somali hunting knife, "manufactured from soft native steel . . . with a handle cut from the tusk of a hippopotamus," this is precisely what she does (315).

Neil Hultgren, one of very few critics to offer a sustained reading of the novel, argues that "Jess stands in for Jantjé"—that is, that her killing of Muller "serves as an act of vengeance for Muller's earlier crimes against

Jantjé's relatives."¹³⁴ To this I would add that by having Jess look first to Jantjé to execute Muller, Haggard gives readers time to come to terms with the heroine's surprising new role; we thus have the chance to accept Jess as "practically . . . a murderess" before accepting her as *actually* a murderess (*J* 317). We see her initial "thirst to be avenged" swiftly followed by her use of logic to determine Muller's fate ("Frank Muller must die"), her cautious reasoning that there is no alternative ("by no other possible means could . . . both Bessie and her old uncle [be] saved"), her reluctance to commit the act herself ("she had not come to that yet"), the "poetic justice" of her decision to recruit Jantjé as assassin, her respect for the gravity of the situation ("it was a dreadful thing to steep her hands in blood, even for Bessie's sake"), and her physical revulsion at the feat itself ("the sight [of the knife] made Jess feel sick") (311, 313, 314, 317, 320). Only when Jantjé falters, terrified of the ghost of Muller's mother whom he believes he has encountered in Muller's tent, does Jess step in, and then only after readers are reminded that she does so "for Bessie's sake, for Bessie's sake!" (325). Having followed Jess from realization to decision, through doubt, dread, and a final summoning of courage, readers fully back her.

Her midnight attack on Muller is a victory for her family, though a costly one. Lying in partial darkness in his tent, "his throat and massive chest . . . quite bare," Muller opens his eyes "full upon [the] face . . . of the woman he [believes he] had murdered, come back to tell him that there *was* a living vengeance and a hell!" (325–26). The deed itself is conveyed through "the flash of falling steel," "the red knife in [Jess's] hand," and an unattributed "shriek"—is it Jess's? is it Muller's?—that "must have awakened every soul within a mile" (326). The dark of night, the sleeping chamber, the exposed flesh, the stain of blood, the African knife, the piercing cry make Jess not a femme fatale but, like the Biblical Jael and the Apocryphal Judith, a war hero.¹³⁵ Her murder of Muller is an act that resonates at both the sexual-cum-domestic and military-cum-political level. If a dead Muller cannot execute the aged Silas or force Bessie to become his wife, neither can he pursue his political aspirations. With the courage Jantjé lacks and the strength the British fail to muster, Jess, avenging the indigenous and British alike, brings an end to his plans "for a United Dutch South Africa, and Frank Muller to rule it!" (314, 113).

But Jess cannot sustain her position of power, and her forceful action is reinscribed as one of sacrifice. Having fled from the scene of the crime, with "all the conscience-created furies" in chase, she collapses, spent and "*dying*," in a cave near her home (326, 335). Having survived the assassination attempt arranged by Muller, spent days on the run in the wet and cold, and plunged a knife into Muller's powerful body,

> her strength was leaving her at last. . . . "Oh, God, forgive me! God forgive me!" she moaned. . . . "Bessie, I sinned against you, but I have washed away my sin. I did it for you, Bessie love, not for myself. I had rather have died than kill him for myself. You will marry John now, and you will never, never know what I did for you." (335)

Acknowledging her sins, as she sees them, Jess repents, even as she justifies the murder, framing it, in part, as atonement for her intimacy with Niel. After awakening to find Niel asleep beside her, Jess dies, leaving him undisturbed, with "her head . . . on her lover's breast as on a pillow" (336). "Poor, dark-eyed, deep-hearted Jess!" laments the narrator. "This was the fruition of her love and this her bridal bed. . . . She had gone, taking with her the secret of her self-sacrifice and crime" (336–37).[136] Jess, however, does not die entirely an unsung hero, as "the night winds moaning amid the rocks sang their requiem over her. . . . 'Think gently of her,'" entreats the narrator, "and let her pass in peace" (337).

In addition to being advised not to condemn Jess, readers are reminded of the political implications of Muller's death—that is, of the welcome reversal that Jess's actions bring about, from a Boer to a British fate for her family. Haggard accomplishes this with four images, each connected with one or both of their deaths. First, Jess writes a farewell note to John on the (back of the) pass (signed by an unnamed but clearly identifiable Paul Kruger) that enabled her and Niel to leave Pretoria. Second, bringing her body home, Niel places it on the very "saw-bench on which Frank Muller had sat as judge upon the previous day" when he condemned Silas to die (338). Third, Jess is buried a mere "ten feet [from] the man on whom she was the instrument of vengeance" (339). And finally, Muller is himself buried in "the very grave that he had caused to be dug to receive the body of Silas Croft" (339). The Boer leader is dead; the British patriot lives on.

Though Jess has given her life to preserve colonial domesticity, her survivors relinquish it once she is gone, just as Haggard severed his "residential and official connection with South Africa" following Britain's surrender (*Days* 2: 265). Willing to fight for his home, though unsupported by his homeland, Haggard felt hamstrung by a metropole with little regard, as he saw it, for loyal colonists.[137] "This is no country for Englishmen," Silas tells his future son-in-law, echoing Haggard's own postwar sentiments (*J* 339).[138] Like Haggard, Silas blames the loss of the Transvaal not on a lack of colonial vigor but on metropolitan disinterest. Leaving southern Africa to "go home to England" after fifty years, Silas is joined by Bessie and Niel (339). Like Haggard, Niel weds his second choice of a wife and takes up residence in the English countryside, and though "on the whole [he] may be considered a happy man[,] [at] times . . . a sorrow . . . gets the better of him, and for a while he is not himself" (340).[139] The contrast between life on a "dim" but "peaceful landscape" with a "sweet" but tepid wife and the foreclosed possibility of life with the "passionate" Jess, whom Niel symbolically wed beneath the "wide, star-strewn heavens" of the South African sky, resonates with Haggard's own frustrated hopes (340).[140] Haunted by southern Africa as Niel is haunted by Jess, Haggard would spend the duration of his life writing about the region on which he could never truly turn his back. He may have chosen the relative security of the metropole, but he constructed his identity from the ashes of the colonial future he had hoped to build.

Jess is something of an aberration in Haggard's oeuvre, not simply because it is one of his few realist novels and his only South African one but also because it is at once "a psychological study of female character" and a tale of adventure.[141] While Haggard typically demonizes female power in his male imperial romances,[142] in *Jess* he craftily marshals it to vindicate the shame he "suffered" as a result of the First Anglo-Boer War (*Days* 1: 201). Though ideologically the female subject of the domestic novel, Jess is also a political player in a story of war. In Jess's renegotiation of domesticity in colonial space and her assumption of the role of war hero, the novel far exceeds the limits of domestic fiction. Haggard's choice of a female protagonist to represent colonial fortitude evinces, on some level, both his awareness of the obstructed position of women and their (largely untapped) strength. Generating a new kind of heroine, one with the strength—of body, mind, and character—to rival man and metropole alike, the novel reflects Haggard's belief in southern Africa's ability to produce empowered subjects *regardless* of gender. Ultimately, then, his evocation of female potency, though unconcerned with women's rights, expands not only generic boundaries but gendered ones as well.

Conclusion

African Farm functions as a critique of the domestic novel both because and in spite of its reliance on its form and conventions. A manifestation of Schreiner's desire for increased opportunities for women, Lyndall rejects the model of femininity provided by the genre's most familiar resident, the angel in the house. Nonetheless, the narrow parameters of *African Farm* give birth but not life to her feminist aspirations. With her limited access to weapons of social warfare—useful education, female community, alliances with other groups of the oppressed—and her self-involvement, Lyndall cannot escape constraint. She awakes not into a satisfying awareness of colonial womanhood, but rather into the realization that adulthood will not, after all, improve her lot. Though Lyndall is a far cry from the "female ideal" of the domestic novel, her transformation from theorizing to acting subject, from observer to agent, is a failure.[143] She dies not a stronger version but rather "a frail shadow of herself."[144]

Jess suggests alternatives to Victorian domesticity both because and in spite of its protagonist, an empowered female quasi-warrior who lacks a feminist agenda. A manifestation of Haggard's faith in colonial strength, she functions as a critique of imperial retrenchment. Equipped with tenacity and a knife, Jess protects the family that Britain deserted. Considered alongside *African Farm*, Jess's successful actions in the face—and place—of a negligent empire highlight Lyndall's inefficacy in implementing her vision of transcendence. At the same time, Jess's inability to see herself as a political actor, despite single-handedly destroying one of the leaders of the rebellion, accentuates the perspicacity of Lyndall's feminist thought. Inversely, Lyndall's lack of achievement draws attention to the magnitude of Jess's political engagement, while Lyndall's trenchant social analysis illuminates Jess's lack of self-conscious reflection.

African Farm enabled Schreiner to express and examine the trauma of growing into colonial womanhood. Acquiring an unusual degree of autonomy (for a Victorian woman) as a result of her celebrity and material success, she could break free from some of the fetters of her early existence. She would, however, remain committed to women's independence. *Jess* allowed Haggard to express and examine the trauma of colonial abandonment. Shaking "the dust of South Africa off [his] feet and return[ing] to England," he could to some extent escape his past sense of disgrace.[145] He would, however, continue to advocate for colonials, henceforward as a colonial-in-exile rather than a colonial-in-residence.

If the role of women in southern Africa is the focus of *African Farm*, in *Jess* it is a means of addressing metro-colonial politics. In *She*, an imperial adventure novel published the same year as *Jess*, Haggard approached the subject more directly. But where its protagonist, Ayesha, is a monstrous projection of female leadership, the heroines of his later South African narratives are not. *Benita: An African Romance* (1906) and *The Ghost Kings* (1908), discussed at length in the next chapter, celebrate female authority and fortitude, while continuing to articulate southern Africa's value to the empire.[146] As *Jess* expresses Haggard's dissatisfaction with Britain's hasty surrender in the First Anglo-Boer War, the female colonial romances that followed two decades later express his concern with maintaining the dominance that victory in the Second Anglo-Boer War (1899–1902) had brought. As the following chapter will show, generic innovation continued to enable Haggard to work through problems of identity, politics, and gender.

Chapter 2

"It Is I Who Have the Power"

The Female Colonial Romance

H. Rider Haggard has long been known as the premier writer of the imperial adventure novel. Specifically, he has been associated with what Patrick Brantlinger has termed the "imperial Gothic," a "blend of adventure story with Gothic elements," and what Elaine Showalter has called "the male quest romance," a genre in which men "explore their secret selves in an anarchic space which can be safely called the 'primitive.'"[1] Of course, "the terrifying exotic journey is . . . as old as Homer and Dante," but a more direct forefather of the nineteenth-century imperial adventure novel is Daniel Defoe, particularly his 1719 novels, *The Life and Strange, Surprising Adventures of Robinson Crusoe* and *The Farther Adventures of Robinson Crusoe*.[2] While nineteenth-century writers like Frederick Marryat and R. M. Ballantyne were publishing imperial adventures decades before Haggard, the latter's inclusion of supernatural elements, dramatic, high-stakes battles, and lost races contributed to a significant rise in the genre's popularity. And while lost world fiction, "tales of forgotten cities, rediscovered races, civilizations, and continents submerged beneath the sea or the ground," predates Haggard, his incorporation of lost world elements into the imperial adventure novel was a significant contribution to both genres.[3] Routinely contrasted with realist fiction, particularly the domestic novel, and typically associated with "the heroic cult of masculinity,"[4] the imperial adventure novel is described by scholars as predominantly devoid of colonial settlers, especially women.[5] The general consensus is that in Haggard's tales of adventure, "male identity is forged at the expense of—and to the exclusion of—women." When present at all, critics concur, "women are either pliantly submissive or fiercely assertive."[6]

While Haggard's best known characters are Allan Quatermain, a Victorian Crusoe-cum-fully-grown-Jim-Hawkins, and Ayesha, the supra-human protagonist of *She* (1887), his most innovative contribution to the genre of adventure fiction is actually his most overlooked: the colonial settler heroine.[7] As a strong, independent, and valiant female colonial, Jess Croft, the eponymous heroine of Haggard's only South African realist novel (discussed in chapter 1) is a clear precursor to the protagonists of what I have termed his *female colonial romances*, in contradistinction to his male imperial romances.[8] If Benita Beatrix Clifford, of *Benita: An African Romance* (1906), and Rachel Dove, of *The Ghost Kings* (1908), are more ideologically complex than the hypermasculine hunter-trader and the ancient Arabic femme fatale, they are also more modern than Jess, whose roots are recognizably Victorian. Where Jess defends British colonial domesticity in southern Africa, Benita and Rachel blaze new territory there, both materially for empire and symbolically for women. Where Jess is an effect of Haggard's dissatisfaction with imperial politics, Benita and Rachel are an effect, like She, of Haggard's anxiety over burgeoning metropolitan female agency.[9] They manifest, however, none of Ayesha's extremes. Confident, where She is imperious, independent, where She is autocratic, powerful, where She is tyrannical, Haggard's colonial heroines expand the British empire's sphere of influence, rather than simply their own. Enabling the author imaginatively to redirect feminist energy—from metropole to colony, from self (as he saw it) to service, from suffragism to soil—these South African frontierswomen nonetheless belie his imaginative mastery. Thwarting or forestalling martial conflict through mystical powers and diplomacy, they domesticate the empire while themselves transcending domestication in novels that foreground female settler heroism.

The year before Haggard's death, an article in a prominent monthly literary journal noted that while he "cannot be ranked among the masters of literature," he made an "impression[] too deep and too genuine on the imagination of [his] time ever to be passed over as negligible."[10] This assertion notwithstanding, Haggard was largely neglected in the half century between his 1925 death and the emergence of modern feminist and postcolonial scholarship.[11] Despite the centrality of feminist criticism to Haggard's resurgence and the "Settler Revolution" to recent postcolonial criticism, his colonial women have remained a largely unexplored terrain.[12] As I began to demonstrate in the previous chapter, however, productive ambivalences can be found in his fiction regarding both empire and women. Gayatri Chakravorty Spivak and Antoinette Burton have shown that white British female—including specifically feminist—agency during the Victorian and Edwardian eras was contingent on imperialist ideology. My examination of Haggard's colonial women demonstrates that imperialist texts can produce feminist effects as a reaction to the feminism they seek to thwart or contain; for rather than appropriating a dominant discourse to challenge marginalization, as Western feminists so often have, Haggard inadvertently broadens a marginalized discourse (of female agency) while opposing its (feminist) agenda.[13]

Scholarship on literary representations of British colonial women is remarkably circumscribed. It has tended to focus on the "memsahib," the British woman living in India, generally as the wife of a colonial administrator. Both by overseeing a British home abroad and by exerting moral influence, the memsahib "replicate[s] the empire on a domestic scale." At the same time, she enhances her own authority, particularly through her oversight of Indian servants. But she is also "in need of protection from potential sexual threat," especially, as both Jenny Sharpe and Nancy Paxton have shown, following the 1857 "Indian Mutiny."[14] As homemaker and potential victim alike, the fictional memsahib displays characteristics and behaviors traditionally associated with her gender.[15] In Haggard's female colonial romances, the colonial woman also furthers an imperialist agenda and expands her own authority, but she does so through qualities and actions traditionally associated with men—leadership, confidence, and diplomacy, most notably—in combination with what I have called "mystical feminism": protective supernatural powers facilitated by female bonds across cultures.[16] She thus challenges gender norms and ethno-racial codes alike. As India's privileged position in scholarship on the British empire has begun to give way, recent work on the British colonial female has examined her domestic authority in the antipodes. There is also a growing body of work on the figure of the colonial girl, whose freedoms exceed those of her metropolitan counterpart.[17] Since Haggard's colonial heroines are adults, the stakes are higher and the implications greater. These are women who, assuming roles unavailable to them in the metropole, extend their own position, even as they extend that of the empire that so often limits them.

The female colonial romance is remarkable in its challenge to multiple, well-established binaries, ideological as well as generic. In addition to pushing against the divide between masculinity and femininity, it counters the distinction between metropolitan and colonial. Unlike the male imperial romance, which is "more aligned with imperial-metropolitan than with colonial ideology," the female colonial romance enabled Haggard to express his South African affiliation, his identity not just as an imperial but also as a *colonial* citizen.[18] Born in or having immigrated to South Africa at a young age and committed to securing colonial domesticity, the heroines of the female romances convey a colonial sensibility generally lacking in his male adventurers, like Horace Holly and Leo Vincey, who remain firmly rooted in the metropolitan base from which they travel "outwards"; Quatermain, perpetually peripatetic though still tied to the metropole, not least through his son; or even Captain John Good and Sir Henry Curtis, who cannot be said to represent colonials, despite making Africa their permanent home. While Haggard's male adventurers are in danger of regression as they reconnect with a "primitive" masculinity, which, properly channeled, ultimately reinvigorates the empire, his female adventurers are in no such peril.[19] For example, while the "power of prescience" that Rachel Dove inherits "from her mother and her Highland forefathers"—or more accurately, foremothers—is strengthened by her association with the indigenous, enabling her influence over them, her supernatural abilities "did not . . . make her weak, any more than the strength of her frame or her spirit made her unwomanly" (*GK* 28, 50).[20] Always eminently womanly and British, whether treading on a crocodile or brandishing an assegai (Zulu spear), Haggard's female colonial heroines reinvent femininity as they reinforce the empire. Carving out new space for female authority, they simultaneously strengthen Britain's colonial position. Security rather than exploration compels them to reach beyond European-settled spaces, where they find powers that at times defy the realistic imagination. For in its entwinement of fantasy and domesticity, the female colonial romance also blurs the generic distinction between "romance," or adventure, and "realism," or the novel, which was particularly strong at the turn of the century.[21] Reading beyond *King Solomon's Mines* (1885), *She*, and *Allan Quatermain* (1887), male imperial romances that have almost exclusively been allowed to represent Haggard's vast body of work, we encounter female colonial leadership on the South African frontier: women who protect white as well as indigenous men and women, domesticating southern Africa not by overseeing home and family but by exerting authority far beyond domestic space.[22]

The Presence of Women

From the start, colonization had been a particularly gendered affair: (white) men explored, set up trading stations, and established military outposts, although, given Britain's strong interest in the proliferation of its own "race,"

British women were necessary for settlement. In 1849, emigrationist Edward Gibbon Wakefield remarked, a "colony that is not attractive to women, is an unattractive colony."[23] Two years later, the census revealed that there were a half million more women than men in Britain, "a statistical surplus" of "redundant"—shorthand for unmarried—women for which society had little use.[24] This "abnormal" number of unmarried women was more than an economic problem (not least for women themselves). In the eyes of many, it was "indicative of an unwholesome social state," for not only did it pose the possibility of adding greater numbers of women to the workforce, it also "threaten[ed] the image of women as dependent and protected." The solution that W. R. Greg famously proposed in an 1862 *National Review* article was female immigration to the colonies.[25] A number of emigration societies specifically for women emerged between the middle of the century and World War I, stressing colonial opportunities for "employment, marriage, home-building, self-fulfillment, moral guardianship, and imperial and racial duty."[26] These emphases varied over time and from organization to organization. The possibility of marriage, never a selling point in the few feminist societies that existed, was touted more frequently at the turn of the century, as was the female civilizing mission, which entailed carrying British culture, upholding the morality of male colonials, and bearing their children.[27] Nonetheless, the bulk of Britain's colonial-bound emigrants continued to be men. Thus, as the empire expanded, so, too, did the ratio of both colonial men to women and metropolitan women to men. By 1911 there were 1.3 million more women than men in Britain and three-quarters of a million more white men than white women in the self-governing dominions, a cause of concern for an empire invested in racial demarcation.[28]

South Africa experienced a sharp rise in its male-to-female ratio as a result of its unprecedented mineral revolution, starting with the 1867 discovery of diamonds and escalating with the 1886 discovery of gold. From then until the 1899 outbreak of the Second Anglo-Boer War (1899–1902), men arrived in large numbers from across the empire (many came from other places as well).[29] "Even before the war," then, "in the total white population the number of men considerably exceeded that of women in every one of the South African colonies; and of the women, the large majority was Boer, the minority British." The gap widened yet further when, following the Boers' 1902 surrender, the imperial government, colonial governments, emigration societies, the press, and South African luminaries like Cecil Rhodes encouraged soldiers to stay and women to immigrate in order to shore up both the region's British population and its "British . . . character [and] sympathies."

Because the "intermarriage of British men with Boer women," it was argued, would "never produce these results," "the emigration of [British] women to South Africa" was soon identified as "a question of national [and] Imperial importance"—the key to "consolidat[ing] British control."[30]

Though supported by the imperial government, the facilitation of female immigration to southern Africa was left mostly to private organizations, which drew funding and other assistance from local South African governments, commercial concerns, private individuals, and only minimally from Westminster.[31] The most successful South African female emigration society was the South African Colonization Society (SACS), which, with "its forerunner SAX [the South African Expansion Committee,] emigrated some 4,250 women to South Africa" between 1901 and 1910.[32] Two years of mass migration and "artificial prosperity" followed the war, only to be succeeded by six years of economic depression. At the same time, Afrikaner political power was on the ascendant, manifest most ostensibly by the "decisive electoral victory" achieved by Afrikaner nationalists in 1907, within a year of the former Boer republics (the South African Republic, or Transvaal, and Orange Free State) being granted self-government.[33] Since it was now clear that reconciliation with rather than domination over the Boers was the only "politically viable" option available to the British in southern Africa, British emigration rhetoric began to focus on the importance of increasing southern Africa's white population as a whole, in order to prevent the indigenous, always numerically greater, from acquiring the rights and authority they actively sought.[34] With the 1910 formation of the Union (of the Transvaal, Orange River Colony, Cape Colony, and Natal), there was again a rise in immigration, though a "small" one, which quickly tapered off with the start of World War I.[35]

Britain's "surplus" of women, the "solution" of female emigration, southern Africa's disproportionate number of (white) men, and Afrikaner political power were all issues in which Haggard was keenly interested. In an interview six months before the end of the Second Anglo-Boer War, he suggested that an "influx of [British] population would" be necessary to "protect . . . the loyals" and "to hold South Africa."[36] As he told the *Times* four years later, shortly before the former Boer republics were granted self-government, he supported

> land settlement in South Africa on a large scale of Anglo-Saxon families as opposed to the emigration of single men. If we could prevail upon numbers of English people with their wives and

children, whatever the cost, whatever the trouble, to settle there so that there might grow up there [*sic*] a large British population capable of holding in check and counterbalancing the Dutch population, then it [is] possible we might still retain our power in South Africa.[37]

While not specifically encouraging the emigration of single British women, Haggard was explicitly advocating the emigration of British women, as a requisite for the preservation of British "power." The previous year, he had presented the British government with a plan for settlement throughout the dominions. Though a committee put together specifically to evaluate it was "unable to recommend that [it] should be adopted," Haggard published a version as *The Poor and the Land* (1905). He found the government's decision "painful," he wrote in his autobiography. "My report was destroyed; the divided recommendations of the Departmental Committee . . . were never acted on; in short, all came to nothing."[38] In the midst of World War I, Haggard visited South Africa, Australasia, and Canada as a representative of the Royal Colonial Institute, "to discover what arrangements could be made for the after-war settlement of ex-soldiers."[39] For the remainder of his life, he would continue to encourage settlement in the dominions broadly, particularly in southern Africa, and especially by women.[40]

As supportive as Haggard was of female emigration, he was equally opposed to the growth of metropolitan female agency. Though the British women's suffrage movement had been struck a hard blow with the passing of the 1884 Reform Act, the emergence of New Woman fiction, discussed in chapter 1, ensured that "women's issues [were at] the forefront of the national consciousness" in fin-de-siècle Britain.[41] Challenging the divide between private and public and the correlative gender disparity that constituted Victorian politics, education, and economics, the New Woman was for many "a model of . . . female independence," while for others she was a source of anxiety. At the same time that the New Woman was variously inspiring and shocking readers, metropolitan women were working in a wider range of roles, most notably in hospitals, shops, and offices.[42] And though the start of the Second Anglo-Boer War, which coincided with the century's close, saw an end to the booming years of New Woman fiction, a decline in the attention given to "women's issues," and a significant lull in the suffrage movement, women were clearly in the public arena to stay. Indeed, the war's termination was accompanied by a renewal of both "the surplus debate" and the suffrage movement.[43]

Haggard's unease with Britain's "superfluous women"—another term for "surplus" or "redundant" women—was less about the numeric imbalance that it reflected than the power imbalance that it threatened.[44] As Margaret Strobel neatly puts it: "The notion of 'surplus' women of marriageable age is, of course, ideologically determined: a patriarchal ideology that prescribed for women the roles of mother, wife, and household manager could conceive no positive outcome for single women."[45] Far from being a positive outcome, as Haggard saw it, the employment opportunities that women were increasingly securing meant "female competition" and thus male "unemployment." "Girls [who] could not marry," he opined, "would simply take the bread from the mouths of the other sex, whose proud tradition it had been to support them." As for female suffrage, women would be "coming to it new, while man, with all his failings, after all had the experience and the instinct of ages to help him to his decisions."[46] Haggard's views are clearly aligned with those of Holly, the self-proclaimed "misogynist" narrator of *She*, who, reflecting on Ayesha's desire to visit England, "absolutely shuddered to think what would be the result of her arrival there." As Ann Ardis has pointed out, Holly's "concerns . . . are precisely those voiced about the New Woman's entrance into the public arena."[47] Haggard articulated his concerns directly in an 1894 article titled, "A Man's View of Woman":

> [W]hen at last she has conquered at the polls, and as a political factor occupies the place that her numbers will give her, what then? Already in the press, in literature, in society appear tokens of an uprising; and though, perhaps fortunately, we of this generation shall not live to see it, all thinking men must wonder as to its ultimate course and direction.[48]

Though Haggard could not in fact alter the course or direction of the "uprising," he could do so in the fictional world of the female colonial romance.

Impelled by the dual exigencies of bolstering South African anglicization and impeding metropolitan female authority, Haggard shunted feminist agency from Britain's streets to South Africa's veld in the pages of his fiction. In these texts, the relation "between the domestic reader and imperial space" is one of attempted mastery not only over colonial territory and autochthonous subjects, as it is in the male imperial romance, but also over British women, who are themselves agents of empire; for while the female colonial romance allows for both female and indigenous strength, it does so with the counterintuitive aim of harnessing both.[49] Nonetheless, in celebrating the accomplishments of female colonials, Haggard suggests opportunities for women beyond the more ostensibly political ones for which many were fighting in the metropole.[50]

Female Adventure

Female adventure stories had long been around.[51] Among these were female military adventures, most famously Daniel Defoe's *The Life and Adventures of Mrs. Christian Davies, Commonly Call'd Mother Ross*, first published in 1740 and reissued regularly throughout the eighteenth and nineteenth centuries.[52] Though "eighteenth century female soldiers' stories," including Davies's, "are often presented as 'biographies,' based on interviews with their subjects," a number of their details are likely fictional. In these stories, women dress and live as men in military settings, usually in order to find missing husbands, a "motive safely within the bounds of wifely devotion." Nonetheless, after locating their husbands, many of these women voluntarily continue to live as men.[53]

Eighteenth- and nineteenth-century Robinsonades, which were often intended for young readers, likewise depict female protagonists, alone or in leadership roles, in situations and locations traditionally gendered male. Even in these texts, however, female power is still partly circumscribed. In R. M. Ballantyne's *The Island Queen* (1885), the girl-heroine Pauline, made queen of the "embryo nation" that she helps to establish, may on occasion "exercise the privilege of [her] position," but her influence is primarily moral. She is chosen, as her brother tells her, because "there are so many strong, determined, and self-willed men [on the island] that there's no chance of their ever agreeing to submit to each other." "Innocent, sensible, gentle, just, sympathetic, and high-minded"—which is to say, traditionally feminine—Pauline is "a sort of good angel before whom [the men] will be only too glad to bow—a kind of superior being, whom they will reverence, and to whom they will submit—a human safety-valve."[54] Isabel, in L. T. Meade's *Four on an Island* (1892), may have "twice [the] pluck, twice [the] courage," and nearly twice the brains of her older brother, but as "housekeeper-in-chief" of White Feather Island, her tasks—knitting, sewing, cleaning, cooking, and nurturing—are fundamentally domestic.[55] *The Island Queen*, which we might loosely call a female Robinsonade, and *Four on an Island* center on girlhood, a transitional period in which masculine traits might be tolerated, since, it was imagined, they would soon disappear.[56] But the heroines of the female colonial romance are adults: the titular protagonist of *Benita* is twenty-five, and Rachel, of *The Ghost Kings*, is fifteen when the story begins and twenty-three for the bulk of its action. Haggard's ability to imagine martial intrepidity in women of marriageable age is certainly unusual, but it is also comparatively limited, given that his male adventurers range in age from eighteen to sixty-eight.[57]

Late Victorian and Edwardian girls who favored adventure stories were, however, flexible readers. They read that which was written, as Haggard puts it in the dedication for *King Solomon's Mines* (1885), for "big and little boys"—that is, for adults as well as for children—by writers like Haggard, Robert Louis Stevenson, and Rudyard Kipling; that which was intended for boys, by prolific authors like Ballantyne and G. A. Henty; and that which was aimed at girls, by equally productive writers like Meade and Bessie Marchant.[58] As mid-Victorian gender codes began to soften, "girls' boyishness developed an acceptable public face" and, on the heels of New Woman fiction, New Girl fiction, stories of modern girls at school, work, and in the colonies, flourished.[59] The Second Anglo-Boer War, during which women served as teachers (in British concentration camps for Boer civilians), nurses, and relief workers, brought female heroism to the fore, generating a spate of girls' fiction and "true stories" depicting heroic girls and young women in southern Africa and the empire more broadly.[60] Increasingly until World War I began to drag on, juvenile literature, even when penned by "boys'" writers, included adventurous heroines.[61] For instance, in Henty's 1906 short story "A Soldier's Daughter," Nita is not simply "a regular tomboy"; donning a uniform and cropping her hair, she passes for a young soldier. A skilled markswoman, she kills at least twenty-five Indian combatants before being taken hostage, escaping confinement, and rescuing an imprisoned lieutenant. Nonetheless, the young heroine states, "a girl's life is not worth anything," and she "keep[s] herself entirely in the background" when providing an "account of [her] wanderings" with the soldier, to whom she "giv[es] all the credit."[62] The text concludes with a brief mention of their engagement, followed by a summary of the lieutenant's military exploits.

The female adventure stories of Marchant, widely known as "the girls' Henty," predate Henty's own, and while at first not particularly daring, they "alter significantly," as Sally Mitchell notes, "between 1900 and 1915. In the earliest books, girls listened and watched while men acted. In Marchant's later books girls have adventures and courageously rescue men," even "shoot[ing] to kill."[63] The "last-minute rescues and hairbreadth escapes," physical exertion, and violence that appear so consistently in both the male imperial romance and the boys' adventure tale can be found in some of Marchant's narratives also. Yet even as the latter "challenge" limitations imposed on "women's identities" and "'women's place,'" the female power that they depict is aimed primarily at restoring the status quo. Like other girls' adventure fiction of the period, Marchant's stories are usually "set on the edge" of rather than *beyond* spaces already "domesticated" by empire, and her colonial heroines tend not to "engage with the indigenous inhabitants at all and rarely with any significant interaction."[64] Such, however, is not the case in the female colonial romance, in which, far beyond the reaches of "civilization," the heroine becomes actively involved in both colonial-indigenous relations and internal indigenous politics.

Though there is no indication that he was aware of the fact, courageous colonial heroines were emerging in Australian romance at the same time that Haggard was experimenting with the figure. David Hennessey's *An Australian Bush Track* (1896), for instance, focuses initially on the heroine's adventures and "begins and ends with her rescuing men." The story, however, is ultimately a male quest, since, as Robert Dixon puts it, "Hennessey apparently could not imagine an adventure tale in which his heroine actually accompanied the male adventurers to the lost world."[65] Consider, as well, Rosa Praed's *Fugitive Anne: A Romance of the Unexplored Bush* (1902). Obviously influenced by Haggard, this female-written adventure story is essentially a male imperial romance with a female colonial protagonist, who is joined, less than halfway through, by a European male. With the important exception that it centers on an independent and courageous woman, it shares little, however, with the female colonial romance.

Before Benita and Rachel, Haggard tried his hand at daring colonial heroines, most notably in *Jess*, a realist novel, and *Swallow* (1898), an incipient version of the female colonial romance. In the former, the heroine murders a powerful Boer leader at the close of the First Anglo-Boer War (1880–1881), making her, if indirectly, a war heroine. Set before and during the Great Trek, the latter is a tale of romance between Suzanne—called Swallow by the indigenous—a Boer of Dutch and Huguenot descent, and her adopted Scottish brother, Ralph.[66] Suzanne mistakenly believes that Ralph is dead; acquires an indigenous name; is perceived by an indigenous group to play a key role in their fate; travels far into indigenous territory; shares a spiritual connection with Sihamba, a Swazi "chieftainess"; repels the advances of a rough colonial; has visions; is given authority by an indigenous ruler; receives a royal salute from an indigenous regiment; and saves her lover's life. These elements strongly ally the story with the female colonial romance, whose chief characteristics are outlined in the following section. However, unlike Rachel and Benita—"I was the seer, not the seen. I have always been like that," says the latter of her clairvoyance, though it also rings true for her subject position (*B* 6)—Suzanne is more sought than seeker, more survivor than savior. Despite her rescue of both Sihamba and Ralph, her strength is mainly in bearing up, not in strategizing or directing. Time and again she is rescued; time and again she swoons. Sihamba and Ralph are the true heroes of *Swallow*, Suzanne the object of their efforts. By the time that Haggard introduced the fully formed female colonial romance eight years later, the Second Anglo-Boer War had come and gone, Afrikaner nationalism had reignited, and feminist agitation in Britain had become militant.[67] In *Benita*, Haggard used a number of the plot points from *Swallow*, but he altered the heroine in two critical ways: she was now British and not merely the story's center but also its central adventurer.

The Female Colonial Romance

The genre, clearly, has a variety of influences, even as it introduces innovations. Where the heroine of the eighteenth-century female military adventure (usually) tries to locate her husband, the heroine of the female colonial romance defends family and colony. Where the heroine (when there is one) of the Robinsonade is typically a girl, the heroine of the female colonial romance is a young woman. Unlike contemporaneous Australian settler heroines, she acts independently of men. Unlike Jess, she lives to tell. Unlike Suzanne, she is more actor than acted upon. Where Meade's Isabel sees herself "as much boy as girl," Henty's Nita "wish[es] [she] had been a boy," and Praed's Anne "wish[es] that [she] had been a man," Benita and Rachel possess traditionally masculine characteristics and function in traditionally masculine roles without identifying as or wishing they had been born men, thus, to some extent, bypassing contemporary expectations of exceptionality.[68] Ultimately, the female colonial romance's nearest relation is the male imperial romance, "the twelve most recurring plot functions" of which have been neatly mapped out by Richard Patteson. They can be summarized as:

1. Adventurers (usually European) journey into the unknown with "clearly defined" "goals" that are generally "both idealistic and materialistic."

2. Protagonists have a series of preliminary adventures.

3. Adventurers descend into caves.

4. Heroes encounter "evidence of previous or current rule by a relatively advanced—and always white or partly white—civilization."

5. Indigenous are divided into political factions.

6. Heroes "establish . . . influence over" the indigenous by the display of technology or the use of scientific knowledge.

7. Indigenous are divided into religio-spiritual factions.

8. Heroes side with the more secular faction of the indigenous.

9. Women are absent, "treacherous," or "helpless."

10. "If one of the Europeans falls in love with a native woman, the woman usually dies."

11. More civilized indigenous faction "emerges victorious . . . with the aid of the Europeans."

12. Adventurers, "having established order . . . , get what they came for and depart."[69]

Patteson, who read multiple "imperialist romances" in compiling his list, offers *King Solomon's Mines* as "a nearly 'pure' example" of the genre.[70]

Using Patteson's list as a model, I have generated a list of the twelve primary plot functions of Haggard's female colonial romances:

1. Young female colonial meets and is separated from her future mate, whom she will at some point erroneously believe to be dead.

2. Heroine has a near-death experience.

3. Heroine undergoes a spiritual (re)birth into colonial womanhood.

4. Preliminary adventures, vigor, perspicacity, and connection to the indigenous establish the heroine's suitability over that of a male relative for the story's principal adventure.

5. Heroine is deeply respected by the indigenous, who give her an indigenous name, believe her to be spiritually affiliated with them, and recognize her supernatural power.

6. Motivated by loyalty and affinity, the heroine travels into the unknown at the request of the indigenous.

7. A spiritual association exists between the colonial heroine and another woman (or other women) from a culture different than her own.

8. Heroine repeatedly rejects romantic advances of a rough colonial male.

9. Heroine experiences psychic invasion by—and ultimately repels—a man or men who seek access to her knowledge and power.

10. Heroine is given authority by an indigenous ruler, wields power from a spot on high, and is saluted by an indigenous regiment.

11. Heroine plays a key role in resolving discord in one or more of the following circumstances: between indigenous groups, within an indigenous group, between the indigenous and colonials.

12. Heroine saves her lover from death, establishes order, and departs.

The remainder of this chapter provides an analysis of these features, paying particular attention to cross-cultural female connections, mystical feminism, and the role of both in mediation and resolution. Woven throughout is a comparison between the male imperial and the female colonial romance. Though my primary goal is to reorient critical understanding of Haggard, whose unintended contributions to feminist literature—literature that values or positively expands the roles of women—have been underacknowledged, I also explore the unexpected ways and places in which female agency registered more broadly around the turn of the century.

Set primarily in the Transvaal and Matabeleland in the 1870s, *Benita* begins on a ship bound for South Africa, the country of the heroine's birth. Thirteen years earlier, after her gambling, alcoholic father, T. Clifford, struck her mother, the latter fled with Benita to England. Her mother recently deceased and her repentant father long since reformed, Benita is on her way to join the latter on his "fine [horse] farm in the Transvaal" (*B* 57). While at sea, she meets Robert Seymour, an Englishman headed to southern Africa to make a living hunting big game. He proposes to her, but before she can accept, the ship is rent. As it sinks, the lovers are separated, and though both survive, Benita receives news of Robert's death. Some months later, she journeys with her father and his business partner, Jacob Meyer, to Bambatse, a Makalanga fortress on the Zambesi River. "A peaceful agricultural people," the Makalanga seek their assistance (in the form of guns) against the aggressive Matabele (Ndebele), then ruled by Lobengula (67). Clifford, "brave" if sometimes "foolish[]," and Jacob, a duplicitous, greedy German whose failings are consistently attributed to the Judaism he has renounced, seek the treasure that they (correctly) believe is hidden at Bambatse (276, 90).[71] Six generations earlier, two hundred Portuguese men, women, and children had fled with "an enormous quantity of gold, all the stored-up treasure of the land which they were trying to carry off," from "the tribes of Monomotapa, [who] rose against [their] rule" (82, 243).[72] "Shut up [atop the] fortress, which it was impossible to storm, [they] slowly perished of starvation" (83). The last to die was Benita da Ferreira, a young woman who, "mad with grief" at the loss of her parents and her lover, jumped from the pinnacle of the stronghold after telling the Makalanga chief that, although "no black man would ever find" the treasure, she "gave it into his keeping, and that of his descendants, to safeguard until she came again" (83). Since that time, the "Spirit of Bambatse" has lingered in the fortress, appearing periodically but revealing the gold's location to no one (304). As the Makalanga and Jacob realize, however, Benita Clifford, who possesses the "gift of clairvoyance," is psychically connected to the deceased woman whose name and appearance she shares (223). Attempting to use this connection to locate the gold, Jacob repeatedly mesmerizes Benita while holding her and her father hostage at the top of the fortress. While Clifford grows ill, Jacob goes mad, and Benita continues to resist the latter's advances, the Matabele attack the Makalanga. In the end, Benita finds the cave-buried treasure, liberating the Spirit of Bambatse from her lonely vigil; escapes confinement; rescues and pledges herself to Robert, a prisoner of the Matabele; saves her father's life; and secures the Matabele's promise that they will leave the Makalanga in peace, thus making the region safer for all.

The Ghost Kings opens in the early 1820s, the first years of the settlement of Natal, where John Dove, a British missionary, has immigrated with his wife and young daughter, Rachel.[73] Out alone during a fierce storm, Rachel meets Richard Darrien, an English boy who immigrated with his widowed father to southern Africa five years earlier and is now on his way to college in Cape Town. Surviving the lightning, flash flood, and lions that prowl outside the cave into which the pair retreat, Rachel acquires both a "supernatural reputation" and a Zulu name, "a very long name that meant Chieftainess or Lady of Heaven, *Inkosazana-y-Zoola*; for Zulu or Zoola, which we know as the title of that people, means Heaven" (*GK* 123, 41). In time, the Zulus come to revere her as the "incarnation of the Spirit of [their] people," whom she resembles and whose name she shares—Inkosazana-y-Zoola being another name for Nomkubulwana, "that mysterious white ghost [whom they believe] control[s] their destinies" (155, 118–19).[74] Several years after the storm, while living near Zululand, Rachel rescues Noie, a young part-Zulu girl pursued by the warriors of Dingaan (Dingane), King of the Zulus.[75] The Dove family adopts Noie, and when she is later kidnapped, Rachel treks into Zululand to retrieve her. There she meets Dingaan, who, because of her reputation as "the traditional white Spirit of their race," seeks Rachel's counsel regarding the encroachment of the Boers, then engaged on the Great Trek (190). Unable to make sense of her intentionally ambiguous advice and fearful that were "the Inkosazana . . . to leave us, . . . with her would go the Spirit of our people, and [our] good luck," Dingaan holds Rachel against her will (154–55). At the same time, however, he gives her power over the Zulus, including the authority to adjudicate internal disputes. Still "troubled about this matter of the Boers, and the meaning of the words [Rachel] spoke as to their waging war on them," Dingaan sends Noie as an envoy to the land of the Ghost-people (the "half human race" after whom the book is named), whose powers of divination he wishes to procure (159, 318). In Noie's absence, Rachel reunites with and is again separated from Richard; discovers that Ishmael, a scheming English hunter-trader who is obsessed with her, caused her parents' murder; and views (false) evidence of Richard's death. As a result of these traumas, her "Spirit" comes unmoored from her body, even as her psychic powers grow stronger (296). Brought by Noie to the Ghost-people for healing, Rachel regains her senses, becomes embroiled in their conflicts, and frees Richard from captivity. The women work together to prevent male usurpation of the ostensibly female-led race, and when this proves impossible, Noie sacrifices herself to destroy them altogether. The two young lovers then begin their life together, as foretold by Rachel's prescient mother.

Colonial Maturation

The heroic feats of will performed by the heroines of the colonial romance are partly an effect of their upbringing in southern Africa, where "girls grow quickly to womanhood" (4). Benita, who has three English grandparents (the other is half Dutch and half Portuguese, one of several factors that link her to Benita da Ferreira), spent her childhood in southern Africa (and her teens in England). Crediting Africa for her "brave heart," she proudly declares, "I am not afraid who was born in Africa. Indeed, often and often have I wished to be back there again, out on the veld, far away from the London streets and fog" (*B* 11). When her father suggests that she might be lonely or frightened on his farm, she again asserts her affinity: "I was born on the veld, father, and I have always hated London" (60). Having "wearied of the monotony of civilisation," she thrives in rural southern Africa (109). A mere six weeks after the shipwreck, her health "was quite come back to her, indeed never before had she felt so strong and well" (75).

Her natural "home," southern Africa is where this "bold-spirited woman" is in best form (100, 220). When she accompanies her father on a four-month trek to the Zambesi, she not only learns to use a gun, she also learns her guides' Makalanga tongue, "which she did not find difficult, for Benita had a natural aptitude for languages, and had never forgotten the Dutch [the *taal*] and Zulu she used to prattle as a child, which now came back to her very fast" (99–100). Though the journey is arduous, "their rough, wild life . . . agree[s] with Benita extraordinarily well, so well that any who had known her in the streets of London would scarcely have recognized her as the sunburnt [*sic*], active and well-formed young woman [sitting] by the camp fire" (102). "Could she be the same woman," Benita wonders herself, "who not a year before had been walking with her cousins down Westbourne Grove, and studying Whiteley's windows? What would these cousins say now if they could see her, white-faced, large-eyed, desperate, splashing through the mud upon the unknown banks of the Zambesi, flying from death to death!" (298).[76] She is the same woman, but faced with challenges she could not have imagined in the metropole. Window-shopping in West London, she is an idle girl warding off boredom. On the banks of the Zambesi, she is a woman who "constant danger had made . . . very cunning" (296).

Though born in England, southern Africa is the only home that the heroine of *The Ghost Kings* can recall. Rachel immigrated with her family to the Cape when she was four—presumably as one of the original 1820 settlers—then moved to Natal in the "first days of [its] settlement" and later to "the Transvaal side of the Drakensberg" mountain range (*GK* 40, 183). Raised by her English father, a "religious enthusiast" gripped by "missionary-fury," and her long-suffering Scottish mother, Rachel is the sole surviving child of four (40, 4). Having grown up among the Zulus, whom her father was perpetually trying to convert, Rachel "spoke their tongue as well as she did her own" (88). A child of the wilderness, Rachel is as comfortable with "her double-barelled [*sic*] gun" as with an assegai (55). At the sound of hyenas in the night, she rises, grabs the weapon by her side, and surveys the land, "resting upon her gun like some Amazon on guard" (53). Yet, neither in *The Ghost Kings* nor in *Benita* is woman equivalent to Africa, a site to be domesticated, which, as has been aptly demonstrated elsewhere, is Haggard's modus operandi in the imperial adventure. Neither is she, like Ayesha or Gagool, the ancient African "witch doctoress" of *King Solomon's Mines*, darkly empowered by land that is "itself . . . the *femme fatale*."[77] She is, rather, strengthened bodily, mentally, and spiritually by her affiliation with Africa, which she makes safer for its European inhabitants through the dissuasion of violence.

Rachel, whose "bodily and mental vigour overshadowed" that of both her parents, is also better suited than they are to colonial life (*GK* 49). Though the local Africans "would laugh at her father," whom they aptly called "Shouter-about-Things-he-does-not-understand," "and mimic him behind his back, . . . Rachel they never laughed at or mimicked" (42). For while she shares her father's "courage and fixity of purpose," she does not share his weaknesses (9). On the contrary, where her father most fails, Rachel most succeeds: adapting to African surroundings and understanding indigenous ways. Keenly interested in the people and places of southern Africa, she listens, learns, and seeks to comprehend those with whom she makes the region home, so that "with all natives from her childhood up, Rachel was on the best of terms[,] . . . intimate in the sense that she could enter into their thoughts and nature" (41). The colonial heroine's natural affinity for and cultivated understanding of the indigenous are the earthy, or secular, components of a mystical connection that will greatly enhance her influence over them.

But it is the arrival and loss of love that transforms the colonial heroine into robust colonial womanhood, anticipating her involvement in political strife.[78] Nearing the coast of Africa, Benita falls in love, has a premonition, is almost killed, is separated from her lover, and undergoes a metamorphosis in rapid sequence. Presuming her lover dead, she declares, "I shall never be myself again. . . . My old self is dead" (*B* 55). Her presentiment, just before their unexpected parting, that there was "about to be a mighty change, and beyond it another life, something new and unfamiliar," proves to be more about her own agency than the separation itself (5).

In *The Ghost Kings*, Haggard offers a much more elaborate description of the (differently ordered, though similarly experienced) process of love, near-death, premonition, loss, and rebirth. Rachel's sudden, orgasmic, and solitary eruption into womanhood takes place outdoors moments before an unexpected "tempest [from] the heavens," during which she first meets her future mate (*GK* 15). It resonates remarkably with the description of Jess's awakening, which in some instances uses identical language and concludes with her realization "that she loved with heart and soul and body, and was a very woman."[79] Walking by the water's edge, Rachel senses that

> the atmosphere was full of electricity struggling to be free. Although she knew not what it was, Rachel felt it in her blood and brain. In some strange way it affected her mind, opening windows there through which the eyes of her soul looked out. She became aware of some new influence drawing near to her life; of a sudden her budding womanhood burst into flower in her breast, shone on by an unseen sun; she was no more a child. Her being quickened and acknowledged the kinship of all things that are. That brooding, flame-threaded sky—she was a part of it, the earth she trod, it was a part of her; the Mind that caused the stars to roll and her to live, dwelt in her bosom, and like a babe she nestled within the arm of its almighty will. . . . [Moments later,] she became aware of a low moaning noise and a stirring of the air about her which caused the leaves and grasses to quiver . . . (13–15)

This extended passage at once invokes the sensual, the sexual, the maternal, the natal, the spiritual, and the natural, as Rachel emerges into a state of organic harmony and agentic womanhood. Simultaneously a narrative of birth and sexual maturation, it hinges as much on "quicken[ing]" and "stirring" as it does on "moaning" and "quiver[ing]." While a reductive analysis might consider only the problematically naturalized associations between adult femininity and heterosexual romance or between femininity and nature, there is more to this cataclysmic maturation. What occurs, in essence, is an awakening, not simply to love but also to powerful forces within.

The young woman who exits the cave the next morning has not only spent her first night in the arms of a man and had her first premonitions—of "her life and this lad's life . . . interwoven," "of blood and terror, . . . of voices crying war," of "rul[ing] [as] a queen," and of power over death—she has also, in surviving, obtained influence (28). "'She is alive,'" exclaim the indigenous Africans who spot her first. "'The lightnings have turned away from her, she rules the waters and the lightnings!' and then and there, after the native fashion, they gave Rachel [the] name which was destined to play a great part in her future. That name was 'Lady of the Lightnings,' or, to translate it more accurately, 'of the Heavens'" (34). The formidable figure that Rachel, as Inkosazana-y-Zoola, becomes seems to have been sanctified by nature, as the region's native inhabitants immediately recognize. When she returns home, her mother observes, "Rachel, you are changed since yesterday. . . . [Y]our life is all before you, whereas mine lies behind me" (37, 39). Jane Dove's life of dependence on the will of a husband is one she neither wishes nor foresees for her strong-minded daughter.

Indeed, exchange is an essential component of the relationship between heroine and lover in the colonial romance, despite the latter's relative absence. Early in *Benita*, Robert, "fasten[s] [a lifebelt] round" an unconscious Benita and carries her to one of the sinking ship's few lifeboats (*B* 27). In doing so, he saves her life, as she later saves his, once inadvertently and once intentionally, when he is a prisoner of the Matabele. In the initial encounter between Richard and Rachel in *The Ghost Kings*, the former saves the latter from a flash flood, by sweeping her from its path. Here, the turnabout is almost immediate, for "the hungry waters sprang at them like a living thing" and Richard almost falls, "but this time it was Rachel who supported him. Then one more struggle and they rolled exhausted on the ground just clear of the lip of the racing flood" (*GK* 17). When they "recover[] their breath" and are able to rise, Rachel leads Richard to a cave, which, unlike the caves of Kukuanaland (in *King Solomon's Mines*) or Kôr (in *She*), is a haven—from animals and the elements—rather than a site of feminized danger (18). "You risked your life to save mine, and therefore," she tells him, "it belongs to you" (22). When Richard "undertake[s] [the] dangerous . . . mission" of retrieving Rachel from Zululand, she saves his life before he even arrives, by sending word that he should be led safely to her, lest she "lay [her] curse upon the land" (171, 177). Reflecting on the "vision" that warned her of his danger, she tells Richard, "I suppose that I was allowed to save your life that I might bring you here to save me"

(183).[80] The pattern repeats itself once again before the tale is out: the hero rescued by the heroine on his journey to bring her home.

Despite the marginal position of the heroine's mate, readers are not for a moment to doubt his courage or vigor. Robert is a "hero" who surrenders his place on a lifeboat to a mother and child (*B* 49). Richard, "untouched by fear" for his own safety, repeatedly puts himself in harm's way to search for Rachel (*GK* 233). Strong, brave, and "sealed with the indescribable stamp of the English gentleman," the male lover in the colonial romance is distinct from both rough colonials, like Jacob and Ishmael, who seek to control the heroine, and quixotic colonials, like Mr. Clifford and John Dove, who unthinkingly put her at risk (*B* 7). "Nursed" back to health by her father, Benita becomes, in the end, his protector (55). After surviving the storm, Rachel focuses not on romance (not least because she and her family move north, while Richard travels south), but on safeguarding her loved ones. Both women effectively become head of household without ever having married. It is a position that comes naturally to them but is only assumed in the absence of a strong British male. Given the efficacy of young British men in the masculine romance, we can tally the male lover's attributes with his minimal presence in the female romance only by taking into consideration its focus: the colonial heroine, who flourishes not in opposition to but in the absence of her man, and to his benefit. Skilled adventurers who function successfully without the assistance of men, these women suggest that British femininity is acceptably masculinized in the service of empire.

Recognition

The occasional villain excepted, the indigenous recognize and respect the authority of the colonial heroine. Predicated on such imperialist assertions as African effeminacy and European supremacy, indigenous respect for whites—often simply because they *are* white—is a racist construct in both the male imperial and the female colonial romance. Nonetheless, its implicit validation of authority in the female colonial romance works to bolster female colonial agency. While such affirmation of the heroine's authority may not be a wholesale affirmation of white supremacy, neither does it challenge racial hierarchies propagated in southern Africa by whites. Unlike the male adventurer, the female colonial heroine has grown up in southern Africa, but her sway over the indigenous hinges on more than her British South African identity. As I discuss in this section, her embodiment of the spirit of, or a spirit associated with, their people is another reason for her influence.

In Haggard's embryonic colonial romance, the eponymous heroine, born Suzanne, is given her "native name [of] Swallow" while still a child, "because of the grace of her movements and her habit of running swiftly hither and thither."[81] As a young woman, she is perceived by the "Red Kaffirs" to be an omen of good luck, "the White Swallow of the Diviner's Dream," whose presence will ensure their victory over the Endwandwe (175, 185).[82] In this capacity, she not only receives the chief's salute but is also given command of his army, which numbers in the thousands.

In *Benita*, the Makalanga messengers who have come to Clifford seeking help immediately recognize his daughter as "the Spirit of the Rock!" and greet her with "profound obeisance," each "touching the floor with his finger-tips, and staring at her face. But her father they only saluted with an uplifted hand" (*B* 88, 89). In addition to sharing the name and appearance of the long-dead Benita de Ferreira, "who haunts Bambatse," Benita's face tells them "that she has the greatest part" to play in events that are about to unfold for their people (88, 90). "Doubtless it is of her that the Spirit told to my father," remarks the son of the Molimo of Bambatse, leader "and hereditary high-priest of [the] tribe" (90, 82). Accepting Benita as the Spirit on sight, the messengers, impromptu, give her the gold cross that once belonged to "Señora da Ferreira"; the common people assert that she is "the White Lady come again to take her own"; and the Molimo grants her access to the site of the buried treasure, their "secret holy place, where for six generations no white man has set a foot" (297, 113, 112). Even the Matabele concede her authority, referring to her as "White Maiden," "ancient Witch of Bambatse," and "Great Lady of Magic, Spirit from of Old" (306, 311).

In *The Ghost Kings*, Rachel's reputation is even more widely acknowledged. The indigenous "always treated her with the utmost respect, even if they had never seen her before," since "the tale of [her childhood] adventure . . . [had] spread all through the country . . . so that throughout that part of South-Eastern Africa Rachel came to enjoy the lofty title of 'Heaven,' the first girl, probably, who was ever so called" (*GK* 55, 40, 41). In addition to the appellations mentioned earlier in this chapter, she is also referred to by the Zulus as "*Udade-y-Silwana* or Sister of Wild beasts," "Lady Zoola," "Princess of the Zulus," and "Princess of the Heavens, Holder of the Spirit of Nomkubulwana," though King Dingaan most often simply calls her "White

One" (41, 229, 87, 118, 175). Rachel's native names stand in contrast to those of her father, Ishmael, and her male counterparts in the imperial romance. " 'Shouter-about-Things-he-does-not-understand,' or more briefly, 'The Shouter,' [was] a name [that John Dove] had acquired from his habit of raising his voice when he grew moved in speaking to" the indigenous, "rudely" as they saw it, most often while condemning their "private customs" (42). Ishmael's native name, "Ibubesi (lion)"—also sometimes translated as "Night-prowler"—is given to him, "not because he is brave, but because he hunts and springs by night" (48, 153, 78). The Zulu sobriquets of Curtis, Good, and Quatermain—respectively translated as Elephant (for his impressive size), Glass Eye (for his monocle), and "Watcher by Night" (for his vigilance)—though undergirded with respect, denote neither the belonging nor the reverence of Rachel's many names; for while they fight alongside the indigenous, the male adventurers do not possess anything like Rachel's power among them.[83] Before he has even met her, Dingaan declares: "Because of her name, . . . all the territories of the Zulus are her kraal [shelter or home] and all the thousands of the Zulus are her servants. Yea, because of her high name I give to her the power of life and death wherever men obey my word" (87).[84] It is a power enacted more than once (see the section "Blood Is a Bad Seed to Sow" later in this chapter).

While the colonial heroine's reputed ties to the fate of the indigenous initially compel their respect for her, her conduct enhances it. Displaying courage, confidence, and savvy in the face of "difficulties and dangers every way one looks," the more that she engages with them, the greater her effect on them (*B* 128). Acting variously as diplomat, judge, and protector, the heroine invokes her authority most often to enable the peaceful resolution of conflict where possible, with the least loss of life where not.

Negotiation and Adjudication

Benita's arrival at Bambatse coincides with that of the Matabele, who threaten war. Pleading for the lives of two brazen Matabele messengers, who, as "by some instinct, . . . throw[] themselves upon the ground, clutch[ing] her dress and pray[ing] for mercy," she impresses them and the Molimo alike with her calm and compassion (124). Granting her request, the Molimo tells those who wish the men killed: "Give mercy to the merciless, for she buys their lives with prayer" (125). It is a fortuitous intercession, for Prince Maduna, one of the men whose life Benita saves, promises her two lives in exchange, "should it chance that you have cause to demand" them, which she later does (125). Negotiating with this "Prince of the royal house," she manages to secure not only Robert's freedom and her own but also twenty oxen (to cart their wagon) and milking cows (to feed her ailing father) (125). "Give them to her and see that they are good ones, before she asks our shields and spears also," Maduna tells his men, "for after all she saved my life" (308–09). In a show of respect for the woman who outmaneuvered them, "the great impi [army] of the Matabele . . . lifted their great spears in salutation to Benita. . . . Indeed, they were a wondrous and imposing spectacle, such a one as few white women have ever seen" (309).[85]

Similarly, in *The Ghost Kings*, Rachel makes a powerful impression on King Dingaan's warriors. When she hears that he has sent an embassy to greet her, her preparations are deliberate, for while she does not dissemble—"I am a woman, not spirit," she tells them—she nonetheless "desired to impress" (*GK* 89, 87). Therefore,

> she threw a white shawl about her. . . . Then, letting her long, golden hair hang down, she went out alone carrying a light assegai in her hand, to the place where the messengers . . . were encamped[,] [nearby] which, as it chanced, lay a great boulder of rock. On this boulder she took her stand, unobserved, waiting there till the full moon shone out from behind a dark cloud, turning her white robe to silver. (87–88)

Every choice is made for the utmost effect. Her position on the rock augments her height. The spear in her hand conveys authority. Her white shawl and flowing hair, which capture the light, together with her sudden appearance give her the aura of the supernatural. The entire picture is one of confident control. So skillfully is her entrance executed, that when the messengers notice her, "they all sprang to their feet and perceiving this beautiful and mysterious figure, by a common impulse lifted their right arms and gave to her what no woman had ever received before—the royal salute" (88). Diplomatically declining the king's invitation to visit him—"one day, perchance, I will come"—she disappears by cloud cover (89). When, eight months later, a second envoy arrives, this time conveying Dingaan's desire for "her counsel upon an important matter" (see the last paragraph of "Blood Is a Bad Seed to Sow"), she again stands her ground, relenting only when Noie is kidnapped (105). Promised safe passage and Noie's release, Rachel is compelled by loyalty to enter indigenous territory. Her motive contrasts with the motives of Haggard's male adventurers, who generally undertake their journeys because of a desire for novelty, personal glory, or individual gain. A self-appraising Quatermain puts it best: "I . . . never . . . leave anything behind that I can possibly carry away."[86]

Though "perhaps the first white woman . . . who had ever entered Zululand," Rachel sets off "without a sign of doubt or fear" (*GK* 203, 118). Her courage—variously described as "extraordinary," "constitutional," "calm," and "characteristic"—may be Rachel's defining trait, but it is her composure that has the greatest effect on her Zulu escort (13, 56, 90, 163). Bidding her father farewell, she keeps her emotions in check, lest she be "lowered" in their eyes (118). Sitting "proud and upright on her horse," and "taking no notice" of "the captains of the regiment [who] r[u]n forward to meet her with lifted shields and crouching bodies," she crosses the Tugela River into Zululand, where two thousand soldiers regard her "with wonder and awe" (118, 119). First, they beat the handles of their spears against their shields, "producing . . . a sound like the sound of thunder"; then, their spears held high, "from every throat came the royal salute—*Bayète*. It was a tremendous and most imposing welcome" (119).[87] Holding her seat as her "terrified" mare "bucked and shied," "sprang . . . and swerved," Rachel further impresses the Zulus (119).

In her first audience with the king, she surmounts substantial disadvantage, assessing his power and displaying her own. Though Dingaan does not identify himself, Rachel deduces that she is "in [his] presence" (127). Drawing her cloak about her, she "walked forward slowly, till she reached the centre of the [open court], where she stopped and stood quite still, . . . uttering no word for a long while, . . . [for] she knew that the one who spoke first would own to inferiority" (127). When after six or seven minutes she turns as though to leave, Dingaan breaks the silence, announcing himself. Rachel controls the conversation, answering his first question with one of her own and his next with an evasion, manipulating him into affirming her name and authority, and confronting him about his dubious tactics in luring her there. Confidently challenging his lie that Noie is dead, she shows no surprise when Noie eventually appears before her. Admitting that she killed one of the king's soldiers (see the section "Unwanted Advances" later in this chapter), Rachel warns him that she could kill him as well. Using her own observations and information she earlier gathered from Noie, Rachel demonstrates knowledge of the king's darkest secrets.[88] "'Thou knowest all,' [the king] gasped, 'thou art Nomkubulwana and no other. Spare us, Spirit who canst summon our dead sins from the grave of time, and make them walk alive before us'" (136). Displaying confidence while working to secure her safety, she "mockingly" responds: "'Take notice, King, and you his captains, that I am no spirit, nothing but a woman who chances to bear a high name, and to have some wisdom. Only,' she added with meaning, 'if any harm should come to me, if I should die, then I think that I should become a spirit, a terrible spirit, and that ill would it go with that people against whom my blood was laid" (136). Her words leave the king shaking with fright, begging her not to mock him, and affirming her powers.

As the Molimo gives Benita jurisdiction over the cave at the top of the fortress, which he refers to as "her house," so Dingaan appoints Rachel "first judge" of Zululand (*B* 140, *GK* 163).[89] Declining his invitation to "help him and his council . . . try cases" in the royal kraal, Rachel instead submits that "if they had cases for her to try, let them be brought before her in her own house," where she alone presides (163). Silently deducing the lying party in her first case, a large inheritance dispute between two "very powerful chiefs," "she asked him how he dared to give false witness before the Inkosazana-y-Zoola, to whom the truth was always open" (164). The man confesses and Rachel, "warn[ing] him to be more upright in future," sentences him justly (164). "The result was that her fame as a judge spread throughout the land, and every day her gates were beset with suitors whose causes she dealt with to the best of her ability, and to their entire satisfaction" (164). Tempering her authority with compassion, Rachel refuses to try cases that might result in a death-sentence; "the Inkosazana [would] not cause blood to flow," for "that judgment is the Lord's" (164, 243). "Thus to her reputation as a spiritual queen, Rachel added that of an upright judge who could not be influenced by fear or bribes" (164). With her "sincere desire to discover the truth and execute justice," her "intimate acquaintance with Kaffir [Bantu] customs," her compassion, and her "knowledge of [the] law"—acquired through observing trials in Durban and studying the handbooks of her father, a former Cape justice—Rachel, the text suggests, brings Zululand the justice that it previously lacked (163).[90]

"Blood Is a Bad Seed to Sow"

The colonial heroine is not merely reluctant to "cause blood to flow," she uses her authority to prevent it (164). Benita, as we have seen, saves the two Matabele messengers heralding war. Watching the Matabele army from atop the fortress as they prepare to attack, she walks away after an old warrior falls victim to Jacob's sniper shot, telling him, "I do not want to see any more" (*B* 230). When he boasts to her of having killed six and wounded ten, she shows him that she is unimpressed, asking, "What is the use when there are so many?" And while Jacob admits, "not much," he also says that it "amuses" him, before reminding her that part of their "bargain" with the Makalanga (who granted them permission to seek the treasure) was "that we should help [them] if they were attacked" (231). Benita's curt response: "I believe that you like killing people" (231). Though Jacob is increasingly a danger to her father and herself—he sees Clifford as an impediment to Benita, access to whose mind and body he alike desires—she twice deters her father from shooting him. "'I will not have it. It would be murder although he has threatened you. After all, father, I believe that the man is half mad and not responsible. . . . [A]t the worst I can always save myself,' and she touched the pistol which now she wore day and night" (260)—signaling the "moral fortitude" of the British woman, who, like those martyrs of the widely circulated but fictitious narratives of the "Indian Mutiny," chooses "death over dishonor."[91]

Rachel, too, carries a gun for protection, and similarly avoids using it. When she first meets Richard, he is a "young hunter who thinks not of the wonderful and happy life" that each shot might bring down (*GK* 30). Rachel, on the other hand, "always shrank from" the sight of a slaughtered animal (30). When Ishmael presents her with a dead buck for her family, she "turned her eyes from it for it was covered with blood"; though she has "no objection to eating [meat], . . . unless she were driven to it, never would she lift her hand against anything that drew the breath of life" (48, 30, 42).

Like Benita, Rachel uses her authority to protect the lives of others, even when they threaten or oppose her. When her Zulu escort spears an angry "*Isanuzi* or witch-doctoress" who has grabbed the reins of her horse, Rachel is struck with "horror" at the realization that it was she herself who caused them to do so by pointing her whip at her (121, 122). "Too late she remembered that in this savage land such a motion when made by the King or one in supreme command [meant] death without pity or reprieve" (121–22). When "the chief of the slayers" asks Rachel whether she wishes the woman's attendants slain, she replies, "I give them life" (122). After a man is killed for the "sacrilege" of coming too near her private residence in "Dingaan's great town," she says it is "her will . . . that no more men should be killed upon her account" (144, 125, 144). When the king orders the execution of warriors who, at Ishmael's command, caused her parents' death, Rachel intervenes on their behalf: "Set them free, set them free! . . . Vengeance is from Heaven, and Heaven will pour it out in plenty. Not on my hands, not on my hands shall be [their] blood" (257).

She even protects Ishmael himself—to a point. When Zulus lift their spears against him because, with an "amorous sneer," he has made her an unwelcome proposal of marriage, Rachel insists that they "leave him to the vengeance of the Heavens. My mantle is over him" (150). When Noie asks Rachel for permission to kill him—the Zulu custom of "spears for battle-axes" compelling her to avenge his role in the murder of Rachel's parents—she stays her hand as well (151). The death of Rachel's parents, however, whose "spirits" tell her that they "were killed by [Ishmael's] order, and in [his] presence," compels a different response. "For that crime," Rachel tells Ishmael, calling on "Heaven above and earth beneath [to] bear witness" and all Zulus near and far to "hear the voice of your Inkosazana," "I sentence you to death!" (211). She takes no further action, however, until she believes he has killed Richard.

Then, in one of the most dramatic scenes in all of Haggard's writing, Rachel stands atop the hut in which Ishmael held her hostage and tries him before an army of Zulus, eager to do her bidding. Gripping the assegai that killed her father, while "lightning blaze[s]" above her and Ishmael, pleading for forgiveness, cowers below, she asks:

> "Have the Zulus forgiven you, the Zulus who believe that judgment is the King's—and the Inkosazana's? Turn now, and ask them, for here they are," and she pointed over his head with her spear. "Turn, Toad, and set out your case and I will stand above and try it, the case of Dingaan against Ibubesi, and one by one I will call up all those who died through you, and they shall give their evidence, and I, the Judge, will sum it up to a jury of sharp spears." (243–44)

In this expression of authority, Rachel lives up to the legend of the Inkosazana, the Lady of the Lightnings. "Drop[ping] the spear as though she needed it no more," she stretches wide her arms and lifts her face up to the sky. "Seen thus . . . , she seemed no woman but what [the Zulus] had fabled her to be, a queen of Spirits" (245). Though she sanctions Ishmael's death, she is more trial judge than sentencing judge. When Tamboosa, the leader of the impi and her chief guard, asks her to "pass judgment on this wild beast," she does not (244). Instead, she reiterates that "there is blood" between her and Ishmael, as there is between her and the Zulus, who failed to keep her parents safe; she reminds Tamboosa of her warning that "from the seed of [such] blood" would come "woe upon woe"; and she says nothing at all about Ishmael's fate (245). Though she does not command the soldiers to kill him, neither does she intercede, either when Tamboosa declares his intent to deliver him "to the King to tell his story ere he die," or when Ishmael, "praying for pity," begs her not to "judge [him] harshly and send [him] to be tortured" (246). "'I judge not,' she answered in Zulu; 'pray to the Great One above who judges'" (246). "Heaven's vengeance," not her own, she prophesies with confidence, will befall Ishmael, as it will befall the Zulus (246). Indeed, Ishmael dies a fiery death as the huts begins to burn around him, sparked by lightning or the hand of a solider "none could tell," and the Zulus endure a series of trials and plagues—including locusts, disease, and famine—that kill hundreds if not thousands (247). If, in the scene described earlier, Rachel is uncharacteristically hard-hearted, it should be understood that she is not quite Rachel. Traumatized by Richard's "death," which followed so soon after that of her parents, her "spirit [has] left her"; the voice that "speaks through [my] lips," she tells Tamboosa, is that of the Inkosazana (267, 245). When, having healed from her "madness," she encounters Ishmael in the City of the Dead (see the section "Mystical Feminism" later in this chapter), the "spirit of pity and of pardon" arises in her and she forgives his "tortured soul" with "every fibre [sic] of her infinite being" (246, 322).

Because, as she sees it, "blood is a bad seed to sow," the heroine of the female colonial romance throws her weight on the side of peace when possible, consequently playing an influential if informal role in the political life of the region (365). For if in the male imperial romance, the white adventurers partake in war (fighting on the side of the indigenous whose ways are most like the colonizers' own), in the female colonial romance, the white female colonists obstruct war, peace rather than victory being the desired outcome. As we saw in chapter 1, Jess, taking the life of Frank Muller, prevents the rise of a Boer leader who wishes to drive the British out of southern Africa. In *Swallow*, Suzanne successfully discourages Chief Sigwe from making war against the Endwandwe. The name given to the conflict thus averted is "the 'War of the White Swallow,' or . . . 'The War of the Clean Spear,' because no blood at all was shed in it" (*S* 211). When Suzanne later learns of an impending Zulu attack, she and her lover forewarn a group of Boers, enabling them to "beat off the Zulus with great loss to Dingaan" (334). While Haggard allows his heroines to reduce the loss of (primarily white) life, he does not entirely rewrite history. So despite Jess's symbolic takedown of a fictional Boer leader, the British still lose the First Anglo-Boer War. And though Suzanne's warning saves Boer lives, as the narrator notes, "there were many [Boers] on that dreadful night whom no [one] . . . warn[ed]. . . . [S]ix hundred of them . . . went down beneath the Zulu assegai in that red dawn. . . . Is not the name of the land Weenen— 'The Land of Weeping'—to this day?" (334). While the War of the White Swallow is a fiction, the Weenen Massacre, as the British called it, was not.

Similarly, while there was a long history of tension between the Makalanga and the Matabele, there is no record of a conflict like the one in which Benita plays such a significant role.[92] Concluding her negotiations with Prince Maduna, she invokes her power to demand that he "bear this message to your king from the White Witch of Bambatse, for I am she and no other. . . . [L]eave these Makalanga, my servants, to dwell unharmed in their ancient home, and . . . lift no spear against the White Men" (*B* 310). In addition, then, to "br[inging] deliverance" to the Makalanga, who were on the verge of annihilation, Benita asserts her authority over the Makalanga and Matabele alike and ensures the safety of the British at a time when "white people"—encroaching into Matabeleland in search of mineral wealth—"were not very popular with the Matabele" (329, 197). She thus paves the way for Rhodes and his British South Africa Company (BSAC), who would ultimately claim the region on behalf of Britain.[93]

One of the principal plot lines of *The Ghost Kings* centers on Rachel's role in forestalling a Zulu attack on the "emigrant Boers"—the *voortrekkers*—whose Great Trek carried them ever further into Zulu territory (*GK* vii).[94] Uncertain as to the best course of action, Dingaan solicits Rachel's opinion on whether or not to "fall upon the Boers or . . . let them be" (136). Feeling the burden of responsibility for the thousands of lives at stake, she offers an ambiguous response: "*Those who lift the spear shall perish by the spear*" (137). In doing so, she temporarily stays the conflict that she knows must come without "fly[ing] in the face of the martial aspirations of the nation and the secret wishes of the King" (155).[95] She describes her words to Noie as a "warn[ing] . . . not to make war upon the Boers" (141). At the same time, Rachel knows that "fight [the Zulus] must and will and pay the price," for she is "sure that not even her hand could hold [the king and his captains] back from their desire" (141, 137). Of course, numerous battles between the two groups ultimately ensued, including the Weenen Massacre, referenced in *Swallow*, and the Battle of Blood River, mentioned in the opening paragraph of *The Ghost Kings*, an extract from a letter written at least seventeen years after the novel's central events. "Who am I to meddle with such matters . . . ?" Rachel may protest to Noie, but she is in a position of power nonetheless, which she consistently uses to encourage peace (140).

Unwanted Advances

With little or no hesitation, the colonial heroine steps up to protect the innocent, using force when other means fail. The first time Suzanne meets Sihamba, she saves her life, unintentionally forming an alliance that time and again saves her own. Finding the young woman stripped of most of her clothing, her hands bound behind her back, her neck encircled with rope, facing a small crowd of men, Suzanne demands an explanation of their leader, Swart (Black) Piet, who, as Sihamba sees it, "born of white blood [Boer] and black, is false to both and a disgrace to both" (*S* 78). "We are about to hang this thief and witch, who has been duly convicted after a fair trial," Piet tells Suzanne, though she quickly ascertains that he is "both accuser and judge" (75, 76). "It is not justice," she asserts, "it is a crime"—one, it turns out, "born of revenge," because Sihamba rejected his advances (76). Accepting the "bargain" that Piet offers, Suzanne, who has likewise rejected him, now kisses him in exchange for Sihamba's release, and though she feels that "the act" has "cost me my honour," she also believes that "if [it] was good . . . [it will] go to my credit in the Book of the Great One who made us" (79, 81).

This "choice between doing [the] will" of an amorous villain and allowing another to die is presented to the colonial heroine not only in *Swallow* but also in *Jess*, where Bessie must choose between marrying Muller and "seeing [her] uncle . . . shot" (see chapter 1); *Benita*, where the heroine must choose between allowing Jacob to mesmerize her (so that the Spirit can tell her where the treasure lies) and her father's "execut[ion]"; and *The Ghost Kings*, where Rachel must choose between marrying Ishmael and Robert's murder.[96] In each case, a man believes he can act with impunity, though only in *Swallow* does the villain get his way. Jess kills Muller, keeping her sister and their uncle safe. Benita retreats with her father into the cave, closing its entrance with a "barricade" of rock that she built herself "with desperate hands" (*B* 325). And in *The Ghost Kings*, one of Ishmael's indigenous wives, whom Rachel has befriended, nurses a poisoned Richard back to health.

The "choice" itself comes after repeated advances and rebuffs. Refusing Jacob's attempts to read her thoughts, Benita declares, "Mr. Meyer . . . my mind is my own property" (170). Objecting to his holding her and her father hostage, she demands, "How dare you, you coward?" (221). Denying his request to mesmerize her, she asserts, "I refuse to deliver my will into the keeping of any living man, and least of all into yours" (224). Preparing for further assault, she takes to wearing a "pistol at her waist" (270). Rachel similarly resists Ishmael, who, "like most brutes and bullies, was a coward" (*GK* 103). When he declares that he has been "hunting" her, she "indignantly" insists that she is "not a wild creature" (93). When he threatens to "marry [her], with [her] will or without it," she responds: " 'Do not try to touch me; you know that I can defend myself if I choose,' and she glanced at the pistol which she always carried in that wild land, 'I am not afraid of you, Mr. Ishmael; it is you who are afraid of me. . . . [Y]ou have no power at all against me; no one has. It is I who have the power' " (94–95).

Rachel uses this power to defend not only herself but also Noie, in a scene reminiscent of that in which Suzanne and Sihamba first meet. Like Sihamba, Noie is pursued by an unwanted lover, refuses him, and is consequently accused of witchcraft. Given that her would-be suitor is none other than the Zulu king, whom she knows will not relent, she flees Zululand with her parents and siblings. Running from one of "the king's men" who will shortly thereafter kill her family, Noie first encounters Rachel (*GK* 60). I include an illustration (figure 2.1) of this powerful scene, which I quote at length:

> . . . reach[ing] Rachel[,] [Noie] flung her arms about her legs gasping:
> "Save me, white lady, save me!"
> "Shoot her if she won't leave go," shouted Ishmael, "and come on."
> But Rachel only sprang from the horse and stood face to face with the advancing Zulu. "Stand," she said, and the man stopped.
> "Now," she asked, "what do you want with this woman?"
> "To take her or to kill her," gasped the soldier.
> "By whose order?"
> "By order of Dingaan the King."
> "For what crime?"
> "Witchcraft; but who are you who question me, white woman?"
> "One whom you must obey," answered Rachel proudly.

Figure 2.1. "The Zulu leapt into the air." Source: H. Rider Haggard, *The Ghost Kings*, Cassell, 1908, opposite page 60. Illustration by A. C. Michael.

"Go back and leave the girl. She is mine."

The man stared at her, then laughed aloud and began to advance again.

"Go back," repeated Rachel.

He took no heed but still came on.

"Go back or die," she said for the third time. . . .

. . . "Noie, will you return with me, or shall I kill you? Say, witch," and he lifted his assegai.

The girl sank in a heap upon the veld. "Kill," she murmured faintly, "I will not go back. I did not bewitch him to make him dream of me, and I will be Death's wife, not his; a ghost in his kraal, not a woman."

". . . Farewell, Noie," and he raised the assegai still higher, adding: "Stand aside, white woman. . . .

By way of answer Rachel put the gun to her shoulder and pointed it at him.

"Are you mad?" shouted Ishmael. "If you touch him they will murder every one of us. Are you mad?"

"Are you a coward?" she asked. . . . Then she said in Zulu, "Listen. The land on this side of the Tugela has been given by Dingaan to the English. Here he has no right to kill. This girl is mine, not his. Come one step nearer and you die."

"We shall soon see who will die," answered the warrior with a laugh, and he sprang forward.

They were his last words. Rachel aimed and pressed the trigger . . . ; the Zulu leapt into the air and fell upon his back, dead. . . .

"My God! What have you done?" exclaimed Ishmael.

"Justice," answered Rachel. (58–60)

Rachel's authority in this situation is predicated on a number of factors: first and foremost, her implicit "rightness," or fair play. When Noie throws herself at her feet, as the Matabele messengers throw themselves at Benita's, Rachel steps up without hesitation. Asking the soldier three questions, she determines the crime, the plea, and (the injustice of) the punishment. Giving him three warnings, she pulls the trigger only when he is on the verge of killing Noie. Another factor enabling Rachel's dominance is her explicit—twice-referenced—whiteness. Standing toe to toe with the man, she twice articulates a proprietary interest in Noie, who, being on the English side of the river, she tells him in Zulu, "is mine, not [the king's]" (59). Calm, courageous, and direct, she displays the traditionally masculine qualities lacking in Ishmael, whose deficiency she points out and who will later, when Dingaan's warriors seek to drag him to the king for judgment, cry out in final words that echo Noie's first words to Rachel: "Save me, Rachel, save me" (246).⁹⁷ Noie, too, shows courage, decrying the false accusation made against her by the king and choosing death over a forced marriage.

Like Robinson Crusoe, Rachel intervenes for the "good" native on behalf of the "bad," and a grateful Noie becomes, in effect, Rachel's Friday. Like Friday, Noie remains by choice subservient to the European who saves her life—"Lady, from henceforth I am your servant"—but Rachel does not, unlike Defoe's hero, encourage this dynamic (67).⁹⁸ Taken into the Dove family home, Noie lives in a qualified version of sisterhood, "notwithstanding the difference of their race and circumstances" (161). Similarly, after Suzanne saves Sihamba's life in *Swallow*, the "black woman, who [knows she is] less than dirt in the eyes of" the Boers, "knelt before [the white woman], kissing her feet and the hem of her robe" (*S* 80, 81).⁹⁹ "I will go home with you and serve you," she vows, "to my life's end" (82). Like Rachel, Suzanne accepts though she does not urge the servitude of the woman who calls herself both "slave" and "sister," but whom she calls only "sister" (82, 267, 185).¹⁰⁰

Mystical Feminism

Haggard's male adventurers develop or deepen relationships with one another in the absence of British women, forming "an all-male family or team [that] replaces the heterosexual romance [of the domestic novel] with strong affective (though also hierarchical) ties between men."¹⁰¹ Often the team brings down a corrupt and unjust indigenous leader or oligarchy through prowess in battle and superior weaponry, with the help of righteous indigenous allies, who are thus able to ascend or secure the throne. Haggard's colonial heroines develop relationships with a non-British woman or women, forming strong affective, even spiritual alliance/s in the temporary absence of heterosexual romance, which bookends their story. They resolve indigenous disputes or indigenous-colonial ones, partly through these psychic sororal connections. Exchange is characteristic of these relationships as well, for the women are not only allies but also guardians of one another, securing each other's liberty and saving each other's lives.

The male grouping augments the strength and enhances the authority that the white men already possess, supercharging their performance of typically masculine acts. The female grouping develops the white women's latent psychic powers, producing something altogether new: *mystical feminism*. A supernatural manifestation of wisdom, insight, and authority, mystical feminism facilitates political authority that the women would not otherwise possess. It contrasts with the brute strength and military prowess of the male team in the imperial adventure as well as with the passionate, selfish command of women in the genre, like Ayesha and Gagool. Rather than demonizing the woman or the feminine, mystical feminism empowers both in the British colonial, channeling female strength toward expanding colonial domains of safety and influence, and thus of course implicating her in imperialism. To some degree this phenomenon, like the affiliation between woman and land, or woman and African, naturalizes the association between femininity, indigeneity, and the mystical, and so perpetuates standard British gender and racial hierarchies; but by valorizing mystical feminism, the colonial romance also implicitly valorizes the potency of female-female and indigenous-colonial synergy.[102]

While in both genres indigenous regard for the protagonists is based partly on their "supernatural powers," the legitimacy and deployment of those powers vary significantly (*GK* 146). The male adventurers merely pretend to possess such powers, while the colonial heroines legitimately do. The male adventurers display them at every opportunity, while the colonial heroines show reserve. And though both employ them defensively, the men are also likely to use them for selfish ends, like obtaining prestige or wealth, while the women tend to deploy them for altruistic ones, like resolving conflict and preserving life. Consider the following examples from the male imperial adventure. In *King Solomon's Mines*, the three male Britons try to convince the Kukuanas that they "come from another world, . . . from the biggest star that shines at night" (84). As "proof," they kill a distant antelope with no more than "a noise" (an express rifle) and cause "deep darkness [to] cover the earth" (an almanac tells them of an imminent eclipse; 86, 85, 128). In *Allan Quatermain*, the same men fire on a herd of (what turn out to be beloved) hippopotami, "to impress the natives with a sense of [their] power."[103]

By way of contrast, the colonial heroine variously refutes, distrusts, and prevaricates about her powers. When Jacob tells Benita that her "spirit can loose itself from the body, . . . see the past and the future[,] [and] discover the hidden things," she rejects his claims (*B* 224). When Zulu messengers describe Rachel's celestial birth story—"as a child you came down from above in the lightning, and . . . these white people with whom you dwell found you lying in the mist on the mountain top, and took you to their home"—she sets the record straight: "I was born as other women are, and my name of 'Lady of the Heavens' came to me by chance, as by chance I resemble the Spirit of your people" (*GK* 106). When Benita wakes from "a torpor" with the details of the gold's location "imprinted on her mind," she surmises the information was "nothing but a dream" (*B* 285, 286). When Rachel has visions of the far and the dead, she wonders whether they were "but a fiction of an overwrought and disordered mind" (*GK* 173). But when life hinges in the balance, the colonial heroine draws on every tool at her disposal, including her reputation. Thus when Rachel negotiates with Dingaan (see pages 85–86), she denies her celestial provenance while hinting at its possibility; and when Benita negotiates with Maduna, she pivots between her roles as "white woman" and "ancient witch of Bambatse" (*B* 311).

The bond between Suzanne and Sihamba in *Swallow* anticipates the bond that enables mystical feminism in *Benita* and *The Ghost Kings*. The women come from different cultural backgrounds, are devoted to one another, save each other's lives, and possess supernatural powers. As we have seen, they meet under circumstances similar to those in which Rachel meets—and saves—Noie, with the indigenous woman feeling that she has accrued a "debt" to the colonial heroine that she "can never repay" (*S* 293). "You . . . are to me father and mother and sister and lover," Sihamba tells Suzanne, much as Noie tells Rachel, "I am yours and no one else's" (293; *GK* 64). Suzanne twice has prescient dreams and Sihamba, "born a doctoress[,] see[s] visions of things that are to happen," but their abilities are neither related nor joined (*S* 81).[104]

In the fully developed colonial romance, psychosensory collaboration amplifies the colonial heroine's psychic powers. "A born clairvoyante [*sic*]," Benita possesses a "strange sixth sense," but only once she comes in contact with the Portuguese Benita does she discover the extent of her powers (*B* 254, 86). She senses impending "catastrophe" before the shipwreck, though she does not know what it means (5). "Her mind and imagination . . . seemed to loose themselves from her . . . [,] entering into the secret thoughts of [Jacob]. She saw them pass before her like living things, and yet she could not read them" (71). A gold coin her father found on an earlier trip to Bambatse "seemed to speak to her, yet, alas! she could not understand its story" (86). "Something within her, . . . [a] voice," compels her to set out for Bambatse, as it later "bid[s] her to stay," but she does not recognize it as the Spirit of the Rock (128). Not so the Molimo, who tells "the English Benita" when they first meet that "out of those eyes of yours I see ["the Portuguese maiden"] gaze at me" (326, 139). Under the mesmeric influence of Jacob, who is desperate to find the gold, the "spirit" of the living Benita "travels backward" to the time when the Portuguese were at Bambatse (239, 241). There, she sees "a beautiful woman. . . . She draws near to me, she enters into me. . . . I am I no more. . . . I am Benita da Ferreira" (240–41). Thus does "the spirit of the dead woman" impart her knowledge and memory to the living (242).

Because the two Benitas work together—to protect the living woman and the buried gold—we must see Benita Clifford as agent rather than vessel. The Spirit of Bambatse may direct her steps, but Benita always takes the action. The Spirit "smote [Jacob] . . . with horror and with madness when he would have . . . made [Benita] a wife," but the living woman "thrust the man aside" when he kissed her, draining him of power, so that she was again "a free woman, mistress of herself" (328, 270). The Spirit "told [Benita] the secret of the treasure-pit," but the living woman bravely crept inside. From the Molimo's vantage point, the Spirit "gave [Benita] wit and power" to rescue Richard (see this chapter's next section, "Recovery and Loss"); from that of readers, it is a joint venture (328). Exchange undergirds this relationship, for as the Spirit has "guided" Benita through danger to safety, so the living woman liberates the Spirit from her "guardian[ship] of [the] gold," a "purgatory" she has long "suffer[ed]" in "atone[ment] for her "sin of self-murder" (328, 246, 245, 246).

Rachel's "power of prescience," like Benita's, predates her mystical feminism (*GK* 28). As her mother sees the future—Rachel's safety among the Zulus, her own violent death, the fire that consumes Ishmael's kraal—so, too, does Rachel. Right after she first meets Richard, "a strange conviction [tells] her . . . that her life and this lad's life were interwoven" (28). In a dream or vision—she is not sure which—her future plays out before her, though she does not recognize it as such. She has the same experience a few years later, just before she first meets Noie, who has also inherited "the second sight" (3). "Although my mother was a Zulu," Noie tells her, she is, like her father, "one of the Dream-people, the Ghost-people. . . . That is why I dream dreams and talk with spirits, as one day I hope that I shall teach you to do, you whose soul is sister to my soul" (158–59). When, on the first day of their acquaintance, Noie tells Rachel, "Your fate and mine are intertwined . . . , for our spirits are sisters which have dwelt together in past days," Rachel affirms only her affection: "Well, Noie, I love you, I know not why" (80–81). Though far from an acceptance of Noie's conviction, her words gesture, if ever so slightly, toward a leveling of status.[105] In time, Rachel comes to recognize that Noie is indeed her "sister in the spirit" and that, like Noie, she herself is "not altogether as others are, there is a power in my blood. I see and hear what should not be seen and heard" (81, 140).

This power grows stronger as she moves among first the Zulus and then the Ghost-people on her travels to and with Noie. In the eyes of Dingaan and Mopo, one of the king's chief advisers, she reads their memories, secrets, and fears.[106] In the depths of a pool, she sees Richard making his way to her across Zululand. "In the roar" of the Tugela River, she hears "the voices of her father and mother calling [to her] . . . in . . . fear and pain"; later, she sees "their spirits," who tell her how they died (207, 211). Into her heart it comes suddenly, "she knew not whence, that fire" would devour Ishmael's home (238). In her gut, she knows that "something strange [and] unhappy" would befall the man himself (40).

After she sees the bodies of her dead parents, views what she believes to be Richard's corpse, and confronts Ishmael, Rachel enters into a dissociative state, or, as one character puts it, "her Spirit had gone" (296). In this condition, "new powers grow within" her, as she makes her way with Noie to the land of the Ghost-people (281). Though the Mother of the Trees leads the Ghost-people, a man can rule *through* her, which is precisely what Eddo, one of its priests, attempts to do. Seeking to take advantage of Rachel's vulnerable state, Eddo aims to "make her mouth to speak my words, and her pure eyes to see things that are denied to mine, even the future" (296). His paramount goal is to establish Rachel as Mother of the Trees in place of Nya, Noie's great-aunt, so that, as Rachel says once she regains her senses, "thou wilt rule and I do thy bidding. . . . I will have none of it" (313). Until she is able to fend for herself, Noie "protect[s] Rachel from him as much as she [is] able, never leaving her side . . . lest he should become the master of her will" (277). Cursing his failure and Noie's intervention—"I have felt thee fighting against me for long," "thou causest this Inkosazana to defy me," "she speaks her own words, not my words. And thou hast done this thing, O Bastard"—Eddo echoes Ishmael's complaints about the intimidating alliance between Rachel and "that black slut whom you are fond of," "your black *ehlosé* (spirit) who whispers in your ears" (296, 95, 217).

Arriving in "the land of the Ghost Kings," Rachel, in the span of just a few minutes, regains her senses, saves Nya from a deadly fall, and not only refuses Eddo's request that she kill Nya but invites her instead to "sit . . . in [her] shadow and be safe" (315, 295). In turn, Nya "protect[s] her with her wisdom" (297). "The Mistress of mysteries, the mother of magic, in whom was gathered a hundred generations of [her] half human race," she "thrice ren[ds] [Rachel's] soul from [her] body and sen[ds] it afar," so that she may seek Richard (318, 336). In one instance, accompanied by Noie, who "follow[s]" "where [her] Sister goes," Rachel travels to "a region where all life was forgotten, beyond the rush of the uttermost comet, beyond . . . the outposts of the universe," to the City of the Dead (318, 319). Though "she heard him not, she saw him not, [and] she knew not where he was," Rachel ultimately finds Richard, during one of these "trances," alive on earth (339). Unbeknownst to herself and with Nya's assistance, Rachel visits Richard first in dreams, then in his waking life, "her face float[ing] before him, . . . her voice call[ing] [to] him" as she guides him toward the land of the Ghost-people (348). Not until her female allies have died, however, does Rachel reconnect with the living man, just as Benita does not reconnect with Robert until Benita da Ferreira has been released from Bambatse, nor Suzanne with Ralph until Sihamba has died. Mystical feminism thus enables but is ultimately not compatible with the colonial domesticity that closes out the text.

Recovery and Loss

While Suzanne, in *Swallow*, sits passively atop a cliff, scanning the horizon for signs of a rescue party, Benita and Rachel actively facilitate their own and their lover's liberation. In one instance, Benita saves Robert by chance. Her appearance "upon [Bambatse's highest] rock, glittering like . . . the angel of the dawn," startles the Matabele, thus buying Robert enough time to bargain for his life (*B* 313). Later, standing atop Robert's wagon after having fled from Jacob, Benita negotiates with the royal prince for Robert's life and her own.[107] "With a tongue of oil and wit that cuts like steel," she presses the Matabele general to honor the promise that he made when she pleaded for his life with the Makalanga (310).[108] " 'Great Heavens!' muttered Robert Seymour to himself, as he looked at Benita standing with outstretched hand and flashing eyes. 'Who would have thought that a starved woman could play such a part with death on the hazard?' " (307). Robert saved, Benita sets about rescuing her father, making her way back through the hidden passage to the top of the fortress. While the two Zulu servants who accompany her and Robert, "bold enough men outside, were shaking with fright," Rachel "walked on boldly" (315). Impatient with Robert, she thrice instructs him to "Come on quickly," and responds brusquely to his questions: "How stupid you are not to understand!" "You know nothing." "I'll show you, and you must be prepared" (316, 318). More confident and capable than both the Zulus and her male lover, Benita demonstrates the claim that she made when Robert proposed aboard ship: "We are all of us adventurers in this world, and I more than you" (23).

The final rescue in *The Ghost Kings* is similarly unconventional, with the British colonial male rescued by instead of rescuing his lover. Discovering Richard tied to the base of a tree, Rachel, "with a few swift cuts of [her] spear . . . severed his bonds, . . . pick[ed] up his own assegai that lay at his feet [and] thrust it into his numbed hand" (*GK* 363). Though now armed and free, it is not Richard who confronts his captor, but Rachel: "In an instant the spear that Rachel held was at Eddo's throat. 'Dwarf,' she cried, 'this is my man, and I am no Mother of the Trees and no pale ghost, but a living woman. Let but one of [your servants] lay a hand upon him, and thou diest. . . . Stir a single inch, and this spear goes through thy heart'" (364).[109] Rejecting the "supernatural reputation" attributed to her as she defends the man she claims as hers, Rachel asserts her human power (123). Placing herself in charge of Eddo's captivity, she offers firm instructions on his management: "Richard, take hold of him by one arm, and Noie, take the other. If he tries to escape kill him at once, or if you are afraid, I will" (364). Marching out of the forest, they form a procession: "Eddo, dragged along between Richard and Noie, and after them, the raised spear in her hand, followed Rachel" (364–65). In contrast to the absent, monstrous, and acquiescent femininity that has long been associated with Haggard, this is a portrait of competent, capable, even-handed female command. Neither a burdensome responsibility, a threat to masculinity, nor a mere supplement to masculine authority, the British colonial woman is a force to be reckoned with in this South African imaginary.

Swallow, *Benita*, and *The Ghost Kings* begin and end with a heterosexual coupling between colonials. In *Swallow*, the British Ralph rescues the Boer Suzanne, who grows little though she is exposed to multiple challenges. In *Benita* and *The Ghost Kings*, the initial encounter catalyzes the heroine's growth into colonial womanhood, a state of resilience, but her strength proves not to be contingent on a man, for in his absence she is called upon to test that resilience, and succeeds. When her mate returns to rescue her, she rescues him instead, and the story ends, like many a domestic novel, with the promise of marriage; yet there are no plans for the white couple to leave southern Africa—to move, that is, to a metropolitan space of traditional domesticity. In *Jess*, the heroine's burial is followed by her family's return to England. In *Allan Quatermain*, Flossie, the young daughter of a Scottish missionary, eventually leaves south central Africa for England, where she will "receive some education and mix with girls of her own race," lest, Allan warns her father, "she . . . grow up wild, shunning her kind."[110] Two decades later, Haggard seems no longer to share Allan's concerns, leaving open the possibility of a frontier future for British colonial women, who, like Rachel, may "[not] wish to say good-bye to Africa" (*GK* 104).

Like many an imperial romance, the colonial romance also concludes with the death of a key ally and the passing of an old regime. In its nascent version, *Swallow*, Sihamba dies at the hands of Swart Piet, and her people at the hands of the Zulus. In *Benita*, "the spirit of her who was Benita da Ferreira" is finally free to join her loved ones, who perished at Bambatse more than two hundred years earlier (*B* 246). Though Benita Clifford has found the "misery-working gold" over which that spirit so long stood vigil, she desires only "the gold of life and liberty" (293). Indeed, the story condemns the pursuit of treasure not only through the heroine's assessment of it but also through the Portuguese Benita's description of "that accursed gold which was wrung from the earth by cruelty and paid for with the lives of men," the horrific deaths of the two-hundred Portuguese in the Makalanga fortress, the madness and cruelty of the avaricious Jacob, Clifford's realization that he had endangered his daughter because of his own "love of lucre," and the Molimo's repeated chiding of the whites for their attraction to wealth (246, 220). As he bids her farewell, the Molimo tells Benita:

> Children shall spring up about you, and children's children, and with them also shall the blessing go. The gold you white folk love is yours, and it shall multiply and give food to the hungry and raiment to those that are a-cold. Yet in your own heart lies a richer store that cannot melt away, the countless treasure of mercy and of love. (329)

In offering this blessing to Benita, the Molimo implicitly approves British colonial settlement, in contradistinction to the imperial rapaciousness represented by the Portuguese. The proliferation of British colonial domesticity—symbolized by Benita's future—marks the decline of the old ways of empire, so that, the Molimo prophecies, "[n]o more shall the White Witch stand upon the pillar point at the rising of the sun, or in the shining of the moon" (328).

Titled "The End and the Beginning," the final chapter of *The Ghost Kings* marks the end of the Ghost-people, along with their use of mysticism for selfish purposes and their self-imposed isolation. "Overcome" by "the magic of the White One," Eddo admits defeat, but the priest who longed "to become master of [Rachel's] will" is ultimately destroyed by Noie (*GK* 374, 277). Sacrificing herself "for love's sake," to save the woman who had "once . . . saved her," Noie dies in the process (375). The immolation of Noie, whose affection for Rachel is laden with sexual undertones, paves the way for the rekindling of heterosexual union between Rachel and Richard.[111] The destruction of the Ghost-people (like that of the priests of Zu-Vendis in *Allan Quatermain*) brings to a close male manipulation of female leadership, but it also (like Nyleptha's marriage to Curtis, who has plans of his own for Zu-Vendis) brings to a close female leadership. For while Benita, Rachel, Nya, and Nyleptha all evince Haggard's capacity to imagine positive female leadership, they also evince the limits of his sexist imagination.

Conclusion

If Africa in Haggard's male romance is the unknowable that Englishmen keep trying to know—Sheba's Breasts that nearly kill them, the veiled Ayesha who dominates them, various caves that threaten to consume them—in the female romance it is made comprehensible by indigenous affiliation and sororal communion. If in the male romance, "the line between the team and its surroundings *must* be maintained," in the female romance the line between the heroine and the "primitive" is done so effortlessly.[112] If Ayesha and Gagool embody fears about the monstrous power of women, the female colonial embodies hopes about the ways in which female power might be used productively—from the point of view of an imperialist—and safely—from the point of view of a misogynist. As Elana Gomel points out in her analysis of *She*, "Vincey and Holly return to England, broken and defeated men," Kôr being "finally and irrevocably lost to appropriation."[113] In the colonial romance that followed two decades later, Haggard empowers British women to appropriate the colonial space that men, alone, could not.

After *The Ghost Kings*, however, southern Africa's most popular authorial informant returned to the male imperial adventure, the historical romance, and the historical novel, as well as to the nonfiction that had particularly occupied him for the last decade. *Marie*, published in 1912, was his first Quatermain story in more than twenty years. Eighteen at the novel's start and twenty-one by its conclusion, Marie, like Suzanne a Huguenot-descended Boer, shoots a gun, treks into Zulu country, and sacrifices her life for her husband, Allan. Drugging him so that she can swap their clothes, she is shot by his Boer rival, who mistakes her for Allan, while he, "grotesque in [her] woman's garments," remains unharmed.[114] Despite Marie's valor, she, like Suzanne, is no figure of authority, no political force, no British colonial heroine.

One can only speculate about Haggard's reasons for abandoning the female colonial romance. His attempts had been successful, in terms of both generic innovation and sales.[115] South Africa's unification, the election of Louis Botha, former Boer general, as its first prime minister, and the consolidation of the (primarily Afrikaner) South African Party, all in 1910, may have been factors; for while southern Africa remained part of the empire, it became increasingly clear that British immigration there had neither led to anglicization nor assured Anglo-leadership. Perhaps the female colonial romance, like New Girl fiction, was a victim of the relative return to gender norms that followed World War I, not least because homecoming soldiers wanted to reclaim the jobs that women had filled in their absence.[116] Or maybe Haggard came to recognize the political implications of the agency with which he had endowed his colonial heroines.

There is no question that he remained anxious about "Britain's 'Superfluous Women'" and their sociopolitical ascendency.[117] Six years after the enactment of women's suffrage in Britain and three years before his death, he spoke on the subject of "Woman and Life" to a London club on the first occasion of its inclusion of women.

> In Parliament, on the Bench, in the professions, women were appearing, and what was going to be the effect of it all? . . . At present there were 2,250,000 more women than men in this country. Presently there would be a vast majority of female voters over male voters, and power would pass into the hands of the female sex. . . . How could we keep on exporting our young adult manhood, leaving the women behind?[118]

Like Greg before him, Haggard supported female emigration—to southern Africa following the Second Anglo-Boer War and to the empire more broadly following the First World War. For a brief period, he employed the female colonial romance toward this end, rewarding rather than punishing white women for their agency.[119]

Strengthening and expanding the British sphere of influence in southern Africa, Haggard's colonial heroines are not self-consciously feminist; they contribute to the imperial project rather than advocate improvements for their own condition, but they do so with an authority rarely seen and elsewhere not affirmed in the pages of British adventure. Haggard sought not to facilitate but to reroute female agency, and in so doing to obstruct the future that metropolitan women were increasingly demanding. Nonetheless, as his novels of South African settlement—and female authority—so clearly demonstrate, even a misogynist effort to harness female power can produce feminist effects, though inadvertently and partially: transformation without self-actualization, agency without a vote.

Chapter 3

Colony of Dreadful Delight

Gertrude Page and the Rhodesian Settler Romance

The death of Gertrude Page in April 1922 was "a loss which the whole country felt," reported the *Buluwayo Chronicle* at the end of that year, not least because "she was . . . one of the best advertisers of the territory that Rhodesia could possibly have had."[1] One of Rhodesia's earliest novelists, Page was also its "first famous" one, with a "world-wide reading public" that included British parliamentarians and royalty, and extended to Australia, where, by one account, she was the country's favorite author.[2] By the time of her death, Page had sold at least 2.5 million copies of the eighteen novels and one collection of short stories that she had written, thirteen of which were set all or primarily in Rhodesia, two of which had been dramatized and staged in London, and three of which had been made into films.[3] In 1919, when one of her stories appeared in the inaugural issue of *Hutchinson's Story Magazine*, her work sat comfortably alongside that of Rudyard Kipling, who had written a poem "specially for the first number," and H. Rider Haggard, whose "'She' Meets Allan" (published in book form as *She and Allan*) began its serialization there.[4] Page was for Rhodesia what Kipling was for India and Haggard was for South Africa: its principal authorial informant. Familiarizing the empire's reading public with Rhodesia while simultaneously asserting her own expertise, Page wrote about it as an insider. The reverend who presided over her burial service remarked: she "served Rhodesia well and . . . spread its fame to the farthest corners of the Empire."[5] As the colony's foremost fictive chronicler, she spread her own fame as well.

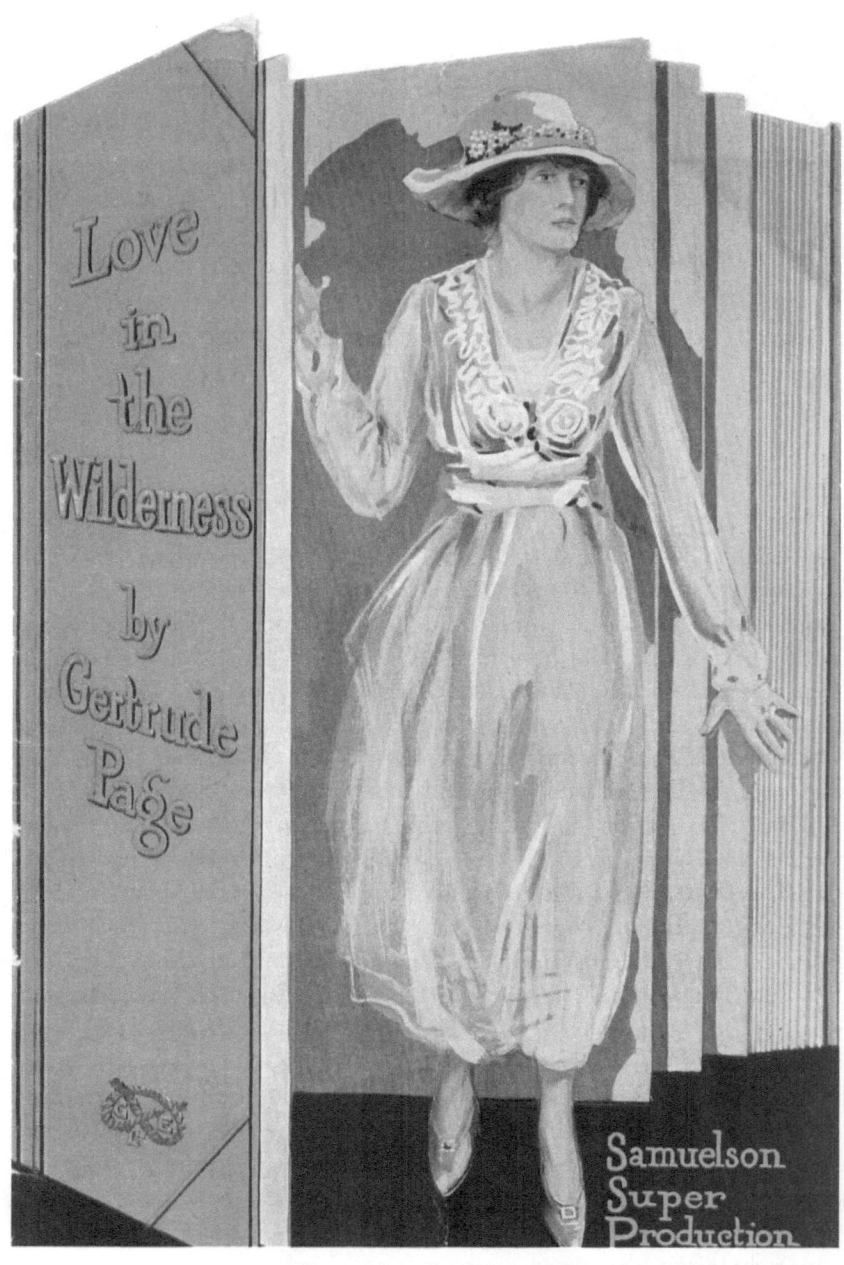

Figure 3.1. From Page to screen. Source: G. B. Samuelson, catalog for *Love in the Wilderness*, directed by Alexander Butler, 1920, cover. BFI National Archive.

Figure 3.2. Page in the company of Kipling and Haggard. Source: *Hutchinson's Story Magazine*, vol. 1, no. 1, July 1919, cover, *Internet Archive*, archive.org/details/hs_1919_07.

Shortly after her 1904 arrival, Page began an endeavor that would occupy her for the remainder of her life: writing about, and promoting immigration to, Rhodesia, particularly for women. In a series of fourteen articles published between 1905 and 1907 in the *Empire Review*, an intra-imperial London-based journal that focused on contemporary domestic and imperial politics and social concerns, she recounted her experience as a new female settler.[6] The final article coincided with the publication of her first novel, *Love in the Wilderness: The Story of Another African Farm* (1907), whose subtitle self-consciously invokes the prototypical New Woman novel, Olive Schreiner's *The Story of an African Farm* (1883). Similarly, the heroine of Page's first published story, which appeared in the *Girl's Own Paper* in 1897, echoes the heroine of Schreiner's novel in her views on gender. Just as Lyndall tries to explain the plight of women to Waldo, so Page's heroine attempts this with her brother:

> When her brothers go out into the world to fight their way, encouraged by the delight of freedom and independence, she must stay at home and mend their socks and do as she is told, spending each day in the same weary round of little duties and little pleasures. Men tell her it is all holidays and she lives like a queen. She knows otherwise, but she soon learns not to say anything; she finds it is simplest to go with the crowd. It doesn't matter in the least, if the monotony and *ennui* crush her best points and develop instead, irritability, discontent and selfishness.[7]

Page, like Schreiner, chose not "to go with the crowd" and as a result found contentedness, not just by immigrating to Rhodesia but by persevering through the many early difficulties of settler life, which she argued were harder for women. An experienced settler by 1907, Page began to publish the fiction that would establish her international reputation. Before long, the woman who had "introduced" Rhodesia to "English readers" had, as one contemporary critic noted, amassed "a wider circle of readers than any other writer on South Africa."[8] In doing so, she not only "attract[ed] valuable attention" to the colony, she also modeled the colonial authority that her fiction ultimately posited for women through colonial trial.[9]

Where the most radical New Woman writers reconceived womanhood by refusing to relegate women to traditional roles, and women's rights advocates reconceived women's position in society by agitating for political power, Page reconceived domesticity by suggesting its liberative possibilities in Rhodesia. In the demanding but compensatory Rhodesia that she depicts, white women function neither exclusively nor even primarily as homemakers and mothers but as partners, mentors, and contributors to a new Rhodesian identity, all within a domestic frame. Cautionary as well as coercive, she maps out both the "pitfalls" of Rhodesian settler life for "women from home, because of a certain sense of freedom from the usual restraint," and its "compensations," precisely for the same reason.[10] Faced with the trials of rugged colonial domesticity, her typical heroine is a new settler tempted by sexual opportunity, which she navigates with the help of another woman, often a more seasoned settler. Compelled by her wish to save the newcomer "for the sake of the country, as well as her own sake," the latter's pedagogical position is inherently political, an alternate form of mothering that produces fully grown women whose focus has been channeled from the self-interest of romance to the larger interest of empire building.[11] The traversal of new sexual terrain, in particular, empowers even as it challenges the novice, facilitating her achievement of the authority possessed by the veteran. Aligning danger with pleasure, and endurance—or recovery—with transformation, Page posits Rhodesian domesticity as an emancipatory modernity for British women; for she not only titillates potential settlers with the illicit possibility of sexual indiscretion, she also holds out the opportunity of guiding those "sister[s] of the lonely veldt" who *Follow After!*[12]

Born in 1872, Gertrude Eliza Page grew up Buckinghamshire, England, the daughter of a local businessman. Her first publication was a "pictorial acrostic" in *Little Folks* when she was eleven years old, followed by several stories, both single-issue and serialized, in the *Girl's Own Paper* in her twenties. In 1902, she married George Alexander "Alec" Dobbin, an engineer from a northern Irish family.[13] Within two years, the couple immigrated to Rhodesia to take up farming. Since they had limited resources and farming ventures in Rhodesia were slow to yield profit, it was nearly a decade before they accrued enough capital to purchase a farm of their own, and another eight years before they saw a return on their investment.[14] Though Page took frequent trips to England and at least one to Spain, Rhodesia was home.[15]

The large-scale British incursion into Rhodesia had begun less than two decades before Page's arrival. It was initiated in the late 1880s by South African immigrant, diamond magnate, and politician Cecil Rhodes. In 1888, Lobengula, leader of the Matabele (Ndebele), gave Rhodes's British South Africa Company (BSAC) exclusive prospecting and mining rights into Mashonaland. In 1889, Queen Victoria granted the BSAC a charter for Mashonaland and Matabeleland, collectively referred to by the British as

Figure 3.3. Gertrude Page. Source: Gertrude Page, *Jill's Rhodesian Philosophy; or, The Dam Farm*, Hurst, 1910, opposite title page.

Zambesia until 1895, when the BSAC named it Rhodesia.[16] The "Chartered Company," or simply "the Company," as the BSAC was sometimes called, thus had trading, colonizing, policing, governmental, infrastructural, and other administrative rights over a region that was close to 200,000 square miles—nearly that of Great Britain.[17] The following year, the BSAC's Pioneer Column marched into Mashonaland. It was comprised of 350 indigenous bearers, guides, and servants; three hundred BSAC police; and 186 "paramilitary settlers," armed men who had been "promised 3,000 acres and 115 gold claims" apiece. A similar offer was made to those white men who, in 1893, pushed farther north into Matabeleland, where this time they were met with resistance, thus commencing the short First Matabele War (1893–1894). Nonetheless, the white men successfully overwhelmed the Matabele, making way for yet more prospectors and settlers, mines and farms.[18] "Over the following three years . . . virtually the whole of the land formerly occupied by the Ndebele [Matabele] and by far the greater part of their cattle passed into white ownership."[19] Less than three years later, the Matabele and Shona joined forces against the whites in the sixteen-month Second Matabele War (1896–1897), or what the Shona call the First Chimurenga (uprising). A much deadlier war, it left 630 whites and six thousand Africans dead. Permanently weakened, the Shona and Matabele population of approximately 500,000 to 750,000 were forced to labor in the mines to pay taxes levied on them by the BSAC.[20]

When Page arrived in early 1904, there were roughly twelve thousand to sixteen thousand whites in Rhodesia, and the ratio of women to men was about one to four. By 1911, the number of whites had risen to twenty-three thousand, and the gender ratio was somewhere between one to two and one to three. By 1923, the year after Page's death, there were thirty-five thousand whites in the colony.[21] Having failed to produce the mineral wealth that the BSAC had initially expected, Rhodesia "was dominated by . . . lower middle class settlers, skilled artisans, small farmers and small miners," most of whom were "of British South African origin," though by at least 1915 and until 1928, more emigrants came from Britain than from South Africa annually.[22]

"Play[ing] . . . the dual *rôle* of a Government and a commercial company," the BSAC was accountable neither to parliament nor to any constituency until 1898, when the colonial office insisted that it include some elected members on its governing body, the legislative council. Though initially there were fewer elected than appointed members, this was soon reversed, giving settlers the majority.[23] In 1919, the Women's Franchise Ordinance gave white women the vote, and by 1920 it was clear that most settlers, Page among them, favored the elimination of Company rule. The question put before them in a 1922 referendum was whether to join the Union of South Africa or to become self-governing. The latter option, which Page had long championed, won the day, and in 1923, Southern Rhodesia—today's Zimbabwe—became a self-governing crown colony.[24]

While best known for writing "light dramatic novels," Page was also a vocal public figure, promoting Rhodesia and speaking to power. Rhodesia was a country in the making and she cared passionately about its future. During World War I, she and her husband "gave lectures and readings on Rhodesia in military hospitals" in Britain.[25] In a 1918 *Times* article, she voiced her objection to the age qualification that excluded forty-six-year-old Alec from military service, asking rhetorically: "Must we lengthen this terrible war by suffering men in high posts at the War office who are so utterly devoid of imagination?"[26] She came out in support of her preferred candidates for the BSAC Legislative Council. For example, in a letter to the *Rhodesian Herald*, Page, as the *Buluwayo Chronicle* put it, "greatly daring, enter[ed] the field as a champion of Col. [Raleigh] Grey."[27] She was the first woman in her district to be elected to the Farmer's Association.[28] She wrote passionately against Rhodesia's joining the Union of South Africa, in the leadup to both the 1910 formation of the Union (of the Transvaal, Orange River Colony, Cape Colony, and Natal) and Rhodesia's 1922 referendum on the matter. Sharing the strong "anti-Afrikaner feeling" of the majority of her fellow Rhodesians, she feared an influx of Afrikaners in what she and so many others saw as southern Africa's most British colony.[29] England, she wrote, had become "tender, not to say effeminate" in its "sensitiveness of her late enemy."[30]

An "ardent supporter of responsible government," Page wrote frequently on the topic. Self-government was, she argued, "our chance to have the spending of our money, the framing of our own land policy, and to make urgent decisions important to the welfare of our country for ourselves." Though she addressed "every voter," in at least one instance she "made a special appeal to women! It is the first time we have been able to vote," she wrote. "Do not be apathetic."[31] When Ethel Tawse Jollie (who in 1924 became the first female parliamentarian in Rhodesia, making her the first in any British colony) "made an appeal for support" of the movement, Page "headed the subscription list with 100 guineas."[32] Page "work[ed] with" the Rhodesian delegation that traveled to England to receive a draft of the constitution for responsible government.[33] And in the "last words" that she wrote for publication, an article that appeared in the *Rhodesian Herald* the day before her death, she took aim at "leading" English newspapers who "publish[ed] leader after leader, paragraph after paragraph, article after article, all with the express intention of proving to dull-witted Rhodesians that it is quite impossible for them to run their own country."[34]

Page is interesting for a number of reasons, including her support of female emigration, her role in colonial politics, the tension in her work between feminism and conservatism, and the generic relationship of her fiction to the New Woman novel that preceded it and the empire romance that followed it—for more on which see this chapter's conclusion. Each of these aspects, some more than others, can be seen in her Rhodesian settler romances, which depict the neophyte's transformation into colonial womanhood as the outcome of navigating the early challenges of colonial life, sexual opportunity chief among them. Page not only illustrates the authority available to Rhodesian women who survive "the trials of this country," she also manifests it, writing fiction that compels female emigration through the very dangers she suggests that women must negotiate.[35] For the authority that she holds out only fully inheres if women continue to feel desire's pull and so to require assistance to resist it.

Metropole and Colony

Since the mid-nineteenth century, England's "surplus" of women had been a cause of national concern, and immigration to the colonies a frequently voiced "solution." Despite the emergence of numerous emigration societies specifically for women, the bulk of Britain's colonial-bound emigrants continued to be male. So where in 1851, there had been roughly 500,000 more women than men in England, a half century later that figure was 1.3 million; it would rise still higher as a result of World War I.[36] The increase in occupational opportunities available to women at the fin de siècle did nothing to alleviate the prevailing sense that single women were a social problem; on the contrary, the concurrent rise of the New Woman and the suffragette, agents and emblems of social change, compounded this belief.[37] Female emigration societies variously stressed colonial opportunities for employment, "marriage, home-building, . . . moral guardianship, and imperial and racial duty," obligations that they suggested would lead to "self-fulfillment."[38] The possibility of marriage, never a selling point in the few feminist societies that existed, was touted more frequently at the turn of the century, as was "imperial and racial duty," or the female civilizing mission, which entailed carrying British culture, upholding the morality of male colonials, and bearing their children.[39]

By way of contrast, Page stressed self-fulfillment through the acquisition of colonial authority. For while she repeatedly referenced both the "superfluous number" of women "at home" (*Jill's* 177) and the "great demand for wives" in Rhodesia, she was not preoccupied with promoting colonial marriage, at least not directly.[40] Nor was she particularly concerned with the cultural influence, moral suasion, or "racial motherhood" that many of her contemporaries felt it was a woman's duty to provide in the colonies, the latter especially in southern Africa following the Second Anglo-Boer War (1899–1902).[41] Instead, she posited an emancipatory domesticity available to British women in Rhodesia, where, single or married, they could live a life "independent of custom and prejudice"; and if it was a life with greater challenges, it was also one with greater rewards (*Strange* 42). "All women in Rhodesia wrestle with difficulties that they never encounter at all in comfortable England," attests the narrator of *Follow After!* (1915). "But the law of compensation holds good, and one may safely say that they often encounter pleasures which could not possibly be their portion in the conventional Homeland" (128–29). Rhodesia is not for all women, Page teasingly and repeatedly warns, but those willing to face the challenges in a colony with "no hard-and-fast lines"[42] would be able to experience "real-life . . . , instead of just playing and frivoling" (*Veldt* 208).

If, for the BSAC and its advocates, Rhodesia is "the land of the future"[43] because it promises wealth and health, it is so for Page because it "give[s]" female immigrants, specifically, "useful, busy, happy lives in place of the narrowness and emptiness of their English conditions" (*Jill's* 178). While Page's writing is certainly emigrationist, it lacks the "paradise complex" that is the genre's hallmark.[44] Where the BSAC promoted Rhodesia as "the Land of Sunshine, and Promise, and Milk and Honey" (*Love* 28), Page describes the many obstacles that challenge its female immigrants, "women who start bravely out from England to face difficulties and disappointments they cannot even conceive in the old country," difficulties that Page herself has faced and overcome.[45] More than one of her heroines calls out the BSAC for its unrealistic portrayal of Rhodesia. For instance, in 1921's *Jill on a Ranch*, Jill complains to her friend that "it's really absurd for the guide books and 'Sunny Rhodesia' books to harp all the time on flowers and fruit and gold and sunshine, and leave people supposing they're going to journey straight to Utopia" (115). Women who come out with "fantastic, high-flown notions that embody chiefly flowers and sunshine, and beautiful aristocrats . . . , and milk and honey," says another, are invariably disappointed (*Strange* 39). "It would be much better to prepare them a little. . . . After all, there are so many things to tear your hair about and rave at in Rhodesia, and it is just as well the new-comers [*sic*] should know" (*Ranch* 115, 70).

While many of the difficulties Rhodesian women confront are environmental, like insects—fleas, flies, mosquitoes, white ants, locusts—snakes, drought, heat, and dust, they must also learn how to manage African servants. Never part of the central action and only rarely individuated, Africans only ever appear as servants; beyond servitude itself, their lives remain a blank.[46] Page makes a couple of references to Bushmen paintings (*Jill's* 102, *Strange* 85), one to the squalor of Africans' living conditions,[47] and one to Matabele violence against whites during the '90s (*Strange* 168). Referring to Africans consistently as "niggers" in her *Empire Review* articles, Page repeatedly complains about "the odour with which they permeate the atmosphere, known to some as *bouquet d'Afrique*."[48] The fictional Jill, who makes her first appearance in the 1910 epistolary novel, *Jill's Rhodesian Philosophy*, jokes about their deaths through brush fire and drowning (*Jill's* 96, 206). Nita Dendale, one of the heroines of *Where the Strange Roads Go Down* (1913), is frustrated not only that she can't force her dissatisfied "house-boy" to remain—"Does a nigger never have to do anything unless he likes? Is a white woman out here of no account?"—but also that "her husband treated the house-boy question lightly, merely begging her not to worry" (121, 122). Jo Latham, the novel's protagonist, thinks herself "a heroine" for putting up with a servant who "is like a rubbed sore to [her] at every point. [Her husband] was not very sympathetic. Since they could not get anything better, it was obviously the only thing to do." She believes, however, that if her husband "would just give the *sjambok* [whip made of hide] once . . . it would do him good" (191). Jill's seasoned female neighbor seems to have matters more in hand, advising Jill: "It's no use scolding and talking at them. One under the left-side jaw from the Boss will give you peace in the kitchen for a whole week. They understand it so much better" (*Jill's* 135). By the second Jill novel, the protagonist herself notes that her servants are now "like faithful dogs waiting upon my lightest [*sic*] sign" (*Ranch* 223).

Page has no sense of the contingency of white women's position on black labor. She sees no contradiction in imputing to her own African servants a hatred of work, though they "fetch wood and water[,] clean, wash, sew, bake, iron, starch, [and] cook, with a temperature at about 96° in the shade."[49] Such work, she admits, would be "almost a physical impossibility" for her to do on her own. Similarly, when her servants leave her employ to seek better-paying jobs in town or, having earned the twenty-shilling hut tax levied by the BSAC, to return to their families, she deems them lazy rather than enterprising.[50] As is so often the case, progressive gender politics do not compel progressive racial politics. Smugly savoring their own authority over Rhodesia's black population, Page's heroines, without a touch of irony, condemn the "arrogant self-satisfaction of the male," who thinks himself superior to women (*Strange* 228).

Nonetheless, as Page unequivocally states in one of her *Empire Review* articles: "let anyone say what they will, the life [of the Rhodesian immigrant] is emphatically not so hard [for] a man as [for] a woman."[51] For while men have a range of distractions—"their shooting[,] . . . their pipes, . . . each other, and a good many jaunts to town," where they can attend their club—women, far more isolated from one another and the local community, do not.[52] As Page trenchantly notes of her own husband's club, its members "are not on the whole gallant in their hospitality. There is no ladies' afternoon, nor ladies' evening, and only on the rarest of occasions are we permitted to cross its sacred precincts."[53]

While women face greater challenges than men, they receive less recognition. They are "so little talked about. . . . They put up a good fight, and no one says, 'Well done!' "[54] Asks one of her heroines rhetorically: "One hears so much of the brave Englishmen who go out into the lonely places of the world and pave the way to Empire—but what is ever said about the women? . . . When the Sons of the Empire are lauded to the skies, the Daughters of the Empire should be remembered also" (*Love* 82–83). The narrator of *Strange Roads* answers this call: "on behalf of the women . . . one pauses a moment longer to offer a special homage" (63).

As Page notes in the *Empire Review*, eventually "the rough places become smooth, fun bubbles up where there looked only the bleakest desolation, enjoyment grows in a truly astonishing fashion . . . , and life smiles quite hopefully again, even if it is from a vastly different perspective."[55] Page and her middle-class heroines might make furniture from packing cases and meals from scraps, but they meet "the little things that worry and fret the stay-at-homes [with] serene complaisan[ce]."[56] The new immigrant should not "expect much beyond knocks and loneliness to begin with," but "any woman who [can] manage to 'hold on' through the first nine months of Rhodesian farm life"—a suggestive length—will not "regret her efforts, or wish then to give [the colony] up."[57] As Page repeatedly illustrates, those who have "staying power" and "grit" develop the "pioneer spirit" needed to "grapple[] with" the "petty cares and worries and annoyances" for which they will be richly recompensed (*Strange* 153, 46, 63).

That "pioneer spirit" is often equated with military might. "The farmer's wife," Page advises, "will do well to go out . . . in a soldier's spirit, prepared for a fight, through which pluck alone will carry her to victory."[58] The heroine sisters of 1914's *The Pathway* are described as "true types of the fine women's battalion of the same army" as male pioneers (19). Male characters in both *Follow After!* and "His Job," one of the stories in Page's 1918 collection, *Far from the Limelight*, suggest that a colonial woman's courage merits something akin to the Victoria Cross, respectively for helping to rescue a Rhodesian garrison besieged by Germans and for birthing thirteen children.

More than one of Page's seasoned heroines points out the necessity of earning the favor of a colony that "doesn't give much away for nothing" (*Strange* 153). "She gives you a jolly bad time at first, to see if you are worth bothering about," one woman attests, "and if you win through she suddenly turns round and smiles at you, and compensations crop up in all directions" (*Jill's* 72–73). "Nothing good is to be had without paying for it," says Jill (129). "Rhodesia laughs . . . jeeringly" at the frustrations of the callow female immigrant, "and says, 'Go home again, you town girl, . . . and scramble for buses and bargains, and leave my wide spaces undisfigured by your gloomy face. Go home and be mediocre and suburban, and lose yourself once more in the crowd'" (155). The comparison Page consistently makes is not between urban and rural spaces, but between metropole and colony; for as much as life in London is "dull, artificial and generally absurd," life in "England's country villages" (*Strange* 13), for unmarried women, anyway, is "empty [and] monotonous" (*Rhodesian* 143).

Rhodesia's relaxation of customs, its stimulation of originality, and its facilitation of freedom are repeatedly contrasted to the "orthodoxy" (*Veldt* 17), "staleness," and constraint of the metropole (*Love* 4). For the middle-class women who form the majority of Page's heroines, the contrast between life in Britain and life in Rhodesia is particularly stark. In the former, they are expected to "achieve little else" than "dress[ing] well, talk[ing] well, [and] danc[ing] well" (*Jill's* 129, *Love* 2). "What [would] I [have] do[ne] with myself for years and years?" wonders Jo, in *Strange Roads*, "trying to kill time in a rotten little London villa, while" her husband spent his days in the City (13). Her life would have been "exactly like countless other lives, . . . hopelessly wanting in individuality" (*Love* 2). "You know instinctively that in England you will, through habit, do what you are told, and be what you are told by that stern censor Public Opinion," notes Jill; "but once get well past Table Mountain, and if you have anything in you that is original it will show itself, and thrive. You feel in your blood it is quite impossible for any one [*sic*] to say what you will be or what you will do, once you are out there in the big spaces with all your fancy running free" (*Jill's* 11).[59] Time and again, the authentic colonial is contrasted with the predictable metropolitan, and the former's "free, unfettered life" with the constraints of metropolitan convention (*Strange* 13).[60] Rhodesia is presented as a geographical solution to a metropolitan problem: saved from conventionality, the female subject achieves satisfaction.

Often in Page's Rhodesian writing, space is a metonym for freedom. Juxtaposed to "the narrow limits of the home country," Rhodesia satisfies the immigrant's "craving for more light, and air, and freedom" (*Love* 9). It is a land of "wide skies, wide hopes, wide thoughts, [and] wide experiences" (*Strange* 42). Able to "think and act with a freedom not possible in the old country," the Rhodesian female immigrant finds she can "attain to a freshness of individualism, untrammelled by any ancient written, or unwritten law: [can] in short be [her]self" (*Love* 4–5). Transformed into someone for whom challenges are easily met, she comes to look upon the metropolitan woman, "mediocre[,] suburban, and los[t] . . . in the crowd," as a shadow version of the contented woman she has become (*Jill's* 155).

But if Rhodesia possesses the power to transform, it also possesses the power to compel. It "cast[s] [an] invincible spell" (*Love* 4), it operates "like a germ in the blood" (*Rhodesian* 113), it calls "like a siren. . . . When you are in her grasp she sometimes almost crushes your spirit; but when you go away she sings to you alluringly, and you have to come back" (*Follow* 209).[61] As the narrator of *The Pathway* explains: "The woman who shakes her annoying red dust from her feet and garments one dry season, and rejoices that she is able to depart, will have a yearning after a time for the riotous beauty of flowers and sunshine, and far blue hills, the wide spaces, the freedom" (95). Again, space and freedom merge, desire for the one equivalent to desire for the other.

Playing with Fire

The majority of requisites (adaptability, patience, hard work) and benefits (open spaces, independence, casualness) of settler life that Page identifies are common enough in immigration literature.[62] What stands out is the way that she conflates practical challenges with moral ones, "heat, and dust, and flies, and worry" with sexual opportunity, and transcending the former with navigating the latter (*Strange* 39). While she condones neither adultery nor premarital sex, she tantalizes readers with the likelihood of these possibilities. Rhodesian farm life can be lonely for women, husbands are preoccupied, social checks are limited, women, unlike men, are often "devoid of occupation," and female immigrants are frequently ill-prepared (189).[63] "These very facts make extenuating circumstances," says Jo in *Strange Roads*, who, after ten years in Rhodesia, does "not judg[e] [its] women one way or the other" (228). After all, she notes, many women new to the colony "find a solution [to its challenges] in finding a lover" (45). What's more, "the wilderness forgave such little breaches . . . more quickly" (188). Of Nita, the recently arrived newlywed immigrant who has left her "thoughtless" husband for her lover,[64] Jo says, "of course . . . she hasn't been very wise or very brave, but perhaps we shouldn't have been in her place. Anyhow, the odds have been against her" (223, 213). Even Jo considers leaving her husband when her old lover reappears. The novel ostensibly commends the women's eventual choices—a more mature Nita returns to her husband and the seasoned Jo never leaves hers—but it nonetheless correlates Rhodesia with sexual opportunity for women. If restraint often wins out—and it does not always—the circumstances of Rhodesian settler life certainly facilitate consideration of the sexual opportunities to which they give rise.

Again and again we see the "extenuating circumstances"—a selfish or simply preoccupied husband, isolation, frustration, boredom, or perhaps all at once—the entreaty not to judge, and the courage associated with resisting temptation if the man in question is not the "rightful mate," or giving in to it when he is (*Limelight* 51). Circumstances are certainly stacked against Nita, who, though "touched by the right spirit" in marrying an emigrant and coming out to Rhodesia to "do her small share of the world's work," is nonetheless "ill-equipped" for its challenges (*Strange* 64). When she grows "tired of eating little else but buck [and] pork, . . . not knowing how to tell one day from another, and scarcely ever seeing anyone but just her own man," an indifferent companion as it is, she "do[es] something desperate" by entering into a "flirtation" (51) with the "lady-killer" Aubrey Dension (90). It soon turns serious, and when

> he folded her in his arms, and covered her face with kisses[,] . . . Nita yielded to him, feeling strangely that some last link with the past was irrevocably broken. In a new land, and a new life,

> with strange unnatural conditions, and a haunting memory of [the] dreadful loneliness [of her first three months in Rhodesia], her frail defences gave way before the combined onslaught, and she was conscious chiefly that the man who ought to have protected her had failed her in every way; and henceforth she must fight for her own hand and make what terms with life she could. (186)

In "yield[ing]" to Aubrey, Nita is breaking with a past linked to Britain and entering the "new" world of Rhodesia. Her husband's neglect, though painful, is the very thing that frees her to make her own "terms." Enid Davenport, the unmarried heroine of *Love in the Wilderness*, similarly feels, initially at least, entitled to give in to passion, as she considers joining Keith Meredith, the unhappily married (and long separated) man she loves, on his travels. "That dangerous sense of isolation" brought about by life on a remote Rhodesian farm "made her feel her world was not as other women's" (*Love* 255). After all, she wonders, "was she any longer . . . bound by their conventions?—a slave to their ties? Was it not partly their fault . . . ?" (254). Since, unable or unwilling to visit her, "they had left her to herself so long, . . . was she therefore the more free to choose her own path?" (255). The answers to these questions are left up to readers.

Strength, or "grit," is associated at least as much with surrender as it is with resistance (*Strange* 46). When Meredith entreats Enid to join him, he appeals to her courage.

> Isn't it rather a question of pluck, darling. Isn't it largely what you are willing to brave for Love's sake? . . . You know in your heart the ordinary home life will never quite appeal to you again—a year ago it might, but now things are changed. . . . Passion . . . cannot always be crushed down into cut-and-dried proportions, twisted this way and that according [*sic*] as Society proclaims. If you were of the ordinary weak, vacillating feminine nature I would not try to persuade you. What I want you to do is to face facts fearlessly and come to me out of your strength. (*Love* 249, 251)

If the "ordinary home life" may once have "appeal[ed]" to Enid, it no longer can. Transformed in and by Rhodesia, she has the "pluck" and the "strength" to follow her own conscience, rather than to accept blindly the rules that

"Society proclaims." Though Meredith seems to speak the language of the cad, readers are not meant to interpret him as one. His proposition—and correlative lack of belief "in the present form of marriage"—is unconventional, but he is inclined to explain rather than to coerce (250). His sincerity, deceitful in-laws, and unreasonable wife (whose financial security he has nonetheless ensured) compel readers' sympathy, though they do not, in the end, compel Enid's consent.[65] In the strictest sense, Meredith's offer may not be respectable, but he certainly is.

In two of the short stories that appear in *Far from the Limelight*, a married heroine is tempted to leave her husband for "the right man" (53). Though one leaves and the other does not, in both cases courage is associated with making the change. In "There Is Nothing of Any Importance," the heroine's husband, though not a bad man, had "persuaded her to marry him against her inner conviction, and afterwards had made no special effort to suit his life and his tastes to hers" (84). So when she falls in love with "a man of heroic stature who matched her own splendid womanhood" (53), she decides to break her vows "without a backward glance" (72). Even her own husband "knew, deep down in his heart, [that] she had shown a fine courage whatever [society] might say" (84). In "The Falling Gods," Mary's choice to stay with her bullying husband, to be true to her "treaty," her "promised word," is seen as tragic and outdated, even in some sense by the heroine herself (135). Admitting a "lack [of] courage," she "choose[s] to fall with the fallings gods," dubious deities that stand in the way of her fulfillment (139).

For sometimes, Page suggests, adultery is justified, as in *The Edge o' Beyond* (1908), in which Joyce Grant leaves her cruel husband permanently for her doctor-lover (played by Basil Rathbone in a London theater production in 1921). The former had "inherited almost intact the comfortable theories of his forefathers concerning the obligations of a wife. In his eyes she had practically no right to any individual will, outside her housekeeping concerns" (*Edge* 17). Joyce's decision to escape her marriage is supported by a number of characters, as well as the narrator. "Everyone knows it takes a certain amount of grit and character to go wrong," says Dinah Webberley, another of the novel's heroines (242). "Joyce was one of those fine souls who could do this thing," reflects one of her male neighbors, "and be none the less pure" (235). She was, thinks another friend, like a "horse in the stable . . . fainting with thirst while the owner [neglects] to bring it water, small blame if it will go in search of healing for itself" (227). And if Joyce's union with her lover is not wholly a physical restorative—she dies five years after leaving her husband, because of his continued refusal to grant her a divorce—it is a spiritual one. "The Lord do so to me, and more also, if aught save death part thee and me," prays the doctor after their first "kiss that was a benediction," from which "moment Joyce was as entirely his as any marriage service could have made her" (233).

More than once readers are entreated *not* to join in society's "outraged morality" (*Limelight* 84). In *Love in the Wilderness*, we are asked to put ourselves in the shoes of, perhaps even to admire, a new female immigrant teetering on the brink of infidelity.

> How can [those who have not been tempted] truly judge? The woman who fought a long, losing game and then gave in, may she not yet be stronger than the woman who never fought at all, never had any occasion to fight, never had the smallest knowledge of what the temptation might be? O, ye Good women of the world! be merciful. . . . No matter who the offender—in her place, dare you absolutely affirm you would not have been as she? (248–49)

While temptation itself is implicitly equated with knowledge, succumbing is explicitly equated with strength. At the same time, the female reader who has never fought against desire is given both the opportunity to imagine herself as "the offender" and the power not to judge. Similarly, in the second Jill novel, the heroine implies the value of temptation. She believes "that the girl who abuses her freedom and makes a mess of things is yet ahead of, and more to be envied, than the girl who has known only a jealously guarded, fiercely circumscribed life, and never really lived at all" (*Ranch* 144–45). Beneath the stated contrast of freedom and circumscription are the implied ones of thriving and existing, modernity and archaism, envy and pity.

Unquestionably in these stories, women have a right to their desire, and for the most part they know it. One of the heroines of *The Pathway* acknowledges kissing other men before kissing her lover, who, she tells him, "does not kiss quite like other men" (208). In *Strange Roads*, the married Jo initiates a kiss with the man she loves. As she thinks of running off with him, "something fierce, primeval, desperate, rose up in her nature . . . heaped derision upon prejudice and conventions, clamoured to her to show herself worthy of the great love that was hers by surmounting all obstacles to reach and hold it" (247). In "His Job," a woman confesses her love before the object of her affection has done so. In *The Silent Rancher* (1909), the newcomer immigrant, taking the initiative with the man she loves, says to him: "one of the chief arts in life is to be able to snatch opportunity when it comes—because I love you—Ranger—snatch me" (305). After all, notes the narrator of *Strange Roads*, Rhodesia has a knack for making men more appealing "by the simple fact of their toil" (61). The novel's heroine, Jo, compares the colony to "a mill. You put a milksop, pink and blue mother's darling in at one end, and, if he is any good at all, she turns him out a man at the other" (39).

For many of Page's heroines, desire is experienced as a "Great Awakening" (*Love* 186), something that "caus[es] a . . . riot in the blood" (*Limelight* 52), a "quicken[ing]" of the "pulses," a "tingling [in the] veins" (*Love* 187). Often it is linked to an appreciation of Rhodesia that they previously lacked, as one sees in highly charged passages that make little distinction between lover and land. As she realizes her passion for Meredith in a chapter titled "The Awakening," Enid notices, "stirring in her heart, a sudden, new sensation almost like love for this sleeping, kopje-strewn [hillock-strewn] world[.] . . . The night whispered among the hills, as a lover murmuring his love. . . . It wrapt itself round her [and] caressed her upturned face" (186–87). In *The Edge o' Beyond*, Dinah, who has left behind Rhodesia and the man she loved there, feels herself "aching for the kopjes" (229). She returns because "Rhodesia beckoned. Beckoned! nay, *called*—called in her blood, called in her heart. . . . She wanted Rhodesia—wanted the kopjes and the vleis and the sunshine. Wanted the free, untrammeled vigorous life," and she wanted it with her lover (229, 218). As we saw in chapter 2, Haggard depicts Jess and Rachel awakening into womanhood in passages that eroticize nature.[66] In the Rhodesian settler romance, Page depicts the heroine awakening specifically, if not always explicitly, to sexual desire, in passages that not only eroticize nature but also convey a newfound love for Rhodesia, an awareness of inner strength, or both. So when, in *The Silent Rancher*, Evelyn Harcourt "awaken[s]" to her desire for Ranger Metcalfe, she feels "the spirit of the land beg[i]n to storm the citadel of her mind and heart. Across the wide spaces voices whispered to her" at once to embrace her "birthright and freedom and rich fulfilment, rather than let them clash with . . . conventionality and . . . prejudice" and, "since you have no fear of a wilderness life if he is there, [to] take your courage in both hands, and—*go to him*!" (301, 298, 303). As we have seen before, Page links wide spaces with freedom, in opposition to metropolitan conformity; in these moments of awakening, she adds desire and fortitude to the coupling.

One wonders if Page's readers did not themselves desire such an awakening, for, as she depicts it, the cost is worth the reward. In a land where "big things happen" (*Love* 262), women may feel compelled to "play with fire" (*Strange* 189), but it brings them "strangely close to the great heart of the world" (*Love* 247). Appealing to circuits of desire that she also forestalls,[67] Page allows readers to envisage this "intoxicating" possibility for themselves, not least the "sense of power" that a woman feels in the presence of her lover (*Strange* 165). "It *is* beautiful," says Jo of Rhodesia, "but it is sometimes cruel too" (50). The temptations that it offers make Rhodesia both at once.

"Woman with a Capital W"

Page's narratives of white Rhodesian women center not on courtship, marriage, or motherhood, but on transformation into colonial maturity, a position of some license. Determined not to function as "white slaves of their household," her heroines strive to attain satisfaction, not through "sacrifice" but through authority; security, not through dependence but through strength; and pleasure, not through romance but through participation in the larger world (*Love* 88, 191). Though, like Enid, Page affirms her distance from "Woman with a capital W," her writing has much in common with New Woman fiction, associated primarily with the fin de siècle (83).[68] Page wrote with "authority about the female experience," sought "to demonstrate the limitations of traditional [gender] roles," and welcomed modernity, particularly as it promised new opportunities for women.[69]

For Page, women's assistance to other women is crucial in Rhodesia, whether in learning to manage servants, "to find abundant compensations" for the colony's hardships, or to traverse the minefields of desire (*Edge* 99). "I'm afraid it's a fallacy that the women in the colonies always hang together, and help each other through thick and thin. I'm afraid often they don't do either all they might, or all they ought" remarks Joyce's lover in *The Edge o' Beyond* (180). Page's heroines, however, rise to the occasion, sharing their knowledge and experience. Jo, who struggled with loneliness in her early years, is determined to "care for the well-being of the women of Rhodesia" (*Strange* 217). Jill's female neighbor, who did not at first love Rhodesia, now tells her: "I love my country. And I want to make other women love it if I can" (*Jill's* 131). Whether the newcomer simply fails to appreciate Rhodesia or encounters temptation, the experience of a more seasoned woman helps her to achieve the self-knowledge and authority that this woman also models.

Sometimes that woman is a veteran colonist, who has herself navigated the landscape of desire. In *Strange Roads*, Jo, thirty-four, married for a decade, and nearly as long an immigrant, serves as a mentor to the naïve Nita, for she "know[s] better than most what it must have been to her, to face the life out here without any reasonable training or knowledge concerning what was before her" (215). When warning Nita away from her lover fails, Jo convinces Nita to leave his home before she has spent the night, "compromising her[self] past redemption" (213). Addressing Nita's husband "man to man" (230), she then convinces him of his part in the affair, forcing him to "wak[e] up to the fact of what he owes to Nita, instead of merely what she owes to him" (223). Changing "a good many of his ideas" as well as his behavior, he thus "win[s] her over again" (223). As a result of her experience and Jo's intervention, both Nita's marriage and Nita herself are stronger. Saving the neophyte "for the sake of the country, as well as her own sake," Jo models for Nita the robustness required of the successful female colonist (213).

In *The Silent Rancher*, Evelyn at first rejects the friendship of Gwendolyn Leven, who divorced her philandering husband and has since remarried. "Nothing can whitewash her faithlessness," says Evelyn. "That is black, and it colours the whole" (91). Over time, however, the young new immigrant learns that some things are "grey," and "thus, with her opening mind and widening experience, Evelyn was able to perceive quietly, and learn not a little from the other woman's . . . fearless, engaging attitude of independence" (91, 171). Treating Evelyn as a "young[er] sister," Gwendolyn advises her against marrying Henry Mahon, a knight commander and a high-placed Rhodesian administrator (258). When her first attempt at dissuasion fails, Gwendolyn reveals to Evelyn the findings of a report about "his black harem" (280). She does so not only for Evelyn's sake but also "for the good of the country" (275). Like so many of Page's heroines, Gwendolyn believes that the happiness of Rhodesia's (white) women is crucial to the country's "future."[70]

A number of Page's heroines value freedom in one form or another, like Enid, who had "always . . . rebelled instinctively against . . . conventionality" (*Love* 4); or Dinah, who "want[s] to see and experience everything—everything!'" (*Edge* 45). Jo may be a farmer's wife, but she "smoke[s] cigarettes anywhere that the fancy took her, . . . regard[s] certain words forbidden to polite vocabularies as merely slang, . . . mak[es] up her mind about things for herself, and declin[es] to be dictated to by recognized laws and codes" (*Strange* 10, 224).[71] Direct in temperament and feminist in sentiment, she teasingly speculates, to a bishop no less, that a group of women once told St. Paul "what they thought of him for saying they were to be meek and humble, and subject to their husbands. . . . I guess they asked him whether it was his business or theirs, anyhow" (30). There is nothing meek about Nurse Evelyn Grey, one of the heroines of the World War I novel *Follow After!*, who is "determin[ed] to play her part as a soldier" (74). After helping her two male companions defend a British garrison near the border with German East Africa, she insists that they treat her as an equal. "Don't you see," she asks them, rhetorically,

> that life in the colonies, as I have lived it for seven years, travelling in all directions, and accustomed to looking after myself, make[s] all the difference in the world? Not but that hundreds of Englishwomen would be ready to take part in the fighting now, . . . even if they had been in England all their lives. You men never seem able to see that we can be manly, without being unwomanly. (73)

Rhodesian life has fostered her self-sufficiency, women back in England share her capacity for courage, and neither quality makes a woman unwomanly.

Nan Johnson, a "high-spirited," strong-willed, independent "young Amazon" (*Love* 67), is "one of the earliest fictional [representations of] a white Rhodesian-born woman."[72] Though associated with masculine habits—shooting, roughhousing, jesting, dressing casually, enjoying the outdoors, and palling around with men—she is not described *as* masculine. After finally agreeing to marry her longtime friend, Dicky, third son of an English aristocrat, she rebelliously asserts: "I'm going to ride to church, and be married in my habit and my old Panama. If you all went down on your knees for a week I wouldn't deck myself out in a mosquito net and a silly train!" (*Love* 303). Ultimately accepting the role of wife, Nan shuns the role of bride, a display of femininity starkly at odds with her no-frills identity. Nan and Enid's double wedding at novel's end serves to underscore the women's symbolic relationship: Nan, "a daughter of Rhodesia, of whom the country had every reason to be proud," functioning as a living ancestor to Enid (65).[73]

Jill proudly asserts that "freedom has always been my fetish" (*Ranch* 144). In her earlier years in Rhodesia, she restricted herself to dresses and skirts, because her husband, "a bit of a prude in those days, . . . objected to a wife in tunic and breeches." In the second Jill novel, published eleven

Figure 3.4. Gertrude Page in modern attire. Source: Gertrude Page, *Jill on a Ranch*, Cassell, 1921, opposite title page.

years after the first, she now works in the "style of costume" worn by the "land girls," as the Women's Land Army was known.[74] For Jill, this practical attire, a khaki "knickerbocker suit" (145), "suggests an atmosphere of freedom to the mind as well as to the limbs. An uplifting sense of having broken away from ancient-received-opinions, from the old ignominious chatteldom to the male sex, from antiquated law-giving, better suited to another age" (144). Recognizing its importance, not merely for herself but also for society, she remarks: "It is possible that the advent of the land girl's dress marks an epoch in the history of woman" (143).[75]

Among the most independent of Page's Rhodesian heroines is the unnamed "Writer-woman," also referred to as "the Neighbour," who appears in the first of the two Jill novels (*Jill's* 166, 106). "Delightfully British," "a sportsman Englishwoman," writer, wife, and mother, she skillfully manages maternity *and* an occupation, marriage *and* autonomy (71, 73).[76] Though she "could shine in any assembly at home," she chose to "give herself to the colonies," where, like Page, she supervises a home while making time to write (73). She rides solo and astride, clothed in a "khaki divided skirt" before the advent of the land girl. She talks of writing a useful handbook for settlers, building a health spa in town, "chiefly for the sake of the women" (179), and of a "great scheme" for bringing single British women to Rhodesia (177). While she wants to "marry off all the lonely men to them," her chief concern is their fulfillment, which will come through the sense of "useful[ness]" that Rhodesia enables (178).

Page might not see herself as "an agitator for Women's Rights," but she nonetheless draws attention to such social injustices as the sexual double standard, marriage inequality, and divorce laws (*Love* 83). While men involved in sexual liaisons "always get off so easily, . . . a woman generally has to pay such a heavy price" (*Strange* 230). "If things grew a little uncomfortable," a man might host a social event, "and everybody accepted his invitations and forgave him. It was hardly the same for the woman," who would "probably [become] the topic of many afternoon tea-tables and much undisguised censure" (179). When Jo facilitates the reconciliation of a young immigrant couple, it is as much through addressing the husband's problematic behavior as the wife's. "I don't see why the right and wrong of [your wife's] part in the question should matter so much more than the right and wrong of your part," she "candid[ly]" tells the "the young fool-husband" (225, 154).

While a number of her stories depict romance, her heroines do not hold traditional views on marriage. Enid rejects the idea that "love is . . . the main object of a woman's life," that "women love sacrifice," and that it is their duty—or pleasure—to function as "housekeeper[s]" to "lordly" husbands (*Love* 96, 191, 95, 83). While she acknowledges that her brother-in-law is "devoted" to her sister, "it so often seemed that he might, with so little trouble, make life pleasanter and easier for her. Why then did he not do it? Looking back, she remembered [similar] cases . . . and she began to feel that all men must be selfish and thoughtless; and single-blessedness with freedom the greater happiness" (88). Her sister Marian "is essentially a family woman. Every thought and interest she has are woven round [her husband] and the children"; and while Enid "admire[s] her tremendously," she has no wish to emulate "Mother Marian," as she is locally known (81, 42). Enid's belief that people like her sister, "so much better than we ordinary sinners . . . , perhaps . . . delay progress" implies that for Enid (as for Page) traditional domesticity, far from being the foundation of civilization, may impede its development (295). Dinah similarly feels that marriage is "distasteful. Not for all the world did [she] intend to put her head under the yoke, and have to consult another as to her coming and going" (*Edge* 111). The problem is that "there was no alternative" (111). She "envie[s]" her doctor friend Cecil Lawson for the "daily . . . satisfaction" that his work gives him and laments the injustice of nature's "giv[ing] [women] brains teeming with life and eagerness, and then so arrang[ing] circumstances that we are tumbled into a vault-like existence almost before we know it" (167, 168, 101). Of course, both Enid and Dinah wind up married—Enid to a man who "do[es] not believe in the present form of marriage" (rather than to the man who "dare[s]" to call her "child") and Dinah to a modern-thinking man with an "independent soul," who respects her own (*Love* 250, 257; *Edge* 26). These are men, in short, who will view—and treat—their wives as partners rather than servants.[77]

As World War I unfolded and women abetted the empire in a variety of roles, Page commended the shift away from "that old worn-out [Victorian] era" (*Ranch* 154) in which the choice for most women lay between marriage and "starved spinsterhood" (*Limelight* 138). Though fear of the latter too often compelled them to "enter upon the treaty [of marriage] blindly . . . [or] in haste" (138), a "joyful era of emancipation" had at last arrived, in which "a girl could go forth in the world, choosing for herself either open-air work or clerical work, and while filling her life with interest, wait cheerfully for the 'right' man" (31). Far from threatening the institution of marriage, "work and independence will make their lives so much fuller and richer and happier, and this will give them greater wisdom and greater opportunity of choice" (138). Trapped in her own bad marriage, Mary, one of the heroines of "The Falling Gods," expects that such women "will see to it that conditions of the treaty are more equalised, and the withdrawal from it, if desired with reason, can be without stigma" (138).

Women, that is, in part through their own efforts, will not only have greater say in the terms of their union, they will also be able to obtain a divorce without social condemnation. Thus, someone like *The Silent Rancher*'s Gwendolyn, happily married in Rhodesia to the man once named as the defendant in her divorce case, would not be "condemn[ed] to ignoring and disgrace" back in England (274).[78] And someone like Joyce would be free from the "petty tyranny [of both] the man who chose to hold his bond intact, [and] a civilization ruled by prejudice" (*Edge* 284). In support of the cause, Joyce's friend Dinah declares her intent "to turn from a passive suffragette to an active one, for the express purpose of protesting against the Divorce Laws" (262). Though on occasion Page lightly mocks the suffragettes,[79] Jo insists: "Emancipation of women. . . . It's got to come—north, south, east and west. And you silly men think you can stay it by being sarcastic and scathing, and talking nonsense generally about what you would like to do to crush the modern spirit" (*Follow* 179). Rhodesia, as Page depicts it, is at the vanguard of social change. "[I]t *is* the battlefield of the future," and those female immigrants who help to build it "play their part in the 'firing-line' of the new order of warfare, which has this great good over other warfares [*sic*], that the man and woman at least fight side by side upon an equal plane, and neither is the head of the other" (*Strange* 63).[80] Though a site of battle, Rhodesia is nonetheless a site of hope—for the woman seeking the level playing field that Page so enticingly promises.

Conclusion

Page's novels continued to explore the issue of female desire that *The Story of an African Farm* had made an acceptable subject for literature. They thus paved the way for the empire romance, which flourished in the 1920s in the Amalgamated Press. Owned until 1926 by Harold Harmsworth, 1st Viscount Rothermere (cofounder of the *Daily Mail*), the press published more than fifty magazines "catering for female audiences." Sometimes set in southern Africa, the empire romance "promised [the female immigrant] not only a challenging life but also, it is hinted, genuine excitement." The neophyte begins the story unmarried, sex is implied, but not explicit, and "the ideal heroine . . . can face hardship like any man." These stories are more fantastical than Page's—the women beautiful, the men dashing, the obstacles less mundane—and the immigrant heroines, unlike Page's, "never develop[] or change[]."[81] The empire romance might also usefully describe the many novels that were increasingly explicit in foregrounding female desire in the colonies. These include those of the contemporary Rhodesian writer Cynthia Stockley—for instance, *Poppy: The Story of a South African Girl* (1910), mentioned in the introduction—W. Somerset Maugham's *The Painted Veil* (1925), Nora Strange's many Kenyan novels, and any number of "amorous adventures" set in India.[82]

Doris Lessing's first novel, *The Grass Is Singing* (1950), owes something to Page as well. Born in southern Africa, the novel's heroine, Mary Turner, leaves her city job to join her new husband on his isolated Rhodesian farm. The dust, heat, and African servants irritate her. She is bored and lonely, has no female companions, and her husband is too busy, tired, and inept to attend to her needs. Mary struggles with the same difficulties as Page's heroines, with one important difference: the man who attracts her attention is black. That man is Moses, one of her husband's African laborers, who comes to work in her home some years after she has hit him across the face with a *sjambok*, sharply enough to leave a scar. Though the deeply racist Mary hates and fears Moses, she is also fascinated by him, following him with her eyes, aware of his presence even when he is in another room, thinking about him when he is elsewhere. It is certainly not love, but it is a kind of passion, something on which to focus beyond her mounting depression and overwhelming sense of powerlessness. Unlike Page's heroines who confront their desires, Mary is unable to acknowledge her complicated feelings for Moses. Doing so would not simply undermine her personal values, it would threaten her very identity as a Rhodesian white woman, which is dependent on a separation between whites and Africans—a separation white society viewed as both necessary and natural, especially when it came to white women. The story that Page tells is one of symbiosis between Rhodesia and the "modern . . . wom[a]n," but there is neither symbiosis nor freedom when Africans emerge from the periphery of a text (*Rhodesian* 102). In 1978 critic Kenneth Parker asked rhetorically: "If you are white, is living in South Africa"—we could just as easily say Rhodesia—"compatible with notions of freedom? Since white privilege is dependent upon black dispossession, to what extent can white South Africans think [of] themselves as being free?"[83] As Lessing novel's illustrates, the answer is resoundingly no to the first question and not with any validity to the second. Because colonial belonging is contingent on the denial of indigenous belonging, it is always threatened not only by whites' awareness of this fact, or their effort to suppress it, but by Africans' awareness of it as well. Writing both out of and against a literary heritage bequeathed to her by Page, Lessing exposes the limitations and contingencies of Rhodesian women's dubious liberation. Despite her effort to escape, Lessing's earliest heroine has more in common with the claustrophobic existence of the feminist Lyndall than with the expansive universe of Page's protagonists. As the stones on which the Bushmen drew their paintings "lie on here, looking at everything," speaking to and through Waldo, and the "Kaffir [Bantu] herd" "wakes thoughts [in Lyndall] that run far out into the future and back into the past," Moses insistently frays the edges of Mary's conscience.[84]

In *City of Dreadful Delight*, Judith Walkowitz argues that the Jack the Ripper murders, which took place in London in 1888, were "shaped . . . into a cautionary tale for women, a warning that the city was a dangerous place when they transgressed the narrow boundary of home and hearth to enter public space."[85] In Page's Rhodesian settler romances, danger and transgression are less a warning than an invitation. Suffusing her novels with the possibility of sexual opportunity, she suggests that experience is the price of authority. And while temptation is not absolutely requisite for the British female immigrant to achieve colonial maturity, it is certainly a means to that end. After six months in Rhodesia, Enid, the heroine of *Love in the Wilderness*, "is an entirely different person to what she was when she came" (261). In *The Edge o' Beyond*, Dinah says of her time in Rhodesia, "It seems as if only in the last year had life taught me anything worth learning" (177). In *The Veldt Trail* (1919), the newcomer Sybil describes her own Rhodesian experience as "the most real time I have ever known—I mean real-life time, instead of just playing and frivoling" (208). "The mysterious fascination of the country," as Page depicts it, is simply this: freedom infused with the prospect of sex (*Edge* 71).

Chapter 4

"There Will Be No More Kings in Africa"

Foreclosing Darkness in *Prester John*

John Buchan's *Prester John* (1910) looks forward to his Hannay quartet, which established "the formula for the modern secret agent story."[1] It also looks backward to the male imperial romance, popularized by H. Rider Haggard.[2] Published in the early years of southern Africa's mineral rush, Haggard's *King Solomon's Mines* (1885) compelled more than a few of its thrill-seeking readers to inquire where precisely (the fictional) Kukuanaland could be located.[3] Published the year that the Union of South Africa was formed, *Prester John* renders South Africa's mystery finite.[4] For while Haggard's Quatermain novels continually extend the frontiers of the unknown, *Prester John* consummately denies them. Casting his hero in an ever-receding past, Haggard laments the demystification of Africa south of the Zambesi.[5] Buchan welcomes it as evidence of the success of the reconstruction that followed the Second Anglo-Boer War (1899–1902). Where Haggard depicts individual Britons of heroic proportions, *Prester John* portrays an imperial social body whose domestication is complete. Though the novel begins as an imperial romance, by the time it concludes there is no treasure left to unearth, no enemy to oppose, no darkness to withstand. The empire's agents are thus free to turn their attention from acquisition to consolidation, to the "edification" of South Africa's black citizens, as in *Prester John*—or to the circumvention of German ambition, as in the quartet. The desuetude of the imperial romance must therefore be understood in the context of southern Africa, which, in Buchan's representation, has been so successfully anglicized that it can no longer satisfy the genre's needs.

If Buchan brings down the curtain on the imperial romance, it is because he must—to achieve his vision of a British southern Africa. "The last word in all matters," he wrote shortly after the Second Anglo-Boer War, "*must* rest with [those] whose interests and sentiment are on the British side, who seek progress on British lines." An imaginative bulwark against the threats, as he saw them, to such progress at the moment of union, *Prester John* creates the conditions that nourish southern Africa's future as "a 'white man's country'; by which," he wrote, "I [mean] a country not only capable of sustaining life, but fit for the amenities of life and the nursery of a nation."[6] Depicting a scant Afrikaner population, ignoring Afrikaner nationalism, and conveying harmony between English and Afrikaner, the novel negates the growth of Afrikaner political power. Depicting indigenous strength as contingent on a single charismatic leader and the fetish that legitimizes him, it acknowledges only to destroy the dreaded swell of organized, collective African nationalism, a unifying concern for the Boers and the British following the war.[7] Depicting southern Africa as less exotic than familiar, less precarious than stable, less a holding than "a homeland," less African than British—a far cry, in short, from the southern Africa of *King Solomon's Mines*—the novel counterintuitively entices possible settlers by suggesting that the goals of British settlement have already been achieved.[8] The net result is an anglicized southern Africa in which British loyalty is the only extant form of South African nationalism. By the close of the novel, not only has southern Africa become successfully British and successfully white, whiteness itself is a function of Britishness. A work of prolepsis on multiple levels, *Prester John* imaginatively forecloses Afrikaner and indigenous threats to southern Africa's political security and British identity, as well as anticipates the shift in imperial politics, from frontier to continent, and in popular fiction, from imperial adventure to spy thriller, that would coincide with the First World War.[9]

A New Sense of Space

As assistant private secretary to Alfred Milner, British High Commissioner to South Africa, from 1901 to 1903, Buchan contributed to the reconstruction efforts that followed the war. A member, as he put it, of Milner's "crèche" rather than of Milner's "Kindergarten," Buchan prepared the way for the men who would organize, agitate for, and shepherd the passing of the Union of South Africa Act, which led to the formation of the Union in 1910.[10] Arriving seven months before the end of the war, Buchan's initial task, in his own words, "was to take over on behalf of the civilian governments the concentration camps for women and children established by the army."[11] Though the British ostensibly created these camps to shelter enemy civilians, they were chiefly concerned with impeding (their assistance to) guerilla fighters. The infamous "scorched earth" policy, which destroyed Boer homesteads, had the same end in mind: inhibiting both physical and moral support to the Boer cause. Deprived of their homes and forced to live behind barriers in excessively close quarters and unsanitary conditions, at least twenty-seven thousand Boers and fourteen thousand black Africans died in the camps.[12] Through the efforts of journalists, healthcare workers, and other campaigners, it soon became clear to an outraged metropolitan public that these camps were no "manifestation of British generosity in sheltering the enemy" but rather poorly run centers for corralled civilians.[13] Under Buchan's watch—though not primarily through his efforts—"irrigation, engineering, medical, culinary and financial" aspects of camp administration were ameliorated and death rates plummeted.[14]

"Next, with the end of the war in sight, we had to prepare for the repatriation of the Boer inhabitants of the commandos, the concentration camps, and the prisoner-of-war camps overseas." Attempting to "adjust the ethnic balance" in the Transvaal and Orange River Colony, Buchan, as head of the Land Settlement Department, also oversaw the settlement of Britons and colonials in these former Boer republics. This immigration opportunity was, he wrote, among the most "serious and well-considered that has been afforded [to Britain] since we first planted a colony."[15] Through a number of articles in a variety of venues, he encouraged, in particular, British and dominion soldiers "who had fallen under the spell of South Africa" to take up farming on these thirty million acres of newly acquired land. While Buchan "saw in the Empire a means of giving to the congested masses at home open country instead of a blind alley," he also believed that the settlement of Britons in southern Africa's rural areas would provide a foundation for "generations [of] affection for the mother-land."[16] Ultimately, he sought to fortify British dominance throughout southern Africa—both by increasing the ratio of British to Boers and by strengthening the bonds between colony and metropole.

Buchan's experience in southern Africa has much in common with that of Haggard, who preceded him there by more than two decades. Arriving in southern Africa as young men, both worked for the colonial administration, traveled extensively (particularly in the Transvaal), learned the *taal*, developed a deep affection for the country, contemplated permanent settlement, and ultimately decided to depart.[17] Unlike Haggard, who actually purchased a farm, Buchan merely considered doing so—first between Pretoria and Johannesburg and later in the Wood Bush, in the Highveld of the northeastern Transvaal. "I resolved to go back in my old age," he wrote of the spot, "build a dwelling, and leave my bones there."[18] While he did not in fact do so, he did make the Wood Bush the site of police headquarters—the hub of white operations against the black rising—in *Prester John*.

Though most sources indicate that Buchan never returned to southern Africa after his mid-1903 departure—if he did it was for a brief visit in 1905—he clearly maintained a lifelong affinity for the country with which he had fallen "so much in love." "I have never got Africa out of my bones," he noted, three decades after his departure.[19] As it had for Haggard, southern Africa inspired multiple works. Besides *Prester John*, these include *The African Colony: Studies in the Reconstruction* (1903), a collection of articles promoting immigration; *A Lodge in the Wilderness* (1906), a "philosophical novel on imperialism"; the Hannay novels; and *The History of the South African Forces in France* (1920).[20] As the latter suggests, southern Africa also compelled his loyalty: written at the request of then prime minister Jan Smuts—former Boer general—the *History* drew from Buchan's experiences with the South African Infantry Brigade as a *Times* correspondent during World War I.[21] When, nearly two decades later, Buchan was offered the governor-generalship of Canada, he requested the same position in South Africa instead. The position not being then vacant, "Buckingham Palace . . . pressed him to take the job in Canada," which he ultimately did.[22]

Southern Africa also informed Buchan's sense of identity, broadening the way he saw both himself and the empire. "I learned a good deal in South Africa," he wrote at the end of his life. "Above all I ceased to be an individualist and became a citizen." Where once he had aspired to work at the Bar, he now "wanted some share in the making of this splendid commonwealth." Where once he had imagined residing exclusively in Britain, he now "hoped to spend most of [his] life" beyond her shores. Where once he had "regarded the Dominions patronizingly as distant settlements of our people who were [striving] to carry on the British tradition," he "now . . . realised that Britain had at least as much to learn from them as they had from Britain."[23] If Buchan had gotten "the sense of space into [his] blood"—the foundation of imperialism according to one of his characters in *A Lodge in the Wilderness*—he had also acquired a new sense of belonging. After two years in southern Africa, he had come to see himself as more than a Scotsman, more even than a Briton; he now saw himself as a citizen of "the Empire, which had hitherto been only a phrase to me."²⁴ "We must learn to regard colonials as . . . our fellow citizens," he said in a speech delivered just a few months after his return to Britain, and to regard individual colonies "as no more a foreign country than Wales or Ireland."²⁵

Claiming both "the colonial view" and the perspective of "the outside spectator"—the enhanced vantage of the authorial informant—Buchan reflected on South African and British identity alike. The newly emerging "South African civilisation," he argued in 1903, "will borrow English principles, but not English institutions, [which] are the incrusted mosses of time." English in spirit but liberated from her sclerotic structures, southern Africa would become, like the Wood Bush, "England, richer, softer, kindlier."²⁶ Inhabited by colonials who were "at once imaginative and realistic," "audacious" and "traditionalist[]," southern Africa was not England replicated, but England remade.²⁷

Generic Deviation

Prester John opens in Scotland, with three twelve-year-old boys in pursuit of adventure. These boys, we learn, comprised "a band," "bore . . . the name[s] of some historic pirate or sailorman," and "were sealed to silence by the blood oath."²⁸ Among "deep caves and pools" along the shore, they searched for "hid treasures," pretended to be smugglers and rebels, and told "mighty tales" (*PJ* 7, 8). "But the . . . truth is," admits the now grown Davie Crawford, narrator and one of the erstwhile boys, "our deeds were of the humblest, and a dozen of fish or a handful of apples was all our booty, and our greatest exploit was a fight with the [local] roughs" (8). Lacking the opportunity for adventure, the boys create their own, until adventure unexpectedly comes to them in the form of an "uncanny . . . great negro," an "interloper [in] our territory" (13, 11). Barefoot and in a state of semi-undress, walking in circles around a fire, bowing toward the moon, making "odd markings" in the sand with a "great knife," the man, angry at being discovered, chases after them, knife in hand (13). Unable to catch them, he hurls "a great stone" at Davie, nearly missing his head; in response, Davie hurls a rock of his own, hitting the man in the face and leaving, he observes years later, a scar on his cheek (15). The man, it turns out, is the Reverend John Laputa, an African minister in town to preach at a local church. In catching him "at his devil-worship," as one character sees it, Davie is "the first man alive to know the Reverend John in his true colors" (70).

Despite the allusions to the imperial romance in this opening—caves, quests, treasures, territory, a band of males, a dangerous "savage"—and parallels throughout the novel, *Prester John* differs from the genre in a number of ways (13). A story of defense rather than conquest, espionage rather than exploration, imperial consolidation rather than acquisition, the novel anticipates the spy thriller that would soon follow. Set in the northern Transvaal a few years after the Second Anglo-Boer War, *Prester John* tracks the adventures of Davie, now nineteen, who has come to southern Africa "to set about earning a living" (19). Exchanging Edinburgh for a remote trading station on a "back-veld dorp," a university education for a job as an assistant storekeeper, and the probability of never earning "much more than a hundred pounds a year" for a starting salary of "three hundred," Davie heads to southern Africa to "better [his] future" (103, 19, 20, 19). In less than eighteen months, he uncovers a far-reaching plot to "dr[i]ve . . . the white man" out of Africa, learns "more about" its leader "than [almost] any man living" (95), is captured, escapes, helps to bring down both leader and rising, is made rich by his share of the indigenous "war chest," returns to Scotland, and reenrolls in university (134, 178). An aberration in an otherwise average life, Davie's South African adventure is the only story, unlike Haggard's Allan Quatermain, he has to tell.

"Little more than a lad," Davie has almost nothing in common with this seasoned professional or his ilk (159). Self-proclaimed "hunter and explorer," Quatermain is the quintessential hero of the male imperial romance, for whom "the excitement of adventure [is] a kind of necessity."[29] Compelled by his affinity for the unknown, Quatermain travels the breadth of southern Africa. An inexperienced shopkeeper newly out from the metropole, Davie stumbles into the path of adventure quite by accident, though he takes to it readily. That his job turns out to include spying on as well as selling to the local indigenous population is an enticement rather than an impediment for Davie, who cheerily narrates: "Things were shaping well for some kind of adventure" (29). And when his sleuthing yields evidence not only of the illicit diamond buying (I.D.B.) that his employers suspected but also of a large-scale indigenous "rising, with diamonds as the sinews of war"—revenue for guns and ammunition—Davie turns his energies to the cause of defense (69).[30]

Though he professes to "believe that every man has deep in his soul a passion for treasure-hunting," Davie's "lust[] for . . . treasure" is derivative of his quest for intelligence. Locating the "headquarters of the rising" is far more important, in other words, than making off with the store of riches therein (95). At one point, Davie claims to think more of his "duty to enrich" himself than of his "duty to [assist his] country," but "patriotism . . . flickers up," reminding him of his primary objective: "saving [his] country from the horrors of rebellion" (95, 134, 135). Capitalizing on the success of the adventure genre, the story's first American publisher released Buchan's tale under the title *The Great Diamond Pipe*,[31] but the treasure plot is nonetheless secondary to the larger, political concerns of the novel, just as the treasure's accumulation is secondary to its purpose: funding the rising that Davie is trying to stop.

That rising is led by none other than John Laputa, the adversary of Davie's boyhood who is now the "arch-enemy" of white Africa (93). An American-educated, widely traveled African Christian "of Zulu blood," Laputa seeks "the overthrow of the alien" and the resurrection of a "golden age . . . for the oppressed" (74, 105). Uniting Africans against "the white man," who has "snatched" Africa "from [its] rightful possessors," his goal is "to lead the African race to conquest and empire" (105, 75). A highly unusual figure in contemporary British writing, Laputa represents both the threat of African nationalism and its futility. And while he may embody the strength of Africa, he is also the end of the line. As he is dying he tells Davie, "there will be no more kings in Africa. . . . My race is doomed. . . . I alone could have saved them. Now . . . the warriors of John become drudges and slaves" (177, 180).

In its depiction of a centralized, nationalist indigenous population, *Prester John* contrasts sharply with the imperial romance, in which the indigenous are often divided into factions; in the lack of attention the novel gives to individual Africans, it is in keeping with the genre. The Africans who live near Blaauwildebeestefontein (Blue Wildebeest's Spring), the site of the main store, are "well conducted," "mostly Christians, and quiet, decent fellows, who farm[] their little gardens" (38). The men who help Davie build the new store are "lusty blacks" (43). The servant Zeeta is a "well trained" female "orphan from a mission station," who tends quietly to the white men's needs (32, 34). There are unnamed Basuto scouts; "loyal natives [on police] pay in most tribes," who provide "early intelligence" (78); and four local chiefs—identified by name—allied with Laputa. The rest are simply "Kaffirs," "dark men who live only for the day and their own bellies" (108, 198).[32]

Past African leaders are mentioned several times: by those delivering the incantation at Laputa's coronation; by Captain James Arcoll, the Transvaal's "chief Intelligence officer among the natives"; and by Mr. Wardlaw, the Scottish schoolteacher who "had read a lot about native history, and was full of the doings of Tchaka and Mosilikatse and Moshesh, and the kings of old" (73, 52).[33] Wardlaw even concedes the native origins of the Zimbabwe ruins, "maintain[ing] that the men who could erect piles like that" must have been part of a great African empire (53). When Europeans encountered these structures in 1871, they supposed them to have been built by whites or Arabs, and though "archaeologists began to controvert [this theory] in 1906," it was decades before many whites would admit the ruins' African provenance.[34] Wardlaw's affirmation thus notably invokes the history of an African empire in African hands.

Africans in *Prester John*, unlike those so often in the imperial romance, are not impressed with the Europeans they encounter. Under Laputa's direction, they have accrued a store of funds, stockpiled guns and ammunition, and gained access to European centers of power. A popular figure in both colony and metropole, Laputa is as likely to be at a meeting of the Royal Geographical Society in London as at a missionary conference in Cape Town or on an "evangelizing tour[] in the back veld" (*PJ* 74). "A good scholar," "a great reader," a "natural orator," and an ordained minister, "he is a favourite speaker at Church meetings" in southern Africa and Britain alike (74). "You will find evidence given by him in Blue-Books on native affairs," Arcoll tells Davie, "and he count[s] many members of [the British] Parliament . . . among his correspondents" (74). "Strongly buttressed by support" in Britain, Laputa is in many ways closer to the seat of imperial power than Arcoll, whose "reputation does not follow [him] home" and who cannot get the "Government [to] act" against the reverend (76, 74, 76). What is more, because of his access to a secret diamond pipe unknown to any whites, his many contacts, and his inside knowledge of Britain's "weaknesses," Laputa succeeds in the I.D.B. business "on a big scale" (76, 75).

Using the tools of the West in his quest to pry its grip from southern Africa, Laputa arouses rather than manifests "awe" (104). "He has the heart of a poet and a king," says Arcoll, "and it is God's curse that he has been born among the children of Ham" (77). Davie is "mesmerized by this amazing man"; impressed by his "commanding" face and figure, and his "rich" and "gentle" voice; "lost in admiration" of his remarkable endurance, "splendid proportions," and "great physique"—with a "deep" chest and "massive" shoulders, he stands "at least six feet and a half" tall (106, 23, 168, 83, 167, 84).[35] But the white men's feelings for Laputa are as riven with contradictions as Buchan's portrayal of the man himself, for while Arcoll "hope[s] to shoot him like a dog," he is "glad to bear testimony to his greatness" (77); while Aitken, a landing agent and former secret service officer, helps to rout him out, he erects his likeness in stone; and while Davie is the cause of his undoing, he is also "hypnotized by the man. To see him going out was like seeing the fall of a great mountain" (177).

At once a version of and a departure from the noble savage, Laputa is more ambitious, more majestic, and more complex a character than any of Haggard's noble "savage[s]."[36] Claiming to "have sucked civilization dry," he "want[s] a simpler and better world" for himself and for his "own people." He envisages this world as an "empire" at once "so majestic that the white man everywhere would dread its name [and] so righteous that all men under it would live in ease and peace" (*PJ* 151, 105). He seeks, then, more an influential kingdom than a primitive idyll.

The conflict having been won by the "good" indigenous faction with the help of the whites, the imperial romance generally ends with the reestablishment of the former and the departure of the latter, now significantly enriched.[37] In *Prester John*, the conflict concludes with victorious whites remaining in Africa alongside pacified Africans whose instruction and labor they superintend. After overseeing, like Buchan, the early stages of resettlement, Davie soon departs southern Africa; and though he leaves with "a very considerable fortune," "the wealth," he says, does "not dazzle so much as . . . solemnize[]" him (178, 200). After a "satiety of action," he begins his journey home, thinking of the "comforting" return to his "old common-place self" rather than of future adventure (201). If heroism in the imperial adventure entails the preservation of spaces beyond the realm of civilization, heroism in *Prester John* entails the foreclosure of such spaces. The one entices Britons with the exotic, the other assures them that civilization is underway. Once resurrected, romance has now been laid to rest.[38]

"Excellent Friends"

Custom, religion, lifestyle, and political ideology had long inspired Afrikaner resistance to British political domination and British culture alike. Hence, the Great Trek.[39] Hence, their establishment of various republics, most of which the British quickly annexed. Hence, the two Anglo-Boer Wars. So while the British had achieved military victory in the Second Anglo-Boer War, they still had to contend with the strong oppositional identity and political agency of the majority white population—not only in the Transvaal and Orange River Colony but also in Natal.[40] In keeping with Milner's early intentions, Buchan had tried to balance unity between British and Boers with British cultural and political domination. Thus, on the one hand he would claim that a post–Boer War southern Africa "must borrow much from the Dutch race" as well as from the "English"—note Buchan's elision, which effaces his native Scotland—and on the other that because the latter's "tradition" was "stronger, wider, [and] resting on greater historical foundations, [it will] more readily attract and absorb the lesser."[41] After Buchan left southern Africa and the postwar dust began to settle, it became clear that Milner's hopes for significant British immigration had failed. Though there had been an initial influx of British and dominion immigrants, by 1904, with South Africa in the midst of an economic recession, departures exceeded arrivals, as they would until the formation of the Union.[42] In 1906, the Liberal government was returned to parliament in England, leading to full self-government for the former Boer republics and the reenfranchisement of Cape rebels. This, in turn, paved the way for the domination of Afrikaner nationalist parties in South Africa.[43]

In *Prester John*, however, not only are Afrikaners numerically negligible, they possess neither political agency nor the desire for it.[44] Davie notes in passing that the five white children who attend the local school "belong[] to Dutch farmers in the mountains" and that he hires "two Dutch masons" to oversee the building of the new store (*PJ* 33, 40). The only Afrikaners readers encounter directly are "old-fashioned farmers" and their families, driving their cattle into the "winter-veld" (40). These "honest companionable fellows" allow Davie, en route to the new store, to hitch his wagons to their caravan (42). Though "at first . . . silent and suspicious of [the] newcomer," they are "soon on good terms" with the young man, who "talked their *taal* fluently" (41). "Lounging," drinking, and "smoking" around the fire after supper, they share hunting stories and other "reminiscences," "verge[] on politics," even joke about former hostilities (41, 42). "Which side are you on in the next war?" asks an old man named Coetzee, shooting a baboon from a tree without sighting it. "Laughing," narrates Davie, "I told him, 'Yours'" (41). This cozy gathering with its easy banter between "excellent friends" suggests a total lack of animosity between the English and the Boers, who just a few years earlier had been at war with one another (42).

Afrikaners in the novel, including Coetzee, are a source of knowledge and wisdom, supplying information that ultimately helps counter the rising. Reflecting that "these were old residenters" from whom he "might learn perhaps something of value," Davie tries to gather intelligence about the area (42). Aitken has described it as a "place [Africans] go to on pilgrimage," perhaps because of "some sort of great witch or wizard living" there

(28). So Davie brings up "a tale [he] said [he] had heard . . . of a great wizard somewhere [nearby], and ask[s] if anyone knew of it" (42). Coetzee points him on the right track: "It is in the Rooirand. There is a devil dwells there. . . . [H]e himself had heard it roaring when he had gone there as a boy to hunt" (42). Following this lead, Davie travels to the Rooirand, where he discovers the source of a great river, the sound of which "descend[ing] into the earth," he correctly deduces, is the "devil" of Coetzee's childhood (48).[45] Trapped in a deep cave there later in the novel, Davie realizes that he is "about to share the experience of all treasure-hunters—to be left with jewels galore and not a bite to sustain life," when he suddenly remembers an old Boer saying: "'Ek sal'n plan maak'" (184). Though Buchan does not translate the phrase in *Prester John*, he implies its meaning in *Greenmantle*, when its hero, Richard Hannay, reflects: "*Ek sal'n plan maak*, says the older Boer when he gets into trouble, and it was up to me now to make a plan." In *The African Colony*, Buchan not only translates it, he also explains the story from which it originated and announces his intention to take the "motto" for his own.[46] Davie, buoyed by his recollection of the aphorism, makes his own plan, which enables him to escape.

If Coetzee and a Boer adage provide indirect assistance, so, too, does the historical figure Christiaan Frederik Beyers. A Boer military leader in the Second Anglo-Boer War and an Afrikaner nationalist politician following it, Beyers is mentioned by Davie five times in the text. As they consider ways to defeat Laputa, both he and Arcoll independently think of "following Beyers's historic precedent" of taking guns up into the mountains (165). When used against the British, this strategy "saved them from our troops" (139). Now, under Arcoll's command and "directed by one of Beyer's old commandants," it is successfully employed to "hold up the bulk of [Laputa's] force" (192, 193). Contra Stephen Gray's claim that Boers "play no role in the balance of power," commandoes of Boer farmers also aid Arcoll, the police, and the companies of regulars, reinforcing their efforts to staunch the rebellion.[47]

No longer threats, Afrikaners are not only allies and assets, they are also martyrs, murdered by local natives, who "wanted blooding," and the villainous Henriques, who killed Coetzee "with [his] own hands" (*PJ* 88). Recalling his "kindly old friends, lying butchered with their kinsfolk out in the bush, hot tears of rage came to [Davie's] eyes" (89).[48] These are the "Dutch companions" with whom he traveled, with whom he did business, and about whom he worried as the rising approached (58). Confederates and victims, the few Afrikaners in the novel are everything that a decade earlier they were imagined *not* to be.

The "Dangerous Spirit" of Ethiopianism

Where the British had initially encouraged "Anglo-Saxon race patriotism" following the war, they soon began to advocate "white South Africanism" instead. The "ideal," wrote an essayist in the *South African Magazine*, "is not to be narrowly Dutch or English, but broadly and tolerantly South African."[49] This new South African identity, however, was neither broad nor tolerant. On the contrary, the push for unity between Afrikaners and English had as much to do with the "black peril" as it did with the disappointing British immigration numbers and the ascendency of Afrikaner political authority.[50] "The Englishman and the Dutchman, sinking their differences, will have to unite," wrote Roderick Jones in a 1904 article titled "The Black Peril in South Africa," not merely "to preserve the domination of the white man over the black" but also to "escape complete annihilation." A slippery but pervasive specter that ranged from a black political majority to a black revolution, from "black men ruling whites" to blacks "whip[ping] the British back to the Thames," from black men raping white women to miscegenation, the "black peril" was imagined in political, military, cultural, and moral terms.[51]

Debates around black voting rights were widespread between the end of the war and the formation of the Union. The Boer republics had never allowed nonwhites the vote. The British colonies, while not explicitly restricting voting rights along racial lines, had essentially done so by tightening franchise qualifications (in 1887 and again in 1892), "mainly because of a vast increase in the potential African vote resulting from the incorporation of new territories." Despite substantial indigenous support in the war, the British turned their backs on the black population by failing to "press the issue of a non-racial franchise as a condition of restoration of full self-government in the former Republics." Thus, the Treaty of Vereeniging, which officially ended the war, stipulated that no decision on African enfranchisement would be made until after the Transvaal and the Orange Free State had been granted full self-government. This betrayal effectively facilitated not only the disenfranchisement of nonwhites throughout South Africa but also a broader range of racist policies that would develop in the Union, leading ultimately to apartheid.[52] For his part, Buchan argued that the denial of the indigenous franchise on the basis of "*radical mental dissimilarity*," rather than "a lack of property or educational qualification," was "the most philosophic as well as the simplest way [to handle the matter]. In any case," he glibly wrote, "it is a matter which must be left for the people of the colony to settle for themselves."[53]

By 1909, white South Africa had done so, with Natal and the Cape (the last holdout) following the former republics' example rather than the other way around. The Union of South Africa Treaty submitted to the British parliament in 1909 stipulated the "rejection of any political representation for black Africans and inclusion of merely symbolic representation for 'Asians' and 'Coloureds.'" "This was no last-minute imposition, smuggled into the polity by illiberal, unscrupulous Afrikaners," writes Bill Schwarz, "but the founding principle on which the Union of South Africa, as a nation, was created, and sanctified by Westminster." In May 1910, the treaty passed unamended, and South Africa moved closer to becoming the "white man's country" that Buchan had envisioned.[54]

Reflecting concerns that went well beyond the possibility of an enfranchised black populace, including the rise of black education, black religious autonomy, pan-Africanism, and, above all, African nationalism, "the black peril" loomed large in the years between the war and the union. African nationalism, in particular, triggered "alarmist fears" in a minority white population that had come to identify almost any attempt on the part of black Africans "to improve [their] religious, educational, and political status" as *Ethiopianism*.[55] At once a "protonationalist movement of religious separatism" and a "pan-tribal political ideology," Ethiopianism had "three broad strands": African American diasporic, West African, and South African. Seeking to return Africa "to its old glory," it looked back to the "achievements of ancient Egypt, Nubia, and Ethiopia. . . . In all incarnations, it fueled black nationalism."[56] Ethiopianism first appeared in southern Africa in the 1870s, when a number of African Christians, breaking off from the region's white churches, began to form churches of their own. Gaining significant support from African American churches in the 1890s, it soon sought to spread "across the entire African continent."[57] It "became more directly political" in 1896, when Abyssinia, one of only two remaining self-ruled African countries, succeeded in defeating the Italians, thus becoming "a symbol of African redemption." The 1897 publication of the missionary Joseph Booth's *Africa for the African*, which "emphasised the need for increased African self-reliance and the role of Afro-Americans in attaining it," gave the movement a "rallying-cry" that exacerbated its reputation among whites as "essentially anti-white."[58]

The Bambatha Rebellion, which broke out in Natal in 1906, intensified white anxiety over Ethiopianism, both because of the involvement of African Christians (who in fact formed only a small portion of the rebels) and the cooperation across chiefdoms, which seemed to some like a kind of "nationalism."[59] The last of the Zulu rebellions, it began as a protest against a new poll tax. After two white policemen were killed, martial law was declared and troops "marched through the lands of Africans reported to be defiant or restless, burning crops and kraals [hutted villages or homes], confiscating cattle, and deposing chiefs." Before long, resistance forces had been organized by Chief Bambatha, for whom the rebellion is named.[60] Ultimately, between thirty-five hundred and four thousand Africans and twenty-four whites were killed, an incommensurability that—like that in India in 1857 and Morant Bay in 1865—reflects the severity of British retaliation. "Play[ing] up" the "threat of black resistance" manifest in the rebellion, the South African administration put increasing rhetorical pressure on "white South Africans to bury their internal differences" and unite.[61] "Ethiopianism, whatever its form, always contained an element of protest," sparking fears in the minority white population.[62]

This concern with the "dangerous spirit" of Ethiopianism, though mentioned by name only three times in *Prester John*, both infuses and is dispelled by the novel.[63] Claiming to be "the incarnated spirit of Prester John," Laputa aspires to retake "Africa for the Africans" (*PJ* 75, 73)—"the keynote to Ethiopianism."[64] Though Prester John—references to whom first appear in Europe in the twelfth century—was originally thought to rule in Asia, by the fourteenth century he was almost always associated with Africa.[65] It is explicitly the latter figure, "the King of Abyssinia" and not "the man that lived in Central Asia," with whom Laputa identifies (*PJ* 71). Sometimes used as a generic title, sometimes as an individual, "who always seemed to be contemporary," from the fourteenth century on Prester John stood above all for the kingdom of African Christians he was imagined to have ruled.[66] Though by the end of the fifteenth century there was evidence to indicate that there may never have been a Prester John, "the demolition of the dream-text," as one scholar put it, "was slow."[67]

Calling himself "the Heir of John," Laputa suggests the very possibility that the novel works so hard to contain: Africans, having "had a great empire in the past, . . . might have a great empire again" (*PJ* 180, 73). A "roving evangelist" who "talked Christianity to the mobs" and African nationalism to their leaders, Laputa uses Prester John's reputation as both "Priest and king" to incite and unite Africans against whites (73, 75, 102). These two roles—Christian leader and "conqueror" (73)—are "umbilically linked" in Laputa,[68] who prays to the "Lord of Hosts" for assistance in his revolution (104). According to Wardlaw, the novel's informal historian, Prester John was both "a sort of Christian" and "a great potentate," making him "a good argument" for Laputa (71, 73). In Arcoll's telling, "under him and his successors, the empire of Ethiopia extended far south," relocating its "centre of authority" over time in the kingdom of Monomotapa (site of the Zimbabwe ruins) and the parts of southern Africa ruled by the Zulus for much of the nineteenth century (73).[69]

Laputa may be the ideological, spiritual, possibly even biological descendent of Prester John, but he is also the last "of his breed left in Africa" (194). Taking with him the symbol of African potency as he jumps to his death in "the underground deeps" of the Rooirand cave, Laputa ensures that no one will rise to take his place (180). This symbol, a "necklace of rubies" shining from his neck like "the flames of [a king's] funeral pyre," was once "the necklet of Prester John" (90, 180, 75). "Always in the hands of the tribe which for the moment held the leadership," once it is gone, so, too, is "the chance of a Kaffir empire" (72). According to the text's revisionist version of history, "the great native wars of the sixteenth century . . . were not for territory but for leadership, and mainly for the possession of this fetich" (72). Tchaka, who "made the Zulus the paramount power in South Africa, . . . owed his conquests" not to his leadership but to the necklet; and Mosilikatse, Tchaka's chief general, fled to Matabeleland not because of their political differences but because he had tried and failed to steal "the collar" from him (72, 90). At the end of Tchaka's reign, "*Ndhlondhlo*" ("the Great Snake"), as the Zulus referred to the necklace, seemed to disappear—that is, until Laputa (72). "The fetich of the whole black world[,] . . . their Ark of the Covenant,"[70] *Ndhlondhlo* does not merely hold, it *is* "the secret of Africa, of Prester John's empire[,] [of] Tchaka's victories," and of Laputa's ascendancy (124, 103). On this point the narrative is clear: possession of "the Prester's Collar" and black dominion over Africa go hand-in-hand (106). Attributing African power to a necklace of fifty-five rubies, "the largest as big as a pigeon's egg, and the least not smaller than [a] thumbnail," this history not only contravenes African agency, it also implies the precariousness of African leadership, for if a necklace can make a king, its loss can unmake him (103). Laputa's possession of *Ndhlondhlo*, in other words, may authorize and facilitate his leadership, but it also underscores its contingency. Buchan's reduction of African power to a collection of gems seems to reflect Britain's overriding (material) interest in southern Africa. "Far from human quest," the necklace may be lost forever in the deeps of the cave, but the store of gold and diamonds elsewhere in the cave, in addition to other as-yet-unmined diamonds throughout southern Africa, are firmly in white hands (181).

Anglo-Eden

Having witnessed Laputa and the Great Snake descend "into the gulf" of the cave, Davie climbs out of the "deep cleft of darkness," emerging into the "clear sunshine" of the "early morning" (189). "All of a sudden," he recalls, "I realized that at last I had come out of savagery. . . . Behind me was the black night, and the horrid secrets of darkness. Before me was my own country" (189–90).[71] He has "looked into the heart of darkness," "conquered terror," and emerged on "the other side of fear" (110, 174). Standing in the morning light, breathing in "the fresh scent of the air," Davie sees before him a land so "fresh [and] clean," so green and serene, that it reminds him of home, making him feel "young again, and cheerful, and brave" (190, 189, 190).

Though the "great Rising" could have become another Isandlwana (a major British loss in the Anglo-Zulu War [1879]) or even "a second and bloodier Indian Mutiny," it becomes instead a story of success (191, 53). Thanks to "the midnight shepherding of the 'heir of John' by Arcoll and his irregulars," an event facilitated by intelligence that Davie provided, Laputa—and thus ultimately the rising—is defeated; for, notwithstanding a force twenty-thousand strong (comprised of Zulus, Swazis, and "men from the north"), "Laputa *is* the Rising" (165, 106, 163). Indeed, as both he and Davie have foreseen, without his leadership the armies "blunder and fight and [are] beaten" and the rising soon "crumble[s]" (179, 160). Its leadership centralized, its warriors foregathered, and its wealth amassed in a single location, indigenous southern Africa's defeat, when it comes, is complete. Its general destroyed, its reserves plundered, and its hopes withered, its glorious crusade degenerates into an inglorious surrender.

Following Laputa's death, Davie proposes an "indaba" (gathering) between himself, Arcoll, and Laputa's chiefs, which, as Davie notes in his one concession to heroism, parallels the indaba between Cecil Rhodes and the Matabele in 1897 (196). Just as Rhodes famously walked unarmed into the Matoppos, so Davie and Arcoll "come in peace" to Inanda's kraal, voluntarily surrendering their pistols (195). Just as Rhodes convinced the Matabele to lay down their arms, so Davie convinces the chiefs to surrender, by claiming, in an "opportunistic interpretation of Laputa's final speech,"[72] that Laputa's "spirit approves"—even "mandate[s]"—his "mission" (197). Just as armed conflict in Mashonaland followed the truce reached in the Matoppos, so "months of guerilla fighting" "around the Swaziland and Zululand borders" follow the peace agreed upon at Inanda's kraal (190, 197). And just as the Second Matabele War (1896–1897) marked the demise of the Matabele kingdom, so the "Kaffir Rising" marks the end of "Africa for the Africans" (198, 73). By the end of the narrative, drums that once beat to signal the coming of the rising—as, notes a minor character, they had beat on the eve of Isandlwana (62)—now beat to "sound a . . . curfew" on "all the Kaffir farms" (203).

Though the bulk of the narrative is concerned with Davie's role in thwarting the rising, he is proudest of "the work of settlement" with which he and Aitken are "entrusted" (197). In the novel's most frequently cited passage, Davie claims:

> The task took many months. . . . Yet it was an experience for which I shall ever be grateful, for it turned me from a rash boy into a serious man. I knew then the meaning of the white man's duty. He has to take all risks, recking [sic] nothing of his life or his fortunes, and well content to find his reward in the fulfillment of his task. That is the difference between white and black, the gift of responsibility, the power of being in a little way a king. . . . Before we had got Laputa's army back to their kraals, with food enough to tide them over the spring sowing, Aitken and I had got sounder policy in our heads than you will find in the towns, where men sit in offices and see the world through a mist of papers. (197–98)

Painting his efforts as altruistic, Davie implies that he has saved rather than stifled the region's indigenous population. Seeing them firsthand rather than "through a mist of papers," deftly arranging for their shelter and sustenance, and caring for their welfare after the fall of their king, Davie has come to understand them in ways, he suggests, that officials never could. In addition, he has come to know himself not only as an adult but also, because he has done his "duty"—borne, that is, the white man's burden—as "in a little way a king."

Aitken and Wardlaw continue "the work [Davie] had a hand in starting" (203), constructing Africa for whites through the "re-education" of blacks, who are taught the skills that make them a useful labor force.[73] With some of the "great fortune" he made from the diamond pipe that had once supported the rising, Aitken establishes "a great native training college" in Blaauwildebeestefontein (202). "It [is] no factory for making missionaries and black teachers, but an institution for giving the Kaffirs the kind of training which fits them to be good citizens of the state. . . . [T]echnical workshop[s]" and "experimental farms" mold black Africans into second-class citizens in a land once their own, while "playing-fields and baths and reading rooms and libraries" attest to the white man's good intent (202). It is overseen by Wardlaw, who, in a letter to Davie, one of its "governors," writes: "I was never a man of war like you, and so I had to bide at home while you and your like were straightening out the troubles. But when it was all over my job began, for I could do what you couldn't do—I was the physician to heal the wounds" (202–03). In this Edenic vision of a modernized southern Africa, there is not a single Afrikaner, though every South African British man has a place: the warrior-governor (Davie), the financier-patron (Aitken), even the educator-healer (Wardlaw). Yet Davie, unlike Laputa, is dispensable, for while Laputa alone represents black dominion, white domination is everywhere apparent. As Davie himself puts it, he is "only one wheel in a great machine" (80). In his absence, the machine continues to function, fitting subjects to meet its needs.

Channeling indigenous "manhood[,]" once "exercise[d] in war," into labor that they oversee, British South Africans secure their place in the Union (203). For Stephen Gray, "the novel . . . goes past the normal resolution in the [adventure] genre into a general pamphleteering about how to pull the savage through into civilization." For Craig Smith, it serves as a "virtual blue-book recommendation[] for the correct administration of a colony."[74] But the novel is at least as much about British South African belonging as it is about indigenous pacification. Laying claim not only to whiteness but also to South African identity for its British inhabitants, *Prester John* is no less arrogation than prescription. According to the logic of the novel, it is the British not Laputa who are the rightful heirs of Prester John. "His last words were that the Rising was over," Davie tells Laputa's chiefs. "Respect that word, my brothers. We come to you not in war but in peace, to offer a free pardon, and the redress of your wrongs" (197). The pardon offered for the sin of rebellion is submission to the demands of an economy predicated not on brotherhood but on oppression.

"The last of the kings of Africa," however, "does not lack his monument" (202). The novel, which begins with the living Laputa circling a blazing fire under "the fitful moonlight" as he praises God on the Scottish shore, ends with the man, now a "big black statue," "looking far over the [Transvaal] plains to the Rooirand," the site of his defeat (7, 203, 202). Engraved "Prester John," though cast in Laputa's image, the monument is "set up" by Davie and Aitken (203). It is a tribute they can easily afford, for not only have they profited from his downfall, they have also turned "the heart of native reserves" into a version of the British countryside: its lake is "stocked with Lochleven trout," its orchards are ripe with fruit, and its pastures are "white with sheep" (21, 203). Gazing eternally over this pastoralized, anglicized, sun-drenched Africa, the immobile black figure "shad[es] his eyes with [both] hands" (300). Though the purpose of the gesture may have been to suggest the African's dazzlement by the splendor grown up about him, it can also be seen as a futile attempt to ward off the glare.

Conclusion

Africa, in Buchan's rendering, belongs not to a past rekindled by the blaze of a final, futile revolution but to a future imagined to have already arrived. Having yielded the "secrets of darkness" borne south from Abyssinia by the "doomed" descendants of Prester John, southern Africa emerges "a land for homesteads and orchards and children" (190, 180, 189). It is a vision that evinces a legacy too often whitewashed by those who, rightly attributing apartheid to Afrikaner nationalism, wrongly overlook its roots in British soil. Treating the anglicization of southern Africa as a foregone conclusion, the occlusion (Afrikaners) and elimination (Africans) of "racial" authority antithetical to Britishness signals an important generic shift. Devoid of darkness and mystery, Buchan's anglicized South Africa cannot sustain a genre contingent on these elements. The genre's demise and the Union's emergence thus go hand in hand.

If "Victorian imperialism and racism . . . painted an entire continent dark,"[75] *Prester John* tells a different story of its southernmost part, one in which darkness has been eliminated and "romance [has] died" (*PJ* 191). It is a perspective illustrated in the opening issue of *South Africa: A Weekly Journal for All Interested in South African Affairs* (1889): "No one may truly . . . call Africa the 'Dark Continent,' or the 'Unknown Land,' or any other of those romantic or unpractical names so much affected by the globe-trotter of the present day."[76] For if the myth of the Dark Continent suggests that a "benighted" Africa stands in need of the "light of civilization," the idea of a white South Africa suggests that civilization has already prevailed. If the myth of the Dark Continent developed, as Patrick Brantlinger has shown, out of the nineteenth-century discourses of abolition, "the great Victorian explorers," and Darwinian social science, the idea of a white South Africa developed out of the discourses of mineral wealth, emigration, and, eventually, union.[77]

"Do[ing] [his] countrymen a service such as no man in Africa could render," Davie not only prevents an "Armageddon," he altogether eliminates the threat of darkness from southern Africa (*PJ* 160, 147). Demolishing the last vestige "of an antique world," he destroys the possibility of opposition to the white southern Africa that he leaves behind (147). For *Prester John*, finally, celebrates not the individual but the empire to whose defense the private citizen readily comes. Ask not what your empire can do for you, the novel seems to suggest, reversing the transformative direction of the imperial romance; ask what you can do for your empire.[78] It is a question that Richard Hannay—the man Davie would have become had he stayed in southern Africa—would soon ask and answer, bringing South African Britishness, forged in opposition to forces poised to eject her, to the aid of the metropole itself now under siege.[79]

Epilogue

Beyond the British South African Novel

Part I: Richard Hannay in Britain and Europe

The closing pages of John Buchan's *Prester John* (1910) include a passage from "a recent letter" sent by Mr. Wardlaw, happily settled in southern Africa, to Davie, now enrolled in university in Scotland. "Come out and visit us soon, man," he writes, "and see the work you had a hand in starting. . . .'" In the novel's concluding sentence, Davie claims to be "thinking seriously of taking Wardlaw's advice."[1] With these final ambivalent words, Davie and southern Africa seemingly disappear from Buchan's fiction. Character and region persist in spirit, however, through Richard Hannay, who spent three decades in southern Africa. A Scottish-born amateur spy and military hero who comes to the empire's rescue in four novels (often referred to as a quartet) published between 1915 and 1924, Hannay illustrates this study's central premise: that southern Africa played an essential role in British literary developments from the 1880s to the 1920s, from the First Anglo-Boer War (1880–1881) and its aftermath to the First World War and its aftermath, from the New Woman novel to the spy thriller.[2] As with the other authorial informants discussed in *Beyond Gold and Diamonds*, so with Buchan: southern Africa remained for him a key point of reference, pervading his fiction and informing his identity. As the encounter between author/authorial informant and southern Africa compelled generic innovation in the form of the New Woman novel, the female colonial romance, and the Rhodesian settler romance, so it enabled *The Thirty-Nine Steps* (1915), "the first major version of the twentieth-century spy story."[3]

This bestselling novel was not only a model of the genre, it also introduced Hannay, the character most associated with its development. Like Lyndall and Jess, Benita and Rachel, and the Rhodesian heroines of Page's novels, Hannay is a product of southern Africa. Indeed, many of the skills that enable his success as a spy stem from his experience there. At the same time, he is "a true-blue English gentleman," "the very model of the 'clubland hero'—a sophisticated denizen of London's elite male clubs who could turn his good breeding, talents, and leisure time to the pursuit of patriotic espionage and, of course, the preservation of King and Country."[4] As it turns out, the Englishman at his best, the Englishman who England most needs, is a Scot who comes to his Englishness by way of southern Africa.

Certainly, *The Thirty-Nine Steps* has precursors, most notably invasion fiction and Buchan's own *Prester John*. Though George Chesney's *The Battle of Dorking* (1871) was perhaps the first novel to anticipate a German invasion of Britain, the genre really took off in the 1890s with popular novels by William Le Queux and E. Phillips Oppenheim that reflect anxieties about Germany's growing industrial and naval power.[5] Many titles have been proffered as the first spy thriller, most frequently Rudyard Kipling's *Kim* (1900), about the Great Game; Erskine Childers's *The Riddle of the Sands: A Record of Secret Service* (1903), about circumventing a German invasion; and Joseph Conrad's *The Secret Agent: A Simple Tale* (1907), about a partly homegrown terror plot in England. Referring to Kipling and Conrad, Michael Denning points out that their "novels about spies did not make them 'spy novelists.'"[6] This observation is also true of Le Queux, who wrote only the one novel. Though "critics generally agree that *The Thirty-Nine Steps* offers the first definitive expression of a previously embryonic popular genre," even those who do not still concede that Buchan established, in the words of novelist Graham Greene, "a pattern for adventure writers" for half a century.[7]

That pattern for British spy fiction persists well into the Cold War. Its elements include the spy in enemy territory, surveillance, the amateur hero, the ticking clock, the foreign villain, the cypher, and international stakes. The plot, centered on a chase, entails repeated close calls, a capture, and a "turnabout," in which "the quarry turns hunter."[8] Unlike the imperial adventure novel, the British spy thriller is "defensive rather than aggressive," "insular" rather than "expansionist," and "vigilan[t]" rather than "confident."[9] Denning writes offhandedly of the transition between the two genres: "it is a shift that we might mark for convenience at the South African War."[10] But there is nothing arbitrary about this shift. As I showed in chapter 4,

Buchan's experience during and after this war compelled him to signal the end of the imperial romance with *Prester John*, a novel that, despite its African setting and hidden treasure, anticipates the spy thriller more than it rehearses the imperial adventure novel. With the exception of the foreign villain, *Prester John* includes all of the genre's central elements. Infused with surveillance, as Yumna Siddiqi has shown, it "frequently dramatizes the clandestine observation of characters."[11]

When we first encounter Hannay, he is like the hero of an imperial adventure novel in the process of turning amateur spy. Years later, Hannay recognizes himself in H. Rider Haggard's most celebrated male quest romance: "I read *King Solomon's Mines* [1885] aloud to [my son] Peter John before a blazing fire, and added comments on it from my own experience."[12] Arriving in England for the first time at the age of thirty-seven, Hannay is initially disappointed with its mundanities. "The best bored man in the United Kingdom," he "ha[s] just about settled to clear out and get back to the veld" when he learns of a plot against Britain he is compelled to prevent.[13] With information that he gathers from deciphering a coded notebook while journeying through England and Scotland, Hannay stops the Germans from acquiring Britain's naval secrets on the eve of World War I. The conspiracy against Britain in *The Thirty-Nine Steps* is only the first of four conspiracies that Hannay thwarts. In *Greenmantle* (1916), set in England, Germany, and the Ottoman Empire in 1915 and 1916, he prevents Germany from inciting Muslims across the Near East and North Africa to join their side. In *Mr. Standfast* (1919), set in England, Scotland, France, and Switzerland in 1917 and 1918, he breaks up a group of German spies menacing the Allies across Europe. And in *The Three Hostages* (1924), set in England, Norway, and Scotland in the early 1920s, he prevents an Erse-speaking, Irish-descended English MP from employing anarchists, socialists, petty criminals, and mind control to destroy Western civilization.

Though Hannay's South African life is already behind him at the start of *The Thirty-Nine Steps*, his varied experiences throughout southern Africa and their utility to his current missions are revealed over the course of the quartet. At six, Hannay emigrated with his father from Scotland to southern Africa. An avid climber, Hannay "scrambled over almost every bit of upland south of the Zambesi, from the Hottentots Holland to the Zoutpansberg, and from the ugly yellow kopjes of Damaraland to the noble cliffs of Mont aux Sources."[14] His mountaineering proficiency means the difference between life and death when he climbs the Alps from Italy into Switzerland in *Mr. Standfast* and the Cuillin on the Isle of Skye in *The Three Hostages*. "Three years prospecting for copper in German Damaraland" made him extremely observant (*Steps* 21). Hunting on the veld along the Zambesi and Pungwe Rivers, he learned to tolerate discomfort with ease, to remain vigilant, and to navigate, skills he uses throughout the quartet. The "hundreds of times [he slept] alone beside [his] horse on the veld" prepare him for his solo journey across Europe in *Greenmantle*.[15] After all, he insists, "a sharp winter night on the high-veld was a long sight chillier than anything I had struck so far in Europe" (*Green* 90). Having "travelled . . . in rough places" and lived long out of doors (*Steps* 104), he can "go to bed supperless on the wet ground and wake whistling from pure light-heartedness" (*Island* 185). Hannay thrives out of doors, which proves essential for his traipses across England, Scotland, and Europe.

His time in southern Africa has equipped him to read both landscape and people. An expert at "veldcraft," he is a practiced map-reader and an able astronomer (*Steps* 21). And while, as he puts it, "my life on the veld has given me the eyes of a kite and I can see things for which most men need a telescope," he can also orient himself in other ways (49). "From long living in the wilds [he has] a kind of sense for landscape without testimony of the eyes" (*Mr.* 243). Similarly, by "a kind of instinct that men get who have lived much in wild countries," he feels the approach of an ally, knows when he is "being pursued," and has a "nose for finding out what [the] enem[y] [is] try[ing] to hide" (*Green* 91, 15). He is also adept at distinguishing truth from falsehood: as he says in *The Thirty-Nine Steps*, "I was enough of a hunter to know a true yarn when I heard it" (92). He has, says a character who enlists his aid in *The Three Hostages*, "a different kind of imagination" than the detectives at Scotland Yard, "and a rarer kind of courage." Mr. Macgillivray of Scotland Yard concurs: "You have a kind of knack of stumbling on truths which no amount of ordinary reasoning can get at."[16]

"Used to rough jobs," Hannay has strong nerves, a "steady heart" (*Steps* 97, 46), and the ability to keep his "wits" under pressure (*Green* 93). Although he is "pleased [by] uncertainty" (155) and imbued with a "devil-may-careness" (*Mr.* 238), he has the "old hunter's notion of order" and is as sound and unimpressionable "as Table Mountain" (*Three* 7, *Green* 169).[17] Having endured numerous bouts of malaria, he is able to stay focused even when weak with hunger, fatigue, or illness. Of this asset he remarks: "Once I had ridden for five days down country with fever on me and the flat bush trees had seemed to melt into one big mirage and dance quadrilles before my eyes" (93). His work as a mining engineer in

Rhodesia—"not a profession that weakens the nerves"—enables him to identify and calculate the force needed to detonate an explosive, and so to free himself from captivity in *The Thirty-Nine Steps* (46). He fought in the Second Matabele War (1896–1897) and worked as an "intelligence officer at Delagoa Bay [in Portuguese East Africa] during the Boer War," winning medals in both campaigns (25).[18] Although the full scope of his South African intelligence work remains hidden from readers, we do learn that he is "a swell at codes," cracking multiple cyphers over the course of the quartet (*Three* 271).

His adventures in southern Africa have also made him an able impersonator and impressive linguist. He goes undercover as a Lowland Scot, an Englishman, an Australian, a German, a Boer, and an American, while employing his knowledge of Dutch, the *taal* (Afrikaans), Sesutu (Sotho), and German. In *Mr. Standfast*, he dresses in "the relics of [his] South African wardrobe" to pass as a Boer (35).[19] Thanks to his "one run down the Zambesi," he manages to pass as a riverboat engineer in *Greenmantle*, bringing him closer to his rendezvous in Constantinople (106). In this guise, he speaks in Sesutu to communicate with his Boer ally without being understood by the Dutch-speaking captain. "Brought up to speak [German] pretty fluently," for his father had German business partners, Hannay also used the language while prospecting in German South West Africa (*Steps* 21). This background not only gives him access to information throughout the first three novels but also enables him to understand the minds and habits of its native speakers. For instance, in *The Thirty-Nine Steps*, he is able to determine the precise time and place where he and his allies can catch their German adversaries red-handed. "I know Germans," Hannay insists, "and they are mad about working to a plan" (94).

Hannay's adaptability extends to accent, affect, and class. On the run in the Scottish Highlands in *Mr. Standfast*, he "fall[s] into the broad Lowland speech" when he encounters a woman who "instinct" tells him is not from these parts (81). When a policeman on the lookout for a South African stops him shortly thereafter, he immediately adopts a new persona. "I advanced with a very stiff air, and asked him what the devil he meant. No Lowland Scots for me now. My tone was that of an adjutant of a Guards battalion" (83). When asked his name, he does "not reply in a colonial accent, but with the *hauteur* of the British officer when stopped by a French sentry" (83). The policeman not only accepts his bluff, he also takes him home, feeds him, puts him up for the night, and sends him on his way with sandwiches. In *The Thirty-Nine Steps*, he "passes himself off in turn as milkman, political candidate, road sweeper, tramp and shepherd," feigning a wide variety of professions and social positions.[20]

Hannay's friend and colleague, Peter Pienaar, a Boer "out of the Old Colony," shares many of these skills (*Green* 36). Hannay often recalls Peter's precepts in *The Thirty-Nine Steps*, while in the two novels that follow, readers see Peter in action. Among the jobs Peter has held in southern and central Africa, sometimes with Hannay at his side, are prospector, transport-rider, big-game hunter, guide, scout, and intelligence operative. Loyal to the empire, Peter uses his talents on its behalf in Europe, as he did in skirmishes in Mashonaland and Swaziland and in both the Second Matabele War and the Second Anglo-Boer War. His "rackety life" has made him an excellent combatant, tracker, map and Morse-code reader, disguise artist, and evader (*Mr.* 14).

"I have never known anyone so brave," notes Hannay of Peter; "all his life he had been facing death, and to take risks seemed to him as natural as to get up in the morning and eat his breakfast" (151). Matching courage with "sense," Peter prevents Germany's best pilot from carrying information "inside his own lines," which would have meant death for Hannay, their allies, and many "muddy British infantrym[e]n" (204, 131). "[T]o make certain of victory . . . he took the only way," crashing his plane into the enemy's at the cost of his own life (319). It is for him, steady to the end and an ardent admirer of John Bunyan's *The Pilgrim's Progress* (1678), that the quartet's third novel is named. Posthumously, he is awarded the Victoria Cross, "the highest honour that can be bestowed upon a soldier of Britain" (320). Hannay later names his son after him.[21] Nonetheless, Peter is a "faithful dog" and Hannay is a master; Peter is ultimately dispensable, while Hannay, now the Englishman, is not (127).[22] "As Hannay becomes more sophisticated, more the man of the world, the leader of Englishmen on the battlefield, the colonel, the brigadier and the general," writes Richard Usborne, "Peter becomes less of an example, less of an elder, less even of an equal."[23] For while Peter is "a kind of English" (*Green* 238), Hannay is quintessentially English, and the England whose banality at first so disappointed him ultimately proves to be the "blessed and happy place" in which he "burie[s] [his] heart" (*Mr.* 223, *Three*, 162).

In less than a decade, "the South African engineer called Dick Hannay" (*Sheep* 67) is transformed into "Sir Richard Hannay, K.C.B., who had commanded a division in France, and was the squire of Fosse Manor, the husband of Mary [an English wife], and the father of Peter John," an English son (*Three* 85). High up in the hills above Fosse Manor, his future home, Hannay realizes that he had become an "Englishman" (138):

> . . . in that hour England first took hold of me. Before my country had been South Africa, and when I thought of home it had been the wide sun-steeped spaces of the veld or some scented glen of the Berg. But now I realised that I had a new home. I understood what a precious thing this little England was, how old and kindly and comforting, how wholly worth striving for. (*Mr.* 17)

Just before this transformative "moment" in the Cotswolds, Hannay reads a letter Peter sent him from a German prisoner-of-war camp, "the smell of the woods behind [which] reminded him of a place in the Woodbush," the Transvaal tableland so beloved by Buchan (and the headquarters of police operations against the African rising in *Prester John*) (*Mr.* 16). "One could read in every sentence," reflects Hannay, "the ache of exile" (16). Though just three or four years earlier, undercover in Europe during the war, the "pleasant smell of wood smoke . . . made [Hannay] sick for the burning veld," it is an ache that Hannay, now at home in England, no longer feels (*Green* 161). Not so Haggard's Allan Quatermain, who in England feels "an almost unaccountable craving" to return to southern Africa.[24] Where Quatermain realizes that he must return, Hannay recognizes that he must remain—that he feels most at home in "the divine English countryside where Mary and I would one day make our home" (*Mr.* 193). Reflecting on Peter's letter while walking in that countryside, he also realizes the purpose of the war,

> what I had been fighting for, what we all were fighting for. It was peace, deep and holy and ancient, peace older than the oldest wars, peace which could endure when all our swords were hammered into ploughshares. . . . I saw not only victory after war, but a new and happier world after victory, when I should inherit something of this English peace and wrap myself in it till the end of my days. (16–17)

For Hannay, England and peace are interchangeable; to fight for the latter is to champion the former. Once the colonial from the edge of empire, he has become the guardian of its central ethos: "the priceless heritage which is England" (29).[25] Though he is initially resentful at being removed from active duty and reluctant "to serve again in the old [spy] game," his bucolic "revelation" shifts his outlook (10, 16). While surely "in for some arduous job, . . . whatever it was, I was ready for it, for my whole being had found new purpose" (17). Hannay, it turns out, needs England as much as England needs Hannay.

Nonetheless, he is initially unfamiliar with certain aspects of English custom, culture, and history. He "discover[s]," for instance, but does not initially know, "the right English manner" with which to greet one's guests—"with . . . friendly casualness"—just as he discovers "the British style" of bidding farewell—"without much to-do" (18, 287). As he embarks on the "pleasant country-gentleman's existence," he undertakes a program of cultural study (*Island* 11). First, he turns his attention to the "English classics," including *The Pilgrim's Progress* (which so infuses *Mr. Standfast*), works by William Hazlitt, and "the songs of the Elizabethans" (*Mr.* 26, 27). Next he focuses on English military history, "the only interest [he] ha[s] left in soldiering" after the world war (*Three* 3). Before long, having "dropped the 'General' " from his title and ensconced himself in Fosse Manor, Hannay is living a "happy vegetable life" (15, 13). "I've settled so deep into the country that I'm just an ordinary hayseed farmer," he insists (19). It is one of many attestations of normalcy: "My mind is weedy and grass-grown"; "I am the eternal average man"; there is "in me now" an "intractable bedrock of commonplaceness" (19, 215, 84).

But as one of his acquaintances pointedly asks in the midst of a reconnaissance: "Do English farmers travel in Norway under false names?" (184). Indeed, however much Hannay wishes himself typical, it is partly through his atypicality that he protects England, and in so doing (further) hybridizes Englishness. For the colonial essence that he only seems to shed attaches itself to the Englishness that he embraces, such that the English identity he ultimately inhabits is, like that of the authorial informant who created him, both metropolitan and colonial—that is, translocal.[26] Under his proprietorship, Fosse Manor is not simply an old squire's domain. It is a site to which more than one influential figure turns for assistance when the Foreign Office or Scotland Yard, bastions of English security, has failed them. Between its walls Hannay's young son builds not a fortress but "a kraal [hutted village or homestead] every morning," out of fabric and furniture (*Three* 7). Its butler is "a fellow [Hannay] had done a good turn to" in Rhodesia and "had inspanned . . . as [his] servant as soon as [he] got to England" (*Steps* 15). Although Hannay, after inhabiting the manor for two and a half years, calls himself "a Tory and a bit of a land-reformer" (*Green* 88), he is no mere "grandee" (*Island* 67). His forearm is "rough with old scars" (*Steps* 51). He can perform "the old Mashona [Shona] trick" of tossing a hunting knife into the air "and catching it in [his] lips" (46). And southern Africa, if decreasingly so, remains a point of reference: the scrub of a hill in Lisbon is "like the veld" (*Green* 36), the sound of guns in battle is "like the low growl of a veld thunderstorm" (*Mr.* 282), and Norwegian mountains are like the Drakensberg (*Three* 180).

Equipped with a broad set of skills that he acquired during his thirty-year residence in southern Africa, Buchan's most popular character defends "the Old Country" as "no one else can" (*Steps* 7, *Mr.* 11).[27] Though his value to the metropole stems primarily from his South African experience, he is rendered increasingly English as he engages his skills, time and again, on Britain's behalf. At the same time, he reinvigorates British identity, infusing it with just enough difference to preserve its integrity, while shutting out other, more radical differences, some of which—such as pacifism, trade unionism, and Eastern mysticism—are manifest in the quartet's villains. Hannay both enables Britain to maintain its "national character and independence" from the encroaching continent and obviates concessions to social and political demands, closely connected in the public imaginary to "threatening foreigner[s]."[28] A peripheral-born metropolitan who flourishes in southern Africa and heads to England once he has "got [his] pile," Hannay is both a vehicle of transformation and a means of defense (*Steps* 7).

On his way across Anatolia in *Greenmantle*, Hannay has a recurring nightmare in which, "hotly pursued [and] straining for some sanctuary," he spies a "little hill with a rocky top: what we call in South Africa a *castrol* or saucepan. I had a notion that if I could get to that *castrol* I should be safe" (243, 191). When Hannay and his companions are in fact chased by the enemy close to the front, they come across "the *castrol* of [his] persistent dream" (247). A concave circle, ten feet in diameter with a four-foot parapet atop a steep, boulder-strewn hill, the *castrol* is a natural fortress. Holding it long enough for Peter to pass intelligence (acquired by Hannay) to their allies across enemy lines, the men not only survive but also see their erstwhile pursuers crushed by the rout Peter's success brings about. The first time Hannay had the dream, he thought perhaps "it was a reminiscence of the veld" (191). Though the dream seems rather to have been a premonition, the *castrol* reminds readers of Hannay's years in southern Africa, as do his reflections while inside it, facing (he believes) imminent death: "The panorama of blue moons on the veld unrolled itself before me, and hunter's nights in the bush, . . . the joy of wild adventure" (260). As a first-rate spy, Hannay does more than recollect his South African experience, he also draws on it, every step of the way. In the First Anglo-Boer War, British South Africa, effectively denied the support that it sought from Britain, lost the Transvaal;

this convinced a young Rider Haggard that southern Africa "was no place for an Englishman."[29] Less than a generation later, Britain turned to southern Africa for assistance in World War I. In *The History of the South African Forces in France* (1920), Buchan documented this assistance. In the character of Hannay, who was born the year that Britain annexed the Transvaal and immigrated to southern Africa a year after its loss, Buchan materialized the importance of southern Africa to Britain's imperial identity. It seems that southern Africa was, after all, a very good place for an Englishman.

Part II: The First Novel in English by a Black South African

While Buchan was writing South Africa into the metropole in the British novel, Solomon Tshekisho Plaatje was writing Britain out of South Africa in the South African novel. Sol T. Plaatje, as he was better known, was a mission-educated Bechuana (Tswana) diarist, journalist, editor, translator, linguist, court interpreter, and founding secretary of what would become the African National Congress (ANC).[30] He was also the author of a single novel, *Mhudi* (1930).[31] The first full-length novel in English by a black South African,[32] *Mhudi* excludes the British, gives the Boers a key role, and makes black Africans the pivot of modern South African history. As others have noted, *Mhudi* is self-consciously hybrid, using both African idiom and the English language; orality and the novel form; African storytelling techniques, such as songs, gossip, anecdotes, folktales, and proverbs, and European literary genres, like the romance and the epic, to resist discursive and other violence against Africans. Shakespeare, Bunyan, Virgil, the Bible, and the imperial romance have all been cited as influences.[33] To this list I would add the female colonial romance, a specifically British South African literary genre. Used by Haggard to deny African claims to belonging, Plaatje deploys it instead to affirm them.

Set in the late 1820s and '30s, *Mhudi* focuses on the eponymous heroine and Ra-Thaga, members of the Barolong (Rolong), a branch of the Bechuana whom the Matabele (Ndebele) attack at Kunana.[34] Each thinking themselves Kunana's sole survivor, Mhudi and Ra-Thaga soon meet and wed, living first in a sylvan paradise they name "Re-Nosi (We-are-alone)" and later joining other Barolong at Thaba Nchu.[35] Following a Matabele attack on a group of *voortrekkers* (see next page), the Boers and the Bechuana combine forces, and with the assistance of the Griqua (mentioned only in passing) manage to defeat the Matabele.[36]

The violence and dispersal that *Mhudi* depicts, which are based on historical events, are part of the *Mfecane* and the Great Trek. The former refers to the "widespread warfare and resultant scattering of [African] ethnic groups" caused by "'state-building' amongst different polities in the region"—particularly the Matabele and the Zulu, of whom the Matabele are an offshoot—and the "disruptions unleashed by the labour demands of Cape colonists and [Portuguese] slave traders based at Delagoa Bay."[37] The Great Trek, which began during the *Mfecane*, refers to the north- and eastward migration in the 1830s and '40s of approximately ten thousand *voortrekkers,* Boers seeking to escape the reach of British authority.[38] ("The English laws of the Cape are not fair to us," says Sarel Cilliers, a historical *voortrekker* leader, in *Mhudi* [70].) While conflict among the various groups appears to be resolved at the novel's end, readers know it will continue. The Matabele will grow stronger, dominating indigenous groups farther north until they are decimated by Cecil Rhodes's British South Africa Company in the 1890s. The Boers (like the British) will far more often fight against than with the indigenous. And though the Boers and the British will ally at various points, war will erupt between them in two Anglo-Boer wars (1880–1881, 1899–1902), in the latter of which thousands of Africans will also participate, mainly on the British side.[39]

Orality, a central component of *Mhudi*, might be described as telling a story or the moral of a story likely to have been told before. In the novel's foreword, Plaatje draws a connection between storytelling and the preservation of history, at the same time establishing himself as both listener and teller. "While collecting stray scraps of tribal history, . . . the writer"—though he begins and ends the foreword in the first person, here he slides into third—"incidentally heard of" the novel's originating events: the death of Matabele "tax collectors" at the hands of the Barolong, from whom they came to collect what was more accurately "tribute" (*Mhudi* xi, 5). "Tracing this bit of information further back, he elicited [specifics] from old people" (xi). It was also from old people—among others, his grandmother—that Plaatje learned about his family history, which includes an ancestor named Mhudi and another named Noto (Notto—with two Ts—is the name of Ra-Thaga's father).[40] Yet in the foreword he neither mentions these familial connections nor suggests that "Mhudi was a 'real' historical figure."[41] It is an interesting lapse in a novel that "foreground[s] oral testimony [both] as a crucial source of historical information [and] as a narrative technique."[42] As the novel is an (enhanced and partly imagined) retelling of the details that Plaatje gathered, so the narrative purports to be a retelling, for readers discover in chapter 5 that the narrator, a "hoary octogenarian" named Half-a-Crown, is none other than the son of Mhudi and Ra-Thaga. From Ra-Thaga, Half-a-Crown learned, as he puts it, "exactly how my father and mother met and became husband and wife" as well as certain details about the *Mfecane*, with which his parents' story is entwined (79, 41).

Proverbs are a prominent form of orality in the novel, which has itself been described as an "enlarged folk-tale."[43] Plaatje first published some of the proverbs and folktales that *Mhudi* contains in *Sechuana Proverbs* (1916) and *A Sechuana Reader* (1916), respectively.[44] As he notes in the novel's foreword, one of the reasons he wrote *Mhudi* was to make money "to collect and print (for Bantu Schools) Sechuana folk-tales which, with the spread of European ideas, are fast being forgotten" (xi). Demonstrating orality's value as a resource and its embeddedness in indigenous South African cultures, the novel also directly helps to preserve "the shape and substance of oral history in its transition into written form."[45] Proverbs and folktales in *Mhudi* influence decision-making, assist in conflict, and predict the future, generally through reminders of the past.[46] As Tim Couzens points out, "there is a marked increase in the number of proverbs used by speakers during the crucial debate amongst the Barolong about whether they should help the Boers."[47] Concluding the matter, Moroka, the Barolong chief at Thaba Nchu, states: "Sarel and I will parry the Matabele assegai [spear] together. Old people say the quarry of two dogs is never too strong" (*Mhudi* 106). But proverbs are not always the best guides. Disregarding "the sober judgement of his clever wife," Ra-Thaga is instead led by a "Sechuana proverb which his comrade used to quote, viz., 'Never be led by a female lest thou fall over a precipice'" (57). He thus goes hunting with a man that "Mhudi warned him against" and nearly gets himself killed (57). The final words of the novel, spoken by Ra-Thaga to his wife, revisit that proverb, turning it on its head: "From henceforth I shall have no ears for the call of war or the chase; my ears shall be open only to one call—the call of your voice" (193). If this statement affirms a woman's value as a partner and her husband's recognition of that value, their male child's decision to close the novel with it suggests its generational resonance. That is to say, readers are witness to a proverb in the making.

Though Plaatje wrote *Mhudi* in the late 1910s and early '20s, he was unable to find a publisher until 1930, when Lovedale, a missionary press, agreed to publish it with some changes.[48] Most significantly, the Lovedale edition makes no mention of Half-a-Crown, thereby disabling the novel's function as a "living oral narrative" and undermining Plaatje's role as "scribe."⁴⁹ Lovedale further undercut the original manuscript's emphasis on orality by eliminating some of the proverbs. For instance, the proverb cited in the previous paragraph ("Old people say . . .") was omitted. And Ra-Thaga tells Mhudi that his "ears shall be open" not only to her but also to his chief.⁵⁰ Despite Plaatje's prominence as a political journalist, *Mhudi* received little attention and its political implications were largely overlooked when it first came out.⁵¹ In 1976, the original typescript was rediscovered and in 1978 the novel was finally published "as it was written."⁵² Since then, it has gained increasing attention from critics and others who view it as "a corrective view on history," for in addition to depicting early mid-nineteenth century events from an indigenous perspective, it engages with early twentieth-century South African politics.⁵³

Specifically, it serves as "an implicit attack on the injustice of land distribution in South Africa" following the Native Land Act of 1913.⁵⁴ This act, passed three years after the formation of the Union of South Africa, made it illegal for indigenous Africans to own or rent land anywhere except on specially designated native reserves. Allotting ninety-two percent of the most desirable land to South Africa's roughly 1.5 million whites, it forced approximately four million blacks onto eight percent of the land. The majority of indigenous Africans were removed from land they called home, which in some cases had been home to their people for centuries. Those pushed onto distant locations were divested of massive amounts of livestock. And many had little choice but to engage in wage labor for whites.⁵⁵ In its retelling of events that took place a century earlier, *Mhudi* draws a parallel between the Bechuana, dispossessed as a result of the *Mfecane*, and modern black South Africans more broadly, dispossessed as a result of the Land Act.⁵⁶

In a letter to his friend Silas Molema, a Barolong writer and ANC member like himself, Plaatje described *Mhudi* as "a novel—a love story after the manner of romances, but based on historical facts."⁵⁷ The novel tells the story of not one but three pairs of lovers: the Bechuana couple, Mhudi and Ra-Thaga; the Matabele couple, Mzilikazi and Umnandi; and the Boer couple, De Villiers and Hannetjie, each of whose ongoing migration is marked at the novel's end. If their various ethnicities represent the ethnic plurality of southern Africa and their continued migration suggests a national identity still in the making, the cross-ethnic friendships that they form point to the possibility of peaceful coexistence. These include both 1) Boer-Bechuana friendships, as between a) De Villiers and Ra-Thaga, and b) Hannetjie and Mhudi; and 2) Matabele-Bechuana friendships, as between a) Umnandi and Mhudi, and b) Umnandi and her servant, Nomsindo.⁵⁸ The novel, then, does more than critique the laws of an all-white government, it also intimates a way forward. Through both cross-ethnic alliances and cross-ethnic friendships, it calls for "co-operation and integration rather than domination and assimilation," even for "an extensive pan-ethnic southern African nationalism."[59]

In addition to being a history and a love story, *Mhudi* is also an adventure tale, as Plaatje himself put it, "like the style of Rider Haggard when he writes about the Zulus."[60] Others have drawn comparisons between *Mhudi* and Haggard's imperial romances, which both contain "romantic elements[,] . . . such as adventures, acts of heroism, love, chance, and supernatural events."[61] Some have suggested that *Mhudi* was influenced by Haggard's Zulu epic, *Nada the Lily* (1892). As Couzens notes, there are "obvious parallels" between the two: "The Eden of the beginning, the sacking of the town, the wanderings of the hero and heroine, the lion stories which are introduced to distinguish courage and cowardice, the tale-telling narrator, the entry of the Boers half-way through, the alliance of blacks and whites against 'cruel dictatorship,' the tales within tales."[62] Two-thirds of the way through *Nada the Lily*, the Weenen Massacre (of the Boers by the Zulus in 1838) and the Battle of Blood River (between the Boers and the Zulus later that year) are described at some length. Not much more, however, is said about the Boers, who, by way of contrast, figure prominently in *Mhudi*. Laura Chrisman identifies another important difference between the two novels: "Against a Haggardian . . . equation of national history with masculine warfare, [*Mhudi*] argues for the central place of African women—as political agents, not static domestic icons of tradition—in building a national narrative."[63] Other feminist critics have similarly noted that *Mhudi* makes women visible as agents of history and their own lives, not least through its portrayal of the heroine herself, who "goes against expected codes of gender behavior."[64] In this, the novel certainly differs from the male imperial romance, with the complicated exception of Haggard's *She* (1887), which paints a portrait of female despotism; but it does not, as some have implied, lack a precedent in adventure fiction.[65]

On the contrary, the female colonial romance, like *Mhudi*, foregrounds female heroism in ways that lays claim to South African belonging. It is a genre that Plaatje seems to have read, given the plot points it shares with his novel. In *Benita* (1906), for instance, the English heroine, her father, and another white man form an alliance with the Makalanga against the Matabele, much as in *Mhudi*, the Boers and Bechuana join forces against the Matabele. In both novels, guns provided by the whites are crucial to the defeat of the Matabele. And in both, a prisoner (or prisoners) of the Matabele (Robert in *Benita*, Sarel van Zyl and Taolo in *Mhudi*) forestalls his death and buys his allies time by claiming to assist the captors he is actually undermining. In both *The Ghost Kings* (1908) and *Mhudi*, a light in the sky—a meteor in the former, Halley's Comet in the latter—is a harbinger of bloody conflict. In *The Ghost Kings*, set at almost exactly the same time as Plaatje's novel, Dingaan (Dingane), King of the Zulus, asks the young white heroine, Rachel, for advice about the *voortrekkers*. "'Shall I fall upon the Boers or let them be?' Rachel looked upwards, studying the stars [and] it chanced that a bright meteor . . . swept across the sky to burst and vanish over the kraal of the king." Commanded by Dingaan to read "the omen," Rachel declines, answering his question about the Boers instead: "*Those who lift the spear shall perish by the spear.* . . . Read you the omen as you will. . . . I also hear the feet of a people travelling over plain and mountain, and *the rivers behind them run red with blood*. Are they black feet or white feet? Read ye the omen as ye will." Intentionally ambiguous, Rachel forestalls the war that she knows "must come."[66] In *Mhudi*, Mzilikazi, King of the Matabele, "ask[s] the principal national wizard to throw bones and communicate any omens he could divine" (135). Examining his bones, the wizard reveals: "Away in the distance I can see a mighty star in the skies, with a long white tail[,] . . . [w]ithin [whose] rays . . . I can clearly see streams of tears and *rivers of blood*" (135; emphasis added). He goes on to predict that the star "would cause terror and destruction unless [the Matabele] move the[ir] nation" (148). Only after being defeated by the Boer-Bechuana-Griqua alliance does Mzilikazi take heed, leading his people across the Limpopo River. Another similarity: in both *Benita* and *The Ghost Kings*, the heroine's lover is mistakenly presumed dead, while in *Mhudi*, Ra-Thaga is erroneously reported dead three times, once as a tiger's (leopard's) prey, once as a captured spy, and once as a warrior on the battlefield.

The most notable characteristic that *Mhudi* has in common with the female colonial romance is female empowerment, which Plaatje supported.[67] In the female colonial romance, the heroine resists the advances of a predatory man who either attempts to kill her lover or threatens to kill her father. Mhudi outwits a Koranna headman who tries to kill her husband and take her as a wife. In the female colonial romance, the heroine saves her lover from death. As Mhudi's Boer friend, Hannetjie, observes to Ra-Thaga: "you bear the scars of a tiger's claws on your face, a tiger's fangs on your arm and Mzilikazi's spear on your shoulder; and, although the wounds were inflicted far out in the wilderness, [Mhudi] turned up each time and nursed you back to health" (*Mhudi* 191). "She made me what I am," Ra-Thaga tells De Villiers; "Mhudi is 'the whole of my pluck'" (160, 191). The heroine of the female colonial romance repeatedly faces danger. Mhudi not only survives the Matabele attack on Kunana, she also "thrice face[s] the king of beasts [a lion] and [ultimately] kill[s] one with her own hand" (47). Two years before she meets Ra-Thaga, she stands calm as the roar of a lion "shook the earth beneath [her] feet, and bathed [her] face in its steaming saliva" (51). It is a story "known far and wide," even to Mzilikazi and Ra-Thaga, who is astonished to learn that she is "the heroine of Motlhokadiste, whose bravery was the pride of the countryside! Why," he predicts, "the thrilling talk of your adventure will live as long as there breathes a member of our tribe" (51). In the second instance, she comes across a lion devouring its prey, manages to flee, then returns with Ra-Thaga to scare it off. And on the final occasion, she drives a spear into a lion's heart, saving her husband's life. In the female colonial romance, indigenous warriors salute the heroine in recognition of her courage. De Villiers gives Mhudi an ox-wagon, for, he says, as "the only Rolong woman who had been to the front, [she] was entitled to some permanent and useful souvenir of her own adventure" (189).

An important component of the female colonial romance is at least one cross-cultural alliance between women. Of the four central cross-ethnic friendships in *Mhudi*, three are between women. As in the female colonial romance, they are founded on trust and affection, emerge or are strongest in the absence of men, and benefit both women. Mhudi and Umnandi for instance, become "beloved friend[s]" as they travel to their husbands, whom they seek to support in their time of need (170). Before the women part, Mhudi advises Umnandi to "urge [Mzilikazi] to give up wars and adopt a more happy form of manly sport" (169). While Mhudi has little regard for the Matabele leader, she blames men more generally. "How wretched [it is] that men in whose counsel we have no share should constantly wage war," she laments to her "Matabele Sister" (169, 170). "What will convince them of the worthlessness of this game, I wonder?" (169). Is it, readers are left to wonder, women like Mhudi herself? The novel's final passage seems to suggest so, as Ra-Thaga promises his wife to listen to her (as quoted on page 166).

Mhudi looks to the past, but it also signals a beginning. As black South Africans were increasingly shut out of the new nation, Plaatje inscribed them into the record as contributors, in his novel as in his nonfiction. Unlike most British South African writers, Plaatje neither marginalizes nor vilifies Africans, nor does he portray a singular, exceptional "noble savage." Rather, he presents in *Mhudi* a variety of African characters, communities, and perspectives. "Against the failures" that result from the "impetuosit[y]" of Chief Tauana, the Barolong chief at Kunana, the autocracy of King Mzilikazi, and the selfishness of his son Langa, he depicts "the democratic wisdom" of others, Bechuana and Matabele alike.[68] Mhudi is only the most heroic of many brave, wise, and above all multifaceted characters whose histories, traditions, and practices, the novel suggests, are an asset to South Africa. Though the government would continue to pass laws excluding Africans, it could not drown out their voices. Joining African orality with elements of British—including specifically British South African—literary forms, *Mhudi* signals the insistent, persistent hybridity of black South African writing and resistance that continues to this day.

Notes

A Note on Terminology

1. James Stewart, "Southern Africa: Past and Present," *Scottish Geographical Magazine*, vol. 7, no. 4, Apr. 1891, 179.

Introduction. A Single Frame: Southern Africa, Britain, and the Authorial Informant

1. Cynthia Stockley, *Poppy: The Story of a South African Girl*, Putnam, 1910, 226. Stockley was the pseudonym of Lillian Julia Webb (1873–1936). Born in South Africa to British emigrants, she wrote more than a dozen romance novels, many of which she set in southern Africa. In *Poppy*, the heroine goes to England to escape a controlling man, only to discover that she is pregnant as the result of a single sexual encounter that she had with someone else in South Africa. Though her "love baby" dies in infancy and Poppy undergoes other hardships in England, she eventually becomes a successful playwright, novelist, and poet (267). "Starved for want of the wind and trees and flowers, anything that smelt of open free spaces such as she had known all her life until now," Poppy returns to South Africa three years after her departure and marries the man who had fathered her child (253). The novel was popular in part for "its frank discussion of sex problems, which was then becoming the vogue among many women-writers" (Manfred Nathan, *South African Literature: A General Survey*, Juta, 1925, 226). For a bit more on Stockley and much more on sexuality in the Rhodesian settler romance, see my chapter 3.

2. These titles might have included *South Africa*; *African Review of Mining, Finance and Commerce*; *European Mail*; *South African Empire*; *South African News*; *African Critic*; and *Cape and Natal News*. See "A Note on Terminology" at the beginning of this book.

3. "*South Africa: A Weekly Journal*," advertisement, *The Guide to South Africa for the Use of Tourists, Sportsmen, Invalids and, Settlers, 1896–1897*, ed. A. Samler Brown and G. Gordon Brown, Juta, 1896, inside cover. Mathers had previously

worked as a journalist in both England and southern Africa and had also published *Golden South Africa* (1887); *Zambesia: England's El Dorado in Africa* (1891); and a guidebook, *South Africa and How to Reach It by the Castle Line* (1889), distributed by Castle Line free of charge.

4. "To Advertisers," supplement to *South Africa: A Weekly Journal for All Interested in South African Affairs*, 9 Nov. 1889, n.p.

5. *South Africa: A Weekly Journal for All Interested in South African Affairs*, 2 July 1898, 7. The journal was produced until 1961, when South Africa, following a 1960 referendum on the matter, proclaimed itself a republic and left the Commonwealth of Nations. The journal was so popular that between 1901 and 1921 it published nearly one hundred separate *"South Africa" Handbooks*, using material that had originally appeared in its pages. Among the handbooks were several on immigration; an eight-part series on "South African Exploration"; and a twenty-nine part series originally titled "South African Stories and Sketches," which was later changed to "South African Sketches and Stories," and later still to "Sketches of South African Life and Incident."

6. Starting with its second issue (Oct. 1906), the short-lived *South African Book Buyer: A Monthly Guide to Literature* (1906–1907) appropriated this notional representation, substituting the ships for a book, encircled by a ribbon bound on one end to St. Paul's Cathedral and on the other to Table Mountain.

7. Under the Boers, the Transvaal was the South African Republic, though the British referred to it as the Transvaal more often than not. After the Boers lost the Second Anglo-Boer War, the British took over the Orange Free State, renaming the erstwhile republic the Orange River Colony. When the Union of South Africa was formed in 1910, the region became the Province of the Orange Free State. See "A Note on Terminology" at the beginning of this book.

8. The Portuguese, Dutch, and British all landed ships on the Cape of Good Hope in the 1600s. And though in 1620 the British even planted a flag on the shore of this "half-way house to India," it only became a European colony in 1652, when the Dutch East India Company took formal possession for Holland (Dorothea Fairbridge, *A History of South Africa*, Oxford UP, 1918, 29; the same phrasing, but without the hyphen, appears in William Greswell, *Our South African Empire*, vol. 1, Chapman, 1885, 29). The Dutch then ceded it to the British in 1795, took it back in 1802, and turned it over once again in 1806. The more than twenty thousand Dutch-, German-, and French Huguenot–descended settlers who had made the Cape their home, as well as many thousands more indigenous, at that point became British subjects (Deryck Schreuder, "Colonial Nationalism and 'Tribal Nationalism': Making the White South African State, 1899–1910," *The Rise of Colonial Nationalism: Australia, New Zealand, Canada and South Africa First Assert Their Nationalities, 1880–1914*, ed. John Eddy and Schreuder, Allen & Unwin, 1988, 205). In 1820, four thousand men, women, and children emigrated from Britain under a government-sponsored scheme, with another one thousand following in the

next two years. In 1867, "the richest diamond fields in the world" were discovered on land that was soon incorporated into British territory, and in 1884, "the first important gold field [was discovered] in the Transvaal," at that time a Boer republic (M. F. W. Reitz, *A Century of Wrong*, Review of Reviews, 1899, 20; George M. Fredrickson, *White Supremacy: A Comparative Study in American and South African History*, Oxford UP, 1981, 284). Two years later, Johannesburg was founded along the nearby Witwatersrand (or "the Rand," as the escarpment was known), the site of the "richest gold-mines in the world" (Fairbridge 272).

9. *Advice to Emigrants*, South Africa, n.d., 14, *"South Africa" Handbook*, no. 1. The quotation is from C. W. de Kiewiet, *A History of South Africa, Social and Economic*, Oxford UP, 1941, 119.

10. Elaine Unterhalter, "Constructing Race, Class, Gender and Ethnicity: State and Opposition Strategies in South Africa," *Unsettling Settler Societies: Articulations of Gender, Race, Ethnicity and Class*, ed. Daiva Stasiulis and Nira Yuval-Davis, Sage, 1995, 217. Schreuder 211. For more statistics, see pages 13–14 in this introduction.

11. See "A Note on Terminology" at the beginning of this book and note 8 in the introduction.

12. The Shona, who fought with the Matabele (Ndebele) against the British in 1896–1897, refer to it as the First Chimurenga (uprising).

13. For more on the colonization of Rhodesia, see Robert H. MacDonald, who provides the 1890 figure (*The Language of Empire: Myths and Metaphors of Popular Imperialism, 1880–1918*, Manchester UP, 1984, 112–43, with figure on 115) and my chapter 3, pages 111–13. Dane Kennedy provides a table of Rhodesia's European population, taken from Southern Rhodesia's 1952 *Official Yearbook of Southern Rhodesia* (Kennedy, *Islands of White: Settler Society and Culture in Kenya and Southern Rhodesia, 1890–1937*, Duke UP, 1987, 197, table 4).

14. Olive Schreiner, *The South African Question by an English South African*, Sergel, 1899.

15. John Buchan, *The African Colony: Studies in the Reconstruction*, Blackwood, 1903, 91; Buchan prefaces the phrase, which he puts in quotation marks, with, "as the phrase goes." He himself uses it on multiple occasions, including: *A Lodge in the Wilderness*, Blackwood, 1906, 171, 237; *Memory Hold-the-Door*, Hodder, 1940, 112; and *Comments and Characters*, ed. W. Forbes Gray, Nelson, 1940, 121. Morag Bell, "A Woman's Place in 'A White Man's Country.' Rights, Duties, and Citizenship for the 'New' South Africa, c. 1902," *Cultural Geographies*, vol. 2, no. 2, 1995, 130. H. H. Johnston, "The White Man's Place in Africa," *The Nineteenth Century and After*, vol. 55, no. 328, June 1904, 942.

16. Harry H. Johnston, "South African Interest in South Africa," *African Monthly*, vol. 1, no. 3, Feb. 1907, 265. "To-day every London shopboy knows what this wilderness of coarse green or brown grasses is like; he can picture the dry streams, the jagged kopjes [small hills], the glare of summer, and the bitter winter cold" (Buchan, *African Colony* 80). "People out here have a very ingenious way of

greeting their friends in the incoming steamers. They flash a welcome by means of a mirror, and it is quite a pretty sight to see the flashes from the various houses" ("A Lady's Trip to South Africa. No. 2," *South Africa: A Weekly Journal for All Interested in South African Affairs*, vol. 26, no. 333, 18 May 1895, 332).

17. *In Darkest Africa* (1890) is the title of a two-volume book by journalist and explorer Henry Morton Stanley, but the concept predated his text. As Patrick Brantlinger explains, "the Myth of the Dark Continent was largely a Victorian invention" based on three central discourses: antislavery, African exploration, and anthropology (the quotation is from *Rule of Darkness: British Literature and Imperialism, 1830–1914*, Cornell UP, 1988, 195, but Brantlinger first and most extensively makes his case in "Victorians and Africans: The Genealogy of the Myth of the Dark Continent," *Critical Inquiry*, vol. 12, no. 1, Autumn 1985, 166–203).

18. Joseph Conrad, *Heart of Darkness*, ed. Ross C. Murfin, 3rd ed., Bedford, 2011, 51, Case Studies in Contemporary Criticism.

19. The phrase "impotent witness of good conscience" was suggested to me by Jed Esty, in conversation.

20. J. M. Coetzee, *White Writing: On the Culture of Letters in South Africa*, Yale UP, 1988, 3. While British whiteness occupies the summary position in a triad of British, black African, and Boer, those of mixed race figure only minimally and Asians almost not at all. See the section "The Fiction of Race" later in this chapter.

21. James Belich, *Replenishing the Earth: The Settler Revolution and the Rise of the Anglo-World, 1783–1939*, Oxford UP, 2009, 153.

22. As a noun, colonial was sometimes used to distinguish the colonial born from the immigrant. I use it more expansively to refer not only to those born and raised in southern Africa (such as Schreiner) but also to those who immigrated there (such as Page, though she continued to spend significant time in Britain), as well as to those who came temporarily but considered remaining permanently (such as Haggard and to a lesser extent Buchan).

23. Robert Fraser, *Victorian Quest Romance: Stevenson, Haggard, Kipling, and Conan Doyle*, Northcote House, 1998, 16. John M. Mackenzie, *Propaganda and Empire: The Manipulation of British Public Opinion, 1880–1960*, Manchester UP, 1984, 2. Paula M. Krebs, *Gender, Race, and the Writing of Empire: Public Discourse and the Boer War*, Cambridge UP, 1999, 145–46. Bill Schwarz, "The Romance of the Veld," *The Round Table, The Empire/Commonwealth and British Foreign Policy*, ed. Andrea Bosco and Alex May, Lothian Foundation, 1997, 69. Krebs 145.

24. John Seeley (whose original [1883] comment seems to have been tongue-in-cheek), quoted (also with skepticism) in James Stewart, "Southern Africa: Past and Present," *Scottish Geographical Magazine*, vol. 7, no. 4, Apr. 1891, 184.

25. "Lord Grey on South Africa," *South Africa: A Weekly Journal for All Interested in South African Affairs*, vol. 1, no. 5, 2 Feb. 1889, 30. Cf. "Except in one or two quarters where timeworn fallacy dies hard, or where conviction born even of facts seems naught but heresy, it is needless in these days to justify the existence of the colonist. No longer can the colonist, when revisiting the Mother Country, regard himself as

a pariah or an alien. No longer need he seek to hide his identity, or slur over his association with things colonial" (John Robinson, "The Colonies and the Century," *Proceedings of the Royal Colonial Institute*, no. 30, Royal Colonial Institute, 1899, 324).

26. Walter Peace, *Our Colony of Natal: A Handbook for the Use of Intending Emigrants and Others*, 2nd (rev.) ed., Stanford, 1884, 7.

27. Gayatri Chakravorty Spivak, *A Critique of Postcolonial Reason: Toward a History of the Vanishing Present*, Harvard UP, 1999, 6.

28. See note 22 in this introduction.

29. Haggard, quoted in Kriston Sites, *In and Out of Africa: The Adventures of H. Rider Haggard*, Lilly Publication, no. 55, Lilly Library, 1995, 59. "Haggard had 10,000 copies of the speech printed for immediate distribution under the title, 'A Call to Arms to the Men of East Anglia'" (59). In contemporary imperial discourse broadly and in southern Africa specifically, English was often used to designate what was more correctly British; it is particularly interesting when this is done by someone Irish, Welsh, or Scottish. Regarding this use of "English" generally, see MacDonald 11; Ian Baucom, *Out of Place: Englishness, Empire, and the Locations of Identity*, Princeton UP, 1999, 10; and John Darwin, *The Empire Project: The Rise and Fall of the British World-System, 1830–1970*, Cambridge UP, 2009, 9. Regarding its use in southern Africa, see Darwin 219; and John Lambert, "'An Unknown People': Reconstructing British South African Identity," *Journal of Imperial and Commonwealth History*, vol. 37, no. 4, 2009, 601, doi.org/10.1080/03086530903327101.

30. Both Haggard and Buchan stood for political office, the former unsuccessfully for the Eastern Division of Norfolk in 1895, the latter successfully for the Combined Scottish Universities in 1927 (a position that he held until he was appointed governor general of Canada in 1935). Schwarz writes that around the turn-of-the-century, "the author-as-celebrity cashed his status as an early media star in order to try for a political career" ("Romance" 69).

31. Krebs 145.

32. Haggard declined to serve as a war correspondent for the *Times* and instead agreed to write a series of articles for the *Daily Express* after the war, though in the end he did not do so (H. Rider Haggard, *The Private Diaries of Sir H. Rider Haggard, 1914–1925*, ed. D. S. Higgins, Cassell, 1980, 134). Schreiner, who had been asked regularly for her opinion by overseas newspapers since the Jameson Raid—Britain's failed 1895–1896 attempt to incite a British rebellion in the Transvaal—turned down a number of requests and offers (Ruth First and Ann Scott, *Olive Schreiner*, Schocken, 1980, 224, 221).

33. John Robinson, *Notes on Natal: An Old Colonist's Book for New Settlers*, Robinson & Vause, 1872, 90. Gertrude Page, *Follow After!*, Hurst, 1915, 142. Robinson, *Notes* 90.

34. Though Buchan would later serve as the first governor general of Canada, a dominion nation that would also shape him, his service there did not diminish the connection he felt with southern Africa.

35. Tony Ballantyne, "Race and the Webs of Empire: Aryanism from India to the Pacific," *Journal of Colonialism and Colonial History*, vol. 2, no. 3, Winter 2001, doi:10.1353/cch.2001.0045. Tony Ballantyne and Antoinette Burton, "The Politics of Intimacy in an Age of Empire," Introduction, *Moving Subjects: Gender, Mobility, and Intimacy in an Age of Global Empire*, ed. Ballantyne and Burton, U of Illinois P, 10. See also Darwin 1. See James Mulholland on the concept's origins in the social sciences ("Translocal Anglo-India and the Multilingual Reading Public," *PMLA*, vol. 135, no. 2, Mar. 2020, 273).

36. See Mary Louise Pratt's foundational *Imperial Eyes: Travel Writing and Transculturation*, Routledge, 1992, especially the introduction.

37. Rhodesia, which did not join the Union of South Africa, became the Republic of Zimbabwe in 1980. See also note 13 in this chapter.

38. Gertrude Page, "Farm Life in Rhodesia: Visit to Victoria Falls," *Empire Review*, vol. 12, no. 68, Sept. 1906, 162.

39. Buchan, *Memory* 118. Cynthia Stockley, *Wild Honey*, Grosset, 1914, 86. "The Call of the South," *Social South Africa: Some Hints to Lady Settlers*, South Africa, n.d., 22, *"South Africa" Handbook*, no. 44, originally published in *South Africa: A Weekly Journal for All Interested in South African Affairs*, May 1908.

40. Lilias Rider Haggard, *The Cloak That I Left: A Biography of the Author Henry Rider Haggard K.B.E.*, Hodder, 1951, 172. H. R. Haggard, *Allan Quatermain* 3. H. R. Haggard, *Private Diaries* 114. "Sir Rider Haggard. Ethics of Literature," *Sydney Morning Herald*, 12 Apr. 1913, 9. Haggard, *Private Diaries* 74.

41. Andrew Lownie, *John Buchan: The Presbyterian Cavalier*, Constable, 1995, 243.

42. Saree Makdisi, "Riding the Whirlwind of Settler Colonialism," review of *Replenishing the Earth: The Settler Revolution and the Rise of the Anglo-World, 1783–1939*, by James Belich, *Victorian Studies*, vol. 53, no. 1, Autumn 2010, 113.

43. Darwin 3. Belich 114.

44. See for example Antoinette Burton, *Burdens of History: British Feminists, Indian Women, and Imperial Culture, 1865–1915*, U of North Carolina P, 1994; Catherine Hall, *Civilizing Subjects: Colony and Metropole in the English Imagination, 1830–1867*, U of Chicago P, 2002; and Philippa Levine, ed., *Gender and Empire*, Oxford UP, 2004, Oxford History of the British Empire Companion Series.

45. Darwin is quite right to point out that "the place of the white dominions has been all but ignored by two generations of imperial historiography" (15). Duncan Bell notes that this has been the case even in the new imperial history ("Victorian Visions of Global Order: An Introduction," *Victorian Visions of Global Order*, ed. Bell, Cambridge UP, 2007, 14).

46. Annie E. Coombes, ed., *Rethinking Settler Colonialism: History and Memory in Australia, Canada, Aotearoa New Zealand, and South Africa*, Manchester UP, 2006.

47. Laura Chrisman, *Rereading the Imperial Romance: British Imperialism and South African Resistance in Haggard, Schreiner, and Plaatje*, Clarendon, 2000, 1–2.

Gayatri Chakravorty Spivak's work, notes Chrisman, "is indicative of the dominant theoretical and literary place accorded to India" (1). See also Sara Suleri, *The Rhetoric of English India*, U of Chicago P, 1992; Jenny Sharpe, *Allegories of Empire: The Figure of Woman in the Colonial Text*, U of Minnesota P, 1993; Nancy L. Paxton, *Writing Under the Raj: Gender, Race, and Rape in the British Colonial Imagination, 1830–1947*, Rutgers UP, 1999; Baucom; and John Plotz, *Portable Property: Victorian Culture on the Move*, Princeton UP, 2008.

48. Jude Piesse, *British Settler Emigration in Print, 1832–1877*, Oxford UP, 2016, 4, 11–12.

49. Jason R. Rudy, *Imagined Homelands: British Poetry in the Colonies*, Kindle ed., Johns Hopkins UP, 2017, introduction. While Rudy's "'colonial laureates,' . . . acted as arbiters of poetic taste and culture," authorial informants innovated generically but had little influence over or interest in "taste."

50. Tamara S. Wagner, ed., *Victorian Settler Narratives: Emigrants, Cosmopolitans and Returnees in Nineteenth-Century Literature*, Pickering & Chatto, 2011, 3, Gender and Genre 5. Tamara S. Wagner, ed., *Domestic Fiction in Colonial Australia and New Zealand*, Pickering & Chatto, 2015, Gender and Genre 13. Tamara S. Wagner, *Victorian Narratives of Failed Emigration: Settlers, Returnees, and Nineteenth-Century Literature in English*, Routledge, 2016.

51. See, for example, Robert Dixon, *Writing the Colonial Adventure: Race, Gender and Nation in Anglo-Australian Popular Fiction, 1875–1914*, Cambridge UP, 1995; Tanya Dalziell, *Settler Romances and the Australian Girl*, U of Western Australia P, 2004; and Janet C. Myers, *Antipodal England: Emigration and Portable Domesticity in the Victorian Imagination*, State U of New York P, 2009.

52. Chrisman, *Rereading* 1.

53. "The phrase *white writing*," Coetzee explains, does not "imply the existence of a body of writing different in nature from black writing. White writing is white only insofar as it is generated by the concerns of people no longer European, not yet African" (11). Afrikaans was not made an official language of South Africa until ten years after the formation of the union. Its forerunner, the *taal* (language), was an antiquated version of Dutch that had morphed over time through contact with other languages in southern Africa. Examples of apartheid-era studies of "black writing" include Ursula A. Barnett, *A Vision of Order: A Study of Black South African Literature in English (1914–1980)*, Browne and U of Massachusetts P, 1983; D. B. Ntuli and C. F. Swanepoel, *Southern African Literature in African Languages: A Concise Historical Perspective*, Acacia, 1993; and A. C. Jordan, *Towards an African Literature: The Emergence of Literary Form in Xhosa*, U of California P, 1973, which is also an example of ethnocentric analysis. See "A Note on Terminology" at the beginning of this book.

54. Nathan 13.
55. Nathan 13, 12–13.
56. Nathan 123.

57. David Attwell, "South African Literature in English," *The Cambridge History of African and Caribbean Literature*, vol. 2, ed. F. Abiola Irele and Simon Gikandi, Cambridge UP, 2008, 507. The final chapter of Gray's book is titled "The Emergence of Black English" (Stephen Gray, *Southern African Literature: An Introduction*, Barnes & Noble, 1979).

58. Coetzee 4.

59. David Attwell and Derek Attridge, Introduction, *The Cambridge History of South African Literature*, ed. Attwell and Attridge, Cambridge UP, 2012, 4.

60. Attwell and Attridge 7. See also Johannes A. Smit, Johan van Wyk, and Jean-Philippe Wade, eds., *Rethinking South African Literary History*, Y, 1996.

61. Michael Chapman, *Southern African Literatures*, Longman, 1996.

62. Christopher Heywood, *A History of South African Literature*, Cambridge UP, 2004. Consider, as well, how in the final section of the introduction to his *South African Textual Cultures*, Andrew van der Vlies lays out what follows under the heading, "From Schreiner to Mda, 1883–2005" (Manchester UP, 2007, 12).

63. There are, however, a handful of monographs that deal, in whole or part, with British writing about southern Africa. In *White Skins/Black Masks: Representation and Colonialism*, Gail Ching-Liang Low convincingly argues that Haggard's African fiction depicts English masculinity reinvigorated through its encounter with African "savagery," specifically the Zulus (Routledge, 1996, 6). Though her focus is on several of the Quatermain novels, she brings *Nada the Lily* (1892), Haggard's long overlooked Zulu epic, into the critical purview. In *Gender, Race, and the Writing of Empire: Public Discourse and the Boer War*, Krebs does a superb job of demonstrating that partly as a result of the Second Anglo-Boer War, "the press and reading publics . . . accord[ed] authority to imaginative writers on questions of empire" (144). As I note on pages 6–7 of this chapter, her argument lends itself to my concept of the authorial informant. Chrisman's *Rereading the Imperial Romance: British Imperialism and South African Resistance in Haggard, Schreiner, and Plaatje* explores the tensions between various mid- and late-century ideologies at work in the authors named in its subtitle. While important, these texts reflect the predominance of Schreiner and Haggard, almost to the exclusion of others, in scholarship on British South African literature.

64. On this literary paucity, see Nathan 200; and J. P. L. Snyman, from whom the novel figure comes, *The South African Novel in English (1880–1930)*, U of Potchefstroom for C.H.E., 1952, 171, U Lig Series. On poetry, see Nathan 169–94.

65. W. T. Stead, "The Novel of the Modern Woman," *Review of Reviews*, vol. 10, 1894, 65.

66. Anne McClintock, *Imperial Leather: Race, Gender and Sexuality in the Colonial Contest*, Routledge, 1995, 283. D. S. Higgins, *Rider Haggard: The Great Storyteller*, Cassell, 1981, 117. Martin Green, *Seven Types of Adventure Novels: An Etiology of a Major Genre*, Penn State UP, 1991, 31.

67. See Cecil Degrotte Eby, *The Road to Armageddon: The Martial Spirit in English Popular Literature, 1870–1914*, Duke UP, 1987, 182–88; and Schwarz, "Romance" 71, 114n19.

68. A. Conan Doyle, "The Mystery of Sasassa Valley: A South African Story," *Peril and Prowess: Being Stories Told by G. A. Henty . . . &c., &c.*, Chambers, 1899, 148. Russell Miller, *The Adventures of Arthur Conan Doyle*, Dunne-St. Martin's, 2008, 58.

69. Reneé Durbach, *Kipling's South Africa*, Chameleon, 1988, 31. On *The Friend*, see Julian Ralph, *War's Brighter Side*, Appleton, 1901. Many of the articles can be found in Rudyard Kipling, *Uncollected Prose*, AMS, 1970, *The Collected Works of Rudyard Kipling*, vol. 23.

70. Kipling, quoted in Ralph 13. Working in conjunction with the *Daily Mail*, which debuted the poem and administered the "Absent-Minded Beggar's Fund," Kipling waived all authorial rights (Rudyard Kipling, *Something of Myself and Other Autobiographical Writings*, Cambridge UP, 1990, 162).

71. Peter Keating, *Kipling: The Poet*, Secker, 1994, 130. Amy Cruse, *After the Victorians*, Allen, 1976, 124.

72. Krebs 157.

73. Kipling's attempt to overlook, to justify, and ultimately to accept Britain's arming people of color during the Anglo-Boer War can be seen, respectively, in "A Burgher of the Free State" (1900), "A Sahibs' War" (1901), and "Mrs. Bathurst" (1904). For an analysis of the first of these stories, see Melissa Free, "Fault Lines of Loyalty: Rudyard Kipling's Boer War Conflict," *Victorian Studies*, vol. 58, no. 2, Winter 2016, 314–23.

74. Paul Rich offers this interesting perspective: "While continuing a British metropolitan tradition of popular romance, Haggard must also be seen as both failed South African settler and would-be South African novelist" ("Romance and the Development of the South African Novel," *Literature and Society in South Africa*, ed. Landeg White and Tim Couzens, Longman, 1984, 123).

75. The majority of the (minority) white population had left the country by the time the Republic of Zimbabwe came into being in 1980, and Page is certainly not a Zimbabwean writer. Though born in Rhodesia, Doris Lessing did not publish her first novel, *The Grass Is Singing* (1950), until after she had immigrated to Britain.

76. Chrisman, *Rereading* 2.

77. "Who could have foreseen that the new, and in many respects the most distinctive note of the literature of the last decade of the nineteenth century, would be sounded by a little chit of a girl reared in the solemn stillness of the Karoo, in the solitude of the African bush?" (Stead 64).

78. Unterhalter estimates that in 1865 those of European descent made up only eight percent of southern Africa's population (217). The Rhodesian figure comes from Stephen Donovan, "Colonial Pedigree: Class, Masculinity, and History in the

Early Rhodesian Novel," *Nordic Journal of English Studies*, vol. 11, no. 2, 2012, 63. "Even in 1939, at their prewar peak, Europeans represented no more than 4.4 percent of Rhodesia's total population" (Kennedy 128).

79. Leonard Monteath Thompson, *A History of South Africa*, 3rd ed., Yale UP, 2001, 99–100, 297, table 1. For the contemporary definition of "Coloured," see page 14 of this introduction.

80. L. M. Thompson 99–100. "Indian South Africans," *South African History Online*, www.sahistory.org.za/article/indian-south-africans.

81. L. M. Thompson 144–45. "Arrival of Chinese Labourers in South Africa," *South African History Online*, www.sahistory.org.za/dated-event/arrival-chinese-labourers-south-africa.

82. L. M. Thompson 65.

83. John Buchan, *Prester John*, ed. David Daniell, Oxford UP, 1994, 152.

84. H. Rider Haggard, *Swallow*, Longmans, 1899, 19, 78, *Internet Archive*, www.archive.org/details/swallowtaleofgre00haggiala. See "A Note on Terminology" at the beginning of this book.

85. Buchan, *Prester John* 116, 23.

86. Buchan, *Prester John* 116, 152. Bear in mind that the words are put into the black character's mouth by a white author.

87. H. Rider Haggard, *The Ghost Kings*, Cassell, 1908, 53, 73.

88. Jennifer DeVere Brody, *Impossible Purities: Blackness, Femininity, and Victorian Culture*, Duke UP, 1998, 11.

89. Coetzee 5.

90. Buchan, *Prester John* 168, 151.

91. Buchan, *Prester John* 32, 140.

92. See Edward W. Said, *Culture and Imperialism*, Vintage-Random, 1994.

93. Harry How, "Illustrated Interviews. No. VII. Mr. H. Rider Haggard," *Strand Magazine*, Jan. 1892, 13. H. Rider Haggard, *Jess*, McKinlay, 1887, 266.

94. See, for example, Rosemary Marangoly George, *The Politics of Home: Postcolonial Relocations and Twentieth-Century Fiction*, Cambridge UP, 1996; and Deirdre David, *Rule Britannia: Women, Empire, and Victorian Writing*, Cornell UP, 1995.

95. The empire romance, which flourished in 1920s magazines, "promised [the female emigrant] not only a challenging life but also, it is hinted, genuine excitement," including (implicitly) sexual excitement (Billie Melman, *Women and the Popular Imagination in the Twenties: Flappers and Nymphs*, Macmillan, 1988, 144). For more on the empire romance, see Melman 140–44 and appendix C, which provides a list of titles, as well as my chapter 3, page 132.

96. CHAM, "Life in a Country Dorp," *South African Stories and Sketches*, 5th series, South Africa, n.d., 12, *"South Africa" Handbook*, no. 41, originally published in *South Africa: A Weekly Journal for All Interested in South African Affairs*, Dec. 1907.

97. Richard Hannay appears in seven of Buchan's novels: *The Thirty-Nine Steps* (1915), *Greenmantle* (1916), *Mr. Standfast* (1919), *The Three Hostages* (1924), *The*

Courts of the Morning (1929), *The Island of Sheep* (1936), and the posthumously published *Sick Heart River* (1941). Though Buchan does not seem to have intended the first four as a quartet, they are often treated as such, probably because Hannay plays a minor role in *The Courts of the Morning* and *Sick Heart River*, and *The Island of Sheep* came out more than a decade after *The Three Hostages*, the last novel in which he had been the protagonist.

Chapter 1. Preterdomesticity and the South African Farm: Women Old and New

1. H stands for Henry. See the introduction, note 7.

2. W. T. Stead, "The Novel of the Modern Woman," *Review of Reviews*, vol. 10, 1894, 65. C. M. Prowse, "By Rail to Johannesburg," *South African Illustrated Magazine*, vol. 12, Sept. 1900, 4. The Karoo (sometimes spelled Karroo) is the vast semi-desert region that occupies most of the Cape; for Schreiner's definition, see note 100 in this chapter. *The Story of an African Farm*, published in the first two editions under the pseudonym Ralph Iron, was issued in three editions in 1893, had been printed seventy-eight thousand times by August 1894, and was issued in twelve more editions over the course of the next forty years (Ruth First and Ann Scott, *Olive Schreiner*, Schocken, 1980, 119; "Literary Gossip," *European Mail*, 8 Aug. 1894, 22). Describing *African Farm* as " 'a work of genius,' " Charles Dilke "placed Schreiner first in importance in a discussion of colonial writing in his two-volume *Problems of Greater Britain* of 1890" (First and Scott 121). Anne McClintock calls Schreiner "the first colonial writer to be widely acclaimed in Britain" (*Imperial Leather: Race, Gender and Sexuality in the Colonial Contest*, Routledge, 1995, 259). Schreiner was also the first female novelist "to attain distinction in . . . South Africa" (John Forest, "South Africa's Favourite Novelists," *African Monthly: A Magazine Devoted to Literature, History, Exploration, Science, Art, Poetry, Fiction, &c.*, vol. 1, Dec. 1906, 72). More than forty years after its publication, *African Farm* was still recognized as "the most distinguished work of fiction which a native-born [South African] writer has thus far produced" (Manfred Nathan, *South African Literature: A General Survey*, Juta, 1925, 204). *African Farm* makes two passing references to the (Kimberly) Diamond Fields.

3. Elaine Showalter, *A Literature of Their Own: British Women Novelists from Brontë to Lessing*, Princeton UP, 1977, 199. Cf. "Lyndall was the first of her kind in fiction" (Doris Lessing, Introduction, *The Story of an African Farm*, by Schreiner, Hutchinson, 1968, xiv). Though the term New Woman was not widely circulated until 1894, *The Story of an African Farm* was retroactively deemed a New Woman novel. In his 1894 article, "The Novel of the Modern Woman," W. T. Stead described *African Farm* as "the forerunner of all the novels of the Modern Woman" and its author as "the founder and high priestess of the school" (64). Modern critics generally

concur. Sally Ledger, for instance, refers to Lyndall as "unmistakably a prototype New Woman" and Schreiner as "the 'mother' of the New Woman fiction" (*The New Woman: Fiction and Feminism at the Fin de Siècle*, Manchester UP, 1997, 2; and "The New Woman and Feminist Fictions," *The Cambridge Companion to the Fin de Siècle*, ed. Gail Marshall, Cambridge UP, 2007, 163).

4. "Literature," *South Africa: A Weekly Journal for All Interested in South African Affairs*, vol. 1, no. 1, 4 Jan. 1889, 10.

5. Olive Schreiner, Preface, *The Story of an African Farm*, Penguin, 1995, 29–30. The preface, which was included from the second edition onward, addresses the success of the novel.

6. Norman Colgan, "Africa's Writer of Romance," *Everybody's: The Popular Weekly*, 12 May 1945, 15. Duly impressed with his own productivity, Haggard noted: "between January 1885 and March 18, 1886, with my own hand, and unassisted by any secretary, I wrote 'King Solomon's Mines,' 'Allan Quatermain,' 'Jess,' and 'She' "—while studying law, no less (H. Rider Haggard, *The Days of My Life: An Autobiography*, ed. C. J. Longman, Longmans, 1926, 2 vols., 1: 246, hereafter cited parenthetically as *Days*).

7. Neil Hultgren also points out the "generic hybridity" of *Jess*, though the central genres he identifies are adventure fiction (more specifically, imperial romance) and melodrama (*Melodramatic Imperial Writing from the Sepoy Rebellion to Cecil Rhodes*, Ohio State UP, 2014, 66). Wendy Katz notes that the novel "deal[s] with love and marriage and may be classified as [a] romance[] of contemporary life," but that it "also give[s] prominence to imperial issues, an emphatic heroism, and a deep vein of fatalism which allow[s] [it] to be placed alongside [Haggard's] romances of adventure" (*Rider Haggard and the Fiction of Empire: A Critical Study of British Imperial Fiction*, Cambridge UP, 1987, 5).

8. The quotation is from Richard F. Patteson, "*King Solomon's Mines*: Imperialism and Narrative Structure," *The Journal of Narrative Technique*, vol. 8, no. 2, Spring 1978, 121. Other critics who compare the two texts do so only in passing. For Paul Rich, "Jess reflects the uncertain and ultimately tragic status of a thinking female in a colonial society, paralleling Lyndall in *The Story of an African Farm*" ("Romance and the Development of the South African Novel," *Literature and Society in South Africa*, ed. Landeg White and Tim Couzens, Longman, 1984, 124). For Gerald H. Monsman, "Jess . . . looks back . . . to Schreiner's strong-willed heroine Lyndall" (*H. Rider Haggard on the Imperial Frontier: The Politics and Literary Contexts of His African Romances*, ELT, 2006, 143). See also LeeAnne Richardson, *New Woman and Colonial Adventure Fiction in Victorian Britain: Gender, Genre, and Empire*, U of Florida P, 2006, 3; and Elizabeth Lee Steere, " 'Become a Sweet and God-Fearing Woman': British Women in Haggard's Early African Romances," *Nineteenth-Century Gender Studies*, vol. 6, no. 3, 2010, par. 19–20, www.ncgsjournal.com/issue63/steere.htm. D. S. Higgins, and Sandra Gilbert and Susan Gubar slightly miss the mark: Higgins speculates that Haggard was "perhaps inspired by his contact with

Olive Schreiner"—the two did not meet until 1885—to "start[] work on . . . *Jess*" (*Rider Haggard: The Great Storyteller*, Cassell, 1981, 86), and Gilbert and Gubar that "Haggard's magnetic Ayesha [the titular She] may have been half-consciously modeled on Schreiner's equally magnetic Lyndall" (*Sexchanges*, Yale UP, 1989, 35, *No Man's Land: The Place of the Woman Writer in the Twentieth Century*, vol. 2, ed. Gilbert and Gubar). Shortly after Haggard's death, someone wrote a letter to the newspaper, stating: "I often recommend his 'Jess' as an 'eye-opener' to those who wish to know what the country was like in '81 and 'the last Boer War' of the same time. These are not romances, but true pictures, as is Olive Schreiner's 'African Farm' of days gone by" (J. Burton Twigg, "A Memory of Sir Rider Haggard," letter, *John O' London's Weekly*, 27 June 1925, 433).

9. Schreiner wrote about their brief 1885 meeting in a letter and Haggard did the same in his diary (Olive Schreiner, *Olive Schreiner Letters, Vol. 1: 1871–1899*, ed. Richard Rive, Oxford UP, 1988, 64, hereafter cited as *Letters*; H. Rider Haggard, *The Private Diaries of Sir H. Rider Haggard, 1914–1925*, ed. D. S. Higgins, Cassell, 1980, 210). Haggard publicly praised *African Farm*, which he said was "written from the heart" (H. Rider Haggard, "About Fiction," *Contemporary Review*, vol. 51, Feb. 1887, 180). Schreiner said of his *Dawn*, which he had sent her, urging her to "write something more cheerful, something *more like this* . . . that would suit the taste of the public better": "Cheerful! . . . Why there was a murder or suicide on every other page!" (S. C. Cronwright-Schreiner, *The Life of Olive Schreiner*, Unwin, 1924, 190).

10. Forest 71.

11. See, for example, Schreiner's *Dreams* (1890), a collection of allegories and short stories; the novels *From Man to Man; or, Perhaps Only . . .* (1926) and *Undine* (1929); and the nonfictional *Woman and Labour* (1911), a (flawed) "social history" of "women's subjection" (McClintock 291), which, like *Dreams*, was embraced by suffragists (Ledger, *New Woman* 72). Haggard's misogyny is most pronounced in the figures of "*She-who-must-be-obeyed*," the protagonist of *She*, and Gagool, the "witch doctoress" in *King Solomon's Mines* (H. Rider Haggard, *King Solomon's Mines*, Modern Library, 2002, 224; H. Rider Haggard, *She*, Oxford UP, 1998, 84). In his nonfiction, see H. Rider Haggard, "A Man's View of Woman," review of *Woman: The Predominant Partner*, by Edward Sullivan, in *She*, by Haggard, ed. Andrew M. Stauffer, Broadview, 2006, 337–40, originally published in *African Review of Mining, Finance and Commerce*, vol. 4, no. 96, 22 Sept. 1894, 407–08; and H. Rider Haggard, "Woman and Life: Sir Rider Haggard's Views," *Daily Telegraph*, 18 Mar. 1922, 7.

12. Stead 64.

13. The statistic is from Ann Ardis, *New Women, New Novels: Feminism and Early Modernism*, Rutgers UP, 1990, 4. Cf. Ledger, "New Woman and Feminist" 157–58. The "female" with whom Schreiner is concerned in this novel is specifically the white British subject. See note 3 in this chapter. In her study of the New Girl, Sally Mitchell notes, "virtually every recollection of pupil-teacher life in the

last decades of the nineteenth century that I have discovered mentions . . . reading . . . *The Story of an African Farm*" (*The New Girl: Girls' Culture in England, 1880–1915*, Columbia UP, 1995, 37).

14. See, for example, Showalter, *Literature* 198; Gerd Bjørhovde, "Modernism in Embryo: Olive Schreiner," *Rebellious Structures: Women Writers and the Crisis of the Novel, 1880–1900*, Norwegian UP, 1987, 21–58; Gilbert and Gubar 53; and Anita Levy, "Other Women and New Women: Writing Race and Gender in *The Story of an African Farm*," *The Victorians and Race*, ed. Shearer West, Scolar, 1996, 178.

15. Susan Fraiman, "The Domestic Novel," *The Nineteenth-Century Novel, 1820–1880*, ed. John Kucich and Jenny Bourne Taylor, Oxford UP, 2012, 170, *The Oxford History of the Novel in English*, vol. 3.

16. Nancy Armstrong, *Desire and Domestic Fiction: The Political History of the Novel*, Oxford UP, 1987, 9. Ardis notes that "Lyndall does not want to detach sexuality from political history" (65).

17. See Schreiner, *The Story of an African Farm* 236, hereafter cited as *SAF*.

18. Fraiman 173, and see 181. Karen Scherzinger, "The Problem of the Pure Woman: South African Pastoralism and Female Rites of Passage," *UNISA English Studies*, vol. 29, no. 2, 1991, 33.

19. The novel went through three editions in its first year of publication; earned Haggard a bonus from his publishers; had reached at least its twenty-seventh edition by 1912, not counting, in Haggard's own words, "the countless [editions] in cheap forms"; and sold more than sixty-four thousand copies between 1911 and 1916 (Higgins, *Great Storyteller* 117; *Days* 1: 266; Morton Cohen, *Rider Haggard: His Life and Works*, Hutchinson, 1960, 233). Over sixty years after it was published, "it still ha[d] a steady sale in cheap editions" (Lilias Rider Haggard, *The Cloak That I Left: A Biography of the Author Henry Rider Haggard, K.B.E.*, Hodder, 1951, 128). It was treated to a full-length parody in 1887 ([John De Morgan], *Bess, A Companion to "Jess,"* Munro, 1887); adapted for the London stage in 1890 (*Jess*, adapted by Erwetta Lawrence and J. J. Bisgood, Adelphi Theatre, London, 1890); and made into films in 1905, 1912 (see figure 1.1), 1914, and 1917, in the latter case set in Puerto Rico during a rebellion against the United States (*Jess*, directed by George O. Nichols, Thanhouser Production, 1912; *Jess*, screenplay by Arthur Maude, Kennedy Features, 1914; *Heart and Soul*, directed by J. Gordon Edwards, screenplay by Adrian Johnson, Fox Film, 1917; the only information I can find about the 1905 film is that, like the other three, it was American-made [D. E. Whatmore, *H. Rider Haggard: A Bibliography*, Mansell, 1987, 226]). Advertisements in periodicals, newspapers, and bibliographic supplements, as well as prefatory remarks to Haggard's speeches and preliminaries to his books frequently described him, especially after the Second Anglo-Boer War (1899–1902), as the "author of *Jess*," along with *She* and *King Solomon's Mines*, a three-part reference described by a reviewer in 1944 as "Haggard's usual" (Roger Lancelyn Green, "'He,' 'She,' and 'It,'" *Times Literary Supplement*, 27 May 1944, 264). Found in Boer trenches after

their 1902 defeat and considered "something of a classic in South Africa" by 1906, *Jess* was described in a 1914 issue of the *Transvaal Leader* as "the most famous of [Haggard's] novels" (*Days* 1: 266; Forest 70; "Sir Rider Haggard's Return. In Pretoria, Then and Now," *Transvaal Leader*, 31 Mar. 1914, 6). Haggard's obituary in the *Times* described *Jess* as one of his two "most successful" "stories of modern life," the same year that a survey of South African literature predicted, "*Jess* is the work of Haggard's which is most likely to achieve permanence" ("Sir Rider Haggard. Novelist, Farmer, and Social Worker," *Times*, 15 May 1925, 18; Nathan 213). As late as 1949, *Jess* was listed with five other titles in the "Select Bibliography" of Haggard in *Novels of Empire*; *She* was *not* one of those titles (Susanne Howe, *Novels of Empire*, Columbia UP, 1949, 169).

20. Harry How, "Illustrated Interviews. No. VII. Mr. H. Rider Haggard," *Strand Magazine*, Jan. 1892, 13. H. Rider Haggard, *Jess*, McKinlay, 1887, 135; hereafter cited parenthetically as *J*.

21. On the history of female adventure, see chapter 2.

22. According to the terms of the peace treaty, Britain maintained suzerainty over the Transvaal, which proved to be a point of contention and ultimately a contributing factor to the Second Anglo-Boer War.

23. Stead 64, 74. A century later, in her study of the New Woman, Gail Cunningham echoed Stead's description: "Heroines who refused to conform to the traditional feminine role, challenged accepted ideals of marriage and maternity, chose to work for a living, or who in any way argued the feminist cause, became commonplace in the works of both major and minor writers and were firmly identified by readers and reviewers as New Women" (*The New Woman and the Victorian Novel*, Macmillan, 1978, 3).

24. Sarah Grand, "The New Aspect of the Woman Question," *North American Review*, vol. 158, Mar. 1894, 271.

25. Stead 65.

26. On her time at the diamond fields, see First and Scott 63–67; on her formal education, see First and Scott 55. In his biography of Schreiner, her husband makes frequent references to authors that she read in childhood (Cronwright-Schreiner, passim). See also Schreiner's *Letters* (passim), and First and Scott.

27. Regarding her husband, see First and Scott 206, and Cronwright-Schreiner 271. The quotations are from Schreiner, quoted in First and Scott 210, and *Letters* 63. Note her (feminist) use of humanity over its far more common synonym, mankind.

28. Cronwright-Schreiner 121n1. Details about the personal losses can be found in Cronwright-Schreiner 136–37, 21; see also *Letters* 24n1.

29. The quotation is from a note by Richard Rive, editor of Schreiner's *Letters* (4n8). Cronwright-Schreiner 77.

30. Rive notes, however, that Schreiner received "an annual allowance" from her brother Fred until she married in 1894 (*Letters* 63n1).

31. Regarding the engagement, see First and Scott 61–62; and *Letters* 6–7n2. Regarding Schreiner's complicated views on marriage, see note 118 in this chapter.

32. See First and Scott 31–33. Schreiner spent the next several years in London and Europe but moved back to southern Africa in 1889, where she continued to write, became involved in politics, and married Samuel Cronwright. She went again to England shortly before World War I, after which she returned to southern Africa, where she died in 1920.

33. Cronwright-Schreiner 156.

34. First and Scott 133.

35. First and Scott describe the onset of Schreiner's illness as a "neurotic" response to a number of factors, including the dissolution of her engagement (67); her "guilts [*sic*] about love[,] . . . attachment," and "sexuality" (68); her fluctuating living conditions (67); and "the culture she had to negotiate" (67), though they also provide several of Schreiner's own explanations, namely, physical causes like exposure and hunger (67). Cronwright-Schreiner, who makes no mention whatsoever of Schreiner's failed engagement, describes the history of her first asthma attack at age "16 or 17. There is no doubt that this fell disease altered her life, handicapped her activities, caused her endless suffering and contributed largely to break down her heart and kill her" (90).

36. Symons, quoted in Cronwright-Schreiner 189. Gilbert and Gubar describe Lyndall's death as "suicidal anorexia" (62).

37. Symons, quoted in Cronwright-Schreiner 189.

38. Olive Schreiner, *Undine*, Harper, 1928, 20.

39. On the child's birth and death, see First and Scott 214. Cronwright-Schreiner quotes the line with emphasis (xi). Though Schreiner later changed the line to read "She never lived to know she was a woman," she clearly equates womanhood with suffering (Olive Schreiner, *From Man to Man; or Perhaps Only . . .* , Harper, 1927, v).

40. Schreiner, Preface, *SAF* 30.

41. Schreiner, *Undine* 293. See my introduction, note 29.

42. Cronwright-Schreiner 124.

43. Considered unpromising by his father, Haggard was the only one of seven brothers not to receive a public school education (McClintock 237; and L. R. Haggard 23–27).

44. "She," review of *She*, by H. Rider Haggard, *Saturday Review*, 8 Jan. 1887, 44.

45. Edward P. Mathers, *South Africa and How to Reach It by the Castle Line*, Simpkin, 1889, 131. For Haggard's explanation of the annexation, see *Days* 1: 80–81.

46. A good critical history of the annexation (and First Anglo-Boer War) is John Laband, *The Transvaal Rebellion: The First Boer War, 1880–1881*, Pearson-Longman, 2005, especially 16–21. Just a few of the *many* accounts offered by Haggard include *Days* 1: 79–107; "Mr. Rider Haggard on South Africa," *Times*, 11 Mar. 1919, 12; "Mr. Rider Haggard on Anglo-Africa," *Daily Telegraph*, 24 Apr. 1894, 3; and H.

Rider Haggard, *Cetywayo and His White Neighbours*, 3rd ed., Trübner, 1890. Gold was discovered in the Transvaal in 1886.

47. H. R. Haggard, *Private Diaries* 34. Although in his autobiography, Haggard omits the detail about his contribution to the *reading* of the proclamation, he does tell a story about how, in one instance, when he was delivering copies of the proclamation to "various public offices," he, "trod upon the foot" of one of the "sullen-looking Boers" blocking his way. Though "half expecting to be shot as I did so, . . . I was the representative of England, and I felt that if I recoiled before [them], inferences might be drawn. I therefore went on" (*Days* 1: 105).

48. H. R. Haggard *Days* 1: 106–07, quotation on 107. Cf. "Sir Rider Haggard's Return" 6. For two other descriptions of this same event, see H. R. Haggard, *Private Diaries* 33 and 111.

49. H. R. Haggard, *Private Diaries* 30. Cf. *Days* 1: 109.

50. Forest 70.

51. How 13.

52. Just as Haggard often referred to being proud of the role he had played in the annexation, he also frequently referred to his shame as a colonist at Britain's surrender. On at least one occasion he referenced both at once: addressing the Canadian Club as a British Royal Commissioner in Ottawa, Canada, in 1901, he said, "I had the honour of hoisting the flag of England over [the Transvaal]. Gentleman, I lived, too, to see the flag pulled down and buried. And I tell you this—and you, as colonists as I was [sic], will sympathise with me—it was the bitterest hour of my life" (*Days* 2: 262). Cf. Silas Croft's "utter humiliation" when the Boers pull down his Union Jack, reverse it, and send it back up at half-mast (*J* 267).

53. H. Rider Haggard, "Boers Are Loyal, Says Rider Haggard," *New York Times*, 18 Oct. 1914, C4, Proquest Historical Newspapers.

54. How 13.

55. "Mr. Rider Haggard on Anglo-Africa" 3. In February 1881, after "some five hundred of the enemy had taken possession of the next farm to [my] own," Haggard writes, he and some of his neighbors—"we colonists"—discussed "forming a volunteer corps" to attack them. They were, however, "forbidden" by "the Government," which informed them "that if we insisted on carrying . . . out [the attack] we should be repudiated; that our wounded would be left to lie where they fell, and that if the Boers chose to shoot any of us whom they took prisoner no remonstrance would be made, and so forth and so forth. . . . So our proposed *coup* came to nothing" (*Days* 1: 183, 184). This passage, like several others, reveals both Haggard's pride in his colonial identity and his sense of betrayal by Britain (also see note 52 in this chapter).

56. "South African Writers," *South African Stories and Sketches*, 22nd series, South Africa, n.d., 12, "*South Africa*" Handbook, no. 73, originally published in *South Africa: A Weekly Journal for All Interested in South African Affairs*, Sept. 1913.

57. Edward Aveling, "A Notable Book," *Progress: A Monthly Magazine of Advanced Thought*, Sept. 1883, 156. Roberta Mazzanti, "Lyndall's Sphinx: Images of

Female Sexuality and Roles in *The Story of an African Farm*," *The Flawed Diamond: Essays on Olive Schreiner*, ed. Itala Vivan, Dangaroo, 1991, 129.

58. Jed Esty, *Unseasonable Youth: Modernism, Colonialism, and the Fiction of Development*, Oxford UP, 2012, 77.

59. Aveling 160.

60. Levy 174.

61. "The dark one" (*J* 131), Jess has "dark eyes" and "brown hair" (9), while "the fair Bessie" (23) has "blue eyes" and "light yellow hair" (242).

62. This dynamic inversely parallels Lyndall's liberation of "the bird"—also an ostrich—"that hates Bonaparte," in the hope that "he would chase him and perhaps kill him" (*SAF* 101). According to one of the author's contemporaries, an ostrich scene was part of "the regular stock-in-trade of the African romancer" ("Another South African Novel," review of *Diamond Dyke, or the Lone Farm on the Veldt: A Story of South African Adventure*, by George Manville Fenn, *African Review of Mining, Finance and Commerce*, 8 Dec. 1894, 821).

63. Bessie is, however, concerned with being valued for something other than her looks: "If you marry me," she tells Niel, "I want you to marry me because you care for *me*, the real *me*, not my eyes and my hair" (*J* 110). Compare Bessie and John's conversation with the one between Lyndall and Gregory in which she concedes to marry him, on her own terms: "'She [Em] is not half so good as you are!' said Gregory, with a burst of uncontrollable ardour. 'She is so much better than I, that her little finger has more goodness in it than my whole body'" (*SAF* 231).

64. "South African Writers" 12.

65. Says Lyndall as a child: "There is nothing helps in this world . . . but to be very wise, and to know everything—to be clever" (*SAF* 45). The heroine of *Undine* similarly "dream[s] of the glorious time when she would be a woman and would know everything and . . . would be free" (*Undine* 20). Bjørhovde notes that at boarding school Lyndall learns "that as a woman she will have to . . . remain always a child" (39).

66. First and Scott 103.

67. Rachel Blau DuPlessis, *Writing Beyond the Ending: Narrative Strategies of Twentieth-Century Women Writers*, Indiana UP, 1985, 26. Preparing to run off with RR, Lyndall leaves the sum of her fortune behind for her cousin. "Fifty pounds for a lover!" Lyndall remarks to herself of her own dubious generosity. "A noble reward!" (*SAF* 242). On at least one occasion, Lyndall does return money that RR sends her (278), but given that she leaves the farm with none of her own and winds up on her own in the Transvaal with "heaps of money" (271), she must have willingly kept at least some he has given her (in addition to that which he privately sends the landlady toward her upkeep [271–72]).

68. Patricia Murphy, *Time Is of the Essence: Temporality, Gender, and the New Woman*, State U of New York P, 2001, 219.

69. Undine similarly claims, "I don't want to be loved; I only want to love something," though she also wonders, "Why should a woman not break through

conventional restraints that enervate her mind and dwarf her body, and enjoy a wild, free, true life, as a man may?" (Schreiner, *Undine* 133, 244). As quoted on page 27, Schreiner expressed comparable sentiments in a personal letter: "No one will ever absorb me and make me lose myself utterly, and unless someone did I should never marry" (*Letters* 22). For Schreiner, it would seem, romantic reverence and social independence were not mutually exclusive for women. Perhaps this is because in the true equality she imagines between man and woman, reverence is mutual, nongendered, and non-abasing.

70. McClintock 271.

71. *Trooper Peter Halket of Mashonaland* is more specifically anti-BSAC. "It was an appeal to the English people and government, in the hope of mobilizing protest against" the BSAC, a chartered company whose economic policies and violent practices Schreiner strongly opposed (Laura Chrisman, *Rereading the Imperial Romance: British Imperialism and South African Resistance in Haggard, Schreiner, and Plaatje*, Clarendon, 2000, 124). For more on the BSAC, see chapter 3, pages 111–13. Schreiner had earlier been an admirer of Rhodes; on her shifting views of the man, see First and Scott 199–200; and Chrisman, *Rereading* 129.

72. The quotation is from Olive Schreiner, *Thoughts on South Africa*, Stokes, 1923, 17. "Mostly written between 1890 and 1892, and published as separate articles in a variety of English and US journals between 1891 and 1900," when "read as a whole the essays in *Thoughts on South Africa* offer a curiously ambivalent exposition. At times Olive seems to be looking to a transformed society free of race oppression; at others she seems to endorse the ideological justifications of white conquest" (First and Scott 194, 197). Schreiner certainly continued to see racial difference, claiming, for instance, that "one finds, with much that is immature and childlike [in "African races"], much that is gracious and charming" (*Thoughts* 24). In *From Man to Man*, Schreiner's heroine invokes her past to instruct her son: "When I was a little girl, . . . I could not bear black or brown people. I thought they were ugly and dirty and stupid; the little naked Kaffirs [see "A Note on Terminology" at the beginning of this book], with their dusty black skins, that played on the walls of the kraal [enclosure], I hated. They seemed so different from me in my white pinafores. . . . I felt I was so clever and they so stupid; I could not bear them. I always played that I was Queen Victoria and that all Africa belonged to me, and I could do whatever I liked. . . . I made believe that I built a high wall right across Africa and put all the black people on the other side" (414). But "as I grew older and older I got to see that it wasn't the color or the shape of the jaw or the cleverness that mattered" but rather people's ability to love and suffer, and so "the wall I had built across Africa had slowly to fall down" (417).

73. Ledger, *New Woman* 65, referencing First and Scott 262. This was particularly significant given that Schreiner was "the most honoured member of the suffrage movement in South Africa in the early twentieth century" (Ledger, *New Woman* 65).

74. The first quotation is from a headnote by Carol Barash to Olive Schreiner, "The Native Question," *An Olive Schreiner Reader: Writings on Women and South Africa*, by Schreiner, ed. Carol Barash, Pandora, 1987, 186. The second is from Schreiner, "The Native Question" 194. It comes from a letter published in 1908 in the *Transvaal Leader* as a response to questions asked by its editors of Schreiner (186). It was then reprinted as a pamphlet the same year, published as *Letter on the South African Union and the Principles of Government* in 1909 and as *A Closer Union in South Africa* in 1960. For more on race and voting rights, see my chapter 4, pages 146–47.

75. Jess's heroics constitute some of the behavior, or practice, that allies her with the New Woman (the focus of the present section), but as they are also key ingredients in this generic mix of adventure and domesticity that constitute the novel, a detailed discussion of them will appear instead in "Genre and Colonial Domesticity II: Expansion and Preservation," this chapter's penultimate section.

76. Erroneously believing that he had succeeded in killing Niel, Muller imprisons both Silas and Bessie, then gives the latter a choice "between consenting to marry me [or] seeing your uncle and benefactor shot. Further, . . . if you [do] not consent to marry me your uncle [will] be shot, and . . . I [will] then make you mine, dispensing with the ceremony of marriage" (*J* 307–08).

77. Ardis 27.

78. Silas Croft uses this designation twice, and John, Bessie, Mrs. Neville, and the narrator each use it once (*J* 54, 65, 47, 66, 168, 54). On the use of the word "odd" to denote the New Woman, see Ardis 10.

79. A contemporary reviewer noted the discrepancy between the heroine and the "unsatisfactory" captain: "it is perhaps true to nature, but nevertheless disappointing . . . that Jess should have placed her happiness in the keeping of such a very prosaic person as the retired captain" ("Mr. Rider Haggard's New Story," review of *Jess*, by H. Rider Haggard, *Pall Mall Gazette*, 15 Mar. 1887, 5).

80. While Jess's thoughts are similar to those of Lyndall, Undine, and Schreiner herself, the narrator of *Jess*, unlike these women, suggests an inherent connection between a woman's love and the subservience that suits *and pleases* her (see page 27 and note 69).

81. Compare Jess's decision to that of Lyndall, who, placing her own interests above those of her sister, agrees to marry Gregory, despite her lack of affection for him and her receipt of an earlier proposal from RR.

82. Niel joins the Pretoria Carbineers. Similarly, during the Anglo-Zulu War (1879), Haggard was lieutenant and adjutant of the Pretoria Horse, then "about sixty strong, and for the most part composed of Colonial-born men of more or less gentle birth" (H. Rider Haggard, "An Incident of African History," *Windsor Magazine*, vol. 13, no. 1, Dec. 1900, 114; cf. How 11; "Sir Rider Haggard's Return" 6; and Malcolm Elwin, *Old Gods Falling*, Macmillan, 1939, 231).

83. Haggard identifies this scene, "the account of the passion of John and Jess as they swung together wrapt [*sic*] in each other's arms," as one of his "best" (*Days* 2: 207, 206).

84. Aveling 160. Ardis 67. First and Scott 102. Cf. Carolyn Burdett, *Olive Schreiner and the Progress of Feminism: Evolution, Gender, Empire*, Palgrave, 2001, 31. Aveling was a friend of Schreiner's, though she eventually grew weary of him (see *Letters* 41 and 49).

85. Fraiman 176.

86. Cunningham 19.

87. Because of the centrality of the colonial estate, Christopher GoGwilt makes a similar claim: "the 'African farm' of the title simultaneously estranges the traditional setting of the Victorian novel and recalls what connects it materially, spiritually, and in its origins, with the familiar space of English fiction, the colonial estate. Schreiner's narrative perspective creates a novel that may then be read simultaneously as the epitome of the Victorian novel and as its death and transfiguration" (GoGwilt, *The Fiction of Geopolitics: Afterimages of Culture, from Wilkie Collins to Alfred Hitchcock*, Stanford UP, 2000, 111–12).

88. Carol L. Barash, "Virile Womanhood: Olive Schreiner's Narratives of a Master Race," *Speaking of Gender*, ed. Elaine Showalter, Routledge, 1989, 272. Cf. Carol Barash, Introduction, *An Olive Schreiner Reader: Writings on Women and South Africa*, by Olive Schreiner, ed. Barash, Pandora, 1987, 2.

89. Fraiman 173.

90. Elizabeth Lawson, "Of Lies and Memory: *The Story of an African Farm*, Book of the White Feather," *Cahiers Victoriens et Édouardiens*, vol. 44, Oct. 1996, 120.

91. Fraiman 182.

92. See Itala Vivan, "The Treatment of Blacks in *The Story of an African Farm*," *The Flawed Diamond: Essays on Olive Schreiner*, ed. Vivan, Dangaroo, 1991, 95–106. As Vivan notes, the text mentions "Hottentots" (Khoikhoi), "Kaffirs" (Bantu), and "Bushmen" (San) (104). See "A Note on Terminology" at the beginning of this book.

93. Just as Schreiner's view of Africans changed over time, so, too, did her "feeling for the Boer" (*Thoughts* 17). So while she offers "disapproving caricatures of Boer society" in *African Farm* (John Kucich, *Imperial Masochism: British Fiction, Fantasy and Social Class*, Princeton UP, 2006, 123), she paints a sympathetic portrait of them in the short story "Eighteen-Ninety-Nine" (Schreiner, *Stories, Dreams and Allegories*, Unwin, 1923, 11–55) and "tenderly describes" their social customs in *Thoughts on South Africa* (First and Scott 197). Throughout the Second Anglo-Boer War, she was passionate in her defense of them (see First and Scott 235–50; and Karel Schoeman, *Only an Anguish to Live Here: Olive Schreiner and the Anglo-Boer War, 1899–1902*, Human & Rousseau, 1992).

94. J. M. Coetzee, *White Writing: On the Culture of Letters in South Africa*, Yale UP, 1988, 66. Esty, *Unseasonable* 78. Cf. Annalisa Oboe, "Contrasts and Harmony: The Antithetical Structure in *The Story of an African Farm*," *The Flawed Diamond: Essays on Olive Schreiner*, ed. Itala Vivan, Dangaroo, 1991, 92.

95. The quotations are from Coetzee 66, 4. Esty points out the "notably anemic rate of reproduction among the settler class" (*Unseasonable* 78), and Laura Chrisman notes that the farm is not a "site of potential regeneration for white

women" ("Empire, 'Race' and Feminism at the Fin de Siècle: The Work of George Egerton and Olive Schreiner," *Cultural Politics at the Fin de Siècle*, ed. Sally Ledger and Scott McCracken, Cambridge UP, 1995, 51). Oboe writes that "the whites are never fully integrated into the South African setting" ("Contrasts" 93) and Loren Anthony that "none of the protagonists can achieve a meaningful relationship with the land, with Africa" ("Buried Narratives: Masking the Sign of History in *The Story of an African Farm*," *Scrutiny2*, vol. 4, no. 2, 1999, 11).

 96. See Gayatri Chakravorty Spivak, "'Can the Subaltern Speak?' Revised Edition from the 'History' Chapter of *Critique of Postcolonial Reason*," *Can the Subaltern Speak? Reflections on the History of an Idea*, ed. Rosalind C. Morris, Columbia UP, 2010, 21–78. See Coetzee 4, 167; Anthony 12; and Rebecca Stott, "'Scaping the Body: Of Cannibal Mothers and Colonial Landscapes," *The New Woman in Fiction and Fact: Fin-de-Siècle Feminisms*, ed. Angelique Richardson and Chris Willis, Palgrave, 2001, 161.

 97. Esty, *Unseasonable* 79. Jed Esty, "The Colonial Bildungsroman: *The Story of an African Farm* and the Ghost of Goethe," *Victorian Studies*, vol. 49, no. 3, Apr. 2007, 426.

 98. Jean Marquard, "The Farm: A Concept in the Writing of Olive Schreiner, Pauline Smith, Doris Lessing, Nadine Gordimer, and Bessie Head," *Dalhousie Review*, vol. 59, no. 2, Summer 1979, 293, see also 295. Marquard goes so far as to argue that in *African Farm*, "the woman question is a secondary theme, a lateral growth shaped by the more profound question of what it means to be a South African" (293). Coetzee, passim, especially 66. Stephen Gray claims that the southern African literary tradition of "permanently alienated beings, white beings who are not part of, and can never be part of . . . [African] land," originates with Schreiner (*Southern African Literature: An Introduction*, Barnes & Noble, 1979, 151–52, quotation on 152); for a discussion of white "guilt at being an interloper, a colonizer," see 158. See also Stott, "'Scaping" 162.

 99. Cronwright-Schreiner 123–24. She did, however, keep the name "Thorn Kloof" for the family farm in *From Man to Man* (75), which she began prior to *African Farm* but which was not published in full until after her death.

 100. The glossary, however, describes the Karoo, mentioned in the novel's second sentence, as "the wide sandy plain in some parts of South Africa" (*SAF* 31). The only place names that are given are places where the farm is not: the Orange Free State (and Bloemfontein, its capital) and the Transvaal (or South African Republic), South Africa's two Boer republics during the years in which the novel is set (as well as the year it was published).

 101. Barash, Introduction 2. Readers with more than passing knowledge of southern Africa might conclude, as does Richard M. Rive, that the novel is set in the eastern part of the Cape ("Olive Schreiner: A Critical Study and a Checklist," *Studies in the Novel*, vol. 4, no. 2, Summer 1972, 238).

102. As GoGwilt notes, "The novel is built around the virtual absence of any lived experience of antagonism between colonial settlers and indigenous peoples" (112). Though I would qualify this slightly—near absence would be more accurate, I think, than "virtual absence"—I essentially concur.

103. Scott McCracken, "Stages of Sand and Blood: The Performance of Gendered Subjectivity in Olive Schreiner's Colonial Allegories," *Rereading Victorian Fiction*, ed. Alice Jenkins and Juliet John, St. Martin's, 2000, 148. Aveling 156.

104. Coetzee 66; my emphasis.

105. Regarding Austen, see Fraiman 174, 176.

106. RR asks Lyndall if she has "forgotten the night in the avenue"—she has not—which suggests that there may have been only one sexual encounter (*SAF* 240).

107. In a chapter called "Gregory's Womanhood," Gregory recounts to Em the bits and pieces of information he gathered—as he "trace[d] their course"—from Boer farmers, their families, and servants, a gentleman at a hotel, and the landlady of the hotel in which he finally locates Lyndall (*SAF* 265).

108. Laurence Lerner, "Olive Schreiner and the Feminists," *Olive Schreiner and After: Essays on Southern African Literature in Honour of Guy Butler*, ed. Malvern van Wyk Smith and Don Maclennan, Philip, 1983, 70.

109. The idea of social progress as process is suggested, sometimes by way of analogy, in *SAF* 171, 188; *From Man to Man* 275; and the allegory "Three Dreams in a Desert" (Schreiner, *Dreams: Three Works by Olive Schreiner*, Roberts Brothers, 1898, 65–85, *Victorian Women Writers Project*, webapp1.dlib.indiana.edu/vwwp/view?docId=VAB7054.xml).

110. Levy 173.

111. For similar analyses of Tant' Sannie's role, see Stott, "'Scaping" 160; Levy 173; Showalter, *Literature* 196; and Nancy L. Paxton, "*The Story of an African Farm* and the Dynamics of Woman-to-Woman Influence," *Texas Studies in Literature and Language*, vol. 30, no. 4, ison 1988, 569.

112. Tant' Sannie's visit to Em is "probably [her] last . . . , as she now weighed two hundred and sixty pounds, and was not easily able to move" (*SAF* 292–93). While Schreiner wrote *African Farm* when her views of the Boers were more critical than they would be later in her life (see note 93 in this chapter), it is by no means only *Boer* courtship and domesticity that she calls into question in the novel.

113. Stott, "'Scaping" 160.

114. Burdett 21. Cf. Gerald Monsman, "The Idea of 'Story' in Olive Schreiner's *Story of an African Farm*," *Texas Studies in Literature and Language*, vol. 27, no. 3, Fall 1985, 254. For Burdett, Otto and Bonaparte "together signify the absence of a proper father on the farm" (21).

115. See Gerald Monsman, "Patterns of Narration and Characterization in Schreiner's *The Story of an African Farm*," *English Literature in Transition*, vol. 28, no. 3, 1985, 255; Burdett 20; Esty, *Unseasonable* 74.

116. On the association between restraint and manliness in the Victorian period, see Joseph Valente, *The Myth of Manliness in Irish National Culture, 1880–1922*, U of Illinois P, 2011, 2–3, passim.

117. Christopher Lane, *The Burdens of Intimacy: Psychoanalysis and Victorian Masculinity*, U of Chicago P, 1999, 103. In Lane's estimation, Lyndall mocks this ritual as well. I would argue that Lyndall mocks Gregory, while Schreiner mocks the courtship plot.

118. Schreiner spoke of her own and of Lyndall's views on marriage in a personal letter in 1895: "I think it [marriage] to be the most holy, the most organic, the most important sacrament in life, and how men and women can enter into with the lighthearted indifference they do, has always been, and is, a matter of endless wonder to me. . . . It was because Lyndall, small child that she was, felt what a sacred and deathless thing true marriage should be that she refused to save her reputation by binding herself for ever" to the father of her child (*Letters* 259–60).

119. Mark Sanders, "Towards a Genealogy of Intellectual Life: Olive Schreiner's *The Story of an African Farm*," *Novel: A Forum on Fiction*, vol. 34, no. 1, Fall 2000, 83. Fraiman 172.

120. Arthur Symons quoted in Cronwright-Schreiner 189 (see page 28 in this chapter). Ardis 65.

121. Levy 177. Lerner 75. Lawson 115; cf. Levy 177. Ardis takes an extreme view: "The woman who metaphorically kills the angel in the house dies anyway, leaving the Victorian social order intact" (66).

122. Roberta Mazzanti, "Lyndall's Sphinx: Images of Female Sexuality and Roles in *The Story of an African Farm*," *The Flawed Diamond: Essays on Olive Schreiner*, ed. Itala Vivan, Dangaroo, 1991, 129. Cf. Lawson 123.

123. Mazzanti 130. Cf. Ardis 66. When Em tells Waldo that her wedding is just three weeks away, "he did not congratulate her; perhaps he thought of the empty box, but he kissed her forehead gravely" (*SAF* 297).

124. Ardis 3.

125. Richardson 20.

126. "Novels of the Week," review of *Jess*, by H. Rider Haggard, *Athenaeum*, 19 Mar. 1887, 375.

127. "The Anglo-African Writers' Club. Mr. Rider Haggard Delivers His Presidential Address. A Remarkable Inauguration," *African Review of Mining, Finance and Commerce*, 28 Apr. 1894, 545, 541. On "The Anglo-African Writers' Club," see the first chapter (3–38) of Gerald H. Monsman, *Colonial Voices: The Anglo-African High Romance of Empire*, UP of the South, 2010.

128. For evidence of the novel's popularity, see note 19 in this chapter.

129. Gregg A. Hecimovich, *Hardy's "Tess of the D'Urbervilles": A Reader's Guide*, Continuum, 2010, 91, 99.

130. "Novels of the Week" 375. Of the surrender, Haggard passionately noted in his 1894 inaugural address as president of the Anglo-African Writers' Club: "Never

gentleman, if I live to the age of 100, shall I forget that scene upon the market square in Newcastle [in the Transvaal] when the news of our surrender went home to the intelligence of the three or four thousand refugees, loyal Boers, English and natives, who were gathered there that night. Never do I wish to see such another scene, or to hear such curses as were uttered by those ruined and dishonoured men. I confess that I felt it myself. *I felt it so much that I left South Africa, which at that time I did not consider fit for an Englishman*" ("The Anglo-African Writers' Club" 542; my emphasis).

131. The distinction is between the Transvaal (South African Republic) and *the whole* of South Africa.

132. Muller's father and mother "were murdered by a party of" Africans approximately eight years later (*J* 82).

133. Jantjé, who has long been loyal to the Croft family, supports the British in their defense of the Transvaal, and before the rebellion's outbreak proudly insists: "The land is English now, and Boers can't kill the black people as they like" (*J* 76). On a more personal note, he prevents Muller from kissing Bessie by using his "ventriloquistic power" to imitate the voice of Muller's now-deceased mother, "wail[ing] . . . '*Frank*, thou shalt die in blood . . . !,' " thus sending him scurrying (122, 123).

134. Hultgren 74. Others include Richardson; Steere; Monsman, *H. Rider Haggard*; and Richard Reeve, "H. Rider Haggard and the New Woman: A Difference in the Genre in *Jess* and *Beatrice*," *ELT: English Literature in Transition, 1880–1920*, vol. 59, no. 2, 2016, 153–74, *Project Muse*, www.jhu.edu/article/603472.

135. Monsman points out the similarity of Jess's action to that of Jael, who, while alone in her tent with Sisera, a Canaanite solider who had long oppressed the Israelites, drives a peg through his skull (*H. Rider Haggard* 143, referencing Judges 4: 17–22). Judith beheads the Assyrian general Holofernes while alone with him in her tent, thereby saving the Hebrew city of Bethulia (Judith 13: 1–10).

136. Suspected by the Boers of having committed the crime, Jantjé has fled "from the ken of the white man far into the wilds of Central Africa" (*J* 339).

137. See pages 30–31 and notes 52 and 55.

138. "After Majuba [the battle that led to British surrender] I said that South Africa was no place for an Englishman, and I left the country" ("Sir Rider Haggard. Ethics of Literature," *Sydney Morning Herald*, 12 Apr. 1913, 9–10). Cf. note 130 in this chapter.

139. Lilly Jackson, whom Haggard had hoped to wed, married another man while Haggard was in southern Africa (Higgins, *Great Storyteller* 33–34). He named one of his daughters after her. Niel settles in the East Midlands, Haggard in Norfolk.

140. "Like Gregory's love for Lyndall, John's prosaic marriage to Bessie will always remain shadowed by his greater love of his lost soul mate [*sic*], Jess" (Monsman, *H. Rider Haggard* 145).

141. "Mr. Rider Haggard's New Story."

142. On this point, see Gilbert and Gubar 48–49, 140; Elaine Showalter, *Sexual Anarchy: Gender and Culture at the Fin de Siècle*, Penguin, 1990, 80–83; McClintock 235–36; Christopher Lane, *The Ruling Passion: British Colonial Allegory and the Paradox of Homosexual Desire*, Duke UP, 1995, 57–64; Patricia Murphy, "The Gendering of History in *She*," *Studies in English Literature*, vol. 39, no. 4, Autumn 1999, 747; and Deirdre David, *Rule Britannia: Women, Empire, and Victorian Writing*, Cornell UP, 1995, especially 192, 197.

143. Armstrong, *Desire* 9.

144. Gilbert and Gubar 60.

145. H. R. Haggard, *Private Diaries* 283.

146. *Benita* was published in the United States as *The Spirit of Bambatse: A Romance*. Like *Benita*, *The Ghost Kings* was published in the United States (in some editions) under an alternate title, *The Lady of the Heavens*.

Chapter 2. "It Is I Who Have the Power": The Female Colonial Romance

1. Patrick Brantlinger, *Rule of Darkness: British Literature and Imperialism, 1830–1914*, Cornell UP, 1988, 230. Elaine Showalter, *Sexual Anarchy: Gender and Culture at the Fin de Siècle*, Penguin, 1990, 81.

2. Stephen E. Tabachnick, "Two Tales of Gothic Adventure: *She* and *Heart of Darkness*," *English Literature in Transition, 1880–1920*, vol. 56, no. 2, 2013, 191.

3. Bradley Deane, "Imperial Barbarians: Primitive Masculinity in Lost World Fiction," *Victorian Literature and Culture*, vol. 36, 2008, 206. Everett F. Bleiler writes that Henry Morton Stanley "may have coined the term 'lost race'" (*Science-Fiction: The Early Years*, Kent State UP, 1990, xx). Deane calculates that "over 200 [lost race] stories were published in Britain between 1871 and the First World War, many times the number that had appeared in all the years before" (206; cf. Bleiler xx; and John Rieder, *Colonialism and the Emergence of Science Fiction*, Wesleyan UP, 2008, 159n4). The most famous early lost race novel is probably Edward Bulwer-Lytton's *The Coming Race* (1871), sometimes published as *Vril*, which was preceded by such "hollow-earth journeys" as Adam Seaborn's *Symzonia; Voyage of Discovery* (1820) (Rieder 36). Incredibly, there is no single extensive critical source on lost world fiction.

4. Gail Ching-Liang Low, *White Skins/Black Masks: Representation and Colonialism*, Routledge, 1996, 59.

5. See, for example, Showalter, *Sexual Anarchy* 83; Deirdre David, *Rule Britannia: Women, Empire, and Victorian Writing*, Cornell UP, 1995, 188n38; John Tosh, "Imperial Masculinity and the Flight from Domesticity in Britain, 1880–1914," *Gender and Colonialism*, ed. Timothy P. Foley et al., Galway UP, 1995, 73, 81; and

Paula M. Krebs, *Gender, Race, and the Writing of Empire: Public Discourse and the Boer War*, Cambridge UP, 1999, 149.

6. G. C. Low 49. David 161. See also Nicholas Daly, *Modernism, Romance, and the Fin de Siècle: Popular Fiction and British Culture, 1880–1914*, Cambridge UP, 1999, 62; Elizabeth Lee Steere, "'Become a Sweet and God-Fearing Woman': British Women in Haggard's Early African Romances," *Nineteenth-Century Gender Studies*, vol. 6, no. 3, 2010, par. 5, www.ncgsjournal.com/issue63/steere.htm; and Christopher Lane, *The Ruling Passion: British Colonial Allegory and the Paradox of Homosexual Desire*, Duke UP, 1995, 57, 64. Gerald Monsman, an exception, describes Haggard's colonial heroines as "feminist" figures, though he differs from me significantly in his view that Haggard broadly "prob[es] and subvert[s] the dominant economic and social forces of imperialism" (*H. Rider Haggard on the Imperial Frontier: The Politics and Literary Contexts of His African Romances*, ELT, 2006, 45, 4).

7. *King Solomon's Mines* (1887), in which Quatermain makes his first appearance, was famously inspired by Stevenson's *Treasure Island* (H. Rider Haggard, *The Days of My Life: An Autobiography*, ed. C. J. Longman, Longmans, 1926, 2 vols., 1: 220).

8. See Melissa Free, "British Women Wanted: Gender, Genre, and South African Settlement," *The Oxford Handbook of Victorian Literary Culture*, ed. Juliet John, Oxford UP, 2016, 284–309; and Melissa Free, "'It Is I Who Have the Power': Settling Women in Haggard's South African Imaginary," *Genre*, vol. 45, no. 3, Fall 2012, 359–93. *Benita* was published in the United States as *The Spirit of Bambatse: A Romance*. That which precedes the colon was Haggard's "original choice" of title, but the British "publishers preferred 'Benita'—a single word being more suitable for advertisement purposes" (J. E. Scott, *A Bibliography of the Works of Sir Henry Rider Haggard, 1856–1925*, Mathews, 1947, 107). "*The Guardian and the Gold. An African Romance*" was also considered, since, Haggard claimed, "the word 'Gold' is always attractive in romance" (Haggard quoted in D. S. Higgins, *Rider Haggard: The Great Storyteller*, Cassell, 1981, 193). I am using the first American edition, *The Spirit of Bambatse: A Romance*, McKinlay, 1906, The Works of H. Rider Haggard, hereafter cited parenthetically as *B*. Like *Benita*, *The Ghost Kings* was published in the United States (in some editions) under another title, *The Lady of the Heavens*. I am using the original (British) edition, *The Ghost Kings*, Cassell, 1908, hereafter cited parenthetically as *GK*.

9. On *She* as a reflection of Haggard's misogyny, see Brantlinger, *Rule of Darkness* 234; Sandra M. Gilbert and Susan Gubar, *Sexchanges*, Yale UP, 1989, 48–49, 140, *No Man's Land: The Place of the Woman Writer in the Twentieth Century*, vol. 2, ed. Gilbert and Gubar; Showalter, *Sexual Anarchy* 83–89; David, especially 188, 192, 196–98; Anne McClintock, *Imperial Leather: Race, Gender and Sexuality in the Colonial Contest*, Routledge, 1995, 235–36; and Patricia Murphy, "The Gendering of History in *She*," *Studies in English Literature*, vol. 39, no. 4, Autumn 1999, 747.

10. Edward Shanks, "Sir Rider Haggard and the Novel of Adventure," *London Mercury*, Nov. 1924, 72. Shanks includes Arthur Conan Doyle and Anthony Hope (Hawkins) in this group.

11. Foundational feminist work on Haggard includes Gilbert and Gubar; McClintock; Showalter, *Sexual Anarchy*; as well as Claudia Crawford, "She," *SubStance*, vol. 9, no. 4, 1981, 83–96; Nina Auerbach, *Woman and the Demon: The Life of a Victorian Myth*, Harvard UP, 1982; and Rebecca Stott, *The Fabrication of the Late Victorian Femme Fatale: The Kiss of Death*, Macmillan, 1992, Women's Studies at York. G. C. Low and Laura Chrisman have done terrific readings of race in Haggard's writing, including some of his lesser-known texts (see Laura Chrisman, *Postcolonial Contraventions: Cultural Readings of Race, Imperialism and Transnationalism*, Manchester UP, 2003; *Rereading the Imperial Romance: British Imperialism and South African Resistance in Haggard, Schreiner, and Plaatje*, Clarendon, 2000; and "The Imperial Unconscious? Representations of Imperial Discourse," *Critical Quarterly*, vol. 32, no. 3, Fall 1990, 38–58).

12. The term comes from James Belich, *Replenishing the Earth: The Settler Revolution and the Rise of the Anglo-World, 1783–1939*, Oxford UP, 2009. Other important recent work in the field includes Janet C. Myers, *Antipodal England: Emigration and Portable Domesticity in the Victorian Imagination*, State U of New York P, 2009; Duncan Bell, *The Idea of Greater Britain: Empire and the Future of World Order, 1860–1900*, Princeton UP, 2007; and Diana C. Archibald, *Domesticity, Imperialism, and Emigration in the Victorian Novel*, U of Missouri P, 2002.

13. In "Three Women's Texts and a Critique of Imperialism," Gayatri Chakravorty Spivak argues that the rise of "the feminist individualist heroine of British fiction" is contingent on the sacrifice of the racialized female other (*Critical Inquiry*, vol. 12, no. 1, Autumn 1985, 251). In *Burdens of History: British Feminists, Indian Women, and Imperial Culture, 1865–1915*, Antoinette Burton documents the ways in which metropolitan women's movements, including the suffrage movement, were predicated, in part, on the imperial premise of superiority to—and authority over—the nonwhite female other (U of North Carolina P, 1994).

14. The first quotation is from Rosemary Marangoly George (50), who also notes that India was "one of the primary arenas in which an identifiable group of English women first achieved the kind of authoritative self associated with the modern female subject" (*The Politics of Home: Postcolonial Relocations and Twentieth-Century Fiction*, Cambridge UP, 1996, 6). The second quotation is from Sara Mills, *Discourses of Difference: An Analysis of Women's Travel Writing and Colonialism*, Routledge, 1991, 59. Jenny Sharpe, *Allegories of Empire: The Figure of Woman in the Colonial Text*, U of Minnesota P, 1993. Nancy L. Paxton, *Writing Under the Raj: Gender, Race, and Rape in the British Colonial Imagination, 1830–1947*, Rutgers UP, 1999, 109–36. On the memsahib, see also Rita S. Krandis, *The Victorian Spinster and Colonial Emigration: Contested Subjects*, St. Martin's, 1999, 52–59; and Margaret Strobel, *European Women and the Second British Empire*, Indiana UP, 1991, 7–9.

15. While the British woman in India was still depicted as sexually vulnerable in E. M. Forster's *A Passage to India* (1924) and other early interwar texts, she was increasingly an agent of her own degradation. An "unresisting victim[] of bad example and bad climate," she often failed to uphold British habits and values, from "dressing for dinner" to maintaining sexual modesty (Susanne Howe, *Novels of Empire*, Columbia UP, 1949, 43).

16. See Free, "British Women" 301–02; Free, " 'It Is I' " 382–83; and the section "Mystical Feminism" later in this chapter.

17. On antipodal colonial narratives, see Tamara S. Wagner, ed., *Domestic Fiction in Colonial Australia and New Zealand*, Pickering & Chatto, 2015, Gender and Genre 13. On the colonial girl, see Michelle J. Smith, *Empire in British Girls' Literature and Culture: Imperial Girls, 1880–1915*, Palgrave Macmillan, 2011; Michelle Smith, "Adventurous Girls of the British Empire: The Pre-War Novels of Bessie Marchant," *The Lion and the Unicorn*, vol. 33, no. 1, Jan. 2009, 1–25; Terri Doughty, "Domestic Goddesses on the Frontier; or, Tempting the Mothers of Empire with Adventure," *Victorian Settler Narratives: Emigrants, Cosmopolitans and Returnees in Nineteenth-Century Literature*, ed. Tamara S. Wagner, Pickering & Chatto, 2011, 193–205, Gender and Genre 5; and Kristine Moruzi, " 'The Freedom Suits Me': Encouraging Girls to Settle in the Empire," *Victorian Settler Narratives: Emigrants, Cosmopolitans and Returnees in Nineteenth-Century Literature*, ed. Tamara S. Wagner, Pickering & Chatto, 2011, 177–91, Gender and Genre 5.

18. Chrisman, *Postcolonial* 47. Speaking broadly of "the romance genre as pursued by Haggard," Chrisman does not, in this otherwise incisive observation, make the generic distinction that I do. For more on Haggard's colonial identity, see the section "South African Ties" in chapter 1.

19. Utterly immersing themselves in the life of Zu-Vendis, completely severing their ties with the metropole, bequeathing all the effects they left behind to their next of kin, and approving the "effectual clos[ur]e" of the last "possible means of ingress or egress from the country," Curtis and Good are opposing, in a critical sense, the imperial project (H. R. Haggard, *Allan Quatermain*, Penguin, 1995, 271). Curtis, as "King-Consort," goes so far as to devote himself to "the total exclusion of all foreigners from Zu-Vendis"; and though he plans to "pave the road for the introduction of true religion [Christianity] in the place of this senseless Sun worship" and to raise his son, the heir to "the throne of Zu-Vendis, . . . to become what an English gentleman should be, and generally is," Zu-Vendis is by no means a model imperial colony (275, 276, 275, 276). As for Quatermain, who dies in Zu-Vendis six months after receiving a battle wound, it seems unlikely that the quintessential "imperialist romancer[]" would have settled there had he lived (Richard F. Patteson, "*King Solomon's Mines*: Imperialism and Narrative Structure," *The Journal of Narrative Technique*, vol. 8, no. 2, Spring 1978, 121). On male "regression" (or "going native"), see Brantlinger, *Rule of Darkness* 190, 194, 229–30, 239, 268–70; Lane, *Ruling Passion* 61; and Norman A. Etherington, "Rider Haggard, Imperialism,

and the Layered Personality," *Victorian Studies*, vol. 22, no. 1, Autumn 1978, 79, 83–87. On "imperial masculinity as a transformative encounter," see Deane 205–25, quotation on 215.

20. Alison Winter notes Victorans' familiarity with the concept of "Scottish 'Second Sight'" (*Mesmerized: Powers of Mind in Victorian Britain*, U of Chicago P, 2000, 120; cf. 124).

21. On the subject of late nineteenth-century generic division, see Daly, *Modernism* 8, 23; Nicholas Daly, "Colonialism and Popular Literature at the Fin de Siècle," *Modernism and Colonialism: British and Irish Literature, 1899–1939*, ed. Richard Begam and Michael Valdez Moses, Duke UP, 2007, 35; Showalter, *Sexual Anarchy* 79; Martin Green, *Dreams of Adventure, Deeds of Empire*, Basic, 1979, 23; and LeeAnne Richardson, *New Woman and Colonial Adventure Fiction in Victorian Britain: Gender, Genre, and Empire*, U of Florida P, 2006, 22–30. Haggard's own stories were labeled either romance or novel by his publishers, understood as such by his reading public, classified in this manner by critics, and referred to in this way by the author himself.

22. Terrence Rodgers incorrectly refers to these three popular works as a "trilogy" ("Empires of the Imagination: Rider Haggard, Popular Fiction and Africa," *Writing and Africa*, ed. Mpalive-Hangson Msiska and Paul Hyland, Longman, 1997, 109). Scholars who have offered extended analyses of some of Haggard's other texts include G. C. Low, Lane, Rodgers, Richardson, Steere, Monsman (*H. Rider Haggard*), Chrisman (*Rereading* and *Postcolonial*), Paul Rich ("Romance and the Development of the South African Novel," *Literature and Society in South Africa*, ed. Landeg White and Tim Couzens, Longman, 1984, 120–37), Heidi H. Johnson ("Agricultural Anxiety, African Erasure: H. Rider Haggard's *Rural England* and *Benita: An African Romance*," *Victorians Institute Journal*, vol. 24, 1996, 113–37), and Neil Hultgren (*Melodramatic Imperial Writing from the Sepoy Rebellion to Cecil Rhodes*, Ohio UP, 2014). Jess, a colonial heroine who predates the female colonial romance by two decades, protects her family but does nothing to assist the indigenous.

23. Wakefield, quoted in A. James Hammerton, *Emigrant Gentlewomen: Genteel Poverty and Female Emigration, 1830–1914*, Croom Helm, 1979, 45.

24. Nan H. Dreher, "Redundancy and Emigration: The 'Woman Question' in Mid-Victorian Britain," *Victorian Periodicals Review*, vol. 26, no. 1, Spring 1993, 3; W. R. Greg, *Why Are Women Redundant?*, Trübner, 1869, *Internet Archive*, archive.org/details/whyarewomenredu00greggoog/page/n3, originally published in *National Review*, vol. 14, no. 28, Apr. 1862, 434–60. The census further revealed that two-thirds of Britain's female population between the ages of twenty and twenty-four, one-third between twenty-four and thirty-five, and more than two-fifths between twenty-four and forty were unmarried (Mary Poovey, *Uneven Developments: The Ideological Work of Gender in Mid-Victorian England*, U of Chicago P, 1988, 4).

25. Greg 5. Sally Ledger, *The New Woman: Fiction and Feminism at the Fin de Siècle*, Manchester UP, 1997, 11.

26. Julia Bush, *Edwardian Ladies and Imperial Power*, Leicester UP, 2000, 147, Women, Power, and Politics. On nineteenth-century female emigration societies, see Dreher; A. James Hammerton, "'Out of Their Natural Station': Empire and Empowerment in the Emigration of Lower-Middle-Class Women," *Imperial Objects: Essays on Victorian Women's Emigration and the Unauthorized Imperial Experience*, ed. Rita S. Krandis, Twayne, 1998, 143–69; Hammerton, *Emigrant*; Vron Ware, *Beyond the Pale: White Women, Racism and History*, Verso, 1992, 126–27; Richardson 35; Julia Bush, "'The Right Sort of Woman': Female Emigrators and Emigration to the British Empire, 1890–1910," *Women's History Review*, vol. 3, no. 3, 1994, 385–409; Jean Jacques Van-Helten and Keith Williams, "'The Crying Need of South Africa': The Emigration of Single British Women to the Transvaal, 1901–10," *Journal of Southern African Studies*, vol. 10, no. 1, Oct. 1983, 17–38; Strobel 26; Ledger, *New Woman* 66; and David 159–60.

27. Hammerton, *Emigrant* 142, 162, 163. Cf. Bush, *Edwardian* 159.

28. Van-Helten and Williams 21. See also Strobel 25; Tosh 75; Carmen Faymonville, "'Waste Not, Want Not': Even Redundant Women Have Their Uses," *Imperial Objects: Essays on Victorian Women's Emigration and the Unauthorized Imperial Experience*, ed. Rita S. Krandis, Twayne, 1998, 66; and Stephen Constantine, "Empire Migration and Social Reform, 1880–1950," *Migrants, Emigrants and Immigrants: A Social History of Migration*, ed. Colin G. Pooley and Ian D. Whyte, Routledge, 1991, 65.

29. W. A. Carrothers, *Emigration from the British Isles*, Cass, 1966, 248.

30. Quotations are from Alicia M. Cecil, "The Needs of South Africa: Female Emigration," *The Nineteenth Century and After*, vol. 51, Apr. 1902, 684, 683, 685; and Constantine 68. Similar contemporary assertions include May Hely Hutchinson, "Female Emigration to South Africa," *The Nineteenth Century and After*, vol. 51, Jan. 1902, 71–87; "The Need of Women Colonists in South Africa," letter, *Saturday Review*, 20 Sept. 1902, 365; and a "confidential [1902] report" by the leading South African female emigration society (qtd. in Cecillie Swaisland, *Servants and Gentlewomen to the Golden Land: The Emigration of Single Women from Britain to Southern Africa, 1820–1939*, Berg / U of Natal P, 1993, 42–43). See also Strobel 26; Van-Helten and Williams 22; and Andrew Thompson, "The Languages of Loyalism in Southern Africa, c. 1870–1939," *The English Historical Review*, vol. 118, no. 477, June 2003, 648. See "A Note on Terminology" at the beginning of this book.

31. See Van-Helten and Williams, passim, esp. 24–25, 28–29, 31–32; Cecil 690–92; and *Useful Information for Emigrants: The Transvaal*, South Africa, n.d., 32, *"South Africa" Handbook*, no. 18. On female immigration to southern Africa in this period, see, in particular, Van-Helten and Williams; Swaisland; and Brian L. Blakeley, "Women and Imperialism: The Colonial Office and Female Emigration to South Africa, 1901–1910," *Albion: A Quarterly Journal Concerned with British Studies*, vol. 13, no. 2, 1981, 131–49.

32. Van-Helten and Williams 31.

33. Carrothers 249–50 (quotation on 250). Nicholas Thomas, *Colonialism's Culture: Anthropology, Travel and Government*, Princeton UP, 1994, 150. Regarding the political shift, see also Craig Smith, "Every Man Must Kill the Thing He Loves: Empire, Homoerotics, and Nationalism in John Buchan's *Prester John*," *Novel: A Forum on Fiction*, vol. 28, no. 2, Winter 1995, 182. See "A Note on Terminology" at the beginning of this book, and the introduction, note 7.

34. Saul Dubow, "How British Was the British World? The Case of South Africa," *Journal of Imperial and Commonwealth History*, vol. 37, no. 1, Mar. 2009, 14. The more extreme rhetoric encouraged unity between Boers and British to serve as a bulwark against the "black peril." A specter that ranged from a black political majority to a black revolution, from "black men ruling whites" to blacks "whip[ping] the British back to the Thames," the "black peril" was imagined in political, military, and cultural terms (Roderick Jones, "The Black Peril in South Africa," *The Nineteenth Century and After*, vol. 55, May 1904, 715; *Voice of Missions*, the official organ of the African Methodist Episcopal Church, quoted in Jones 717). See also chapter 4, page 146.

35. Carrothers 250. Cf. Swaisland 43.

36. Frederick A. McKenzie, "After the War: Mr. H. Rider Haggard's Prophecies," *Daily Mail*, 7 Dec. 1901, 8.

37. "Mr. Rider Haggard on the Transvaal Constitution," *Times*, 7 Aug. 1906, 8. See my introduction, note 29.

38. The Report of the Committee on Agricultural Settlements in the British Colonies, 1906, quoted in H. R. Haggard, *Days* 2: 196. Cf. Carrothers 251–52. Other quotations are from H. R. Haggard, *Days* 2: 197, 202–03. Haggard's investigation of Salvation Army colonies led him to visit the United States and to urge settlement in particular to Canada, whose government had great "confidence" in the organization (H. Rider Haggard, *The Poor and the Land*, Longmans, 1905, xv). Haggard also "suggest[ed] that a Commissioner be sent to South Africa and especially to Rhodesia, to examine these Colonies and see what they are prepared to do to help" (H. R. Haggard, *Days* 2: 199).

39. D. S. Higgins, Introduction, *The Private Diaries of Sir H. Rider Haggard, 1914–1925*, by H. Rider Haggard, ed. Higgins, Cassell, 1980, ix.

40. See, for example, H. Rider Haggard, *The Private Diaries of Sir H. Rider Haggard, 1914–1925*, ed. D. S. Higgins, Cassell, 1980, 191; and H. Rider Haggard, "Woman and Life: Sir Rider Haggard's Views," *Daily Telegraph*, 18 Mar. 1922, 7.

41. Richardson 3.

42. Hammerton, *Emigrant* 152. Cf. Sally Mitchell, *The New Girl: Girls' Culture in England, 1880–1915*, Columbia UP, 1995, 35, 43.

43. Sally Ledger, "The New Woman and the Crisis of Victorianism," *Cultural Politics at the Fin de Siècle*, ed. Ledger and Scott McCracken, Cambridge UP, 1995, 35. Faymonville 66. The suffrage movement gained enormous momentum in 1903, when Emmeline and Christabel Pankhurst formed the Women's Social and Political Union, which had become "militant" by 1905 and violent by 1908 (Sophia A.

van Wingerden, *The Women's Suffrage Movement in Britain, 1866–1928*, Palgrave Macmillan, 1999, 71–72, 83–84).

44. Haggard, quoted in Ernestine Evans, "Britain's 'Superfluous Women' Driving Men Out, Says Haggard," *New York Tribune*, 22 July 1916, 1. On the phrase "superfluous women," see Ledger, *New Woman* 11; and Ardis 3, 10.

45. Strobel 25.

46. Haggard, quoted in Evans 1. Haggard, quoted in "Woman and Life" 7.

47. H. Rider Haggard, *She*, Oxford UP, 1998, 88, 256. Ardis 140.

48. H. Rider Haggard, "A Man's View of Woman," review of *Woman: The Predominant Partner*, by Edward Sullivan, in *She*, by Haggard, ed. Andrew M. Stauffer, Broadview, 2006, 340, originally published in *African Review of Mining, Finance and Commerce*, vol. 4, no. 96, 22 Sept. 1894, 407–08.

49. Daly, *Modernism* 26.

50. Though there had been "a brief debate on the subject of women's suffrage in the Cape Legislative Assembly" in 1892, the issue was not taken seriously in South Africa until 1907, when it came before the Cape House of Assembly, where it was defeated sixty-six to twenty-four. The Women's Christian Temperance Union, founded in 1889, was "the first society to advocate actively [for] women's suffrage," when it "established a 'Franchise Department'" in 1895, which led to the Cape Town Women's Enfranchisement League in 1907 (Cheryl Walker, *The Women's Suffrage Movement in South Africa*, Centre for African Studies, U of Cape Town, 1979, quotations on 23, 22–23).

51. See the work of historian Julie Wheelwright, "'Amazons and Military Maids': An Examination of Female Military Heroines in British Literature and the Changing Construction of Gender," *Women's Studies International Forum*, vol. 10, no. 5, 1987, 489–502; geographer Richard Phillips, *Mapping Men and Empire: A Geography of Adventure*, Routledge, 1996, 102–03; and a number of literary critics on the Robinsonade, such as Laura M. Stevens, "Reading the Hermit's Manuscript: *The Female American* and Female Robinsonades," *Approaches to Teaching Defoe's "Robinson Crusoe,"* ed. Maximillian E. Novak and Carl Fisher, MLA, 2005, 140–51.

52. It has long been rumored that Daniel Defoe wrote Davies's story, but this has never been confirmed (Wheelwright 502n5). Library catalogs, including the British Library's, generally list Defoe as the work's author.

53. Wheelwright 491, 492.

54. R. M. Ballantyne, *The Island Queen*, chapter 8, 11, 8, 7, 8, Project Gutenberg, 2007, www.gutenberg.org/files/21741/21741-h/21741-h.htm.

55. L. T. Meade, *Four on an Island: A Story of Adventure*, Chambers, n.d., 201, 110, see also 277.

56. See Mitchell 3, 25; and Bush, "'Right Sort'" 406n7.

57. Allan Quatermain, who appears in a number of short stories and novels, is eighteen at the start of *Marie* (1912) and twenty-one at its conclusion; he dies at the end of *Allan Quatermain* (1887) at the age of sixty-eight. Haggard's other male adventurers are generally in their twenties, thirties, or forties.

58. H. Rider Haggard, dedication to *King Solomon's Mines*, Modern Library, 2002, n.p. On girls reading adventure fiction intended primarily for boys and men, see Mitchell 112, 114; Kimberley Reynolds, *Girls Only? Gender and Popular Children's Fiction in Britain, 1880–1910*, Temple UP, 1990, 93; Judith Rowbotham, *Good Girls Make Good Wives: Guidance for Girls in Victorian Fiction*, Blackwell, 1989, 218; Edward Salmon, *Juvenile Literature as It Is*, Drane, 1888, 28, *Internet Archive*, archive.org/details/juvenileliterat00salmgoog/page/n10; Florence B. Low, "The Reading of the Modern Girl," *The Nineteenth Century and After*, vol. 59, Feb. 1906, 281; and Constance Barnicoat, "The Reading of the Colonial Girl," *The Nineteenth Century and After*, vol. 60, no. 358, Dec. 1906, 943.

59. Mitchell 104.

60. For example, "True Stories of Girl Heroines," a series by Evelyn Everett Green, appeared in *Girl's Realm* between 1899 and 1901, and "True Tales of Brave Women," a series by T. C. Bridges, in the same magazine between 1906 and 1907. Mitchell (105, 113) and Kristine Moruzi discuss the relationship between the Second Anglo-Boer War and girls' periodicals ("Feminine Bravery: The *Girl's Realm* (1898–1915) and the Second Boer War," *Children's Literature Association Quarterly*, vol. 34, no. 3, Fall 2009, 241–54). On British women teachers during the war, see Eliza Reidi, "Teaching Empire: British and Dominions Women Teachers in the South African War Concentration Camps," *English Historical Review*, vol. 120, no. 489, 2005, 1316–47.

61. Sheila Egoff and Judith Saltman note an increase in juvenile heroines of all types during the Edwardian era (*The New Republic of Childhood: A Critical Guide to Canadian Children's Literature in England*, 3rd ed., Oxford UP, 1990, 10). Regarding the effects of World War I on juvenile fiction, see Mitchell 182–88.

62. G. A. Henty, *A Soldier's Daughter and Other Stories*, Blackie, 1906, 8, 47, 108, *Internet Archive*, www.archive.org/details/soldiersdaughter00hentiala. See also G. A. Henty, "A Frontier Girl: A Tale of the Backwood Settlements," *In the Hands of the Malays and Other Stories*, by Henty, Blackie, 1905, 149–76.

63. The original source for the commonly used phrase "the girls' Henty" appears to be the *Daily Chronicle*, date unknown, which is quoted in frontispiece advertisements to a number of Marchant novels (see Doughty 252n4; and Phillips 91). Other quotations are from Mitchell 137, 117.

64. Quotations are from Phillips 100, 92, 105; and M. Smith, "Adventurous Girls" 10. Phillips describes Bessie Marchant's *Daughters of the Dominion* (1910), set in Canada, as being "on the edge" of wilderness, as many of her stories are. Marchant's work is generally considered to be ambivalent, roundly so by Phillips (89–112) and J. S. Bratton ("British Imperialism and the Reproduction of Femininity in Girls' Fiction, 1900–1930," *Imperialism and Juvenile Literature*, ed. Jeffrey Richards, Manchester UP, 1989, 201–06). For M. Smith (2), as well as for Mary Cadogan and Patricia Craig, Marchant falls somewhat on the traditional side (Cadogan and Craig, *You're a Brick, Angela! The Girls' Story, 1839–1985*, Gollancz,

1986, 57). For Mitchell (116–17) and Doughty, she is slightly more progressive, but even Doughty concedes that Marchant "does not seem to stray too far from contemporaneous notions of British womanhood, despite playing to her girl readers' resentment of sexism" (203).

65. Robert Dixon, *Writing the Colonial Adventure: Race, Gender and Nation in Anglo-Australian Popular Fiction, 1875–1914*, Cambridge UP, 1995, 94.

66. Following the first government-sponsored migration of the British to southern Africa (1820) and the abolition of slavery throughout the British empire just over a decade later (1833), approximately ten thousand Boers (mostly farming families) sought to escape the reach of British authority by heading north and east in the 1830s and early '40s. This years-long event is referred to as the Great Trek, and those migrant Boers as *voortrekkers* (George M. Fredrickson, *White Supremacy: A Comparative Study in American and South African History*, Oxford UP, 1981, 169).

67. See note 43 in this chapter.

68. Meade 172. Henty, *Soldier's* 9. Rosa Praed, *Fugitive Anne: A Romance of the Unexplored Bush* (1904), 119, *ManyBooks.net*, www.manybooks.net/titles/praedrosother08fugitive_ann.html. Only the craven Ishmael views "the calm courage" that Rachel displays as "unusual in a woman" (*GK* 90).

69. Patteson 112–13. While condensed, my rendition includes each of his twelve points. Fifty years earlier, Edward Shanks provided a comparable outline of Haggard's stories specifically: "There is again and again the white adventurer who has some motive for seeking his fortune in unknown lands. There is the hidden race, guarding a treasure of one sort or another. There are the strange customs and religious beliefs of this race, which, generally, is divided against itself at the moment when the adventurers arrive, so that they can establish themselves by throwing their weight on the side of one part or the other. This pattern makes the essential framework of more stories than I can enumerate off-hand" (74–75).

70. Patteson 113.

71. See "A Note on Terminology" at the beginning of this book. Lobengula, King of the Matabele from 1868 to 1894, appeared frequently in the British press in the 1890s. Heidi H. Johnson makes an interesting case for reading "the novel's subplot" as a conflict between industrialization and rural agriculture, respectively represented by the Matabele and the Makalanga, who, she claims, "serv[e] only as symbolic understudies in a decidedly British drama" (114). Though not an extant designation, early twentieth-century British historians described the Makalanga as the southernmost branch of the Mashona (Shona), who had early contact with the Portuguese and were decimated by the Matabele over the course of many years, beginning in 1826, when Moselekatse (Mosilikatse/Mzilikazi) split with Tchaka (Chaka/Shaka), King of the Zulu. See George McCall Theal, *The Beginning of South African History*, Unwin, 1902, 211–12, *Google Books*, books.google.com/books?id=I_UQW4RSs4sC&printsec=frontcover&dq=beginning+of+south+african+history&hl=en&ei=d1cnToeaAub20gHJm-HMCg&sa=X&oi=book_result&ct=result

&resnum=1&ved=0CC0Q6AEwAA#v=onepage&q&f=false; and "The British South Africa Company Historical Catalogue and Souvenir of Rhodesia Empire Exhibition, Johannesburg, 1936–37," *The Great North Road*, bsac.greatnorthroad.org/bsac.pdf. Haggard's suggestion that the Makalanga were descended from "some ancient people such as Egyptians or Phoenicians; men whose forefathers had been wise and civilised," is consistent with his tendency in the male imperial romance—and that of Europeans generally—to attribute signs of what they deemed "civilization" (such as mines, stone structures, or artwork) in Africa to people who did not have "negro-blood" (*B* 89). See also *B* 291; H. R. Haggard, *King Solomon's Mines* 116, 202–03, 207; H. R. Haggard, *Allan Quatermain* 149; H. R. Haggard, *She* 129, 178–79; and Haggard's short story "Allan's Wife" (1889) (H. Rider Haggard, "Allan's Wife," *Hunter Quatermain's Story: The Uncollected Adventures of Allan Quatermain*, ed. Peter Haining, Peter Owen, 2003, 200, 207). Anti-Semitism, a frequent trope in British South African fiction of the period, was often employed to offload avarice onto those other than the British.

72. The Kingdom of Monomotapa flourished from the mid-fifteenth through the early mid-seventeenth centuries between the Limpopo and Zambesi Rivers.

73. Recovering from a minor surgery and the major disappointment of his failed emigration proposal, Haggard spent a couple of days in the fall of 1906 at the home of Rudyard Kipling. "Here . . . we compounded the plot of 'The Ghost Kings' together, writing down our ideas in alternate sentences upon the same sheet of foolscap" (H. R. Haggard, *Days* 2: 208). According to Haggard biographer D. S. Higgins, Kipling's major contribution was the realm of the Ghost Kings, which, its titular status notwithstanding, Haggard ultimately "relegated . . . to a small section at the end of the book" (*Great Storyteller* 196).

74. In the "Extract" from an unattributed "letter headed 'The King's Kraal, Zululand, 12th May, 1855,' " which opens the novel, readers learn that "[t]he Zulus . . . have a strange story of a white girl who in Dingaan's (Dingane's) day was supposed to 'hold the spirit' of some legendary goddess of theirs who is also white" (*GK* vii). We later learn that the name of that goddess is Nomkubulwana, and that she is not simply a goddess, but, as Dingaan tells Rachel at their first meeting, "the Spirit of our People" (127). In the Zulu tradition, Nomkhubulwane, as it is more commonly spelled in English, is a goddess, but she is neither white nor the primary deity. She is, rather, "the goddess of rain, nature and fertility" ("The Goddess, the Festival and Virginity Testing," *Alan Paton Centre & Struggle Archives*, U of Kwazulu-Natal, paton.ukzn.ac.za/Collections/Nomkhubulwane.aspx).

75. Dingaan was king of the Zulus from 1828 to 1840.

76. Comparisons between the British on the frontier and the British in the metropole, as well as between frontier space and metropolitan space, occur in both the male imperial and the female colonial romance. Holly, for instance, wonders more than once what his "fossil friends down at Cambridge" would think if they could see him among the Amahagger (H. R. Haggard, *She* 76, see also 103).

77. Haggard, *King Solomon's Mines* 224. Stott, *Fabrication* 102. See also Patteson 120–21; David Bunn, "Embodying Africa: Woman and Romance in Colonial

Fiction," *English in Africa*, vol. 15, no. 1, 1988, 1–27; Rebecca Stott, "The Dark Continent: Africa as Female Body in Haggard's Adventure Fiction," *Feminist Review*, no. 32, Summer 1989, 69–89; Nancy Armstrong, "The Occidental Alice," *differences*, vol. 2, no. 2, 1990, 31; McClintock 1–4; G. C. Low 6, 49; and Rodgers 116. For more on Ayesha, see note 9 in this chapter. For more on Gagool, see Gilbert and Gubar, *Sexchanges* 48–49, 140; David 194–97; McClintock 235–36, 245–48, 254; and Murphy, "Gendering of History" 747.

78. For the Boer heroine of *Swallow*, who expects that her lover will rescue her, love and loss compel waiting more than acting, patience more than growth.

79. The passage reads in full: "And as she lay and heard, her youthful blood, drawn by Nature's magnetic force, as the moon draws the tide, rose in her veins like the sap in the *budding* trees, and *stirred* her virginal serenity. All the bodily natural part of her caught the tones of Nature's happy voice that bade her break her bonds, live and love, and be a woman. And lo! the spirit within her answered to it, and flung wide her bosom's doors, and of a sudden, as it were, something *quickened* and lived in her heart that was of her and yet had its own life—a life apart; something that sprang from her and another, and that would always be with her now and could never die; and she rose pale and trembling, as a woman trembles at the first *stirring* of the child that she shall bear, and clung to the flowery bough of the beautiful bush above and then sank down again, feeling the spirit of her girlhood had departed from her, and that another angel had entered there; knew that she loved with heart and soul and body, and was a very woman" (H. Rider Haggard, *Jess*, McKinlay, 1887, 51; my emphases).

80. His arrival gives Rachel the determination to demand that she be allowed to leave Zululand, but it is a demand she makes herself. As the Zulus note, Richard "dwell[s] in the shadow of the Inkosazana" (*GK* 351).

81. H. Rider Haggard, *Swallow*, Longmans, 1899, 308, 80, *Internet Archive*, www.archive.org/details/swallowtaleofgre00haggiala, hereafter cited parenthetically as *S*.

82. The term "Red Kaffir" was sometimes used by the British to refer to the Ngwane, a branch of the Swazi, and the Endwandwe to refer to the Ndwandwe, tribes with a history of conflict. See "A Note on Terminology" at the beginning of this book.

83. H. Rider Haggard, *The Holy Flower*, Ward, 1915, 76. Quatermain's name is also translated as "he who keeps his eyes open" (H. R. Haggard, *King Solomon's Mines* 34).

84. Allan Quatermain, who narrates *The Holy Flower*, notes, "owing to a queer native custom, . . . Sir Theophilus Shepstone [Haggard's mentor], whom I used to know very well, [was] recognized as the holder of the spirit of the great Chaka [see note 71 in this chapter] and therefore as the equal of the Zulu monarchs" (196).

85. Regarding the "tremendous and most imposing welcome" that the Zulus give to Rachel (*GK* 119), see page 85 in this chapter. In the male romances, sights described as never-before-seen-by-whites are usually unpeopled vistas.

86. H. R. Haggard, *Holy Flower* 332. Cf. H. R. Haggard, *Allan Quatermain* 216. There is the occasional exception to the motivations of Haggard's British men: Curtis's journey to Kukuanaland (in *King Solomon's Mines*), for instance, is motivated entirely by love, the love of a brother, who was himself, however, on a quest for wealth.

87. As quoted on page 84 of this chapter, Haggard similarly describes Benita's salutation by the Makalanga as "a wondrous and imposing spectacle" (*B* 309).

88. Specifically, Rachel alludes to Dingaan's role in the death of his brother, King Tchaka (Chaka/Shaka), which Haggard describes in his 1892 novel, *Nada the Lily*.

89. Compare to Haggard's own position as Master and Registrar of the High Court of the Transvaal at "barely twenty-one years of age and [having] received no legal training" (H. R. Haggard, *Days* 1: 108).

90. See "A Note on Terminology" at the beginning of this book.

91. Sharpe 73.

92. See "A Note on Terminology" at the beginning of this book.

93. Following the discovery of diamonds in southern Africa (1867), the British began surveying in Matabele (Ndebele) territory, which, after the subsequent discovery of gold (1886), the Rudd Concession (1888), and the Royal Charter of the British South Africa Company (1889), would ultimately lead to the First and Second Matabele Wars, or the Chimurengas (uprisings) of 1893–1894 and 1896–1897. For more on this, see chapter 3, pages 111–13.

94. See note 66 in this chapter.

95. Rachel's position is comparable to that of Theophilus Shepstone, Haggard's beloved mentor, who annexed the Transvaal in 1877, when, as Haggard put it, referencing the Zulu King, "Cetewayo's great standing army of fifty or sixty thousand warriors were clamouring to be allowed 'to wash their spears,' and as he did not wish to fight the English and we would not allow him to fight the Swazis, only the Boers remained. In considering the history of the annexation of the Transvaal it should never be forgotten that Shepstone was aware of this fact" (H. R. Haggard, *Days* 1: 81).

96. H. R. Haggard, *Benita* 277. H. R. Haggard, *Jess* 308. H. R. Haggard, *Benita* 276. For more on *Jess*, see chapter 1.

97. As Bratton has noted, the young colonial heroine in girls' fiction of the period may "pull[] the trigger, or strike[] the blow," but then she "instantly faints away, overcome by the conflicting imperatives of Englishness and femininity" (201). For Haggard's heroines, there is no such conflict, English femininity being acceptably masculinized on the South African frontier. In a rare outpouring of emotion, Benita, immediately following her rescue of Robert, "her part played and the victory won, . . . burst into tears and fell upon her lover's breast." The very next sentence, however, sees her "free[ing] herself from his arms" to lead her father's rescue (*B* 311). For further discussion of this scene, see "Recovery and Loss," this chapter's penultimate section.

98. A caveat. Three words and a question mark follow the words offered above, so that the sentence reads in full: "Lady, from henceforth I am your servant, *am I not?*" (*GK* 67; my emphasis). The question Noie poses is one that Rachel does not directly answer. Noie has other things in common with Friday: fairer skin than others of her "race" (descended on one side from Ghost-people, Noie is fairer than most Zulus), broken English (even after years of speaking the language), the assumption of a Christian name (significantly not used by Rachel), and the willingness literally to bow down before her rescuer. But whereas Friday places his head beneath Crusoe's foot, Noie "presse[s] her forehead *on* [Rachel's] feet" (129; my emphasis). Later on, Noie "knelt before Rachel and kissed the hem of her robe, bur Rachel bent down and lifted her up in her strong arms, embracing her *as a mother embraces a child*" (261; my emphasis). Their status, clearly, is never equal.

99. Haggard tends to depict Boers as racist in comparison to the British.

100. The difference in status between Sihamba and Suzanne is significantly more pronounced than that between Rachel and Noie, an effect, in part, of the strong racial prejudice of *Swallow*'s Boer narrator. Haggard was by no means alone, either in ascribing to the majority of his Boer characters prejudice against both indigenous Africans and the British, or in condemning such prejudice through the judgments and behaviors of, and comparisons to, many of his British South African characters. The narrative of white-woman-saving-indigenous-girl-and-earning-her-loyalty can also be seen in "Imbabala," a short story (whether fiction, fact, or a combination of both is unclear) published in South Africa the same year as *The Ghost Kings*. Written by a female colonist living with her husband near Zululand, it describes how, negotiating with Imbabala's father, she rescued the young "Zulu maiden" from being forced into marriage with a man "of uncertain temper and uncertain years." "In the end," she writes, "Imbabala became my 'property,' and for nearly six years [until Imbabala married a man of her own choosing] served me well and faithfully" (R. R., "Imbabala," *South African Stories and Sketches*, 8th series, South Africa, n.d., 14, 15, 18, *"South Africa" Handbook*, no. 45, originally published in *South Africa: A Weekly Journal for All Interested in South African Affairs*, July 1908).

101. Daly, *Modernism* 62.

102. While Benita da Ferreira is Portuguese, not African, and "the one appointed" to whom alone she will reveal the gold's location is European, her multi-century vigil at Bambatse and her equally long relationship with the Makalanga associate her with indigeneity (*B* 91).

103. H. R. Haggard, *Allan Quatermain* 126. The indigenous are horrified by this senseless assault on "a family of tame animals . . . daily fed by priests. . . . Thus it came about that in attempting to show off we had committed sacrilege of a most aggravated nature" (141).

104. Sihamba uses savvy and sacrifice rather than supernatural abilities to save Suzanne.

105. No similar utterance, to my knowledge, is made in Haggard's male imperial romances, where the quality of white-indigenous, male-male relationships is often marked by loyalty but not necessarily by love. Umslopogaas may be an exception, but only partly, for although "there is that between [them] that cannot be seen, and yet is too strong for breaking," Umslopogaas, as Allan knows, "wouldst [sic] split [him] to the chin if [he] stood in [his] path" (H. R. Haggard, *Allan Quatermain* 209, 210).

106. Mopo and Dingaan were both involved in the death of Tchaka (Chaka/Shaka). Mopo narrates this story in *Nada the Lily* (1892). See note 88 in this chapter.

107. The scene resonates with the one in *The Ghost Kings*, described on pages 88–89 in this chapter, in which Rachel commands a Zulu impi from atop the hut where Ishmael had held her captive.

108. See pages 83–84.

109. Haggard's English translation of the (fictional) language of the "ancient People of the Ghosts" resembles an older form of English, likely to denote their antiquity and relative isolation (*GK* 342). My reasoning is as follows: in *King Solomon's Mines*, the (fictional) Kukuana, an ancient, self-isolating tribe from whom the Zulus are descended, speak "an old-fashioned form of the Zulu tongue, bearing about the same relationship to it that the English of Chaucer does to the English of the nineteenth century" (H. R. Haggard, *King Solomon's Mines* 82).

110. H. R. Haggard, *Allan Quatermain* 92.

111. See, in particular, *The Ghost Kings* 159, 328–29. To a lesser extent, the same is true of Sihamba's love for Suzanne (see *S* 81, 150, 219, 293).

112. Daly, *Modernism* 64; my emphasis. Cf. note 19 in this chapter.

113. Elana Gomel, "Lost and Found: The Lost World Novel and the Shape of the Past," *Genre*, vol. 40, no. 1/2, Spring/Summer 2007, 119.

114. H. Rider Haggard, *Marie*, Wildside, n.d., 344. Marie is strictly "of the Huguenot stock," while Suzanne has both Dutch and Huguenot ancestry (4).

115. In Haggard's lifetime, at least six editions of *Benita* were published in Britain (others appeared in Germany, Sweden, Poland, the United States, and India) and seven of *The Ghost Kings*.

116. See Mitchell 187.

117. Evans 1.

118. H. R. Haggard, "Woman and Life" 7.

119. G. C. Low writes, "women who possess agency in Haggard are inevitably punished for it" (48).

Chapter 3. Colony of Dreadful Delight: Gertrude Page and the Rhodesian Settler Romance

1. "The Closing Year," *Buluwayo Chronicle*, Dec. 30, 1922, 6. "Gertrude Page," *Buluwayo Chronicle*, 8 Apr. 1922, 1. The newspaper, like Page herself much of the time, refers to the colony as a country.

2. The quotations are from Colin Black, *The Legend of Lomagundi*, North-Western Development Association, 1976, 61; and "Closing Year." Frederick Glyn, 4th Baron Wolverton, praised *The Edge o' Beyond* (1908) in the *Daily Telegraph* ("The Novels of Gertrude Page," advertisement, *The Rhodesian*, by Gertrude Page, Hurst, 1912, 14, n.p.). Walter Long, MP, recommended *Jill's Rhodesian Philosophy* to King George V (Untitled, *Buluwayo Chronicle*, 15 July 1910, 3). Page was a favorite author of the king's wife, Queen Mary, who had "read most of her books" ("Death of Miss Gertrude Page," *Bedfordshire Times and Woburn Reporter*, 7 Apr. 1922, page unknown). Page's prominence in Australia is mentioned in "Day by Day," *Buluwayo Chronicle*, 9 Feb. 1912, 4. Of her Rhodesian novels, *Love in the Wilderness* was translated into Dutch, *The Edge o' Beyond* into Czech and Polish, and *The Pathway* into Norwegian. There is also a braille copy of *The Veldt Trail*. Though Page's first novel followed Cynthia Stockley's *Virginia of the Rhodesians* (1903) by four years—and appeared the same year as *God's Outpost* (1907), a novel by British South Africa Company administrator Henry Cullen Gouldsbury—Manfred Nathan wrote in 1925 that Stockley "followed in the footsteps of Gertrude Page" (*South African Literature: A General Survey*, Juta, 1925, 225). This likely reflects Page's greater influence and readership more so than it does the format of *Virginia of the Rhodesians*, which was a collection of linked stories rather than a novel. For a brief discussion of Rhodesian novels between 1920 and 1930, see J. P. L. Snyman, *The South African Novel in English (1880–1930)*, U of Potchefstroom for C.H.E., 1952, 161–66, U Lig Series.

3. Beatrice Powell notes that by 1920 Page's sales in books "already exceed[ed] two million copies" (Preface, *Gleanings from the Writings of "Gertrude Page,"* by Gertrude Page, Hurst, 1920, v), and according to Colin Black, "her total sales exceeded 2 ½ million copies" (61). Her obituary in the *Times*, however, states that she had "millions [of] readers" ("A Popular Novelist: Death of Miss Gertrude Page," *Times*, 3 Apr. 1922, 5), and according to Anthony Chennells she sold "millions of copies of [her] novels" ("Imperial Romances and Narratives of White Rhodesian Nationalism. Cynthia Stockley, Gertrude Page and Doris Lessing," *Anglistica: An Interdisciplinary Journal of English Studies*, vol. 3, no. 2, 1999, 79). More precisely, Page published eleven Rhodesian novels; one collection of Rhodesian short stories, *Far from the Limelight* (1918); and one cowritten Rhodesian novel, 1918's *The Course of My Ship*, with Robert Aubrey Foster-Melliar. Two of Page's Rhodesian novels were made into films: *Edge o' Beyond*, directed by Fred W. Durrant, Samuelson, 1919; and *Love in the Wilderness*, directed by Alexander Butler, Samuelson, 1920.

4. *Hutchinson's Story Magazine*, vol. 1, no. 1, July 1919. The quotation appears in a brief editorial introduction to Rudyard Kipling, "The Supports," pages 11–13 of that issue. Page's story, set aboard a passenger ship to southern Africa, is titled "Her Man" and appears on pages 55–60.

5. "Gertrude Page. Burial at Umvukwe," *Buluwayo Chronicle*, 22 Apr. 1922, 8.

6. The articles appeared between 1905 and 1907, usually with a three-to-four-month lag between writing and publication. In her accounts of her experience

as a new immigrant, housekeeping and farming challenges figure prominently, while her encounters with the British community in nearby Salisbury, travel, and growing knowledge of Rhodesian economic prospects also have a place.

7. The story appears in twenty-six installments, with a particularly relevant passage in the second. Here are a few additional highlights from that passage: "She happened to be born a woman and she must abide by the consequences. If she feels she is capable of something nobler and better than the life assigned to her by custom and society, the sooner she crushes the feeling the better it will be; it is madness to cherish it; there is no place in the ranks for her. She is a woman, and woman's place is at home, be it never so uncongenial and disheartening. What more can she possibly want than household duties; and for pleasures, pretty clothes, tea-parties, and entertainments, with her chief aim to look nice and marry well? It is not an aim to treat lightly either, for if she fails to secure a husband there is nothing for her but the 'martyrdom of spinsterhood'" (Gertrude Page, "If Loving Hearts Were Never Lonely—; or, Madge Harcourt's Desolation," *Girl's Own Paper*, vol. 19, no. 928, 9 Oct. 1897, 23).

8. Nathan 225. S. G. Liebson, "The South Africa of Fiction," *The State*, vol. 7, no. 2, Feb. 1912, 139. Liebson then qualifies his claim, offering Richard Dehan (Clotilde Graves), author of *The Dop Doctor* (1910), as the most popular writer of the moment (139). Page specifically mentions Schreiner's writing in *The Veldt Trail*, Cassell, n.d., 4, hereafter cited parenthetically as *Veldt*.

9. "Gertrude Page," *Buluwayo Chronicle*, 8 Apr. 1922, 1.

10. Gertrude Page, *Where the Strange Roads Go Down*, Hurst, 19–, 228, hereafter cited parenthetically as *Strange*. Gertrude Page, *Jill's Rhodesian Philosophy; or, The Dam Farm*, Hurst, n.d., 73, hereafter cited parenthetically as *Jill's*.

11. Gertrude Page, *Love in the Wilderness: The Story of Another African Farm*, Hurst, n.d., 213, hereafter cited parenthetically as *Love*.

12. Gertrude Page, "Second Impressions of Rhodesian Farm Life," *Empire Review*, vol. 10, no. 56, Sept. 1905, 137. Both the title of Page's 1915 novel *Follow After!* and 1913's *Where the Strange Roads Go Down* are taken from Rudyard Kipling's poem "Song of the Dead" (1893), which commends the sacrifices of empire builders.

13. Gertrude Page, "Pictorial Acrostic," "Our Little Folks' Own Puzzles," *Little Folks: The Magazine for Boys and Girls*, 1 Jan. 1884, 61. It is possible the writer is a different Gertrude Page, since she gives her age as "15¼" and her residence as "Hay, R.S.O., Breconshire," which is just inside the border of Wales. The answer to the puzzle: coal! "Death of Miss Gertrude Page." Wade Burgess, "Gertrude Page," *SouthAfricaBooks.com*, 2010, 18 May 2014. Powell vii. Page indicates that her husband is a mechanical engineer in "Enlistment of Men Over Age," *Buluwayo Chronicle*, 1 Apr. 1918, 7.

14. Powell vii. Powell seems to be off with her dates, for if it was eighteen years before the Dobbins cleared a profit, that would mean that they did not do so until the year of Page's death. Why, then, didn't Powell write that rather than writing that by the time the couple was in the black Page had become famous

(which was in fact many years earlier)? Cf. Jock McCulloch, *Black Peril, White Virtue: Sexual Crime in Southern Rhodesia, 1902–1935*, Indiana UP, 2000, 17. The Woburn Sands Collection places Page's emigration in 1904 ("Gertrude Page: 'The Kipling of Rhodesia,'" *Woburn Sands Collection*, n.d., www.mkheritage.co.uk/wsc/docs/gertpage.html), and while Page's essays did not appear in the *Empire Review* until 1905, a reference that she makes in her final article (at the end of 1907) to having been in Rhodesia for at least four years suggests that she may have immigrated as early as late 1903 (Gertrude Page, "Advance, Rhodesia: Farming Prospects," *Empire Review* vol. 14, no. 82, Nov. 1907, 305). The BSAC sold land at about three shillings per acre at the time that the Dobbins purchased theirs (*Useful Information for Emigrants: Rhodesia*, 2nd ed., South Africa, n.d., 7, "South Africa" Handbook, no. 6). Contemporary references to the economic aspects of Rhodesian farming include "Emigration to South Africa," *African Review of Mining, Finance and Commerce*, 7 July 1894, 14; H. Marshall Hole, "Rhodesia, by a Resident," *British Africa*, Kegan, 1899, 28, The British Empire Series 2; Gertrude Page, "Life in Rhodesia," *Empire Review* vol. 10, no. 60, Jan. 1906, 564; Gertrude Page, "Farm Life in Rhodesia," *Empire Review* vol. 12, no. 67, Aug. 1906, 55; and Gertrude Page, *Jill's* 181. I also consulted Deborah Kirkwood, "Settler Wives in Southern Rhodesia," *The Incorporated Wife*, ed. Hilary Callan and Shirley Ardener, Croom Helm, 1984, 153.

15. A short piece in the *Times* mentions that Page was in Spain in early 1921 ("Court Circular," *Times*, 5 Apr. 1921, 13, *Times Digital Archive*).

16. Robert H. MacDonald, *The Language of Empire: Myths and Metaphors of Popular Imperialism, 1880–1918*, Manchester UP, 1994, 114, 118, Studies in Imperialism. Anthony Chennells notes that settlers were referring to themselves as Rhodesians by the turn of the century ("Imagining and Living the Exotic: A Context for Early Rhodesian Novels," *Journal of Literary Studies*, vol. 19, no. 2, June 2003, 137). See "A Note on Terminology" at the beginning of this book

17. MacDonald 114. Stephen Donovan, "Colonial Pedigree: Class, Masculinity, and History in the Early Rhodesian Novel," *Nordic Journal of English Studies*, vol. 11, no. 2, 2012, 62.

18. MacDonald 115–19. The quotations are respectively from Chennells, "Imagining" 137; and Martin Green, *Dreams of Adventure, Deeds of Empire*, Basic, 1979, 399n16.

19. Ruth First and Ann Scott, *Olive Schreiner*, Schocken, 1980, 225. See "A Note on Terminology" at the beginning of this book.

20. MacDonald 118–19. A 1906 guidebook puts the black population at 600,000 (*How to See South Africa* 285). McCulloch estimates that the black population in 1911 was 500,000 (*Black Peril* 13–14), while Kirkwood estimates it at greater by half (146).

21. The 1904 and 1911 settlement figures are from McCulloch, *Black Peril* 88, 219n19, 17. McCulloch puts the 1911 gender ratio at one to three in *Black Peril* and one to two in "Empire and Violence, 1900–1939," *Gender and Empire*, ed. Philippa Levine, Oxford UP, 2004, 228, Oxford History of the British Empire

Companion Series. According to Kirkwood, there were 23,606 whites in Rhodesia in 1911 and the female-to-male gender ratio was one to two (146). The 1923 figure is from Donal Lowry, "Shame Upon 'Little England' While 'Greater England Stands!': Southern Rhodesia and the Imperial Idea," *The Round Table, the Empire/Commonwealth and British Foreign Policy*, ed. Andrea Bosco and Alex May, Lothian Foundation, 1997, 306. Dane Kennedy provides a table of Rhodesia's European population, taken from Southern Rhodesia's 1952 *Official Yearbook of Southern Rhodesia*; its figures match those stated here, though it puts the 1904 population at the lower end of the twelve thousand to sixteen thousand number that McCulloch provides (Dane Kennedy, *Islands of White: Settler Society and Culture in Kenya and Southern Rhodesia, 1890–1937*, Duke UP, 1987, 197, table 4).

22. Lowry 311, 309. Cf. McCulloch, *Black Peril* 17. In his carefully researched book on settler society in Kenya and Rhodesia, Kennedy notes that the majority of Rhodesia's early settlers came from South Africa, but he also provides an appendix showing that this had changed by 1915 (7, 203, table 9). As Lowry points out, "moreover, the settler population remained constantly shifting, with a high-rate of migration between Rhodesia and South Africa" (309).

23. *Useful Information for Emigrants: Rhodesia* 3. Lowry 309.

24. Though there were financial qualifications, the ordinance gave the vote to women over twenty-one, whether married or single. In Britain, women over thirty (and those with property) gained this right a year earlier, but it would be another decade before all single women between the ages of twenty-one and thirty could vote there. In 1924, Northern Rhodesia—today's Zambia—became a British protectorate. Neither region, then, was any longer administered by the BSAC. The north had significantly fewer settlers than the south: 1,497 in 1911, for instance, compared to twenty-three thousand. See R. R. Kuczynski, *South Africa High Commission Territories, East Africa, Mauritius and the Seychelles*, Oxford UP, 1949, 104, table 1, *Demographic Survey*, vol. 2. As Lowry notes, when people wrote or spoke about Rhodesia without a prefix, they were almost always referring to the south/South (307).

25. "A Popular Novelist."

26. "Enlistment of Men Over Age." Gertrude Page recounts: "My husband came home from Rhodesia in 1917 to try to get into the British Army. He is a full trained mechanical engineer, a first-class shot, in excellent health, with two years' service in the Volunteers to his credit." After being rejected by the army and mechanical transport, he went "to France as a voluntary driver with the Red Cross; no pay, to find his own uniform, and to do work—in spite of all his incontestable qualifications—that is efficiently done by women." Her objection to the military's deeming willing men " 'unfit' for some more or less trifling reason" (like age) appears in her fiction as well (Gertrude Page, *Follow After!*, Hurst, 1915, 191, hereafter cited parenthetically as *Follow*). For instance: Jack Desborough in *Follow After!* and Edgar Whitehead in "The Falling Gods" (Gertrude Page, *Far from the Limelight*, Cassell, 1918, 138; hereafter cited parenthetically as *Limelight*).

27. "Mashonaland News. The Political Campaign. Enter 'Gertrude Page,'" *Buluwayo Chronicle*, 31 Mar. 1911, 5. The article references Page's letter of March 24, 1911.

28. Black 61.

29. Lowry 316. "Rhodesia is more British than any other South African colony," wrote Page in a 1909 *Times* article titled "The Future of Rhodesia" (*Times*, 11 Oct. 1909, 4, *Times Digital Archive*). "It is so intensely British (God grant we can keep it so!)," echoes the heroine of *Jill's Rhodesian Philosophy* (129). "The last loyal white colony," was how regular visitor Rudyard Kipling described it; "a bit of England," claimed Lord Buxton, British High Commissioner to South Africa; "our most imperial possession in South Africa," wrote another statesman; according to a third, Rhodesians were "more manifestly proud" of their association with England "than . . . any other of our colonists" (C. E. Carrington, *The Life of Rudyard Kipling*, Doubleday, 1955, 302; Buxton, quoted in Lowry 311; G. Seymour Fort, "British South Africa," *The Scottish Geographical Magazine* vol. 12, no. 6, June 1896, 289; Charles W. Boyd, "Rhodesia," *British Africa*, Kegan, 1899, 10, The British Empire Series 2). See my introduction, note 7.

30. Gertrude Page, "Future." Sir James, a political leader in her 1913 novel *The Pathway*, similarly opposes Rhodesia's "inclusion in the South African Union," on the basis that it would lead to "bi-lingualism and an influx of undesirable poor settlers from the south" (Gertrude Page, *The Pathway*, 4th ed., Ward, 1914, 25, hereafter cited parenthetically as *Pathway*).

31. "Sudden Death of Gertrude Page at Salisbury on Saturday: Famous Novelist Dies at Meikle's Hotel (From Our Own Correspondent)," *Buluwayo Chronicle*, 8 Apr. 1922, 3. "From Gertrude Page, Apathy Denounced, to the Editor, *Buluwayo Chronicle*," *Buluwayo Chronicle*, 23 Apr. 1920, 5.

32. "Rhodesian Life," *Buluwayo Chronicle*, 4 Feb. 1922, 5. The heroine of Page's 1921 novel, *Jill on a Ranch*, makes an oblique reference to Jollie: "I am glad to say that a woman has [been . . .] travelling up and down the country rousing people. . . . [S]he has done wonders in rallying them, and I believe this next election is going to be a staggering revelation to many" (Gertrude Page, *Jill on a Ranch*, Cassell, 1921, 201, hereafter cited parenthetically as *Ranch*).

33. "Slow Progress," *Buluwayo Chronicle*, 24 Dec. 1921, 1.

34. "Sudden Death." The *Buluwayo Chronicle* republished the *Herald* piece in this announcement of Page's death.

35. Gertrude Page, "Life in Rhodesia," *Empire Review*, vol. 11, no. 63, Apr. 1906, 253.

36. The 1851 census, from which the 500,000 figure is taken (Nan H. Dreher, "Redundancy and Emigration: The 'Woman Question' in Mid-Victorian Britain," *Victorian Periodicals Review*, vol. 26, no. 1, 1993, 3–7), further revealed that two-thirds of Britain's female population between the ages of twenty and twenty-four, one-third between twenty-four and thirty-five, and more than two-fifths between twenty-four and forty were unmarried (Mary Poovey, *Uneven Developments: The*

Ideological Work of Gender in Mid-Victorian England, U of Chicago P, 1988, 4). The 1911 figure is from Jean Jacques Van-Helten and Keith Williams, "'The Crying Need of South Africa': The Emigration of Single British Women to the Transvaal, 1901–10," *Journal of Southern African Studies*, vol. 10, no. 1, 1983, 21. On the influence of World War I, see Billie Melman, *Women and the Popular Imagination in the Twenties: Flappers and Nymphs*, Macmillan, 1988, 5. The most famous early proponent of female immigration to the colonies was W. R. Greg (see *Why Are Women Redundant?*, Trübner, 1869, *Internet Archive*, archive.org/details/whyarewomenredu00greggoog/page/n3, originally published in *National Review*, vol. 14, no. 28, Apr. 1862, 434–60).

37. Since the late nineteenth century, hospitals, shops, and offices had begun hiring women (A. James Hammerton, *Emigrant Gentlewomen: Genteel Poverty and Female Emigration, 1830–1914*, Croom Helm, 1979, 152). Ann Ardis writes: "the New Woman [was both an] agent (and representative) of social change" (*New Women, New Novels: Feminism and Early Modernism*, Rutgers UP, 1990, 10).

38. Julia Bush, *Edwardian Ladies and Imperial Power*, Leicester UP, 2000, 147, Women, Power, and Politics.

39. Hammerton, *Emigrant Gentlewomen* 142, quotation on 162, 163. Cf. Bush, *Edwardian Ladies* 159. In the century's first decade, female emigration societies immigrated approximately three hundred (mostly single) women to Rhodesia (Van-Helten and Williams 31).

40. Gertrude Page, "Life in Rhodesia," *Empire Review* vol. 14, no. 81, Aug. 1907, 42.

41. Sally Ledger, *The New Woman: Fiction and Feminism at the Fin de Siècle*, Manchester UP, 1997, 64. On "imperial motherhood," see Anna Davin, "Imperialism and Motherhood," *History Workshop Journal*, vol. 5, no. 1, Spring 1978, 9–66; Deirdre David, *Rule Britannia: Women, Empire, and Victorian Writing*, Cornell UP, 1995, 182; and Van-Helten and Williams 17–38. On women as a cultural force, see Margaret Strobel, *European Women and the Second British Empire*, Indiana UP, 1991, 17. On women as a "moral force," see Alicia M. Cecil, "The Needs of South Africa: Female Emigration," *The Nineteenth Century and After*, vol. 51, no. 302, Apr. 1902, 692; and David 159. For various representations of "the Englishwoman abroad," see Vron Ware, *Beyond the Pale: White Women, Racism, and History*, Verso, 1992, 120. On philosophies of Anglo-Afrikaner coexistence, see my chapter 4, pages 143–44.

42. Gertrude Page, *The Silent Rancher*, Hurst, 1909, 303, hereafter cited parenthetically as *Silent*.

43. Liebson 139.

44. James Belich, *Replenishing the Earth: The Settler Revolution and the Rise of the Anglo-World, 1783–1939*, Oxford UP, 2009, 153.

45. Page, "Second" 140.

46. Cf. Anthony Chennells, "The Mimic Women: Early Women Novelists and White Southern African Nationalisms," *Historia*, vol. 49, no. 1, May 2004, 86.

47. Page, "Farm Life in Rhodesia" 54.
48. Gertrude Page, "Life in Rhodesia," *Empire Review*, vol. 14, no. 81, Oct. 1907, 183. Cf. Gertrude Page, "A Lady's First Impressions of South Africa," *Empire Review*, vol. 9, no. 53, June 1905, 468; and Gertrude Page, *The Edge o' Beyond*, Hurst, n.d., 43, hereafter cited parenthetically as *Edge*.
49. Gertrude Page, "Life in Rhodesia," *Empire Review*, vol. 11, no. 63, Apr. 1906, 250.
50. Page, "Life," Oct. 1907, 183. Page, "Life," Apr. 1906, 250.
51. Gertrude Page, "Farm Life in Rhodesia: Visit to Victoria Falls," *Empire Review*, vol. 12, no. 68, Sept. 1906, 160.
52. Gertrude Page, "Life in Rhodesia," *Empire Review*, vol. 11, no. 65, June 1906, 455.
53. Page, "Life," Apr. 1906, 252. Page's husband is mentioned surprisingly few times in her articles, and when he is, he is unnamed. Perhaps she is one of the "many" women like Jill, who says: "I am one of those wives who never shine when their spouse is present. There are many of us" (*Ranch* 215).
54. Gertrude Page, *The Rhodesian*, Hurst, 1912, 343, 131, hereafter cited parenthetically as *Rhodesian*.
55. Page, "Second" 140.
56. Page, "Life," Aug. 1907, 38.
57. Page, "Second" 146.
58. Page, "Life," June 1906, 456.
59. The heroine of Haggard's *Jess* similarly contends: people in the metropole, "shackled by custom, restrained by law, pruned and bent by the force of public opinion, . . . grow as like one to another as the fruit-bushes on a garden wall," while those in southern Africa "become outwardly that which the spirit within would fashion [them] to" (H. Rider Haggard, *Jess*, McKinlay, 1887, 248).
60. Mary Anne Barker uses almost identical phrasing—"free unconventional life"—to describe southern Africa in *A Year's Housekeeping in South Africa* (Tauchnitz, 1877, 133, *Collection of British Authors*, Tauchnitz Edition, vol. 1670).
61. In an *Empire Review* article, Eleanor Wilson Fox writes: "No one can escape from its [Rhodesia's] spell, which is difficult to define, but is undeniably there" ("Impressions of Scenery in Rhodesia," *Empire Review*, vol. 16, no. 91, Aug. 1908, 43). In *Virginia of the Rhodesians*, Stockley writes that those who have "once lived this queer free life, and breathed this 'Oh-let-things-rip' atmosphere," but have left, "can never rest content until they're back in the thick of it again" (4th ed., Hutchinson, 1903, 109).
62. On the enhanced freedoms of female emigrants, partly through a relaxation of gender codes, see Ware 120; and Ronald Hyam, *Empire and Sexuality: The British Experience*, Manchester UP, 1990, Studies in Imperialism. Hyam "argues that the opportunities for sexual contact in the Empire made a difficult environment more attractive to colonists," but he is speaking primarily of men (Philippa Levine,

"Sexuality, Gender, and Empire," *Gender and Empire*, ed. Levine, Oxford UP, 2004, 134, Oxford History of the British Empire Companion Series).

63. In *Where the Strange Roads Go Down*, Nita believes that if she had had an occupation—writing articles for instance, or making blouses, both of which occupied Page (regarding the latter task, see "Life," June 1906, 456)—"she would not have been lost" (*Strange* 187).

64. I use the term "lover" as Page did, to suggest not a sexual but a romantic partner.

65. Rejecting adultery, Enid is allowed, in the end, both marriage to Meredith—a "formula" he "go[es] through . . . to please her"—once his wife dies and, implicitly, the unconventional life that she sought (*Strange* 250).

66. See chapter 2, page 79 and note 79.

67. "Appealing to circuits of desire that she also forestalls" is a phrase formulated by Joseph Valente, in conversation.

68. Whether one wants to contend, like Gail Cunningham, that "the New Woman heroine did not outlast the Victorian age" (*The New Woman and the Victorian Novel*, Macmillan, 1978, 152), or, like Lyn Pykett, that "the New Woman remained a prominent figure in the early twentieth century" (*Engendering Fictions: The English Novel in the Early Twentieth Century*, Arnold, 1995, 16), Page's heroines share many of her qualities.

69. Ardis 64. LeeAnne Richardson, *New Woman and Colonial Adventure Fiction in Victorian Britain: Gender, Genre, and Empire*, U of Florida P, 2006, 20. "The New Woman of the late nineteenth century was repeatedly associated with modernity" (Sally Ledger, "The New Woman and Feminist Fictions," *The Cambridge Companion to the Fin de Siècle*, ed. Gail Marshall, Cambridge UP, 2007, 165).

70. When aid comes to the struggling Rhodesian woman, it is neither always from a more seasoned colonist nor even from a settler. In *The Edge o' Beyond*, Dinah abets Joyce, though the latter has been in the country longer. In *Where the Strange Roads Go Down*, Jo helps to reconcile Nita and her husband, while Dinah tries to help Joyce obtain a divorce. Though unsuccessful in convincing Joyce's husband to grant her one, Dinah does help Joyce to run off with her lover, "giv[ing] her a little real happiness" (240). In *Love in the Wilderness*, Enid's sister, Marian, "had been one of the pioneers of the place, and gone through a term of roughing it," but she is nonetheless too traditional to serve as a model for Enid (17). Marian does, however, provide her with the journal of their mother, who died years before in the England that she never left; offering evidence of a similar temptation narrowly averted, the journal enables Enid to avert her own.

71. Smoking, a common characteristic of the New Woman, was considered a symbol of freedom (Ardis 182n38). Dinah smokes in *The Edge o' Beyond*, as does Diana in *The Rhodesian*.

72. Chennells, "Mimic" 85.

73. Unlike the metropolitan-born Enid who successfully adjusts to colonial life, Nan, who "had been born on [her father's Rhodesian] farm, and grown up there[,] . . . would no more bear transplanting than the flower of the soil" (*Love* 75). Her year at boarding school in England was a disaster; the school's principal told her that while she "like[d] [her] very much," she was "almost as out of place [t]here as an aborigine"; and Nan herself declares that "Daddy ought to have had more sense than to send me to England" (66). The text thus suggests that while the metropolitan-born woman can expand to fill the contours of Rhodesian life, her colonial-born counterpart cannot contract to fit the contours of "the little home island" (133).

74. Members of the Women's Land Army, begun in 1915, did agricultural work while the men were away at war. Not only did they help to feed Great Britain, they did it wearing pants.

75. Both of the heroines of *The Veldt Trail* wear "knickerbocker suits and ride astride" (116). In another instance we are told that their "rational dress of grey or khaki linen, [was] very like the land-girls of the old country" (3).

76. The Writer-woman embodies the ideal imagined by the heroine of Stockley's *Virginia of the Rhodesians*, who says that she would like to be "as free and unattached as a married woman" (178).

77. While the "odious" man believes that only a woman "unspoilt by modern notions [is] worth marrying" (*Edge* 101, 240), the commendable one believes that "a man has no right to expect a clever interesting woman to be satisfied with his companionship only" (*Silent* 145). In advance of the event itself, the narrator informs readers that someday Enid "would find that Real Thing—meet and go down before the Best—lose herself and her striving in what must ever be the only true consummation of a woman's life" (88). In another early novel, *The Rhodesian*, the narrator similarly reflects on Diana's relationship to love: "like all women of her independent character and fearlessness, she dreaded the mere thought of losing her liberty or yielding her independence. And at the same time she knew that the thought which held a dread held a charm also. Diana would never lose her grit and personality, she would never submit for a moment to any overshadowing, but deep in her heart she knew she was true woman enough to like to be conquered by the right man" (330). These descriptions echo the thoughts of Lyndall in Olive Schreiner's *The Story of an African Farm*, who yearns to "find . . . something nobler, stronger than I, before which I can kneel down," "to love so . . . that to lie under the foot of the thing I loved would be . . . heaven" (Penguin, 1995, 279, 232).

78. Though divorced herself, Gwendolyn says: "Society must set its face against divorce at present, for the welfare of the multitude; but by and by, when women are braver and stronger and more dependable, there will dawn a day of wider and deeper significance. There is always a violent oscillation each way before the happy mean is reached, and it seems to me that the passionate revolt of to-day is the

outcome of the cramped narrowness and bigotry of half a century ago. Presently things will simmer down to a workable level" (*Silent* 274). Such qualifications do not appear in Page's later fiction.

79. For instance, the passage cited in the previous sentence continues: "I shall lead a huge procession, probably on stilts, to the Houses of Parliament, and there, waving my stilts wildly in the air, I shall demand redress. My point will be that any man who refuses to free his wife, when she asks him, shall explain his reasons to not less than five hundred suffragettes, and after that, if anything is left of him, it ought to be put in the British Museum, among the Nation's Antiquities, as representing the last of his order" (*Edge* 262). In a 1907 *Empire Review* article, Page describes suffragettes as "strenuous ladies in appalling khaki helmets" ("Advance" 306). And in *Where the Strange Roads Go Down*, when Jo tells two men at a social event, "If the Bible were to be written afresh to-day, we all know who would pick the apple first and do the persuading!" the first replies that "there'd be a suffragette in the tree," and the second that "the apple would turn out to be a bomb . . . and the only man in the world would be blown to smithereens, and then where would you all be! . . .'" (184; ellipses in original).

80. The language is strikingly similar to a passage in a 1913 article focused on Schreiner's *The Story of an African Farm*, Stockley's *Poppy*, and Richard Dehan's (pseudonym of Clotilde Graves) *The Dop Doctor* (1910): "nothing is more noticeable in these three novels than the evolution of woman and the freedom and equality she claims in the new nation. By the very accidents of environment the Afrikaner [in this context, the word is used to mean white and African-born] woman walks beside—and not behind—the man. The Heroines of these tales of African veld and townships have alike evolved from the muddy places of existence into a charming and intellectual womanhood, they have 'built their own ladders to reach the sky,' thus asserting their equal right with men to drop a worn-out past behind them, and where women face the world as untrammelled [*sic*] by conventional restrictions as men, the country is a strong one . . ." ("South African Writers," *South African Stories and Sketches*, 22nd series, South Africa, n.d., 10–11, "*South Africa*" Handbook, no. 73, originally published in *South Africa: A Weekly Journal for All Interested in South African Affairs*, Sept. 1913).

81. Melman 16, 144, 140, 142. For more on the genre, see Melman 140–44 and appendix C, which provides a list of titles.

82. Susanne Howe, *Novels of Empire*, Columbia UP, 1949, 43–46, quotation on 46. On sexuality in Strange's fiction, see Elizabeth W. Williams, "Queering Settler Romance: The Reparative Eugenic Landscape in Nora Strange's Kenyan Novels," *Archiving Settler Colonialism: Culture, Space, and Race*, ed. Yuting Huang and Rebecca Weaver-Hightower, Routledge, 2019, 190–204.

83. Kenneth Parker, "The South African Novel in English," *The South African Novel in English: Essays in Criticism and Society*, ed. Parker, Africana, 1978, 17.

84. Schreiner, *African Farm* 50, 227, 228. "I know that it is I who am thinking," says Waldo, "but it seems as though it were they who were talking" (50). See "A Note on Terminology" at the beginning of this book.

85. Judith R. Walkowitz, *City of Dreadful Delight: Narratives of Sexual Danger in Late-Victorian London*, U of Chicago P, 1992, 3.

Chapter 4. "There Will Be No More Kings in Africa": Foreclosing Darkness in *Prester John*

1. John G. Cawelti and Bruce Rosenberg, *The Spy Story*, U of Chicago P, 1987, 80. Cf. Robin W. Winks, "John Buchan: Stalking the Wilder Game," *The Four Adventures of Richard Hannay*, by Buchan, ed. Winks, Godine, 1988, xi; and Adrian Wisnicki, "Reformulating the Empire's Hero: Rhodesian Gold, Boer Veld-Craft, and the Displaced Scotsman in John Buchan's *The Thirty-Nine Steps*," *Journal of Colonialism and Colonial History*, vol. 8, no. 1, Spring 2007, par. 1, doi:10.1353/cch.2007.0025. See my introduction, note 97.

2. See chapter 2 for an extended discussion of the male imperial romance. See also Richard F. Patteson on the "imperialist romance" ("*King Solomon's Mines*: Imperialism and Narrative Structure," *The Journal of Narrative Technique*, vol. 8, Spring 1978, 112); Patrick Brantlinger on the "imperial Gothic" (*Rule of Darkness: British Literature and Imperialism, 1830–1914*, Cornell UP, 1988, 230); and Elaine Showalter on "the male quest romance" (*Sexual Anarchy: Gender and Culture at the Fin de Siècle*, Penguin, 1990, 81). Tim Couzens notes that Haggard was "an important influence on Conrad and Buchan" (" 'The Old Africa of a Boy's Dream': Towards Interpreting Buchan's *Prester John*," *English Studies in Africa*, vol. 24, no. 1, 1981, 21).

3. Daniel Karlin, Introduction, *She*, by H. Rider Haggard, ed. Karlin, Oxford UP, 1998, xiii.

4. Andrew Lownie claims that Buchan started the novel while still in southern Africa—that is, before the end of July 1903—and David Daniell that he wrote it during the second half of 1909 (*John Buchan: The Presbyterian Cavalier*, Constable, 1995, 111; David Daniell, Introduction, *Prester John*, by Buchan, ed. Daniell, Oxford UP, 1994, vii). The novel was published in August 1910, though a heavily modified serialization, "The Black General," had begun its run in April of that year, concluding in October (Lownie, *Presbyterian* 111). The Union of South Africa Treaty was passed in September 1909 and came into effect in May 1910.

5. Allan Quatermain dies at the end of the 1887 novel bearing his name. He appears, however, in a dozen more novels, which, though mostly published after 1910—to far less success—are set prior to 1887.

6. John Buchan, *The African Colony: Studies in the Reconstruction*, Blackwood, 1903, 338, 91; my emphasis.

7. See "A Note on Terminology" at the beginning of this book.

8. Buchan, *African Colony* 91.

9. According to David Trotter, the spy thriller "established itself as a market leader in Britain at the turn of the century, gradually displacing the imperial adventure story, as the focus of anxiety shifted from frontier wars to Great Power rivalry" (*The English Novel in History, 1895–1920*, Routledge, 1993, 167).

10. Andrew Lownie, "John Buchan, the Round Table and Empire," *The Round Table, the Empire/Commonwealth and British Foreign Policy*, ed. Andrea Bosco and Alex May, Lothian Foundation, 1997, 57. The moniker "Milner's Kindergarten," coined after Buchan's departure, was given to those (mostly) young Oxonian men working for Milner (and later his successor) in southern Africa after the war (Janet Adam Smith, *John Buchan and His World*, Thames, 1979, 42; Daniel Gorman, *Imperial Citizenship: Empire and the Question of Belonging*, Manchester UP, 2007, 81).

11. John Buchan, *Memory Hold-the-Door*, Hodder, 1940, 108.

12. On the misrepresentation of the camps, see Eliza Reidi, "Teaching Empire: British and Dominions Women Teachers in the South African War Concentration Camps," *English Historical Review*, vol. 120, no. 489, 2005, 1318. On the numbers of deaths, see Elizabeth van Heyningen, "Costly Mythologies: The Concentration Camps of the South African War in Afrikaner Historiography," *Journal of Southern African Studies*, vol. 34, no. 3, Sept. 2008, 496n5; and Elizabeth van Heyningen, "A Tool for Modernisation? The Boer Concentration Camps of the South African War, 1900–1902," *South African Journal of Science*, vol. 106, no. 5/6, May/June 2010, page 2 of 10, archive.sajs.co.za/index.php/SAJS/article/view/242. On black camps, see Elizabeth van Heyningen, " 'Hewers of wood and drawers of water': The Black Camp Experience," *The Concentration Camps of the Anglo-Boer War: A Social History*, by van Heyningen, Jacana, 2013, 150–78.

13. J. A. Smith 40. Laili Dor, "Conflicting Visions of War: Winston Churchill and Rudyard Kipling's Evocation of the Boer War," *Cahiers Victoriens et Édoudardiens*, vol. 66, Oct. 2007, 223.

14. J. A. Smith 40. When Buchan arrived, the death rate in the camps was 344 per thousand; the following year, it was thirty-two per thousand (37, 40). Lownie contends that the improvements were chiefly due to "the work of Millicent Fawcett and the arrival of doctors and nurses from Britain and the Indian Medical Service rather than Milner's officials" (*Presbyterian* 75).

15. Buchan, *Memory* 109. Graham Law, "The Romance of Empire: John Buchan's Early Writings," page 9 of 14, *Waseda University*, www.f.waseda.jp/glaw/arts/re.pdf. Buchan, quoted in Peter Henshaw, "John Buchan from the 'Borders' to the 'Berg': Nature, Empire and White South African Identity, 1901–1910," *African Studies*, vol. 62, no. 1, July 2003, 10. See my introduction, note 7.

16. Buchan, *Memory* 109–10, 125. Buchan, quoted in Henshaw 10.

17. See "A Note on Terminology" at the beginning of this book.

18. Lownie, *Presbyterian* 80. J. A. Smith 42. The quotation is from Buchan, *Memory* 120. Buchan described the Wood Bush in other publications, including a chapter titled "The Wood Bush" in *The African Colony* (113–28). Of its description there, Jeremy Foster writes: "the place of the Woodbush stands for the sensory world of the Highveld, while the illimitable Highveld stands for the whole of British South Africa" (*Washed with Sun: Landscape and the Making of White South Africa*, U of Pittsburgh P, 2008, 139). Though Woodbush is now one word, I use two, in the style of Buchan and his contemporaries (unless, as in the epilogue, I am quoting someone else).

19. According to Lownie, Buchan left southern Africa on July 26, 1903, never to return, while Foster writes (without citing his source) that he "visited South Africa once again, briefly, in 1905" and Henshaw (also without providing a source) that he "made a secretive four month return visit in 1905" (Lownie, *Presbyterian* 80; Foster 286n85; Henshaw 21). Buchan, quoted in Lownie, *Presbyterian* 84, 241.

20. Craig Smith, "Every Man Must Kill the Thing He Loves: Empire, Homoerotics, and Nationalism in John Buchan's *Prester John*," *Novel: A Forum on Fiction*, vol. 28, no. 2, Winter 1995, 177. *A Lodge in the Wilderness* has also been described as "a tedious fictional debate about the nature of imperialism" (Nicholas Thomas, *Colonialism's Culture: Anthropology, Travel and Government*, Princeton UP, 1994, 152), a "country-house discussion novel" (Jefferson Hunter, *Edwardian Fiction*, Harvard UP, 1982, 109; cf. Lownie, *Presbyterian* 90), "a fictional philosophical-political symposium" (David Daniell, *The Interpreter's House: A Critical Assessment of John Buchan*, Nelson, 1975, 90), "an extended pamphlet on empire" (Henshaw 29n38), and a "static political discussion novel" (Hermann Wittenberg, "Occult, Empire and Landscape: The Colonial Uncanny in John Buchan's African Writing," *Journal of Colonialism and Colonial History*, vol. 7, no. 2, Fall 2006, par. 31, doi:10.1353/cch.2006.0049).

21. Buchan, who suffered from duodenal ulcers, was "disqualified on medical grounds for combatant service" (David Stafford, "John Buchan's Tales of Espionage: A Popular Archive of British History," *Canadian Journal of History*, vol. 18, no. 1, Apr. 1983, 6).

22. Lownie, *Presbyterian* 243.

23. Buchan, *Memory* 124, 125, 112.

24. John Buchan, *A Lodge in the Wilderness*, Blackwood, 1906, 93. Buchan, *Memory* 112.

25. Gorman 96, quoting "The Empire of South Africa," 27, a speech Buchan delivered in Edinburgh in January 1904. Compare to the speech Haggard delivered in Ditchingham, quoted on page 6 of the introduction.

26. Buchan, *African Colony* xviii, 389, 126.

27. Buchan, *Memory* 112.

28. John Buchan, *Prester John*, ed. David Daniell, Oxford 1994, 7, hereafter cited parenthetically as *PJ*.

29. H. Rider Haggard, *The Holy Flower*, Ward, 1915, 57.

30. Though Aitken, a former secret service officer, tells Davie that I.D.B. is short for "illicit diamond broking," it was much more commonly understood to be short for illicit diamond buying (*PJ* 28). All three terms refer to illegal diamond trading. Designed to keep profits exclusively in the hands of the capitalist industrialists, I.D.B. laws were targeted primarily at laboring miners, the majority of whom were black. As per J. A. Hobson: "The most vital principles of personal liberty are violated by the monstrous Illicit Diamond Buying Law [Trade in Diamonds Consolidation Act of 1882], according to which any person in the Colony may be arrested for being found in possession of an uncut diamond, and is assumed to be guilty of wrongful possession unless he can bring proof to the contrary" ("Capitalism and Imperialism in South Africa," *Contemporary Review*, vol. 77, Jan./June 1900, 6).

31. Lownie, *Presbyterian* 111. John Buchan, *The Great Diamond Pipe*, Dodd, 1911.

32. The text names Sikitola, Majinje, 'Mpefu, and Magata. The last two, whom Buchan also mentions in *The African Colony*, are actual historical figures (286). See "A Note on Terminology" at the beginning of this book.

33. Buchan's readers would likely have been familiar with the names Tchaka (Chaka/Shaka), King of the Zulus in the early nineteenth century; Mosilikatse (Moselekatse/Mzilikazi), leader of the Matabele (Ndeble) in the mid-nineteenth century; and Moshesh, the Basuto king for much of the nineteenth century.

34. Brantlinger, *Rule of Darkness* 195. "As late as the 1960s works published in Rhodesia and South Africa were still insisting that the builders of the ruins were non-African" (292n61). An example of the prevailing Victorian claim that the ruins were Phoenician can be found in A. Wilmot's *Monomotapa*, originally published in 1896, with a preface by H. Rider Haggard (*Monomotapa: Its Monuments, and Its History from the Most Ancient Times to the Present Century*, Negro UP, 1969).

35. Of his feelings during Laputa's coronation, Davie says, "I longed for a leader who should master me and make my soul his own, as this man mastered his followers" (*PJ* 106).

36. The word is Haggard's own. See H. Rider Haggard, *King Solomon's Mines*, Modern Library, 2002, 38; and H. Rider Haggard, *Allan Quatermain*, Penguin, 1995, 256.

37. See Patteson 113.

38. Between the two is the notoriously ambivalent *Heart of Darkness*, in which romance, "a realm beyond the reach of rationalization," perseveres, while heroism is nowhere to be found (John A. McClure, "Late Imperial Romance," *Raritan*, vol. 10, no. 4, Spring 1991, 9). "Subvert[ing] the notion of the Empire as the location

of utopian dreams," Conrad critiques the facile fantasy of the imperial romance (Linda Dryden, *Joseph Conrad and the Imperial Romance*, Macmillan, 2000, 14). Nonetheless, he remains wedded to the centrality of the individual subject in the adventure story, whereas Buchan, for all his obvious support of imperialism, rejects this generic convention by treating empire itself as his principal subject.

39. See chapter 2, note 66.

40. Cf. Thomas 151. James Belich notes that in 1910 all electorates except for Natal were dominated by Afrikaners (*Replenishing the Earth: The Settler Revolution and the Rise of the Anglo-World, 1783–1939*, Oxford UP, 2009, 379).

41. Buchan, *African Colony* 389, 390. See "A Note on Terminology" at the beginning of this book, and the introduction, note 29.

42. The war had not only brought men to southern Africa, it had also brought women, mostly serving as nurses or English teachers in the concentration camps (see Reidi). On the decline in immigration numbers, see W. A. Carrothers, *Emigration from the British Isles*, Cass, 1966, 250. After the Union was formed there was again a rise in immigration, which quickly tapered off at the start of World War I (250).

43. See C. Smith 182; Thomas 150; and Paul Rich, "'Milnerism and a Ripping Yarn': Transvaal Land Settlement and John Buchan's Novel 'Prester John' 1901–1910," *Town and Countryside in the Transvaal: Capitalist Penetration and Popular Response*, ed. Belinda Bozzoli, Ravan, 1983, 413.

44. Bill Schwarz describes them as "all but absent" (*The White Man's World*, Oxford UP, 2011, 272, *Memories of Empire*, vol. 1).

45. "I will write to the Royal Geographical Society," Davie tells himself, "and they will give me a medal" (*PJ* 46). As noted on page 142 of this chapter, Laputa has himself attended meetings at the society.

46. John Buchan, *Greenmantle*, Penguin, 1956, 87. "Once upon a time, as the story goes, a Dutchman talked with a predikant [preacher] about the welfare of his soul. 'You will assuredly be damned,' said the predikant, 'and burn in hell.' 'Not so,' said the Dutchman. 'If I am so unfortunate as to get in there, I shall certainly get out again.' 'But that is folly and an impossibility,' said the predikant. 'Ah,' said the other with confidence, 'wait and see: I shall make a plan.' *Ek sal 'n plan maak*—this must be my motto" (Buchan, *African Colony* 120).

47. Stephen Gray, *Southern African Literature: An Introduction*, Barnes & Noble, 1979, 127.

48. Though Davie mentions the women and children only in passing—they were "snug in the covered wagons" while he sat around the fire with the men—they are clearly the "kinsfolk" to whom he is referring (*PJ* 42, 89).

49. Saul Dubow, "How British Was the British World? The Case of South Africa," *Journal of Imperial and Commonwealth History*, vol. 37, no. 1, Mar. 2009, 14. George F. Judd, "South African Types. No. 5—The Predikant," *South African Magazine*, Nov. 1906, 131. On the shift in rhetoric, see also Carrothers 250; and

A. James Hammerton, *Emigrant Gentlewomen: Genteel Poverty and Female Emigration, 1830–1914*, Croom Helm, 1979, 165.

50. Saul Dubow, "Colonial Nationalism, the Milner Kindergarten, and the Rise of 'South Africanism,' 1902–10," *History Workshop Journal*, vol. 43, no. 1, Spring 1997, 78.

51. Roderick Jones, "The Black Peril in South Africa," *The Nineteenth Century and After*, vol. 55, no. 327, May 1904, 718, 719, 715. *Voice of Missions*, the official organ of the African Methodist Episcopal Church, quoted in Jones 717. Jones was a Reuters correspondent and "close friend" of Buchan and Smuts (Schwarz, *White* 239). Anxiety over black men raping white women was really, writes Norman Etherington, "the fear of losing control," itself "a constant undercurrent in the thinking of the settler minority. This substratum of anxiety rose to the surface in the form of a moral panic whenever disturbances in the economy or the body politic were severe enough to unsettle the mask of composure worn by the face of public authority" ("Natal's Black Rape Scare of the 1870s," *Journal of Southern African Studies*, vol. 15, no. 1, Oct. 1988, 36). In his 1921 pamphlet, *The Mote and the Beam: An Epic on Sex-Relationship 'twixt White and Black in British South Africa*, Sol Plaatje asks rhetorically, "Is it a "Black' or a 'White' Peril?" (quoted in *Sol Plaatje: Selected Writings*, ed. Brian Willan, Ohio UP, 1996, 283). "By 'Black Peril,'" Plaatje writes, "the South African whites mean 'assaults by black men upon white women.' It is an unsavoury subject" about which he does not wish to write but feels that he must, as "white contributors to the daily press . . . usually give only one side" (274). Presenting another, he points out that while interracial marriage is forbidden in the Transvaal, white men "find[] no paradox in procreating illegitimate half-castes with the girls of a race [they] look[] down upon" (279). Further, he notes, while black men are often convicted "on the specious testimonies" of white women—sexual contact of any sort between a black man and a white woman being not only illegal but presumptively nonconsensual—"white men who rape Native women are almost invariably allowed to go unpunished" (280).

52. George M. Fredrickson, *White Supremacy: A Comparative Study in American and South African History*, Oxford UP, 1981, 184. Andrew Thompson, "The Languages of Loyalism in Southern Africa, c. 1870–1939," *The English Historical Review*, vol. 118, no. 477, June 2003, 637. See also Bill Schwarz, "The Romance of the Veld," *The Round Table, the Empire/Commonwealth and British Foreign Policy*, ed. Andrea Bosco and Alex May, Lothian Foundation, 1997, 79; Hannah Arendt, *The Origins of Totalitarianism*, new ed., Harvest-Harcourt, 1968, 199–200; Saul Dubow, *Scientific Racism in Modern South Africa*, Cambridge UP, 1994, 4; and Peter Keating, *Kipling: The Poet*, Secker, 1994, 138, 148. See my introduction, note 7.

53. Buchan, *African Colony* 340; my emphasis. Buchan goes so far as to praise the *Grondwet* (constitution) of the former South African Republic, "which declared, 'There shall be no equality between black and white'" (340).

54. C. Smith 175. Schwarz, *White* 212. Buchan uses this phrase not only in *The African Colony* (91), in the passage from which I quote on page 136 of this chapter, but also in *Comments and Characters*, ed. W. Forbes Gray, Nelson, 1940, 121; *Lodge* 171, 237; and *Memory* 112. See pages 13–14 of the introduction for information about South Africa's ethnic composition and demarcation. Nominally overseen by a governor-general representing the crown, the new Union governed itself through a parliament and prime minister.

55. Brian V. Street, *The Savage in Literature: Representations of "Primitive" Society in English Fiction, 1858–1920*, Routledge, 1975, 143. J. Mutero Chirenje, *Ethiopianism and Afro-Americans in Southern Africa, 1883–1916*, Louisiana State UP, 1987, 2.

56. Paul Rich, "Romance and the Development of the South African Novel," *Literature and Society in South Africa*, ed. Landeg White and Tim Couzens, Longman, 1984, 126. Ogbu U. Kalu, "Ethiopianism and the Roots of Modern African Christianity," *The Cambridge History of Christianity, World Christianities, c. 1815–1914*, vol. 8, ed. Sheridan Gilley and Brian Stanley, Cambridge UP, 2008, 581.

57. Street 143. Cf. Chirenje 1.

58. Street 143. Ogbu U. Kalu, "Ethiopianism in African Christianity," *African Christianity: An African Story*, ed. Kalu, Africa World, 2007, 234. "Booth, Joseph," *Mundus: Gateway to Missionary Collections in the United Kingdom*, www.mundus.ac.uk/cats/1/52.htm. Street 143. Jones 716. *Africa for the African* was written by Joseph Booth, a white English missionary who spent significant time in New Zealand, Australia, and southern Africa and also traveled to the United States.

59. Shula Marks, *Reluctant Rebellion: The 1906–8 Disturbances in Natal*, Clarendon, 1970, 331, quotation on 336.

60. Marks xv–xvi, quotation on xv. Bambatha, a Zulu leader, was killed long before the end of the unrest. Dinuzulu was actually the "head of the Zulu Royal family and heir to the great military tradition of the Zulu people" (251). Though he was rumored to have been behind the rebellion (for which he was tried and found guilty), his exact role remains uncertain (251).

61. Dubow, "Colonial Nationalism" 78.

62. Pilvi Rajamäe, "John Laputa: The Ethiopian Solar Hero of *Prester John*," *John Buchan Journal*, no. 38, Summer 2008, 13.

63. Jones 717. On one occasion, Wardlaw calls it "a kind of bastard Christianity" (*PJ* 54). Henry Cullen Gouldsbury's novel *God's Outpost* (1907), set in Rhodesia, contains a short scene in which "an apostle of the Ethiopian Mission" shares his "fanaticism" with another: "To-day in this continent, we outnumber the white men by half a million to one, and once we learn to combine, nothing can withstand us. The land shall run red with blood, *their* blood. . . . [T]he day will come when we will deny them the franchise, and be ourselves a law unto ourselves" (Nash, 271, 268, 269).

64. January 1908 Natal government notice, quoted in Marks 26.

65. H. D. Kaplan, *The Rise of the Black Magus in Western Art*, UMI Research, 1985, 54.

66. Kaplan 43. Buchan himself notes that the name was "a generic title for any supposed Christian monarch in unknown countries" (*African Colony* 21n1).

67. Mary Baine Campbell, "Asia, Africa, Abyssinia: Writing the Land of Prester John," *Travel Writing, Form, and Empire: The Poetics and Politics of Mobility*, ed. Julia Kuehn and Paul Smethurst, Routledge, 2009, 31.

68. Justin Livingstone, "Buchan and the Priest King: Nelson's New Novels, 'The Mountain,' and Religious Revolution in *Prester John*," *English in Africa*, vol. 40, no. 2, Oct. 2013, 191. Cf. Kaplan 58.

69. Both Wardlaw and Arcoll situate the historical figure in the fifteenth century.

70. The parallel between the necklace and the ark hinges on each bringing victory to the side who possesses it.

71. "This moment of vision," writes Thomas, "marks the end of the uprising" (149). Buchan similarly depicts proximate contrasting landscapes in his 1910 short story, "The Grove of Ashtaroth," set in southern Africa.

72. C. Smith 195. See "A Note on Terminology" at the beginning of this book.

73. C. Smith 176.

74. Gray 131. C. Smith 174, 176.

75. Brantlinger, *Rule of Darkness* 262.

76. "Literature," *South Africa: A Weekly Journal for All Interested in South African Affairs*, vol. 1, no. 1, 4 Jan. 1889, 10.

77. Patrick Brantlinger, "Victorians and Africans: The Genealogy of the Myth of the Dark Continent," *Critical Inquiry*, vol. 12, no. 1, Autumn 1985, 167.

78. If earlier imperial adventure fiction was somewhat less direct, luring its young readers into colonial service with the implied promise of personal glory, *Prester John* makes its point in no uncertain terms: your empire, your obligation. Everything else is secondary. On adventure fiction as a recruitment tool for boy readers, see Martin Green, *Dreams of Adventure, Deeds of Empire*, Basic, 1979; John M. Mackenzie, *Propaganda and Empire: The Manipulation of British Public Opinion, 1880–1960*, Manchester UP, 1984; and Joseph Bristow, *Empire Boys: Adventures in a Man's World*, HarperCollinsAcademic-Harper Collins, 1991. Buchan's autobiography, published in the United States as *Pilgrim's Way: An Essay in Recollection* (Houghton, 1940), was a favorite of John F. Kennedy ("ask not what your country can do for you . . .") (Stafford, "Tales of Espionage" 20).

79. In the third installment of the Hannay quartet, Hannay, undercover in an artist/pacifist community, attends a lecture by "a great buck nigger who had a lot to say about 'Africa for the Africans.' I had a few words with him in Sesutu afterwards, and rather spoiled his visit" (John Buchan, *Mr. Standfast*, Popular Library-Houghton, 1947, 34). Although Davie never employs this particular derogatory term, we can imagine

him otherwise acting in this fashion. As I discuss in the epilogue, the threats against which Hannay defends Britain are primarily, though by no means only, European.

Epilogue. Beyond the British South African Novel

1. John Buchan, *Prester John*, ed. David Daniell, Oxford UP, 1994, 202, 203; ellipses in original.

2. See the introduction, note 97.

3. John G. Cawelti and Bruce Rosenberg, *The Spy Story*, U of Chicago P, 1987, 41. A few months prior to the publication of the novel, the narrative was serialized in *Blackwood's* under the pseudonym H. de V.

4. Colin Storer, "'The German of caricature, the real German, the fellow we were up against': German Stereotypes in John Buchan's *Greenmantle*," *Journal of European Studies*, vol. 39, no. 1, 2009, 41. Brett F. Woods, "The Last Victorian: John Buchan and the Hannay Quartet," *California Literary Review*, 19 Apr. 2020, originally published 26 Mar. 2007. See also Richard Usborne, *Clubland Heroes: A Nostalgic Study of Some Recurrent Characters in the Romantic Fiction of Dornford Yates, John Buchan, and Sapper*, Constable, 1953. On the conflation of English and British, see the introduction, note 29.

5. See I. F. Clarke, *Voices Prophesying War: Future Wars, 1763–3749*, 2nd ed., Oxford UP, 1992, in particular, chapters 2 and 3. Cf. Cawelti and Rosenberg 38–39; and Susanne Howe, *Novels of Empire*, Columbia UP, 1949, 94–95. Clarke provides a "Checklist of Imaginary Wars, 1763–1990" (224), of which the most significant precursor to Chesney is *The History of the Sudden and Terrible Invasion of England by the French, in the month of May, 1852*, published anonymously in Britain in 1851 (28). Le Queux's most famous invasion novel is *The Great War in England in 1897* (1894) and Oppenheim's is *Mysterious Mr. Sabin* (1898). "At least as early as 1906 (and 1904 in the Admiralty), it was accepted that a German war seemed to be inevitable" (Ronald Hyam, "The British Empire in the Edwardian Era," *The Twentieth Century*, ed. Judith M. Brown and William Roger Louis, Oxford UP, 1999, 55, *The Oxford History of the British Empire*, vol. 4). On the rivalry between England and Germany, see Donald Read, "Crisis Age or Golden Age?," Introduction, *Edwardian England*, ed. Read, Rutgers UP, 1982, 19–20.

6. Michael Denning, *Cover Stories: Narrative and Ideology in the British Spy Thriller*, Routledge and Kegan Paul, 1987, 26, Popular Fiction Series.

7. Adrian Wisnicki, "Reformulating the Empire's Hero: Rhodesian Gold, Boer Veld-Craft, and the Displaced Scotsman in John Buchan's *The Thirty-Nine Steps*," *Journal of Colonialism and Colonial History*, vol. 8, no. 1, Spring 2007, par. 1, doi:10.1353/cch.2007.0025. Graham Greene, quoted in Denning 10. Robin W. Winks marks the shift with John le Carré's *The Spy Who Came in from the Cold*

(1963) ("John Buchan: Stalking the Wilder Game," *The Four Adventures of Richard Hannay*, by Buchan, ed. Winks, Godine, 1988, xi).

8. Cawelti and Rosenberg 63. For a discussion of the formula, see Cawelti and Rosenberg 56–63; and Winks xi–xii. Obviously there were variations. For instance, Ian Fleming's James Bond is a professional spy.

9. Roy Turnbaugh, "Image of Empire: G. A. Henty and John Buchan," *Journal of Popular Culture*, vol. 9, no. 3, Winter 1975, 738. Denning 41. Cf. David Trotter, *The English Novel in History, 1895–1920*, Routledge, 1993, 167.

10. Denning is referring to the Second Anglo-Boer War (41).

11. Yumna Siddiqi, *Anxieties of Empire and the Fiction of Intrigue*, Columbia UP, 2008, 108. Siddiqi provides a robust list of examples on 115.

12. John Buchan, *The Island of Sheep*, Stratus, 2001, 23, hereafter cited parenthetically as *Island*.

13. John Buchan, *The Thirty-Nine Steps*, Oxford UP, 1999, 7, hereafter cited parenthetically as *Steps*.

14. John Buchan, *Greenmantle*, Penguin, 1956, 201–02, hereafter cited parenthetically as *Green*. The Hottentots Holland Mountains are in the Cape; the Zoutpansberg (Soutpansberg) are in what was then the Transvaal (in a portion that is now the Province of Limpopo); Damaraland is in what was then German South West Africa (Namibia); and the Mont aux Sources (Mont-aux-Sources) is in the Drakensberg, in what was then Basutoland (Lesotho), Natal, and either the Orange Free State, Orange River Colony, or Province of the Orange Free State (see my introduction, note 7). Kopjes are small, generally rocky hills.

15. John Buchan, *Mr. Standfast*, Popular Library-Houghton, 1947, 97, hereafter cited parenthetically as *Mr.*

16. John Buchan, *The Three Hostages*, Bantam, 1946, 18, 26, hereafter cited parenthetically as *Three*.

17. A doctor "who dabbled in hypnotism told me that I was the most unsympathetic person he had ever struck. He said I was about as good a mesmeric subject as Table Mountain" (*Green* 169).

18. See note 12 in the introduction.

19. See "A Note on Terminology" at the beginning of this book.

20. Andrew Lownie, *John Buchan: The Presbyterian Cavalier*, Constable, 1995, 122.

21. Peter John Hannay's middle name is of course Buchan's own first name; it is also the first name of the Reverend John Laputa, otherwise known as Prester John, in Buchan's 1910 novel of the same name.

22. The following sentence, in which Hannay reflects on "the defence of Erzurum," demonstrates his sense of both Peter's value and his inferiority: "It depended on Peter, now slumbering like a tired dog on a couch of straw" (*Green* 215).

23. Usborne 129.

24. H. Rider Haggard, *Allan Quatermain*, Penguin, 1995, 11.

25. Where David Stafford argues that Hannay's "captivation by England leads to the inexorable severing of his remnant links with southern Africa," I contend that it instantiates an English identity drawing heavily on a South African-ness that Hannay continues to deploy ("John Buchan's Tales of Espionage: A Popular Archive of British History," *Canadian Journal of History*, vol. 18, no. 1, Apr. 1983, 13).

26. See the introduction, page 7.

27. The Hannay novels sold better than anything else Buchan wrote (Stafford, "Tales of Espionage" 4).

28. David Stafford, "Spies and Gentlemen: The Birth of the British Spy Novel, 1893–1914," *Victorian Studies*, vol. 24, no. 4, Summer 1981, 509, and see 491.

29. "Sir Rider Haggard. Ethics of Literature," *Sydney Morning Herald*, 12 Apr. 1913, 9. See my introduction, note 7.

30. Plaatje kept a diary during the Second Anglo-Boer War, which was not published until 1973 (*The Boer War Diary of Sol T. Plaatje: An African at Mafeking*, ed. John L. Comaroff, Macmillan, 1975). Founded in 1912 as the South African Native National Congress (SANNC), the organization changed its name to the African National Congress in 1923. Plaatje founded (and edited) the first English/Setswana newspaper—*Koranta ea Becoana* (*The Bechuana Gazette*)—shortly after the Second Anglo-Boer War, edited a Bechuana newspaper in Kimberley, and wrote for every major European newspaper in South Africa (Tim Couzens and Brian Willan, "Solomon T. Plaatje, 1876–1932: An Introduction," *English in Africa*, vol. 3, no. 2, Sept. 1976, 4). He could speak at least eight languages and write in four (Brian Willan, *Sol Plaatje: South African Nationalist, 1876–1932*, Heinemann, 1984, vii).

31. He began but did not finish a second novel (Willan, *South African Nationalist* 364–71).

32. Tim Couzens and Stephen Gray, "Printers and Other Devils: The Texts of Sol T. Plaatje's *Mhudi*," *Research in African Literatures*, vol. 9, no. 2, Fall 1978, 198. Three Sesotho novels by Thomas Mofolo appeared before *Mhudi*, as did *An African Tragedy* (1928), an English novella by Zulu writer R. R. R. Dhlomo.

33. On the intentional hybridity of *Mhudi*, see Willan, *South African Nationalist* 352; and Richard Samin, "Sol Plaatje's *Mhudi* and the Emergence of Black Political Fiction in South Africa," *Commonwealth*, vol. 22, no. 1, Fall 1999, 37. For an overview of the novel's influences, see Tim Couzens, "Sol Plaatje and the First South African Epic," *English in Africa*, vol. 14, no. 1, May 1987, 198–215. On the influence of Shakespeare in particular, see Stephen Gray, "Plaatje's Shakespeare," *English in Africa*, vol. 4, no. 1, Mar. 1977, 1–16; Samin 37–45; and Laura Chrisman, *Rereading the Imperial Romance: British Imperialism and South African Resistance in Haggard, Schreiner, and Plaatje*, Clarendon, 2000, 197, 200–02. On romance, see Annalisa Oboe, "From South Africa to Europe to North America and Back: Sol Plaatje, W. E. B. Du Bois, and the Routes of Romance," *Recharting the Black Atlantic: Modern Cultures, Local Communities, Global Connections*, ed. Oboe and Anna Scacchi, Routledge, 2008, 20–44. On the imperial romance specifically, see Lindy

Stiebel, "The Return of the Lost City: The Hybrid Legacy of Rider Haggard's African Romances," *Multiculturalism and Hybridity in African Literatures*, ed. Hal Wylie and Bernth Lindfors, Africa World, 2000, 281–96; and Chrisman, *Rereading*, 163–86. On orality, see Chrisman, *Rereading*, 187–208; Phaswane Mpe, "'Naturally these stories lost nothing by repetition': Plaatje's Mediation of Oral History in *Mhudi*," *Current Writing: Text and Reception in Southern Africa*, vol. 8, no. 1, 1996, 75–89; and Mpe, "Sol Plaatje, Orality and the Politics of Cultural Representation," *Current Writing: Text and Reception in Southern Africa*, vol. 11, no. 2, 1999, 75–91.

34. The attack on Kunana (today called Setlagole) took place on August 6, 1832 (Mpe, "'Naturally'" 88n2). See "A Note on Terminology" at the beginning of this book.

35. Sol T. Plaatje, *Mhudi*, Waveland, 2014, 41, hereafter cited parenthetically as *Mhudi*.

36. The attack on the *voortrekkers* took place on October 16, 1836, at the Battle of Vechtkop. The allies fought the Matabele (Ndebele) in January and November 1837, contributing significantly to the latter's migration from the region. See R. Kent Rasmussen, *Migrant Kingdom: Mzilikazi's Ndebele in South Africa*, Collings, 1978, 97–132. The Griqua are descended primarily from early Dutch settlers and indigenous Africans, the Khoikhoi in particular.

37. Michael Cawood Green, "Generic Instability and the National Project: History, Nation, and Form in Sol T. Plaatje's *Mhudi*," *Research in African Literatures*, vol. 37, no. 4, Winter 2006, 36. Bhekizizwe Peterson, "Black Writers and the Historical Novel: 1907–1948," *The Cambridge History of South African Literature*, ed. David Attwell and Derek Attridge, Cambridge UP, 2012, 291n1. Peterson mentions "debates" on the causes, but does not himself weigh in.

38. George M. Fredrickson, *White Supremacy: A Comparative Study in American and South African History*, Oxford UP, 1981, 169.

39. "100,000 Africans acted as scouts, spies, patrols, transport drivers, messengers, and labourers on the British side," while as many as thirty thousand were armed by the British (Christopher Saunders and Iain R. Smith, "Southern Africa, 1795–1910," *The Nineteenth Century*, ed. Andrew Porter, Oxford UP, 1999, 618–19, *The Oxford History of the British Empire*, vol. 3). Fourteen thousand Africans "lost their lives in the fighting" and as many in concentration camps (Michael Chapman, *Southern African Literatures*, Longman, 1996, 207; Elizabeth van Heyningen, "A Tool for Modernisation? The Boer Concentration Camps of the South African War, 1900–1902," *South African Journal of Science*, vol. 106, no. 5/6, May/June 2010, 2 of 10, archive.sajs.co.za/index.php/SAJS/article/view/242). For more on the black camps, see Elizabeth van Heyningen, "'Hewers of wood and drawers of water': The Black Camp Experience," *The Concentration Camps of the Anglo-Boer War: A Social History*, by van Heyningen, Jacana, 2013, 150–78.

40. Couzens, "Sol Plaatje and the First" 50, 55.

41. Willan, *South African Nationalist* 359. By way of contrast, Rider Haggard purports to be both a friend and editor of (the fictional) Allan Quatermain,

through such literary devices as editor's footnotes, editor's headnotes, and even, in one instance—1917's *Finished*—a personal cameo.

42. Mpe, " 'Naturally' " 75.

43. Couzens, "Sol Plaatje and the First" 61.

44. *Sechuana Proverbs* contains 732 proverbs. *A Sechuana Reader* was the first phonetically spelled Setswana reader. Plaatje coauthored the book with Daniel Jones, a reader in phonetics at London University. Couzens, "Sol Plaatje and the First" 42.

45. Couzens and Gray 206; I have omitted the italics that the authors used for the entire phrase.

46. Couzens, "Sol Plaatje and the First" 42.

47. Tim Couzens, "Sol Plaatje's *Mhudi*," *Journal of Commonwealth Literature*, vol. 8, no. 1, June 1973, 5.

48. On writing dates, see Couzens and Gray 201–02. On publication difficulties, see Couzens and Gray 198–215; and Gray, *Southern African Literature: An Introduction*, Barnes & Noble, 1979, 172–81. Brian Willan has recently disputed the view that Plaatje resisted these changes ("What 'Other Devils'? The Texts of Sol T. Plaatje's *Mhudi* Revisited," *Journal of Southern African Studies*, vol. 41, no. 6, 2015, 1331–47, doi:10.1080/03057070.2015.1116234).

49. Gray, *Southern African Literature* 176, 175.

50. Gray, *Southern African Literature* 176, 181.

51. See Willan, *South African Nationalist* 361–64; Green 38; and David Johnson, "Literature for the Rainbow Nation: The Case of Sol Plaatje's *Mhudi*," *Journal of Literary Studies*, vol. 10, no. 3/4, Dec. 1994, 347.

52. Couzens and Gray 201. Sol T. Plaatje, *Mhudi*, ed. Stephen Gray, Heinemann, 1978, African Writers Series 201.

53. Tim Couzens, Introduction, *Mhudi*, by Plaatje, ed. Stephen Gray, Heinemann, 1978, 17, African Writers Series 201.

54. Couzens, Introduction 17.

55. The figures are from Ruth First and Ann Scott, *Olive Schreiner*, Schocken, 1980, 305. Myrtle Hooper, "Two Sides of Empire: *Heart of Darkness* and *Mhudi*," *The Conradian*, vol. 17, no. 1, Autumn 1992, 41.

56. On this point, see, for instance, Samin 43; and Anthony Chennells, "Plotting South African History: Narrative in Sol Plaatje's *Mhudi*," *English in Africa*, vol. 24, no. 1, May 1997, 43. As the Union had made no provision for black voting rights, which had long existed in the Cape Colony, they were swiftly eroded; not long after Plaatje's death, they were entirely eliminated (54).

57. Plaatje, quoted in Couzens, "Sol Plaatje and the First" 53.

58. Oboe, "From South Africa" 34–35.

59. Shane Moran, "Plaatje's Resistance," *English in Africa*, vol. 42, no. 3, Dec. 2015, 52. Oboe, "From South Africa" 28. Cf. Couzens, "Sol Plaatje and the First" 53; and Couzens, Introduction 11.

60. Plaatje, quoted in Couzens, "Sol Plaatje and the First" 53.

61. Samin 41.

62. Couzens, "Sol Plaatje and the First" 53–54.

63. Chrisman, *Rereading* 14.

64. Oboe, "From South Africa" 29. Cf. Tina Steiner, "Traversing Social Landscapes: Sol Plaatje's *Mhudi* and the Question of Community," *English in Africa*, vol. 41, no. 3, Dec. 2014, 8; Willan, *South African Nationalist* 385–60; and Samin 41.

65. For instance, Oboe, "From South Africa" 34; and Samin 41.

66. H. Rider Haggard, *The Ghost Kings*, Cassell, 1908, 136–38; the first emphasis is in the original, the second is mine. For more on this scene, see chapter 2, pages 85–86, 90.

67. For instance, he objected to women's exclusion as SANNC (ANC) delegates (Steiner 17) and he named his daughter after Olive Schreiner, the New Woman novelist who had by then come to see gender and racial equality as corollaries (Willan, *South African Nationalist* 134). See also Elleke Boehmer, "Failure to Connect: Resistant Modernities at National Crossroads—Solomon Plaatje and Mohandas Gandhi," *Beyond the Black Atlantic: Relocating Modernization and Technology*, ed. Walter Goebel and Saskia Schabio, Routledge, 2006, 52; and Laura Chrisman, "Fathering the Black Nation of South Africa: Gender and Generation in Sol Plaatje's *Native Life in South Africa* and *Mhudi*," *Social Dynamics*, vol. 23, no. 2, 1997, 63.

68. J. M. Phelps, "Sol Plaatje's *Mhudi* and Democratic Government," *English Studies in Africa*, vol. 36, no. 1, Jan. 1993, 55.

Works Cited

Advice to Emigrants. South Africa, n.d. *"South Africa" Handbook,* no. 1.
"The Anglo-African Writers' Club. Mr. Rider Haggard Delivers His Presidential Address. A Remarkable Inauguration." *African Review of Mining, Finance and Commerce,* 28 Apr. 1894, pp. 541–45.
Anonymous. *The History of the Sudden and Terrible Invasion of England by the French, in the Month of May, 1852.* Bosworth, 1851.
"Another South African Novel." Review of *Diamond Dyke, or the Lone Farm on the Veldt: A Story of South African Adventure,* by George Manville Fenn. *African Review of Mining, Finance and Commerce,* 8 Dec. 1894, p. 821.
Anthony, Loren. "Buried Narratives: Masking the Sign of History in *The Story of an African Farm.*" *Scrutiny2,* vol. 4, no. 2, 1999, pp. 3–13.
Archibald, Diana C. *Domesticity, Imperialism, and Emigration in the Victorian Novel.* U of Missouri P, 2002.
Ardis, Ann. *New Women, New Novels: Feminism and Early Modernism.* Rutgers UP, 1990.
Arendt, Hannah. *The Origins of Totalitarianism.* New ed., Harvest-Harcourt, 1968.
Armstrong, Nancy. *Desire and Domestic Fiction: The Political History of the Novel.* Oxford UP, 1987.
———. "The Occidental Alice." *differences,* vol. 2, no. 2, 1990, pp. 3–40.
"Arrival of Chinese Labourers in South Africa." *South African History Online,* www.sahistory.org.za/dated-event/arrival-chinese-labourers-south-africa.
Attwell, David. "South African Literature in English." *The Cambridge History of African and Caribbean Literature,* vol. 2, edited by F. Abiola Irele and Simon Gikandi, Cambridge UP, 2008, pp. 504–29.
Attwell, David, and Derek Attridge. Introduction. *The Cambridge History of South African Literature,* edited by Attwell and Attridge, Cambridge UP, 2012, pp. 1–13.
Auerbach, Nina. *Woman and the Demon: The Life of a Victorian Myth.* Harvard UP, 1982.

Aveling, Edward. "A Notable Book." *Progress: A Monthly Magazine of Advanced Thought*, Sept. 1883, pp. 156–65.

Ballantyne, R. M. *The Island Queen*. Project Gutenberg, 2007, www.gutenberg.org/files/21741/21741-h/21741-h.htm.

Ballantyne, Tony. "Race and the Webs of Empire: Aryanism from India to the Pacific." *Journal of Colonialism and Colonial History*, vol. 2, no. 3, Winter 2001, doi:10.1353/cch.2001.0045.

Ballantyne, Tony, and Antoinette Burton. "The Politics of Intimacy in an Age of Empire." Introduction. *Moving Subjects: Gender, Mobility, and Intimacy in an Age of Global Empire*, edited by Ballantyne and Burton, U of Illinois P, pp. 1–28.

Barash, Carol. Introduction. *An Olive Schreiner Reader: Writings on Women and South Africa*, by Olive Schreiner, edited by Barash, Pandora, 1987, pp. 1–20.

Barash, Carol L. "Virile Womanhood: Olive Schreiner's Narratives of a Master Race." *Speaking of Gender*, edited by Elaine Showalter, Routledge, 1989, pp. 269–81.

Barker, [Mary Anne]. *A Year's Housekeeping in South Africa*. Tauchnitz, 1877. Collection of British Authors, Tauchnitz Edition, vol. 1670.

Barnett, Ursula A. *A Vision of Order: A Study of Black South African Literature in English (1914–1980)*. Browne / U of Massachusetts P, 1983.

Barnicoat, Constance. "The Reading of the Colonial Girl." *The Nineteenth Century and After*, vol. 60, no. 358, Dec. 1906, pp. 939–50.

Baucom, Ian. *Out of Place: Englishness, Empire, and the Locations of Identity*. Princeton UP, 1999.

Belich, James. *Replenishing the Earth: The Settler Revolution and the Rise of the Anglo-World, 1783–1939*. Oxford UP, 2009.

Bell, Duncan. *The Idea of Greater Britain: Empire and the Future of World Order, 1860–1900*. Princeton UP, 2007.

———. "Victorian Visions of Global Order: An Introduction." *Victorian Visions of Global Order*, edited by Bell, Cambridge UP, 2007, pp. 1–20.

Bell, Morag. "A Woman's Place in 'A White Man's Country.' Rights, Duties, and Citizenship for the 'New' South Africa, c. 1902." *Cultural Geographies*, vol. 2, no. 2, 1995, pp. 129–48.

Bjørhovde, Gerd. "Modernism in Embryo: Olive Schreiner." *Rebellious Structures: Women Writers and the Crisis of the Novel, 1880–1900*. Norwegian UP, 1987, pp. 21–58.

Black, Colin. *The Legend of Lomagundi*. North-Western Development Association, 1976.

Blakeley, Brian L. "Women and Imperialism: The Colonial Office and Female Emigration to South Africa, 1901–1910." *Albion: A Quarterly Journal Concerned with British Studies*, vol. 13, no. 2, 1981, pp. 131–49.

Bleiler, Everett F. *Science-Fiction: The Early Years*. Kent State UP, 1990.

Boehmer, Elleke. "Failure to Connect: Resistant Modernities at National Crossroads—Solomon Plaatje and Mohandas Gandhi." *Beyond the Black Atlantic:*

Relocating Modernization and Technology, edited by Walter Goebel and Saskia Schabio, Routledge, 2006, pp. 47–62.

Booth, Joseph. *Africa for the African*. N.p., [1897]. *HathiTrust*, babel.hathitrust.org/cgi/pt?id=ien.35556012349940&view=1up&seq=3.

"Booth, Joseph." *Mundus: Gateway to Missionary Collections in the United Kingdom*, www.mundus.ac.uk/cats/1/52.htm.

Boyd, Charles W. "Rhodesia." *British Africa*. Kegan, 1899, pp. 9–26. The British Empire Series 2.

Brantlinger, Patrick. *Rule of Darkness: British Literature and Imperialism, 1830–1914*. Cornell UP, 1988.

———. "Victorians and Africans: The Genealogy of the Myth of the Dark Continent." *Critical Inquiry*, vol. 12, no. 1, Autumn 1985, pp. 166–203.

Bratton, J. S. "British Imperialism and the Reproduction of Femininity in Girls' Fiction, 1900–1930." *Imperialism and Juvenile Literature*, edited by Jeffrey Richards, Manchester UP, 1989, pp. 195–215.

Bristow, Joseph. *Empire Boys: Adventures in a Man's World*. HarperCollinsAcademic-Harper Collins, 1991.

"The British South Africa Company Historical Catalogue and Souvenir of Rhodesia Empire Exhibition, Johannesburg, 1936–37." *The Great North Road*, bsac.greatnorthroad.org/bsac.pdf.

Brody, Jennifer DeVere. *Impossible Purities: Blackness, Femininity, and Victorian Culture*. Duke UP, 1998.

Buchan, John. *The African Colony: Studies in the Reconstruction*. Blackwood, 1903.

———. *Comments and Characters*, edited by W. Forbes Gray, Nelson, 1940.

———. *The Courts of the Morning*. Hodder, 1929.

———. *The Great Diamond Pipe*. Dodd, 1911.

———. *Greenmantle*. Penguin, 1956.

———. "The Grove of Ashtaroth." *John Buchan: The Complete Short Stories*, vol. 2, edited by Andrew Lownie, Thistle, 1997, pp. 145–66. 3 vols.

———. *The Island of Sheep*. Stratus, 2001.

———. *A Lodge in the Wilderness*. Blackwood, 1906.

———. *Memory Hold-the-Door*. Hodder, 1940.

———. *Mr. Standfast*. Popular Library-Houghton, 1947.

———. *Pilgrim's Way: An Essay in Recollection*. Houghton, 1940.

———. *Prester John*, edited by David Daniell, Oxford UP, 1994.

———. *Sick Heart River*. Hodder, 1941.

———. *The Thirty-Nine Steps*. Oxford UP, 1999.

———. *The Three Hostages*. Bantam, 1946.

Bulwer-Lytton, Edward. *The Coming Race*, edited by Peter Simmema, Broadview, 2008.

Bunn, David. "Embodying Africa: Woman and Romance in Colonial Fiction." *English in Africa*, vol. 15, no. 1, 1988, pp. 1–27.

Bunyan, John. *The Pilgrim's Progress*. Oxford UP, 2003.
Burdett, Carolyn. *Olive Schreiner and the Progress of Feminism: Evolution, Gender, Empire*. Palgrave, 2001.
Burgess, Wade. "Gertrude Page." *SouthAfricaBooks.com*, 2010.
Burton, Antoinette. *Burdens of History: British Feminists, Indian Women, and Imperial Culture, 1865–1915*. U of North Carolina P, 1994.
Bush, Julia. *Edwardian Ladies and Imperial Power*. Leicester UP, 2000. Women, Power, and Politics.
———. "'The Right Sort of Woman': Female Emigrators and Emigration to the British Empire, 1890–1910." *Women's History Review*, vol. 3, no. 3, 1994, pp. 385–409.
Cadogan, Mary, and Patricia Craig. *You're a Brick, Angela! The Girls' Story, 1839–1985*. Gollancz, 1986.
"The Call of the South." *Social South Africa: Some Hints to Lady Settlers*. South Africa, n.d., pp. 22–25. "*South Africa*" Handbook, no. 44. Originally published in *South Africa: A Weekly Journal for All Interested in South African Affairs*, May 1908.
Campbell, Mary Baine. "Asia, Africa, Abyssinia: Writing the Land of Prester John." *Travel Writing, Form, and Empire: The Poetics and Politics of Mobility*, edited by Julia Kuehn and Paul Smethurst. Routledge, 2009, pp. 21–37.
Carrington, C. E. *The Life of Rudyard Kipling*. Doubleday, 1955.
Carrothers, W. A. *Emigration from the British Isles*. Cass, 1966.
Cawelti, John G., and Bruce Rosenberg. *The Spy Story*. U of Chicago P, 1987.
Cecil, Alicia M. "The Needs of South Africa: Female Emigration." *The Nineteenth Century and After*, vol. 51, no. 302, Apr. 1902, pp. 683–92.
CHAM. "Life in a Country Dorp." *South African Stories and Sketches*, 5th series, South Africa, n.d., pp. 10–13. "*South Africa*" Handbook, no. 41. Originally published in *South Africa: A Weekly Journal for All Interested in South African Affairs*, Dec. 1907.
Chapman, Michael. *Southern African Literatures*. Longman, 1996.
Chennells, Anthony. "Imagining and Living the Exotic: A Context for Early Rhodesian Novels." *Journal of Literary Studies*, vol. 19, no. 2, June 2003, pp. 137–58.
———. "Imperial Romances and Narratives of White Rhodesian Nationalism. Cynthia Stockley, Gertrude Page and Doris Lessing." *Anglistica: An Interdisciplinary Journal of English Studies*, vol. 3, no. 2, 1999, pp. 77–90.
———. "The Mimic Women: Early Women Novelists and White Southern African Nationalisms." *Historia*, vol. 49, no. 1, May 2004, pp. 71–88.
———. "Plotting South African History: Narrative in Sol Plaatje's *Mhudi*." *English in Africa*, vol. 24, no. 1, May 1997, pp. 37–58.
Chesney, George. *The Battle of Dorking: Reminiscences of a Volunteer*. Blackwood, 1871.
Childers, Erskine. *The Riddle of the Sands: A Record of Secret Service*. Penguin, 2011.
Chirenje, J. Mutero. *Ethiopianism and Afro-Americans in Southern Africa, 1883–1916*. Louisiana State UP, 1987.

Chrisman, Laura. "Empire, 'Race' and Feminism at the Fin de Siècle: The Work of George Egerton and Olive Schreiner." *Cultural Politics at the Fin de Siècle*, edited by Sally Ledger and Scott McCracken, Cambridge UP, 1995, pp. 45–65.

———. "Fathering the Black Nation of South Africa: Gender and Generation in Sol Plaatje's *Native Life in South Africa* and *Mhudi*." *Social Dynamics*, vol. 23, no. 2, 1997, pp. 57–73.

———. "The Imperial Unconscious? Representations of Imperial Discourse." *Critical Quarterly*, vol. 32, no. 3, Fall 1990, pp. 38–58.

———. *Postcolonial Contraventions: Cultural Readings of Race, Imperialism and Transnationalism*. Manchester UP, 2003.

———. *Rereading the Imperial Romance: British Imperialism and South African Resistance in Haggard, Schreiner, and Plaatje*. Clarendon, 2000.

Clarke, I. F. *Voices Prophesying War: Future Wars, 1763–3749*. 2nd ed., Oxford UP, 1992.

"The Closing Year." *Buluwayo Chronicle*, 30 Dec. 1922, p. 6.

Coetzee, J. M. *White Writing: On the Culture of Letters in South Africa*. Yale UP, 1988.

Cohen, Morton. *Rider Haggard: His Life and Works*. Hutchinson, 1960.

Colgan, Norman. "Africa's Writer of Romance." *Everybody's: The Popular Weekly*, 12 May 1945, p. 15.

Conrad, Joseph. *Heart of Darkness*, edited by Ross C. Murfin, 3rd ed., Bedford, 2011. Case Studies in Contemporary Criticism.

———. *The Secret Agent: A Simple Tale*, edited by Peter Lancelot Mallios, Modern Library, 2004.

Constantine, Stephen. "Empire Migration and Social Reform, 1880–1950." *Migrants, Emigrants and Immigrants: A Social History of Migration*, edited by Colin G. Pooley and Ian D. Whyte, Routledge, 1991, pp. 62–83.

Coombes, Annie E., editor. *Rethinking Settler Colonialism: History and Memory in Australia, Canada, Aotearoa New Zealand, and South Africa*. Manchester UP, 2006.

"Court Circular." *Times*, 5 Apr. 1921, p. 13. *Times Digital Archive*.

Couzens, Tim. Introduction. *Mhudi*, by Sol T. Plaatje, edited by Stephen Gray, Heinemann, 1978, pp. 1–20. African Writers Series 201.

———. " 'The Old Africa of a Boy's Dream': Towards Interpreting Buchan's *Prester John*." *English Studies in Africa*, vol. 24, no. 1, 1981, pp. 1–24.

———. "Sol Plaatje and the First South African Epic." *English in Africa*, vol. 14, no. 1, May 1987, pp. 198–215.

———. "Sol Plaatje's *Mhudi*." *Journal of Commonwealth Literature*, vol. 8, no. 1, June 1973, pp. 1–19.

Couzens, Tim, and Stephen Gray. "Printers and Other Devils: The Texts of Sol T. Plaatje's *Mhudi*." *Research in African Literatures*, vol. 9, no. 2, Fall 1978, pp. 198–215.

Couzens, Tim, and Brian Willan. "Solomon T. Plaatje, 1876–1932: An Introduction." *English in Africa*, vol. 3, no. 2, Sept. 1976, pp. 1–6.
Crawford, Claudia. "She." *SubStance*, vol. 9, no. 4, 1981, pp. 83–96.
Cronwright-Schreiner, S. C. *The Life of Olive Schreiner*. Unwin, 1924.
Cruse, Amy. *After the Victorians*. Allen, 1976.
Cunningham, Gail. *The New Woman and the Victorian Novel*. Macmillan, 1978.
Daly, Nicholas. "Colonialism and Popular Literature at the Fin de Siècle." *Modernism and Colonialism: British and Irish Literature, 1899–1939*, edited by Richard Begam and Michael Valdez Moses, Duke UP, 2007, pp. 19–40.
———. *Modernism, Romance, and the Fin de Siècle: Popular Fiction and British Culture, 1880–1914*. Cambridge UP, 1999.
Dalziell, Tanya. *Settler Romances and the Australian Girl*. U of Western Australia P, 2004.
Daniell, David. *The Interpreter's House: A Critical Assessment of John Buchan*. Nelson, 1975.
———. Introduction. *Prester John*, by John Buchan, edited by Daniell, Oxford UP, 1994, pp. vii–xxvi.
Darwin, John. *The Empire Project: The Rise and Fall of the British World-System, 1830–1970*. Cambridge UP, 2009.
David, Deirdre. *Rule Britannia: Women, Empire, and Victorian Writing*. Cornell UP, 1995.
Davin, Anna. "Imperialism and Motherhood." *History Workshop Journal*, vol. 5, no. 1, Spring 1978, pp. 9–66.
"Day by Day." *Buluwayo Chronicle*, 9 Feb. 1912, p. 4.
Deane, Bradley. "Imperial Barbarians: Primitive Masculinity in Lost World Fiction." *Victorian Literature and Culture*, vol. 36, 2008, pp. 205–25.
"Death of Miss Gertrude Page." *Bedfordshire Times and Woburn Reporter*, 7 Apr. 1922, p. unknown.
Defoe, Daniel. *The Farther Adventures of Robinson Crusoe, Being the Second and Last Part of His Life*. Constable, 1925.
———. *The Life and Adventures of Mrs. Christian Davies, Commonly Call'd Mother Ross*. Montagu, 1740.
———. *Robinson Crusoe*. Penguin, 2003.
Dehan, Richard. *The Dop Doctor*. Heinemann, 1936.
[De Morgan, John.] *Bess, A Companion to "Jess."* Munro, 1887.
Denning, Michael. *Cover Stories: Narrative and Ideology in the British Spy Thriller*. Routledge and Kegan Paul, 1987. Popular Fiction Series.
Dhlomo, R. R. R. *An African Tragedy*. Lovedale, 1928. *Empire Online*, www.empire.amdigital.co.uk.
Dixon, Robert. *Writing the Colonial Adventure: Race, Gender and Nation in Anglo-Australian Popular Fiction, 1875–1914*. Cambridge UP, 1995.

Donovan, Stephen. "Colonial Pedigree: Class, Masculinity, and History in the Early Rhodesian Novel." *Nordic Journal of English Studies*, vol. 11, no. 2, 2012, pp. 57–79.

Dor, Laili. "Conflicting Visions of War: Winston Churchill and Rudyard Kipling's Evocation of the Boer War." *Cahiers Victoriens et Édoudardiens*, vol. 66, Oct. 2007, pp. 211–28.

Doughty, Terri. "Domestic Goddesses on the Frontier; or, Tempting the Mothers of Empire with Adventure." *Victorian Settler Narratives: Emigrants, Cosmopolitans and Returnees in Nineteenth-Century Literature*, edited by Tamara S. Wagner, Pickering & Chatto, 2011, pp. 193–205. Gender and Genre 5.

Doyle, A. Conan. *The Great Boer War*. Nelson, n.d. *HathiTrust*, babel.hathitrust.org/cgi/pt?id=mdp.39015086882282&view=1up&seq=9.

———. "The Mystery of Sasassa Valley: A South African Story." *Peril and Prowess: Being Stories Told by G. A. Henty . . . &c., &c*. Chambers, 1899, pp. 145–61.

———. *The War in South Africa: Its Cause and Conduct*. Tauchnitz, 1902. *Hathi-Trust*, babel.hathitrust.org/cgi/pt?id=mdp.39015019049421&view=1up&seq=7.

Dreher, Nan H. "Redundancy and Emigration: The 'Woman Question' in Mid-Victorian Britain." *Victorian Periodicals Review*, vol. 26, no. 1, 1993, pp. 3–7.

Dryden, Linda. *Joseph Conrad and the Imperial Romance*. Macmillan, 2000.

Dubow, Saul. "Colonial Nationalism, the Milner Kindergarten, and the Rise of 'South Africanism,' 1902–10." *History Workshop Journal*, vol. 43, no. 1, Spring 1997, pp. 53–85.

———. "How British Was the British World? The Case of South Africa." *Journal of Imperial and Commonwealth History*, vol. 37, no. 1, Mar. 2009, pp. 1–27.

———. *Scientific Racism in Modern South Africa*. Cambridge UP, 1994.

DuPlessis, Rachel Blau. *Writing Beyond the Ending: Narrative Strategies of Twentieth-Century Women Writers*. Indiana UP, 1985.

Durbach, Reneé. *Kipling's South Africa*. Chameleon, 1988.

Eby, Cecil Degrotte. *The Road to Armageddon: The Martial Spirit in English Popular Literature, 1870–1914*. Duke UP, 1987.

Edge o' Beyond. Directed by Fred W. Durrant. Samuelson, 1919.

Egoff, Sheila, and Judith Saltman. *The New Republic of Childhood: A Critical Guide to Canadian Children's Literature in England*. 3rd ed., Oxford UP, 1990.

Ellis, Peter Beresford. *H. Rider Haggard: A Voice from the Infinite*. Routledge and Kegan Paul, 1978.

Elwin, Malcolm. *Old Gods Falling*. Macmillan, 1939.

"Emigration to South Africa." *African Review of Mining, Finance and Commerce*, 7 July 1894, p. 14.

Esty, Jed. "The Colonial Bildungsroman: *The Story of an African Farm* and the Ghost of Goethe." *Victorian Studies*, vol. 49, no. 3, Apr. 2007, pp. 407–30.

———. *Unseasonable Youth: Modernism, Colonialism, and the Fiction of Development.* Oxford UP, 2012.

Etherington, Norman. "Natal's Black Rape Scare of the 1870s." *Journal of Southern African Studies*, vol. 15, no. 1, Oct. 1988, pp. 36–53.

Etherington, Norman A. "Rider Haggard, Imperialism, and the Layered Personality." *Victorian Studies*, vol. 22, no. 1, Autumn 1978, pp. 71–87.

Evans, Ernestine. "Britain's 'Superfluous Women' Driving Men Out, Says Haggard." *New York Tribune*, 22 July 1916, pp. 1–2.

Fairbridge, Dorothea. *A History of South Africa*. Oxford UP, 1918.

Faymonville, Carmen. "'Waste Not, Want Not': Even Redundant Women Have Their Uses." *Imperial Objects: Essays on Victorian Women's Emigration and the Unauthorized Imperial Experience*, edited by Rita S. Krandis, Twayne, 1998, pp. 64–84.

First, Ruth, and Ann Scott. *Olive Schreiner*. Schocken, 1980.

Forest, John. "South Africa's Favourite Novelists." *African Monthly: A Magazine Devoted to Literature, History, Exploration, Science, Art, Poetry, Fiction, &c.*, vol. 1, Dec. 1906, pp. 69–73.

Forster, E. M. *A Passage to India*. Harcourt, 1952.

Fort, G. Seymour. "British South Africa." *The Scottish Geographical Magazine*, vol. 12, no. 6, June 1896, pp. 281–89.

Foster, Jeremy. *Washed with Sun: Landscape and the Making of White South Africa*. U of Pittsburgh P, 2008.

Fox, [Eleanor] Wilson. "Impressions of Scenery in Rhodesia." *Empire Review*, vol. 16, no. 91, Aug. 1908, pp. 43–49.

Fraiman, Susan. "The Domestic Novel." *The Nineteenth-Century Novel, 1820–1880*, edited by John Kucich and Jenny Bourne Taylor, Oxford UP, 2012, pp. 169–84. *The Oxford History of the Novel in English*, vol. 3.

Fraser, Robert. *Victorian Quest Romance: Stevenson, Haggard, Kipling, and Conan Doyle*. Northcote House, 1998.

Fredrickson, George M. *White Supremacy: A Comparative Study in American and South African History*. Oxford UP, 1981.

Free, Melissa. "British Women Wanted: Gender, Genre, and South African Settlement." *The Oxford Handbook of Victorian Literary Culture*, edited by Juliet John, Oxford UP, 2016, pp. 284–309.

———. "Fault Lines of Loyalty: Rudyard Kipling's Boer War Conflict." *Victorian Studies*, vol. 58, no. 2, Winter 2016, pp. 314–23.

———. "'It Is I Who Have the Power': Settling Women in Haggard's South African Imaginary." *Genre*, vol. 45, no. 3, Fall 2012, pp. 359–93.

"From Gertrude Page, Apathy Denounced, to the Editor, *Buluwayo Chronicle*." *Buluwayo Chronicle*, 23 Apr. 1920, p. 5.

George, Rosemary Marangoly. *The Politics of Home: Postcolonial Relocations and Twentieth-Century Fiction*. Cambridge UP, 1996.

"Gertrude Page." *Buluwayo Chronicle*, 8 Apr. 1922, p. 1.

"Gertrude Page. Burial at Umvukwe." *Buluwayo Chronicle*, 22 Apr. 1922, p. 8.
"Gertrude Page: 'The Kipling of Rhodesia.'" *Woburn Sands Collection*, www.mkheritage.co.uk/wsc/docs/gertpage.html.
Gilbert, Sandra, and Susan Gubar. *Sexchanges*. Yale UP, 1989. *No Man's Land: The Place of the Woman Writer in the Twentieth Century*, vol. 2, edited by Gilbert and Gubar.
"The Goddess, the Festival and Virginity Testing." *Alan Paton Centre & Struggle Archives*, U of Kwazulu-Natal, paton.ukzn.ac.za/Collections/Nomkhubulwane.aspx.
GoGwilt, Christopher. *The Fiction of Geopolitics: Afterimages of Culture, from Wilkie Collins to Alfred Hitchcock*. Stanford UP, 2000.
Gomel, Elana. "Lost and Found: The Lost World Novel and the Shape of the Past." *Genre*, vol. 40, no. 1/2, Spring/Summer 2007, pp. 105–29.
Gorman, Daniel. *Imperial Citizenship: Empire and the Question of Belonging*. Manchester UP, 2007.
Gouldsbury, [Henry] Cullen. *God's Outpost*. Nash, 1907.
Grand, Sarah. "The New Aspect of the Woman Question." *North American Review*, vol. 158, Mar. 1894, pp. 271–76.
Gray, Stephen. "Plaatje's Shakespeare." *English in Africa*, vol. 4, no. 1, Mar. 1977, pp. 1–16.
———. *Southern African Literature: An Introduction*. Barnes & Noble, 1979.
Green, Martin. *Dreams of Adventure, Deeds of Empire*. Basic, 1979.
———. *Seven Types of Adventure Novels: An Etiology of a Major Genre*. Penn State UP, 1991.
Green, Michael Cawood. "Generic Instability and the National Project: History, Nation, and Form in Sol T. Plaatje's *Mhudi*." *Research in African Literatures*, vol. 37, no. 4, Winter 2006, pp. 34–47.
Green, Roger Lancelyn. "'He,' 'She,' and 'It.'" *Times Literary Supplement*, 27 May 1944, p. 264.
Greg, W. R. *Why Are Women Redundant?* Trübner, 1869. *Internet Archive*, archive.org/details/whyarewomenredu00greggoog/page/n3. Originally published in *National Review*, vol. 14, no. 28, Apr. 1862, pp. 434–60.
Greswell, William. *Our South African Empire*. Vol. 1, Chapman, 1885.
Haggard, H. Rider. "About Fiction." *Contemporary Review*, vol. 51, Feb. 1887, pp. 172–80.
———. *Allan Quatermain*. Penguin, 1995.
———. "Allan's Wife." *Hunter Quatermain's Story: The Uncollected Adventures of Allan Quatermain*, edited by Peter Haining, Peter Owen, 2003, pp. 129–256.
———. "Boers Are Loyal, Says Rider Haggard." *New York Times*, 18 Oct. 1914, p. C4. *ProQuest Historical Newspapers*.
———. *Cetywayo and His White Neighbours*. 3rd ed., Trübner, 1890.
———. *The Days of My Life: An Autobiography*, edited by C. J. Longman, Longmans, 1926. 2 vols.

———. *Finished*. Project Gutenberg, 2004, www.gutenberg.org/files/1724/1724-h/1724-h.htm.

———. *The Ghost Kings*. Cassell, 1908.

———. *The Holy Flower*. Ward, 1915.

———. "An Incident of African History." *Windsor Magazine*, vol. 13, no. 1, Dec. 1900, pp. 112–19.

———. *Jess*. McKinlay, 1887.

———. *King Solomon's Mines*. Modern Library, 2002.

———. "A Man's View of Woman." Review of *Woman: The Predominant Partner*, by Edward Sullivan. *She*, by Haggard, edited by Andrew M. Stauffer, Broadview, 2006, pp. 337–40. Originally published in *African Review of Mining, Finance and Commerce*, vol. 4, no. 96, 22 Sept. 1894, pp. 407–08.

———. *Marie*. Wildside, n.d.

———. *Nada the Lily*. Project Gutenberg, www.gutenberg.org/ebooks/1207.

———. *The Poor and the Land*. Longmans, 1905.

———. *The Private Diaries of Sir H. Rider Haggard, 1914–1925*, edited by D. S. Higgins, Cassell, 1980.

———. *She*. Oxford UP, 1998.

———. *The Spirit of Bambatse: A Romance*. McKinlay, 1906. The Works of H. Rider Haggard.

———. *Swallow*. Longmans, 1899. *Internet Archive*, www.archive.org/details/swallowtaleofgre00haggiala.

———. "Woman and Life: Sir Rider Haggard's Views." *Daily Telegraph*, 18 Mar. 1922, p. 7.

Haggard, Lilias Rider. *The Cloak That I Left: A Biography of the Author Henry Rider Haggard, K.B.E.* Hodder, 1951.

Hall, Catherine. *Civilizing Subjects: Colony and Metropole in the English Imagination, 1830–1867*. U of Chicago P, 2002.

Hammerton, A. James. *Emigrant Gentlewomen: Genteel Poverty and Female Emigration, 1830–1914*. Croom Helm, 1979.

———. "'Out of Their Natural Station': Empire and Empowerment in the Emigration of Lower-Middle-Class Women." *Imperial Objects: Essays on Victorian Women's Emigration and the Unauthorized Imperial Experience*, edited by Rita S. Krandis, Twayne, 1998, pp. 143–69.

Heart and Soul. Directed by J. Gordon Edwards, screenplay by Adrian Johnson. Fox Film, 1917.

Hecimovich, Gregg A. *Hardy's "Tess of the D'Urbervilles": A Reader's Guide*. Continuum, 2010.

Henshaw, Peter. "John Buchan from the 'Borders' to the 'Berg': Nature, Empire and White South African Identity, 1901–1910." *African Studies*, vol. 62, no. 1, July 2003, pp. 3–32.

Henty, G. A. "A Frontier Girl: A Tale of the Backwood Settlements." *In the Hands of the Malays and Other Stories*, by Henty. Blackie, 1905, pp. 149–76.

———. *A Soldier's Daughter and Other Stories*. Blackie, 1906. *Internet Archive*, www.archive.org/details/soldiersdaughter00hentiala.

Heywood, Christopher. *A History of South African Literature*. Cambridge UP, 2004.

Higgins, D. S. Introduction. *The Private Diaries of Sir H. Rider Haggard, 1914–1925*, by H. Rider Haggard, edited by Higgins, Cassell, 1980, pp. ix–xv.

———. *Rider Haggard: The Great Storyteller*. Cassell, 1981.

Hobson, J. A. "Capitalism and Imperialism in South Africa." *Contemporary Review*, vol. 77, Jan./June 1900, pp. 1–17.

Hole, H. Marshall. "Rhodesia, by a Resident." *British Africa*. Kegan, 1899, pp. 27–36. The British Empire Series 2.

Hooper, Myrtle. "Two Sides of Empire: *Heart of Darkness* and *Mhudi*." *The Conradian*, vol. 17, no. 1, Autumn 1992, pp. 37–43.

How, Harry. "Illustrated Interviews. No. VII. Mr. H. Rider Haggard." *Strand Magazine*, Jan. 1892, pp. 3–17.

How to See South Africa: The Official Guide to South Africa. Gilchrist, 1906.

Howe, Susanne. *Novels of Empire*. Columbia UP, 1949.

Hultgren, Neil. *Melodramatic Imperial Writing from the Sepoy Rebellion to Cecil Rhodes*. Ohio State UP, 2014.

Hunter, Jefferson. *Edwardian Fiction*. Harvard UP, 1982.

Hutchinson, May Hely. "Female Emigration to South Africa." *The Nineteenth Century and After*, vol. 51, Jan. 1902, pp. 71–87.

Hutchinson's Story Magazine, vol. 1, no. 1, July 1919. *Internet Archive*, archive.org/details/hs_1919_07.

Hyam, Ronald. "The British Empire in the Edwardian Era." *The Twentieth Century*, edited by Judith M. Brown and William Roger Louis, Oxford UP, 1999, pp. 47–63. *The Oxford History of the British Empire*, vol. 4.

———. *Empire and Sexuality: The British Experience*, Manchester UP, 1990. Studies in Imperialism.

"Indian South Africans." *South African History Online*, www.sahistory.org.za/article/indian-south-africans.

Jess. Adapted by Erwetta Lawrence and J. J. Bisgood. Adelphi Theatre, London, 1890.

Jess. Directed by George O. Nichols. Thanhouser Production, 1912.

Jess. Screenplay by Arthur Maude. Kennedy Features, 1914.

"Jess: A Tale of the South African War, by Rider Haggard." Advertisement for *Jess*, directed by George O. Nichols, Thanhouser Production, 1912. *Bioscope*, vol. 17, no. 318, 14 Nov. 1912, pp. xx–xxi. *British Newspaper Archive*, www.britishnewspaperarchive.co.uk.

Johnson, David. "Literature for the Rainbow Nation: The Case of Sol Plaatje's *Mhudi*." *Journal of Literary Studies*, vol. 10, no. 3/4, Dec. 1994, pp. 345–58.

Johnson, Heidi H. "Agricultural Anxiety, African Erasure: H. Rider Haggard's *Rural England* and *Benita: An African Romance*." *Victorians Institute Journal*, vol. 24, 1996, pp. 113–37.

Johnston, Harry H. "South African Interest in South Africa." *African Monthly*, vol. 1, no. 3, Feb. 1907, pp. 259–65.

Johnston, H. H. "The White Man's Place in Africa." *The Nineteenth Century and After*, vol. 55, no. 328, June 1904, pp. 937–46.

Jones, Roderick. "The Black Peril in South Africa." *The Nineteenth Century and After*, vol. 55, no. 327, May 1904, pp. 712–33.

Jordan, A. C. *Towards an African Literature: The Emergence of Literary Form in Xhosa*. U of California P, 1973.

Judd, George F. "South African Types. No. 5—The Predikant." *South African Magazine*, Nov. 1906, pp. 122–31.

Kalu, Ogbu U. "Ethiopianism and the Roots of Modern African Christianity." *World Christianities, c. 1815–1914*, edited by Sheridan Gilley and Brian Stanley, Cambridge UP, 2008, pp. 576–92. *The Cambridge History of Christianity*, vol. 8.

———. "Ethiopianism in African Christianity." *African Christianity: An African Story*, edited by Kalu, Africa World, 2007, pp. 227–43.

Kaplan, H. D. *The Rise of the Black Magus in Western Art*. UMI Research, 1985.

Karlin, Daniel. Introduction. *She*, by H. Rider Haggard, edited by Karlin, Oxford UP, 1998, pp. vii–xxxi.

Katz, Wendy. *Rider Haggard and the Fiction of Empire: A Critical Study of British Imperial Fiction*. Cambridge UP, 1987.

Keating, Peter. *Kipling: The Poet*. Secker, 1994.

Kennedy, Dane. *Islands of White: Settler Society and Culture in Kenya and Southern Rhodesia, 1890–1937*. Duke UP, 1987.

Kiewiet, C. W. de. *A History of South Africa, Social and Economic*. Oxford UP, 1941.

Kipling, Rudyard. "The Absent-Minded Beggar." *Beira Post*, 13 Dec. 1899, p. 4. *Nineteenth Century Collections Online*, www.gale.com/primary-sources/nineteenth-century-collections-online.

———. *The Five Nations*. Doubleday Page, 1903. *HathiTrust*, babel.hathitrust.org/cgi/pt?id=coo1.ark:/13960/t5z613734&view=1up&seq=7.

———. *Just So Stories for Little Children*. Morang, 1902. *HathiTrust*, babel.hathitrust.org/cgi/pt?id=aeu.ark:/13960/t4vh6vp88&view=1up&seq=1.

———. *Kim*, edited by Harish Trivedi, Penguin, 2011.

———. *Something of Myself and Other Autobiographical Writings*. Cambridge UP, 1990.

———. *Traffics and Discoveries*. Macmillan, 1904. *HathiTrust*, babel.hathitrust.org/cgi/pt?id=uc1.b4658797&view=1up&seq=1.

———. *Uncollected Prose*. AMS, 1970. *The Collected Works of Rudyard Kipling*, vol. 23.

Kirkwood, Deborah. "Settler Wives in Southern Rhodesia." *The Incorporated Wife*, edited by Hilary Callan and Shirley Ardener, Croom Helm, 1984, pp. 143–64.

Krandis, Rita S. *The Victorian Spinster and Colonial Emigration: Contested Subjects*. St. Martin's, 1999.

Krebs, Paula M. *Gender, Race, and the Writing of Empire: Public Discourse and the Boer War*. Cambridge UP, 1999.
Kucich, John. *Imperial Masochism: British Fiction, Fantasy and Social Class*. Princeton UP, 2006.
Kuczynski, R. R. *South Africa High Commission Territories, East Africa, Mauritius and Seychelles*. Oxford UP, 1949. *Demographic Survey*, vol. 2.
Laband, John. *The Transvaal Rebellion: The First Boer War, 1880–1881*. Pearson-Longman, 2005.
"A Lady's Trip to South Africa. No. 2." *South Africa: A Weekly Journal for All Interested in South African Affairs*, vol. 26, no. 333, 18 May 1895, p. 332.
Lambert, John. "'An Unknown People': Reconstructing British South African Identity." *Journal of Imperial and Commonwealth History*, vol. 37, no. 4, 2009, pp. 599–617, doi.org/10.1080/03086530903327101.
Lane, Christopher. *The Burdens of Intimacy: Psychoanalysis and Victorian Masculinity*. U of Chicago P, 1999.
———. *The Ruling Passion: British Colonial Allegory and the Paradox of Homosexual Desire*. Duke UP, 1995.
Law, Graham. "The Romance of Empire: John Buchan's Early Writings," 14 pp., *Waseda University*, www.f.waseda.jp/glaw/arts/re.pdf.
Lawson, Elizabeth. "Of Lies and Memory: *The Story of an African Farm*, Book of the White Feather." *Cahiers Victoriens et Édouardiens*, vol. 44, Oct. 1996, pp. 111–26.
Le Carré, John. *The Spy Who Came in from the Cold*. Dell, 1963.
Ledger, Sally. "The New Woman and the Crisis of Victorianism." *Cultural Politics at the Fin de Siècle*, edited by Ledger and Scott McCracken, Cambridge UP, 1995, pp. 22–44.
———. "The New Woman and Feminist Fictions." *The Cambridge Companion to the Fin de Siècle*, edited by Gail Marshall, Cambridge UP, 2007, pp. 153–68.
———. *The New Woman: Fiction and Feminism at the Fin de Siècle*. Manchester UP, 1997.
Le Queux, William. *The Great War in England in 1897*. Tower, 1894.
Lerner, Laurence. "Olive Schreiner and the Feminists." *Olive Schreiner and After: Essays on Southern African Literature in Honour of Guy Butler*, edited by Malvern van Wyk Smith and Don Maclennan, Philip, 1983, pp. 67–79.
Lessing, Doris. *The Grass Is Singing*. Harper Perennial Modern Classics, 2004.
———. Introduction. *The Story of an African Farm*, by Olive Schreiner, Hutchinson, 1968, pp. vi–xxv.
Levine, Philippa, editor. *Gender and Empire*. Oxford UP, 2004. Oxford History of the British Empire Companion Series.
———. "Sexuality, Gender, and Empire." *Gender and Empire*, edited by Levine, Oxford UP, 2004, pp. 134–55. Oxford History of the British Empire Companion Series.

Levy, Anita. "Other Women and New Women: Writing Race and Gender in *The Story of an African Farm*." *The Victorians and Race*, edited by Shearer West, Scolar, 1996, pp. 171–79.
Liebson, S. G. "The South Africa of Fiction." *The State*, vol. 7, no. 2, Feb. 1912, pp. 135–39.
"Literary Gossip." *European Mail*, 8 Aug. 1894, p. 22.
"Literature." *South Africa: A Weekly Journal for All Interested in South African Affairs*, vol. 1, no. 1, 4 Jan. 1889, p. 10.
Livingstone, Justin. "Buchan and the Priest King: Nelson's New Novels, 'The Mountain,' and Religious Revolution in *Prester John*." *English in Africa*, vol. 40, no. 2, Oct. 2013, pp. 47–78.
"Lord Grey on South Africa." *South Africa: A Weekly Journal for All Interested in South African Affairs*, vol. 1, no. 5, 2 Feb. 1889, p. 30.
Love in the Wilderness. Directed by Alexander Butler. Samuelson, 1920.
Low, Florence B. "The Reading of the Modern Girl." *The Nineteenth Century and After*, vol. 59, Feb. 1906, pp. 278–87.
Low, Gail Ching-Liang. *White Skins/Black Masks: Representation and Colonialism*. Routledge, 1996.
Lownie, Andrew. *John Buchan: The Presbyterian Cavalier*. Constable, 1995.
———. "John Buchan, the Round Table and Empire." *The Round Table, the Empire/ Commonwealth and British Foreign Policy*, edited by Andrea Bosco and Alex May, Lothian Foundation, 1997, pp. 56–63.
Lowry, Donal. "Shame Upon 'Little England' While 'Greater England Stands!': Southern Rhodesia and the Imperial Idea." *The Round Table, the Empire/ Commonwealth and British Foreign Policy*, edited by Andrea Bosco and Alex May, Lothian Foundation, 1997, pp. 305–41.
MacDonald, Robert H. *The Language of Empire: Myths and Metaphors of Popular Imperialism, 1880–1918*. Manchester UP, 1994. Studies in Imperialism.
Mackenzie, John M. *Propaganda and Empire: The Manipulation of British Public Opinion, 1880–1960*. Manchester UP, 1984.
Makdisi, Saree. "Riding the Whirlwind of Settler Colonialism." Review of *Replenishing the Earth: The Settler Revolution and the Rise of the Anglo-World, 1783–1939*, by James Belich. *Victorian Studies*, vol. 53, no. 1, Autumn 2010, pp. 108–15.
Marks, Shula. *Reluctant Rebellion: The 1906–8 Disturbances in Natal*. Clarendon, 1970.
Marquard, Jean. "The Farm: A Concept in the Writing of Olive Schreiner, Pauline Smith, Doris Lessing, Nadine Gordimer, and Bessie Head." *Dalhousie Review*, vol. 59, no. 2, Summer 1979, pp. 293–307.
"Mashonaland News. The Political Campaign. Enter 'Gertrude Page.'" *Buluwayo Chronicle*, 31 Mar. 1911, p. 5.
Mathers, Edward P. *Golden South Africa*. Whittingham / Davis, 1888.
———. *South Africa and How to Reach It by the Castle Line*. Simpkin, 1889.
———. *Zambesia, England's El Dorado in Africa*. King, Sell, & Railton / Juta, 1895.
Maugham, W. Somerset. *The Painted Veil*. Heinemann, 1949.

Mazzanti, Roberta. "Lyndall's Sphinx: Images of Female Sexuality and Roles in *The Story of an African Farm.*" *The Flawed Diamond: Essays on Olive Schreiner*, edited by Itala Vivan, Dangaroo, 1991, pp. 121–34.

McClintock, Anne. *Imperial Leather: Race, Gender and Sexuality in the Colonial Contest.* Routledge, 1995.

McClure, John A. "Late Imperial Romance." *Raritan*, vol. 10, no. 4, Spring 1991, pp. 111–30.

McCracken, Scott. "Stages of Sand and Blood: The Performance of Gendered Subjectivity in Olive Schreiner's Colonial Allegories." *Rereading Victorian Fiction*, edited by Alice Jenkins and Juliet John, St. Martin's, 2000, pp. 145–58.

McCulloch, Jock. *Black Peril, White Virtue: Sexual Crime in Southern Rhodesia, 1902–1935.* Indiana UP, 2000.

———. "Empire and Violence, 1900–1939." *Gender and Empire*, edited by Philippa Levine, Oxford UP, 2004, pp. 220–39. Oxford History of the British Empire Companion Series.

McKenzie, Frederick A. "After the War: Mr. H. Rider Haggard's Prophecies." *Daily Mail*, 7 Dec. 1901, p. 8.

Meade, L. T. *Four on an Island: A Story of Adventure.* Chambers, n.d.

Melman, Billie. *Women and the Popular Imagination in the Twenties: Flappers and Nymphs.* Macmillan, 1988.

Miller, Russell. *The Adventures of Arthur Conan Doyle.* Dunne-St. Martin's, 2008.

Mills, Sara. *Discourses of Difference: An Analysis of Women's Travel Writing and Colonialism.* Routledge, 1991.

Mitchell, Sally. *The New Girl: Girls' Culture in England, 1880–1915.* Columbia UP, 1995.

Monsman, Gerald H. *Colonial Voices: The Anglo-African High Romance of Empire.* UP of the South, 2010.

———. *H. Rider Haggard on the Imperial Frontier: The Politics and Literary Contexts of His African Romances.* ELT, 2006.

———. "The Idea of 'Story' in Olive Schreiner's *Story of an African Farm.*" *Texas Studies in Literature and Language*, vol. 27, no. 3, Fall 1985, pp. 249–69.

———. "Patterns of Narration and Characterization in Schreiner's *The Story of an African Farm.*" *English Literature in Transition*, vol. 28, no. 3, 1985, pp. 253–70.

Moran, Shane. "Plaatje's Resistance." *English in Africa*, vol. 42, no. 3, Dec. 2015, pp. 9–42.

Moruzi, Kristine. "Feminine Bravery: The *Girl's Realm* (1898–1915) and the Second Boer War." *Children's Literature Association Quarterly*, vol. 34, no. 3, Fall 2009, pp. 241–54.

———. "'The Freedom Suits Me': Encouraging Girls to Settle in the Empire." *Victorian Settler Narratives: Emigrants, Cosmopolitans and Returnees in Nineteenth-Century Literature*, edited by Tamara S. Wagner, Pickering & Chatto, 2011, pp. 177–91. Gender and Genre 5.

Mpe, Phaswane. "'Naturally these stories lost nothing by repetition': Plaatje's Mediation of Oral History in *Mhudi*." *Current Writing: Text and Reception in Southern Africa*, vol. 8, no. 1, 1996, pp. 75–89.

———. "Sol Plaatje, Orality and the Politics of Cultural Representation." *Current Writing: Text and Reception in Southern Africa*, vol. 11, no. 2, 1999, pp. 75–91.

"Mr. Rider Haggard on Anglo-Africa." *Daily Telegraph*, 24 Apr. 1894, p. 3.

"Mr. Rider Haggard on South Africa." *Times*, 11 Mar. 1919, p. 12.

"Mr. Rider Haggard on the Transvaal Constitution." *Times*, 7 Aug. 1906, p. 8.

"Mr. Rider Haggard's New Story." Review of *Jess*, by H. Rider Haggard. *Pall Mall Gazette*, 15 Mar. 1887, p. 5.

Mulholland, James. "Translocal Anglo-India and the Multilingual Reading Public." *PMLA*, vol. 135, no. 2, Mar. 2020, pp. 272–98.

Murphy, Patricia. "The Gendering of History in *She*." *Studies in English Literature*, vol. 39, no. 4, Autumn 1999, pp. 747–72.

———. *Time Is of the Essence: Temporality, Gender, and the New Woman*. State U of New York P, 2001.

Myers, Janet C. *Antipodal England: Emigration and Portable Domesticity in the Victorian Imagination*. State U of New York P, 2009.

Nathan, Manfred. *South African Literature: A General Survey*. Juta, 1925.

"The Need of Women Colonists in South Africa." Letter, *Saturday Review*, 20 Sept. 1902, pp. 364–65.

"The Novels of Gertrude Page." Advertisement. *The Rhodesian*, by Gertrude Page. Hurst, 1912, n.p.

"Novels of the Week." Review of *Jess*, by H. Rider Haggard. *Athenaeum*, 19 Mar. 1887, p. 375.

Ntuli, D. B., and C. F. Swanepoel. *Southern African Literature in African Languages: A Concise Historical Perspective*. Acacia, 1993.

Oboe, Annalisa. "Contrasts and Harmony: The Antithetical Structure in *The Story of an African Farm*." *The Flawed Diamond: Essays on Olive Schreiner*, edited by Itala Vivan, Dangaroo, 1991, pp. 84–94.

———. "From South Africa to Europe to North America and Back: Sol Plaatje, W. E. B. Du Bois, and the Routes of Romance." *Recharting the Black Atlantic: Modern Cultures, Local Communities, Global Connections*, edited by Oboe and Anna Scacchi, Routledge, 2008, pp. 20–44.

Oppenheim, E. Phillips. *Mysterious Mr. Sabin*. Ward, n.d., *HathiTrust*. babel.hathitrust.org/cgi/pt?id=hvd.hwkyuv&view=1up&seq=5.

Page, Gertrude. "Advance, Rhodesia: Farming Prospects." *Empire Review*, vol. 14, no. 82, Nov. 1907, pp. 304–07.

———. *The Edge o' Beyond*, Hurst, n.d.

———. "Enlistment of Men Over Age." *Buluwayo Chronicle*, 1 Apr. 1918, p. 7.

———. *Far from the Limelight*. Cassell, 1918.

———. "Farm Life in Rhodesia." *Empire Review*, vol. 12, no. 67, Aug. 1906, pp. 49–55.

---. "Farm Life in Rhodesia: Visit to Victoria Falls." *Empire Review*, vol. 12, no. 68, Sept. 1906, pp. 155–62.
---. *Follow After!* Hurst, 1915.
---. "The Future of Rhodesia." *Times*, 11 Oct. 1909, p. 4. *Times Digital Archive*.
---. "Her Man." *Hutchinson's Story Magazine*, vol. 1, no. 1, July 1919, pp. 55–60.
---. "If Loving Hearts Were Never Lonely—; or, Madge Harcourt's Desolation." *Girl's Own Paper*, vol. 19, nos. 927–52, 2 Oct. 1897–26 Mar. 1898, pp. 8+.
---. *Jill on a Ranch*. Cassell, 1921.
---. *Jill's Rhodesian Philosophy; or, The Dam Farm*. Hurst, n.d.
---. "A Lady's First Impressions of South Africa." *Empire Review*, vol. 9, no. 53, June 1905, pp. 461–71.
---. "Life in Rhodesia." *Empire Review*, vol. 10, no. 60, Jan. 1906, pp. 561–65.
---. "Life in Rhodesia." *Empire Review*, vol. 11, no. 63, Apr. 1906, pp. 249–55.
---. "Life in Rhodesia." *Empire Review*, vol. 11, no. 65, June 1906, pp. 448–57.
---. "Life in Rhodesia." *Empire Review*, vol. 14, no. 81, Aug. 1907, pp. 38–42.
---. "Life in Rhodesia." *Empire Review*, vol. 14, no. 81, Oct. 1907, pp. 181–84.
---. *Love in the Wilderness: The Story of Another African Farm*. Hurst, n.d.
---. *The Pathway*. 4th ed., Ward, 1914.
---. "Pictorial Acrostic." "Our Little Folks' Own Puzzles." *Little Folks: The Magazine for Boys and Girls*, 1 Jan. 1884, p. 61.
---. *The Rhodesian*. Hurst, 1912.
---. "Second Impressions of Rhodesian Farm Life." *Empire Review*, vol. 10, no. 56, Sept. 1905, pp. 136–46.
---. *The Silent Rancher*. Hurst, 1909.
---. *The Veldt Trail*. Cassell, n.d.
---. *Where the Strange Roads Go Down*. Hurst, 19–.
Parker, Kenneth. "The South African Novel in English." *The South African Novel in English: Essays in Criticism and Society*, edited by Parker, Africana, 1978, pp. 1–26.
Patteson, Richard F. "*King Solomon's Mines*: Imperialism and Narrative Structure." *The Journal of Narrative Technique*, vol. 8, no. 2, Spring 1978, pp. 112–23.
Paxton, Nancy L. "*The Story of an African Farm* and the Dynamics of Woman-to-Woman Influence." *Texas Studies in Literature and Language*, vol. 30, no. 4, Winter 1988, pp. 562–82.
---. *Writing Under the Raj: Gender, Race, and Rape in the British Colonial Imagination, 1830–1947*. Rutgers UP, 1999.
Peace, Walter. *Our Colony of Natal: A Handbook for the Use of Intending Emigrants and Others*. 2nd (rev.) ed., Stanford, 1884.
Peterson, Bhekizizwe. "Black Writers and the Historical Novel: 1907–1948." *The Cambridge History of South African Literature*, edited by David Attwell and Derek Attridge, Cambridge UP, 2012, pp. 291–307.
Phelps, J. M. "Sol Plaatje's *Mhudi* and Democratic Government." *English Studies in Africa*, vol. 36, no. 1, Jan. 1993, pp. 47–56.

Phillips, Richard. *Mapping Men and Empire: A Geography of Adventure*. Routledge, 1996.
Piesse, Jude. *British Settler Emigration in Print, 1832–1877*. Oxford UP, 2016.
Plaatje, Sol T. *The Boer War Diary of Sol T. Plaatje: An African at Mafeking*, edited by John L. Comaroff, Macmillan, 1975.
———. *Mhudi*, edited by Stephen Gray, Heinemann, 1978. African Writers Series 201.
———. *Mhudi*. Waveland, 2014.
———. *Sol Plaatje: Selected Writings*, edited by Brian Willan, Ohio UP, 1996.
Plotz, John. *Portable Property: Victorian Culture on the Move*. Princeton UP, 2008.
Poovey, Mary. *Uneven Developments: The Ideological Work of Gender in Mid-Victorian England*. U of Chicago P, 1988.
"A Popular Novelist: Death of Miss Gertrude Page." *Times*, 3 Apr. 1922, p. 5.
Powell, Beatrice. Preface. *Gleanings from the Writings of "Gertrude Page,"* by Gertrude Page. Hurst, 1920, pp. v–viii.
Praed, Rosa. *Fugitive Anne: A Romance of the Unexplored Bush*. ManyBooks.net, www.manybooks.net/titles/praedrosother08fugitive_ann.html.
Pratt, Mary Louise. *Imperial Eyes: Travel Writing and Transculturation*. Routledge, 1992.
Prowse, C. M. "By Rail to Johannesburg." *South African Illustrated Magazine*, vol. 12, Sept. 1900, pp. 1–5.
Pykett, Lyn. *Engendering Fictions: The English Novel in the Early Twentieth Century*. Arnold, 1995.
Rajamäe, Pilvi. "John Laputa: The Ethiopian Solar Hero of *Prester John*." *John Buchan Journal*, no. 38, Summer 2008, pp. 12–20.
Ralph, Julian. *War's Brighter Side*. Appleton, 1901.
Rasmussen, R. Kent. *Migrant Kingdom: Mzilikazi's Ndebele in South Africa*. Collings, 1978.
Read, Donald. "Crisis Age or Golden Age?" Introduction. *Edwardian England*, edited by Read, Rutgers UP, 1982, pp. 14–39.
Reeve, Richard. "H. Rider Haggard and the New Woman: A Difference in the Genre in *Jess* and *Beatrice*." *ELT: English Literature in Transition, 1880–1920*, vol. 59, no. 2, 2016, pp. 153–74.
Reidi, Eliza. "Teaching Empire: British and Dominions Women Teachers in the South African War Concentration Camps." *English Historical Review*, vol. 120, no. 489, 2005, pp. 1316–47.
Reitz, M. F. W. *A Century of Wrong*. Review of Reviews, 1899.
Reynolds, Kimberley. *Girls Only? Gender and Popular Children's Fiction in Britain, 1880–1910*. Temple UP, 1990.
"Rhodesian Life." *Buluwayo Chronicle*, 4 Feb. 1922, p. 5.
Rich, Paul. "'Milnerism and a Ripping Yarn': Transvaal Land Settlement and John Buchan's Novel 'Prester John' 1901–1910." *Town and Countryside in the Transvaal: Capitalist Penetration and Popular Response*, edited by Belinda Bozzoli, Ravan, 1983, pp. 412–33.

———. "Romance and the Development of the South African Novel." *Literature and Society in South Africa*, edited by Landeg White and Tim Couzens, Longman, 1984, pp. 120–37.

Richardson, LeeAnne. *New Woman and Colonial Adventure Fiction in Victorian Britain: Gender, Genre, and Empire*. U of Florida P, 2006.

Rieder, John. *Colonialism and the Emergence of Science Fiction*. Wesleyan UP, 2008.

Rive, Richard M. "Olive Schreiner: A Critical Study and a Checklist." *Studies in the Novel*, vol. 4, no. 2, Summer 1972, pp. 231–51.

Robinson, John. "The Colonies and the Century." *Proceedings of the Royal Colonial Institute*, no. 30. Royal Colonial Institute, 1899, pp. 324–54.

———. *Notes on Natal: An Old Colonist's Book for New Settlers*. Robinson & Vause, 1872.

Rodgers, Terrence. "Empires of the Imagination: Rider Haggard, Popular Fiction and Africa." *Writing and Africa*, edited by Mpalive-Hangson Msiska and Paul Hyland, Longman, 1997, pp. 103–21.

Rowbotham, Judith. *Good Girls Make Good Wives: Guidance for Girls in Victorian Fiction*. Blackwell, 1989.

Rudy, Jason R. *Imagined Homelands: British Poetry in the Colonies*. Kindle ed., Johns Hopkins UP, 2017.

R. R. "Imbabala." *South African Stories and Sketches*, 8th series, South Africa, n.d., pp. 14–18. "*South Africa*" Handbook, no. 45. Originally published in *South Africa: A Weekly Journal for All Interested in South African Affairs*, July 1908.

Said, Edward W. *Culture and Imperialism*. Vintage-Random, 1994.

Salmon, Edward. *Juvenile Literature as It Is*. Drane, 1888. *Internet Archive*, archive.org/details/juvenileliterat00salmgoog/page/n10.

Samin, Richard. "Sol Plaatje's *Mhudi* and the Emergence of Black Political Fiction in South Africa." *Commonwealth*, vol. 22, no. 1, Fall 1999, pp. 37–45.

Samuelson, G. B. Catalogue for *Love in the Wilderness*, directed by Alexander Butler, 1920.

Sanders, Mark. "Towards a Genealogy of Intellectual Life: Olive Schreiner's *The Story of an African Farm*." *Novel: A Forum on Fiction*, vol. 34, no. 1, Fall 2000, pp. 77–97.

Saunders, Christopher, and Iain R. Smith. "Southern Africa, 1795–1910." *The Nineteenth Century*, edited by Andrew Porter, Oxford UP, 1999, pp. 597–623. *The Oxford History of the British Empire*, vol. 3.

Scherzinger, Karen. "The Problem of the Pure Woman: South African Pastoralism and Female Rites of Passage." *UNISA English Studies*, vol. 29, no. 2, 1991, pp. 29–35.

Schoeman, Karel. *Only an Anguish to Live Here: Olive Schreiner and the Anglo-Boer War, 1899–1902*. Human & Rousseau, 1992.

Schreiner, Olive. *Dreams: Three Works by Olive Schreiner*. Roberts Brothers, 1898, pp. 65–85. *Victorian Women Writers Project*, webapp1.dlib.indiana.edu/vwwp/view?docId=VAB7054.xml.

---. "Eighteen-Ninety-Nine." *Stories, Dreams and Allegories*. Unwin, 1923, pp. 11–55.
---. *From Man to Man; or Perhaps Only.* . . . Harper, 1927.
---. "The Native Question." *An Olive Schreiner Reader: Writings on Women and South Africa*, by Schreiner, edited by Carol Barash, Pandora, 1987, pp. 186–97.
---. *Olive Schreiner Letters, Vol. 1: 1871–1899*, edited by Richard Rive, Oxford UP, 1988.
---. *The South African Question by an English South African*. Sergel, 1899.
---. *The Story of an African Farm*. Penguin, 1995.
---. *Thoughts on South Africa*. Stokes, 1923.
---. *Undine*. Harper, 1928.
---. *Woman and Labour*. Unwin, 1911.
Schreuder, Deryck. "Colonial Nationalism and 'Tribal Nationalism': Making the White South African State, 1899–1910." *The Rise of Colonial Nationalism: Australia, New Zealand, Canada and South Africa First Assert Their Nationalities, 1880–1914*, edited by John Eddy and Schreuder, Allen & Unwin, 1988, pp. 192–226.
Schwarz, Bill. "The Romance of the Veld." *The Round Table, the Empire/Commonwealth and British Foreign Policy*, edited by Andrea Bosco and Alex May, Lothian Foundation, 1997, pp. 65–125.
---. *The White Man's World*. Oxford UP, 2011. *Memories of Empire*, vol. 1.
Scott, J. E. *A Bibliography of the Works of Sir Henry Rider Haggard, 1856–1925*. Mathews, 1947.
Seaborn, Adam. *Symzonia; Voyage of Discovery*. Seymour, 1820. *Project Gutenberg*, www.gutenberg.org/files/54485/54485-h/54485-h.htm.
Shanks, Edward. "Sir Rider Haggard and the Novel of Adventure." *London Mercury*, Nov. 1924, pp. 71–79.
Sharpe, Jenny. *Allegories of Empire: The Figure of Woman in the Colonial Text*. U of Minnesota P, 1993.
"She." Review of *She*, by H. Rider Haggard. *Saturday Review*, 8 Jan. 1887, p. 44.
Showalter, Elaine. *A Literature of Their Own: British Women Novelists from Brontë to Lessing*. Princeton UP, 1977.
---. *Sexual Anarchy: Gender and Culture at the Fin de Siècle*. Penguin, 1990.
Siddiqi, Yumna. *Anxieties of Empire and the Fiction of Intrigue*. Columbia UP, 2008.
"Sir Rider Haggard. Ethics of Literature." *Sydney Morning Herald*, 12 Apr. 1913, pp. 9–10.
"Sir Rider Haggard. Novelist, Farmer, and Social Worker." *Times*, 15 May 1925, p. 18.
"Sir Rider Haggard's Return. In Pretoria, Then and Now." *Transvaal Leader*, 31 Mar. 1914, p. 6.
Sites, Kriston. *In and Out of Africa: The Adventures of H. Rider Haggard*. Lilly Library, 1995. Lilly Publication, no. 55.
"Slow Progress." *Buluwayo Chronicle*, 24 Dec. 1921, p. 1.

Smit, Johannes A., Johan van Wyk, and Jean-Philippe Wade, eds. *Rethinking South African Literary History*. Y, 1996.
Smith, Craig. "Every Man Must Kill the Thing He Loves: Empire, Homoerotics, and Nationalism in John Buchan's *Prester John*." *Novel: A Forum on Fiction*, vol. 28, no. 2, Winter 1995, pp. 173–200.
Smith, Janet Adam. *John Buchan and His World*. Thames, 1979.
Smith, Malvern van Wyk. *Grounds of Contest: A Survey of South African English Literature*. Jutalit, 1990.
Smith, Michelle. "Adventurous Girls of the British Empire: The Pre-War Novels of Bessie Marchant." *The Lion and the Unicorn*, vol. 33, no. 1, Jan. 2009, pp. 1–25.
Smith, Michelle J. *Empire in British Girls' Literature and Culture: Imperial Girls, 1880–1915*. Palgrave Macmillan, 2011.
Snyman, J. P. L. *The South African Novel in English (1880–1930)*. U of Potchefstroom for C.H.E., 1952. U Lig Series.
"*South Africa: A Weekly Journal*." Advertisement. *The Guide to South Africa for the Use of Tourists, Sportsmen, Invalids and, Settlers, 1896–1897*, edited by A. Samler Brown and G. Gordon Brown, Juta, 1896, inside cover.
"South African Writers." *South African Stories and Sketches*, 22nd series, South Africa, n.d., pp. 9–16. "*South Africa*" Handbook, no. 73. Originally published in *South Africa: A Weekly Journal for All Interested in South African Affairs*, Sept. 1913.
Spivak, Gayatri Chakravorty. " 'Can the Subaltern Speak?' Revised Edition from the 'History' Chapter of *Critique of Postcolonial Reason*." *Can the Subaltern Speak? Reflections on the History of an Idea*, edited by Rosalind C. Morris, Columbia UP, 2010, pp. 21–78.
———. *A Critique of Postcolonial Reason: Toward a History of the Vanishing Present*. Harvard UP, 1999.
———. "Three Women's Texts and a Critique of Imperialism." *Critical Inquiry*, vol. 12, no. 1, Autumn 1985, pp. 243–61.
Stafford, David. "John Buchan's Tales of Espionage: A Popular Archive of British History." *Canadian Journal of History*, vol. 18, no. 1, Apr. 1983, pp. 1–21.
———. "Spies and Gentlemen: The Birth of the British Spy Novel, 1893–1914." *Victorian Studies*, vol. 24, no. 4, Summer 1981, pp. 489–509.
Stanley, Henry M. *In Darkest Africa, or, the Quest, Rescue, and Retreat of Emin, Governor of Equatoria*. Scribner's, 1890. 2 vols.
Stead, W. T. "The Novel of the Modern Woman." *Review of Reviews*, vol. 10, 1894, pp. 64–74.
Steere, Elizabeth Lee. " 'Become a Sweet and God-Fearing Woman': British Women in Haggard's Early African Romances." *Nineteenth-Century Gender Studies*, vol. 6, no. 3, 2010, www.ncgsjournal.com/issue63/steere.htm.
Steiner, Tina. "Traversing Social Landscapes: Sol Plaatje's *Mhudi* and the Question of Community." *English in Africa*, vol. 41, no. 3, Dec. 2014, pp. 7–26.

Stevens, Laura M. "Reading the Hermit's Manuscript: *The Female American* and Female Robinsonades." *Approaches to Teaching Defoe's "Robinson Crusoe,"* edited by Maximillian E. Novak and Carl Fisher, MLA, 2005, pp. 140–51.

Stewart, James. "Southern Africa: Past and Present." *Scottish Geographical Magazine*, vol. 7, no. 4, 1891, pp. 177–91.

Stiebel, Lindy. "The Return of the Lost City: The Hybrid Legacy of Rider Haggard's African Romances." *Multiculturalism and Hybridity in African Literatures*, edited by Hal Wylie and Bernth Lindfors, Africa World, 2000, pp. 281–96.

Stockley, Cynthia. *Poppy: The Story of a South African Girl*. Putnam, 1910.

———. *Virginia of the Rhodesians*. 4th ed., Hutchinson, 1903.

———. *Wild Honey*. Grosset, 1914.

Storer, Colin. "'The German of caricature, the real German, the fellow we were up against': German Stereotypes in John Buchan's *Greenmantle*." *Journal of European Studies*, vol. 39, no. 1, 2009, pp. 36–57.

The Story of "South Africa" Newspaper and Its Founder, Told by Others. South Africa, 1903. *Internet Archive*, archive.org/details/storyofsouthafri00londuoft/page/n1/mode/2up.

Stott, Rebecca. "The Dark Continent: Africa as Female Body in Haggard's Adventure Fiction." *Feminist Review*, no. 32, Summer 1989, pp. 69–89.

———. *The Fabrication of the Late Victorian Femme Fatale: The Kiss of Death*. Macmillan, 1992. Women's Studies at York.

———. "'Scaping the Body: Of Cannibal Mothers and Colonial Landscapes." *The New Woman in Fiction and Fact: Fin-de-Siècle Feminisms*, edited by Angelique Richardson and Chris Willis, Palgrave, 2001, pp. 150–66.

Street, Brian V. *The Savage in Literature: Representations of "Primitive" Society in English Fiction, 1858–1920*. Routledge, 1975.

Strobel, Margaret. *European Women and the Second British Empire*. Indiana UP, 1991.

"Sudden Death of Gertrude Page at Salisbury on Saturday: Famous Novelist Dies at Meikle's Hotel (From Our Own Correspondent)." *Buluwayo Chronicle*, 8 Apr. 1922, p. 3.

Suleri, Sara. *The Rhetoric of English India*. U of Chicago P, 1992.

"The Supports." *Hutchinson's Story Magazine*, vol. 1, no. 1, July 1919, pp. 11–13.

Swaisland, Cecillie. *Servants and Gentlewomen to the Golden Land: The Emigration of Single Women from Britain to Southern Africa, 1820–1939*. Berg / U of Natal P, 1993.

Tabachnick, Stephen E. "Two Tales of Gothic Adventure: *She* and *Heart of Darkness*." *English Literature in Transition, 1880–1920*, vol. 56, no. 2, 2013, pp. 189–200.

Theal, George McCall. *The Beginning of South African History*. Unwin, 1902. *Google Books*, books.google.com/books?id=I_UQW4RSs4sC&printsec=frontcover&dq=beginning+of+south+african+history&hl=en&ei=d1cnToeaAub20gHJm-HMCg&sa=X&oi=book_result&ct=result&resnum=1&ved=0CC0Q6AEwAA#v=onepage&q&f=false.

Thomas, Nicholas. *Colonialism's Culture: Anthropology, Travel and Government.* Princeton UP, 1994.
Thompson, Andrew. "The Languages of Loyalism in Southern Africa, c. 1870–1939." *The English Historical Review*, vol. 118, no. 477, June 2003, pp. 617–50.
Thompson, Leonard Monteath. *A History of South Africa.* 3rd ed., Yale UP, 2001.
"To Advertisers." Supplement in *South Africa: A Weekly Journal for All Interested in South African Affairs*, 9 Nov. 1889, n.p.
Tosh, John. "Imperial Masculinity and the Flight from Domesticity in Britain, 1880–1914." *Gender and Colonialism*, edited by Timothy P. Foley et al., Galway UP, 1995, pp. 72–85.
Trotter, David. *The English Novel in History, 1895–1920.* Routledge, 1993.
Turnbaugh, Roy. "Image of Empire: G. A. Henry and John Buchan." *Journal of Popular Culture*, vol. 9, no. 3, Winter 1975, pp. 734–40.
Twigg, J. Burton. "A Memory of Sir Rider Haggard." Letter, *John O' London's Weekly*, 27 June 1925, p. 433.
Unterhalter, Elaine. "Constructing Race, Class, Gender and Ethnicity: State and Opposition Strategies in South Africa." *Unsettling Settler Societies: Articulations of Gender, Race, Ethnicity and Class*, edited by Daiva Stasiulis and Nira Yuval-Davis, Sage, 1995, pp. 207–40.
Untitled. *Buluwayo Chronicle*, 15 July 1910, p. 3.
Usborne, Richard. *Clubland Heroes: A Nostalgic Study of Some Recurrent Characters in the Romantic Fiction of Dornford Yates, John Buchan, and Sapper.* Constable, 1953.
Useful Information for Emigrants: Rhodesia. 2nd ed., South Africa, n.d. "South Africa" Handbook, no. 6.
Useful Information for Emigrants: The Transvaal. South Africa, n.d. "South Africa" Handbook, no. 18.
Valente, Joseph. *The Myth of Manliness in Irish National Culture, 1880–1922.* U of Illinois P, 2011.
van der Vlies, Andrew. *South African Textual Cultures.* Manchester UP, 2007.
Van-Helten, Jean Jacques, and Keith Williams. "'The Crying Need of South Africa': The Emigration of Single British Women to the Transvaal, 1901–10." *Journal of Southern African Studies*, vol. 10, no. 1, Oct. 1983, pp. 17–38.
van Heyningen, Elizabeth. "Costly Mythologies: The Concentration Camps of the South African War in Afrikaner Historiography." *Journal of Southern African Studies*, vol. 34, no. 3, Sept. 2008, pp. 495–513.
———. "'Hewers of wood and drawers of water': The Black Camp Experience." *The Concentration Camps of the Anglo-Boer War: A Social History*, by van Heyningen. Jacana, 2013, pp. 150–78.
———. "A Tool for Modernisation? The Boer Concentration Camps of the South African War, 1900–1902." *South African Journal of Science*, vol. 106, no. 5/6, May/June 2010, 10 pp., archive.sajs.co.za/index.php/SAJS/article/view/242.

Vivan, Itala. "The Treatment of Blacks in *The Story of an African Farm*." *The Flawed Diamond: Essays on Olive Schreiner*, edited by Vivan, Dangaroo, 1991, pp. 95–106.

Wagner, Tamara S., editor. *Domestic Fiction in Colonial Australia and New Zealand*. Pickering & Chatto, 2015. Gender and Genre 13.

———. *Victorian Narratives of Failed Emigration: Settlers, Returnees, and Nineteenth-Century Literature in English*. Routledge, 2016.

———, editor. *Victorian Settler Narratives: Emigrants, Cosmopolitans and Returnees in Nineteenth-Century Literature*. Pickering & Chatto, 2011. Gender and Genre 5.

Walker, Cheryl. *The Women's Suffrage Movement in South Africa*. Centre for African Studies, U of Cape Town, 1979.

Walkowitz, Judith R. *City of Dreadful Delight: Narratives of Sexual Danger in Late-Victorian London*. U of Chicago P, 1992.

Ware, Vron. *Beyond the Pale: White Women, Racism, and History*. Verso, 1992.

Whatmore, D. E. *H. Rider Haggard: A Bibliography*. Mansell, 1987.

Wheelwright, Julie. "'Amazons and Military Maids': An Examination of Female Military Heroines in British Literature and the Changing Construction of Gender." *Women's Studies International Forum*, vol. 10, no. 5, 1987, pp. 489–502.

Willan, Brian. *Sol Plaatje: South African Nationalist, 1876–1932*. Heinemann, 1984.

———. "What 'Other Devils'? The Texts of Sol T. Plaatje's *Mhudi* Revisited." *Journal of Southern African Studies*, vol. 41, no. 6, 2015, pp. 1331–47, doi:10.1080/0305 7070.2015.1116234.

Williams, Elizabeth W. "Queering Settler Romance: The Reparative Eugenic Landscape in Nora Strange's Kenyan Novels." *Archiving Settler Colonialism: Culture, Space, and Race*, edited by Yuting Huang and Rebecca Weaver-Hightower, Routledge, 2019, pp. 190–204.

Wilmot, A. *Monomotapa: Its Monuments, and Its History from the Most Ancient Times to the Present Century*. Negro UP, 1969.

Wingerden, Sophia A. van. *The Women's Suffrage Movement in Britain, 1866–1928*. Palgrave Macmillan, 1999.

Winks, Robin W. "John Buchan: Stalking the Wilder Game." *The Four Adventures of Richard Hannay*, by John Buchan, edited by Winks, Godine, 1988, pp. v–xxii.

Winter, Alison. *Mesmerized: Powers of Mind in Victorian Britain*. U of Chicago P, 2000.

Wisnicki, Adrian. "Reformulating the Empire's Hero: Rhodesian Gold, Boer Veld-Craft, and the Displaced Scotsman in John Buchan's *The Thirty-Nine Steps*." *Journal of Colonialism and Colonial History*, vol. 8, no. 1, Spring 2007, doi:10.1353/cch.2007.0025.

Wittenberg, Hermann. "Occult, Empire and Landscape: The Colonial Uncanny in John Buchan's African Writing." *Journal of Colonialism and Colonial History*, vol. 7, no. 2, Fall 2006, doi:10.1353/cch.2006.0049.

Woods, Brett F. "The Last Victorian: John Buchan and the Hannay Quartet." *California Literary Review*, 19 Apr. 2020. Originally published 26 Mar. 2007.

Index

"Absent-Minded Beggar, The" (Kipling), 12
Abyssinia, 147–48
adventure fiction, 21, 69–70, 167, 206n58. *See also* female colonial romance; imperial romance
Africa for the African (Booth), 147
African Colony, The (Buchan), 138
African continent: and empire, 142, 148; perceptions of, 4, 8, 135; symbols of, 78. *See also* Dark Continent, myth of the
African National Congress (ANC), 164, 233n30, 236n67. *See also* South African Native National Congress (SANNC)
African nationalism, 4, 12, 15, 18, 136, 141, 147. *See also* Ethiopianism
African Tragedy, An (Dhlomo), 233n32
Afrikaners: nationalism, 72, 144; political authority of, 66, 143–46; population demographics of, 136; resistance, 143; and terminology, xv; writers, 10. *See also* Boers
agency, 25, 63, 78–79, 81–83, 126, 143, 149, 168. *See also* feminism
Allan Quatermain (character), 7, 62, 64, 83, 85, 103, 135, 140, 161, 180n63, 199n7, 201n19, 205n57, 209nn83–84, 223n5, 235n41

Allan Quatermain (Haggard), 11, 20, 64, 96, 101, 103, 184n6, 201n19, 205n57, 212n105, 223n5
angel in the house, 21, 25, 32, 41, 44, 47, 51–53, 59, 69, 196n21
angel on the frontier, 53–54
Anglo-African Writers' Club, 53, 196–97n130
Anglo-Zulu War, 3, 19, 150, 192n82
Anthony, Loren, 194n95
anti-Semitism, 75, 208n71
apartheid, 10, 14, 146, 153
Ardis, Ann, 44, 68, 185n13
Athenaeum, 53
Atlee, Clement, 11
Attwell, David, 9
Australian Bush Track, An (Hennessey), 71
authorial informant, 3–8, 11–12, 20, 103, 107, 139, 155, 162, 180n63. *See also* native informant
authority: of the authorial informant, 3–8, 12, 107, 139, 180n63; of the colonial heroine, 81–83, 92–94, 115; symbols of, 84; of white men, 95; of writers, 5
Aveling, Edward, 32, 43–44

Baldwin, Stanley, 11
Balfour, Arthur, 11

Balfour Declaration of 1926, 10
Ballantyne, R. M., 61, 69–70
Ballantyne, Tony, 7
Bambatha Rebellion, 147–48
Barker, Mary Anne, 219n60
Barolong, 164–71
Basutoland, 232n14
Battle of Blood River, 90
Battle of Dorking, The (Chesney), 156
Bechuana, 164–71
Bechuana Gazette, 233n30. See also *Koranta ea Becoana*
Belgian Congo, 4
Belich, James, 8
Bell, Duncan, 178n45
Benita (Haggard), 60, 62, 70–72, 74–84, 86–87, 90–92, 96–103, 156, 168–69, 198n146, 199n8, 201n97, 211n102. See also *Spirit of Bambatse, The* (Haggard)
Beyers, Christiaan Frederik, 145
"Black General, The" (Buchan), 223–24n4. See also *Prester John* (Buchan)
"black peril," 146–47, 204n34, 228–29n51
"Black Peril in South Africa, The" (Jones), 146
Boers: depictions of, 32–34, 40, 43, 45, 48–49, 54–57, 144–45, 164, 211nn99–100, 227n48; political power of, 4, 29–30, 89, 174n7; population demographics, 3, 65; and terminology, xv; traditions and ancestry of, 14, 48. See also Afrikaners
Boer War Diary of Sol T. Plaatje, The (Plaatje), 233n30
booster literature, 5, 116–17. See also rhetoric of promise
Booth, Joseph, 147, 229n58
Botha, Louis, 104

Brantlinger, Patrick, 61, 153, 176n16
British identity, 2–4, 6, 18, 53, 57, 130, 143, 162, 185n13, 217n29; and the term English, 144, 160–61, 177n29
British Settler Emigration in Print (Piesse), 8
British South Africa Company (BSAC), 3, 40, 90, 111–14, 116, 118 165, 191n71, 210n93, 215n14, 216n24. See also Rhodes, Cecil
British South African literature field, 8–13
Brody, Jennifer DeVere, 15
Buchan, John: and Haggard, H. Rider, 223n2; legacy of, 3–4, 7–8, 11–12, 135, 153–56, 164; and politics, 18, 29, 136–39, 177n30, 177n34, 224n14; and race, 143, 146–47, 224n14; and sense of identity, 138; and the Second Anglo-Boer War, 135–37, 156–57; and World War I, 138, 225n21. See also Hannay novels; specific works
Bulwer, Henry, 29
Bulwer-Lytton, Edward, 198n3
Bunyan, John, 160, 164
Burton, Antoinette, 7, 63, 200n13
Bushmen paintings, 46, 117, 134

"Call to Arms" (Haggard), 6
Canada, 8, 67, 138, 177n34, 189n52, 206n64
Cape Argus, 53
Cape of Good Hope, 174n8
Cape Colony, 1–4, 10, 14, 19, 26, 46, 66, 76–77, 86, 142, 144, 147, 165, 174n8, 183, 194n101, 205n50, 232n14, 235n56
Cetewayo, 210n95
Chapman, Frederic, 27

Chapman, Michael, 10
"Chartered Company." *See* British South Africa Company (BSAC)
Chennells, Anthony, 215n16
Chesney, George, 156
Childers, Erskine, 156
childhood, 26–28, 37, 45, 63, 69, 77–81. *See also* girlhood
Chinese, 14
Chrisman, Laura, 9, 180n63, 193–94n95, 200n11, 201n18, 202n22
Churchill, Winston, 11
Cilliers, Sarel, 165
City of Dreadful Delight (Walkowitz), 133–34
clothing, 15, 84, 128–30, 159, 221n75
Coetzee, J. M., 9–10, 15, 46–47, 179n53
Cold War, 156
colonial domesticity, 25, 43, 53, 57, 62, 64, 100, 102, 111
colonial exile, 7, 59
colonization: characteristics of, 6, 20, 59, 63–64; depictions of, 61; discourse of, 13; and gender, 21, 64–66; and power, 7, 116, 137; and terminology, 176n22
"Coloureds," 13–14, 147
Coming Race, The (Bulwer-Lytton), 198n3
Commonwealth of Nations, 174n5
concentration camps, 11, 137, 224n12, 224n14, 227n42, 234n39. *See also* Second Anglo-Boer War
Conrad, Joseph, 4–5, 156; and Haggard, H. Rider, 223n2
Coombes, Annie E., 8
Courts of the Morning, The (Buchan), 182–83n97
Couzens, Tim, 166, 168, 223n2
Cunningham, Gail, 187n23, 220n68

Daily Express, 7, 177n32

Daily Mail, 132, 181n70
Dark Continent, myth of the, 4, 153, 176n16. *See also* African continent
Darwin, John, 8, 178n45
Darwinian social science, 153
Defoe, Daniel, 61, 69. *See also* specific works
Dehan, Richard, 222n80
demographics: of gender, 65, 115, 217n36; of race, 3, 13, 66, 113, 136–37, 143–44, 181n75, 181n78
Denning, Michael, 156
Dhlomo, R. R. R., 233n32
diamonds, 3, 19, 26, 29–30, 38, 65, 175n8, 210n93, 226n30. *See also* illicit diamond buying (I.D.B.)
Dickens, Charles, 5, 49
Dingaan, 208n75; depictions of, 76, 82–90, 92, 94–95, 97, 99, 169, 208n74, 210n88, 212n106
Dingane. *See* Dingaan
Dixon, Robert, 71
Dobbin, George Alexander "Alec," 111
Domestic Fiction in Colonial Australia and New Zealand (Wagner), 9
domesticity, 17, 21, 24, 35, 43–60, 62, 71, 78, 111, 116, 135
domestic novel, 16, 21, 44–45, 48, 52–53, 58, 95. *See also* angel in the house
dominions, 65, 67, 137–38, 144, 177n34, 178n45
Dop Doctor, The (Dehan), 222n80
Doyle, Arthur Conan, 11, 200n10
Dreams (Schreiner), 185n11
Dutch, xv, 3, 14, 71, 77, 174n8, 234n36; and terminology, xv
Dutch East India Company, 174n8

Edge o' Beyond, The (Page), 123, 125–27, 131–32, 134, 213n2, 213n3, 220n70

education, 26, 34, 37–40, 48–49, 70, 76, 141, 151–52, 162, 187n26, 188n43, 221n73
Edwardian era, 63, 70
Ellis, Havelock, 26
emigration, 9, 17, 64–67, 75–76, 104, 110–15, 124, 138, 144, 174n5, 174n8, 203n26, 213n6, 214n14, 219n62, 227n42
Empire Project, The (Darwin), 8
Empire Review, 110, 117–18, 219n61, 222n79
empire romance, 11, 17, 115, 132–33, 182n95
Endwandwe. *See* Ndwandwe
enfranchisement: of indigenous Africans, 40, 146–47, 235n56; of Rhodesian women, 113–14, 216n24. *See also* suffrage movement
Esty, Jed, 46, 176n19, 193n95
Etherington, Norman, 228n51
Ethiopianism, 147–48

Fairbridge, Dorothea, xiv
"Falling Gods, The" (Page), 123, 131–32. See also *Far From the Limelight* (Page)
Far from the Limelight (Page), 119, 123–25. *See also* "Falling Gods, The" (Page); "His Job" (Page); "There Is Nothing of Any Importance" (Page)
Farther Adventures of Robinson Crusoe, The (Defoe), 61
Fawcett, Millicent, 224n14
female adventure stories, 69–70. *See also* female colonial romance
female colonial romance, 4, 15–17, 35, 62, 71–74, 101–102, 155, 168, 170. *See also* imperial romance
femininity, 32, 36, 38, 49–50, 53, 59, 63–64, 79, 81, 95, 128, 195n107, 210n97. *See also* gender; masculinity
feminism, 16–17, 20, 32, 37, 44, 52, 62, 68, 115, 127, 168, 199n6.

See also agency; mystical feminism; New Woman; New Woman novel; suffrage movement
femme fatale, 56, 62, 78
Finished (Haggard), 235n41
First, Ruth, 28, 38, 44, 187n26
First Anglo-Boer War, 3, 11, 16, 19, 24, 30, 35–36, 42, 58–60, 71, 155, 163–65, 181n73, 196–97n130. *See also* Second Anglo-Boer War
First Chimurenga. *See* First Matabele War
First Matabele War, 3, 113, 210n93
Five Nations, The (Kipling), 12
Follow After! (Page), 119, 128
Forster, E. M., 201n15
Foster, Jeremy, 225n18
Four on an Island (Meade), 69, 72
Fox, Eleanor Wilson, 219n61
Friend, The, 11
From Man to Man (Schreiner), 27–29, 40, 185n11, 188n39, 191n72, 194n99
Fugitive Anne (Praed), 71

gender: and colonization, 20, 64, 81; demographics of, 65, 115, 217n36; flexibility of, 29; inequalities of, 4, 24–28, 34–35, 39, 51, 67, 236n67; perceptions of, 15, 110; and politics, 32, 118; and race, 24; roles of, 21, 26, 28, 33, 37, 41, 50, 63, 69, 81, 104, 131. *See also* femininity; girlhood; masculinity; men; New Woman; womanhood; women
Gender and Empire (Levine), 8
genre. *See* adventure fiction; domestic novel; female colonial romance; imperial romance; invasion fiction; lost world fiction; New Woman novel; realist novel; spy thriller
George, Rosemary Marangoly, 200n14
George V, King, 11

German East Africa, 128
Germans, xv, 3, 14, 45, 75, 119, 135, 156–57, 159–60, 174n8
German South West Africa, 157–59, 232n14
Ghost Kings, The (Haggard), 15, 60–62, 70, 75–103, 169, 199n8, 211n100. See also *Lady of the Heavens, The* (Haggard)
Gilbert, Sandra, 184–85n8, 188n36
girlhood, 69, 72, 77–81. See also childhood
Girl's Own Paper, 110–11
Gladstone, William, 11, 31
God's Outpost (Gouldsbury), 213n2, 229n63
GoGwilt, Christopher, 193n87, 195n102
gold, 3, 19, 30, 65, 75, 174n8, 199n8, 210n93
Golden South Africa (Mathers), 173–74n3
Gomel, Elana, 103
Gouldsbury, Henry Cullen, 213n2, 229n63
Grand, Sarah, 25
Grass Is Singing, The (Lessing), 133, 181n75
Gray, Stephen, 9, 46, 152, 194n98
Great Boer War, The (Doyle), 11
Great Diamond Pipe, The (Buchan), 141. See also *Prester John* (Buchan)
Great Trek, 71, 76, 90, 143, 165, 207n66
Greene, Graham, 156
Greenmantle (Buchan), 145, 157–58, 160–63, 182–83n97
Greg, W. R., 65, 104
Griqua, 14, 164, 169, 234n36
Grounds of Contest (van Wyk Smith), 10
"Grove of Ashtaroth, The" (Buchan), 230n71

Gubar, Susan, 184–85n8, 188n36

Haggard, H. Rider: and emigration, 66–68; and gender, 64–69, 71, 73, 103–105, 125, 185n11, 199n9, 212n105; legacy of, 3–7, 11–12, 19–20, 61–62, 107, 135, 168, 181n74, 185–86n13; 186n19, 199n6, 207n69, 223n2; and politics, 30–31, 35–36, 58, 62, 67, 137, 163–64, 177n30, 189n47, 189n52, 189n55, 196–97n130, 209n73; and Schreiner, Olive, 20, 185n9; writing style of, 78, 155–57, 210n87, 235n41. See also *specific works*
Haggard, Lilias Rider, 7
Hannay novels (Buchan), 138, 154–64, 182n97, 230n79, 232n21, 233n25, 233n27. See also *specific works*
Hardy, Thomas, 53
Harmsworth, Harold, 132
Hawkins, Anthony Hope. See Hope, Anthony
Hazlitt, William, 162
Heart of Darkness (Conrad), 4–5, 226n38
Hennessey, David, 71
Henty, G. A., 70, 72
heroines: colonial, 17, 20, 32, 62–64, 70–74, 81, 95–96, 104–105, 199n6, 210n97; domestic, 35, 58. See also domestic novel; femininity; New Woman; *specific authors and works*
Hertzog, Barry, 10
Heywood, Christopher, 10
Higgins, D. S., 184–85n8, 208n73
"His Job" (Page), 119, 124. See also *Far from the Limelight* (Page)
History of South African Literature, A (Heywood), 10
History of the South African Forces, The (Buchan), 138, 164
Hobson, J. A., 226n30

Holy Flower, The (Haggard), 209n84
Hope, Anthony, 200n10
Huguenots, xv, 14, 71, 103, 174n8
Hultgren, Neil, 55, 184n7
Hutchinson's Story Magazine, 107, 109
Hyam, Ronald, 219–20n62

illicit diamond buying (I.D.B.), 140, 142, 226n30. *See also* diamonds
Imagined Homelands (Rudy), 9, 179n49
"Imbabala" (R. R.), 211n100
imperial adventure fiction. *See* imperial romance.
imperialism, 3, 6, 25, 31, 42, 62–63, 66, 135, 138–40, 153. *See also* colonization
imperial romance, 16, 18, 59, 61, 64, 72–73, 78, 84–85, 95–96, 101–103, 135–36, 140, 142, 156–57, 168, 208n71, 212n105, 224n9, 230n78. See also *Allan Quatermain* (Haggard); female colonial romance; *King Solomon's Mines* (Haggard)
Imperial South African Association, 12
In Darkest Africa (Stanley), 176n16
India, 12–14, 63, 107, 133, 148, 174n8, 200n14, 201n15, 212n115
"Indian Mutiny," 63, 150
Indians, 13–14, 70
indigenous Africans: absence of, 13, 15, 45; and British identity, 146, 174n8; depictions of, 15, 18, 95, 117, 139–54, 164–71, 195n102, 211n100; and enfranchisement, 40, 146–47, 235n56; and naming, 71, 74, 76, 78, 80, 82–83; and the Second-Anglo Boer War, 165, 234n39; and terminology, xv–xvi. *See also* Barolong; Bechuana; "black peril"; Griqua; Khoikhoi; Makalanga; Matabele; Ndwandwe; Shona; Swazis; Zulus

individualism, 120, 138, 140, 153, 227n38
invasion fiction, 156, 231n5
Iron, Ralph, 183n2. *See also* Schreiner, Olive
Isandlwana, 150–51
Island of Sheep, The (Buchan), 182–83n97
Island Queen, The (Ballantyne), 69

Jackson, Lilly, 197n139
Jess (Haggard), 34–37; adaptations of, 21–23, 186n19; and genre, 16, 20–21, 25, 40–43, 53–60, 71, 101, 184n7; legacy of, 25, 30–31, 91, 184n8, 186–87n19, 192n79, 219n59; writing of, 184n6
Jill on a Ranch (Page), 116, 129, 217n32
Jill's Rhodesian Philosophy (Page), 117
Johnson, Heidi H., 207n71
Jollie, Ethel Tawse, 114
Jones, Roderick, 146, 204n34, 228n51
Just So Stories for Little Children (Kipling), 11
juvenile literature, 70–71. See also *Girl's Own Paper*; *Little Folks*; New Girl fiction

Karoo, 19, 181n77, 183n2, 194n100
Katz, Wendy, 184n7
Kennedy, Dane, 216n22
Khoikhoi, 14, 55, 193n92, 234n36
Kim (Kipling), 12, 156, 208n73
King Solomon's Mines (Haggard), 19, 64, 70, 73, 78, 80, 96, 135–36, 157, 184n6, 185n11, 186n19, 199n7, 210n86, 212n109
Kipling, Rudyard, 11–12, 70, 107, 156, 209n73, 214n12, 217n29
Koranta ea Becoana, 233n30. See also *Bechuana Gazette*
Krebs, Paula M., 6–7

Kruger, Paul, 54, 57

Lady of the Heavens, The (Haggard), 198n146, 199n8. See also *Ghost Kings, The* (Haggard)
Land Settlement Department, 137
language, 9–10, 35–36, 46, 49, 77, 122–23, 137, 144–45, 159, 179n53, 212n109, 213n2, 222n80, 233n30; and terminology, xv
Le Carré, John, 231n7
Ledger, Sally, 183n3
Le Queux, William, 156
Lerner, Laurence, 47, 51
Lesotho. See Basutoland
Lessing, Doris, 13, 133–34, 181n75
Levine, Philippa, 8
Life and Adventures of Mrs. Christian Davies, The (Defoe), 69
Life and Strange, Surprising Adventures of Robinson Crusoe, The (Defoe), 61, 62, 95, 211n98
Little Folks, 111
Lobengula, 75, 111, 207n71
Lodge in the Wilderness, A (Buchan), 138
lost race fiction. See lost world fiction
lost world fiction, 61, 198n3
Lovedale, 166–67
Love in the Wilderness (Page), 108, 110, 122, 124–25, 134, 213n2, 213n3, 220n70
Low, Gail Ching-Liang, 180n63

Makalanga, 75, 77, 82–83, 90, 97–98, 100, 102, 168, 207n71. See also Shona
male imperial romance. See imperial romance
"Man's View of Woman, A" (Haggard), 68, 185n11
Marchant, Bessie, 70–71, 206–207n64

Marie (Haggard), 103–104, 205n57, 212n114
Marquard, Jean, 46, 194n98
marriage: and choice, 21, 26–28, 41, 80–81, 91, 190n63, 192n81, 211n100; depictions of, 33, 48, 50–51, 54, 58, 69–70, 122–23, 128, 130–32, 196n118, 220n65; and emigration rhetoric, 65–66, 115–16; and inequality, 130, 216n24; and race, 228–29n51
masculinity, 35–36, 50, 63, 69–72, 81, 95, 128, 152, 180n63, 201–202n19, 210n97. See also femininity; gender; men
Mashona. See Shona
Mashonaland, 3, 111–13, 150, 160. See also British South Africa Company; Rhodesia
Matabele, 3, 90, 110–11, 113, 117, 150, 175n12, 207n71, 210n93, 234n36; depictions of, 74–75, 80, 82–84, 86–87, 90, 92–95, 149–51, 164–71
Matabeleland, 3, 74, 90, 111–13, 149
maternity, 17, 26, 32, 35, 39, 48–52, 68, 79, 97, 99, 111, 116, 126, 130–31, 173n1, 211n98
Mathers, Edward P., 1, 173–74n3
Maugham, W. Somerset, 133
Meade, L. T., 69–70, 72
memsahib, 63, 200n14
men, 26, 33, 61–62, 80, 95, 118, 130. See also gender; masculinity; women
metro-colonial issues, 32, 59, 63–64, 115–20, 139, 219n59
metropole, 8, 26, 38, 62, 64, 68, 140, 163–64, 201n19
Mfecane, 165–66
Mhudi (Plaatje), 18, 164–72, 233n33
Milner, Alfred, 136, 143–44, 224n10

mineral revolution, 3, 13–14, 19, 29, 65, 135, 153. See also diamonds; gold
Mitchell, Sally, 70, 185n13
mixed-race population, 14, 147; depictions of, 14–15, 32, 91, 102, 176n20. See also "Coloureds"
modernization, 151–52
Mofolo, Thomas, 233n32
Molema, Silas, 167
Monomotapa, 75, 149, 208n72, 226n34
Monsman, Gerald, 184n8, 197n135, 199n6
Moselekatse. See Mzilikazi
Moshesh, 142, 226n33
Mote and the Beam, The (Plaatje), 228n51
Mr. Standfast (Buchan), 157–63
"Mystery of Sasassa Valley, The" (Doyle), 11
mystical feminism, 17, 63, 74, 95–100. See also feminism
Mzilikazi, 207n71, 226n33; depictions of, 169–71

Nada the Lily (Haggard), 15, 168, 180n63, 210n88, 212n106
Namibia, 232n14. See also German South West Africa
Natal, 14, 29–30, 35, 75, 78, 147
Nathan, Manfred, 9
National Party, 10
native informant, 6. See also authorial informant
Native Land Act of 1913, 167
"Native Question, The" (Schreiner), 40
Ndebele. See Matabele
Ndwandwe, 82, 89, 209n82
New Girl fiction, 70, 104. See also juvenile fiction; New Woman novel
New Woman, 38, 40–41, 53, 115, 183n3, 187n23, 192n75, 220n68, 220n71. See also femininity; gender; New Woman novel; women

New Woman novel: conventions of, 47, 51–52; emergence of, 4, 13, 19–21, 25, 32, 44, 67; legacy of, 16–17, 67, 70, 110, 115, 126, 155. See also New Girl fiction; *Story of an African Farm, The* (Schreiner)
Ngwane. See Swazis
"Novel of the Modern Woman, The" (Stead), 183n3

Oboe, Annalisa, 194n95
Oppenheim, E. Phillips, 156
orality, 18, 164–67, 171
Orange Free State, 11, 66, 146, 174n7, 232n14. See also Orange River Colony
Orange River Colony, 3, 137, 232n14. See also Orange Free State

Page, Gertrude: and extra-marital sex, 120–26, 220n70; and gender, 115–16, 118, 126, 130–32; legacy of, 3–4, 11–12, 107, 110, 125–26, 132–34, 181n75, 213n3; photographs of, 112, 129; style of, 128–30; and politics, 114–15; and World War I, 114, 216n26. See also specific works
Painted Veil, The (Maugham), 133
"Palatial, The," 30, 36
Parker, Kenneth, 133
Passage to India, A (Forster), 201n15
Pathway, The (Page), 124
Patteson, Richard F., 72–73, 184n8
Paxton, Nancy, 63
"Pictorial Acrostic" (Page), 111, 214n13
Piesse, Jude, 8
Pilgrim's Progress, The (Bunyan), 160, 162
Plaatje, Sol T., 18, 164–72, 233n30; and feminism, 169, 236n67; and Schreiner, Olive, 236n67. See also specific works

Poor and the Land, The (Haggard), 67
Poppy (Stockley), 1, 133, 173n1, 222n80
Portuguese, 75, 77, 98, 102, 165, 174n8, 207n71
Portuguese East Africa, 159, 165
postcolonialism, 7, 62
Praed, Rosa, 71–72
Prester John (Buchan), 12, 14–15, 18, 135–36, 138–56, 161; and genre, 156–57, 227n38; legacy of, 135, 151; writing of 223n4, 232n21. *See also* "Black General, The" (Buchan)
Prester John (mytho-historical figure), 148–49, 152–53
Progress, 43
provincial novel, 47
publication process, 27, 107, 141, 166–67, 198n146
Pykett, Lyn, 220n68

race: demographics of, 3, 13–14, 66, 113, 136–37, 143–44, 181n75, 181n78; and enfranchisement, 40, 146–47, 235n56; and gender, 24, 38–40; and inequality, 34–35, 38–39, 117, 211n100; and maternity, 116. *See also* "Coloureds"; indigenous Africans; mixed-race population; whiteness
readers, 11, 43, 53, 57, 67, 70, 107, 110, 125–26, 132, 165–66, 206n58
realist novel, 16, 20–21, 51, 58, 61. *See also* domestic novel
Reform Act of 1884, 67
Replenishing the Earth (Belich), 8
Rethinking Settler Colonialism (Coombes), 8
Review of Reviews, 25
rhetoric of promise, 26, 28–29, 111, 116–17. *See also* booster literature
Rhodes, Cecil, 3, 40, 111, 150, 165. *See also* British South Africa Company (BSAC)

Rhodesia: colonization of, 175n13; culture of, 119; demographics of, 113, 215n21, 216n24; departure from, 125; and emigration, 107, 110, 130; and gender, 110, 126, 128; and identity, 114, 215n16, 217n29; perceptions of, 12, 111, 116, 119–21; and social change, 122–23, 132; and the Union of South Africa, 10, 114, 178n37. *See also* Zambia; Zimbabwe
Rhodesian, The (Page), 221n77
Rhodesian Herald, 114–15
Rhodesian settler romance, 4, 16, 110–34, 155
Rich, Paul, 181n74, 184n8
Riddle of the Sands, The (Childers), 156
Robinson Crusoe (Defoe). *See Life and Strange, Surprising Adventures of Robinson Crusoe, The* (Defoe)
Robinsonade, 69, 72
Rolong. *See* Barolong
Royal Colonial Institute, 31, 67
Royal Geographical Society, 1, 142, 227n45
Royal Infirmary of Edinburgh, 27
Rudd Concession, 210n93
Rudy, Jason R., 9

Said, Edward, 16
Saturday Review, 36
Schreiner, Ettie, 26
Schreiner, Fred, 187n30
Schreiner, Olive: and Boers, 193n93, 195n112; and feminism, 25–29, 191n73; and Haggard, H. Rider, 20, 185n9; and illness, 28, 188n35; legacy of, 4–8, 11–12, 19, 28–29, 32, 44, 185n11, 221n77, 236n67; and marriage, 26–27, 196n118; and Plaatje, Sol T., 236n67; and racial inequality, 38–40, 191nn72–73; and romance, 190–91n69;

Schreiner, Olive *(continued)*
   writing style of, 193n87, 222n80.
   See also Iron, Ralph; *specific works*
Schreiner, Theo, 26
Schwarz, Bill, 147, 177n30, 227n44
Scotland, 27, 139–40, 144, 155, 157–58
Scotland Yard, 158, 162
Scott, Ann, 28, 38, 44, 187n26
Scottish, 64, 144
Second Anglo-Boer War: and indigenous Africans, 165, 234n39; end of, 18, 60, 104, 116, 174n7; fictional characters and, 160; legacy of, 3, 14, 70, 135–36, 143, 180n63, 233n30; start of, 65–66, 187n22; and women, 70; and writers, 6–7, 11, 135–36, 180n63, 193n93, 206n60. *See also* concentration camps; First Anglo-Boer War
Second Matabele War, 3, 113, 151, 159–60, 210n93
Secret Agent, The (Conrad), 156
Sepoy Rebellion. *See* "Indian Mutiny"
sex: and autonomy, 28; and awakening, 79, 125; and desire, 17, 43, 111, 124–25, 127; extramarital, 28, 40, 43, 47, 120–26, 173n1, 195n106, 201n15, 220n70; and inequality, 28, 130, 228–29n51; and opportunity, 121, 132, 134, 201n15; as personal expression, 42; and violence / threat of violence, 63, 91–95, 146, 228–29n51; and vulnerability, 201n15
Shaka. *See* Tchaka
Shakespeare, 26, 164, 233n33
Shanks, Edward, 200n10, 207n69
Sharpe, Jenny, 63
She (Haggard), 20, 59–60, 62, 64, 68, 80, 103, 168, 184n6, 185n11, 186n19, 208n76
She and Allan (Haggard), 107

Shepstone, Theophilus, 29, 209n84, 210n95
Shona, 113, 162, 175n12, 207n71. *See also* Makalanga
Showalter, Elaine, 61
Sick Heart River (Buchan), 182n97
Siddiqi, Yumna, 157
Silent Rancher, The (Page), 124–25, 127, 132
Smith, Craig, 152
Smith, James, 53
Smuts, Jan, 138, 228n51
"Soldier's Daughter, A" (Henty), 70, 72
South Africa: anglicization of, 66–68, 136, 146, 150–54, 164; authorial informants of, 107; and British identity, 3, 18, 31; demographics of, 46, 65, 135, 167; domestication of, 64; perceptions of, 1, 4, 9–10, 26, 29, 46, 77, 101–102, 136; and race, 66, 136, 146–47; women in, 26, 29, 40, 59. *See also* Union of South Africa
South Africa and How to Reach It (Mathers), 173–74n3
South Africa: A Weekly Journal, 1–2, 19, 153, 274n5
South African Book Buyer, 174n6
South African Colonization Society (SACS), 66
South African Expansion Committee (SAX). *See* South African Colonization Society (SACS)
South African Literature (Manfred), 9
South African Native National Congress (SANNC), 233n30, 236n67. *See also* African National Congress (ANC)
South African Party, 104
South African Republic, 3, 19, 30, 54, 66, 174n7, 194n100, 197n131, 228n53. *See also* Transvaal

South African Women's
  Enfranchisement League, 40
Southern African Literature (Gray), 9
Southern African Literatures (Chapman),
  10
Spirit of Bambatse, The (Haggard),
  198n146, 199n8. See also *Benita*
  (Haggard)
Spivak, Gayatri Chakravorty, 6, 62–63,
  179n47
spy thriller, 4, 18, 135, 140, 155–57,
  224n9
Spy Who Came in from the Cold, The
  (Le Carré), 231n7
Stafford, David, 233n25
Stanley, Henry Morton, 176n16,
  198n3
Stead, W. T., 11, 13, 25, 183n3,
  187n23
Stevenson, Robert Louis, 62, 70
Stockley, Cynthia, 1, 7, 133, 173n1,
  222n80
Story of an African Farm, The
  (Schreiner): and feminism, 19, 21,
  25–27, 32–34, 36–39, 50–53, 59;
  and genre, 21, 25, 28, 32, 43–53;
  influence of, 15–16, 25, 110,
  221n77; international reception of,
  19, 183n2; as New Woman novel,
  4, 13, 16, 19, 21, 25–26, 32–34,
  37–38, 44, 51–53; perception of,
  11, 25, 43, 183n3, 184n8, 194n98,
  222n80; preface of, 19–20, 28–29,
  51, 184n5; publication process of,
  27, 183n2; writing of, 27, 29, 46,
  195n112
Strange, Nora, 133
Strobel, Margaret, 68
suffrage movement, 40, 67–69, 115,
  132, 191n73, 204–205n43, 205n50,
  216n24, 222n79
Sullivan, Arthur, 12

Swallow (Haggard), 14, 71–72, 89–92,
  97, 100–103, 209n78, 211n100
Swazis, 71, 91–92, 95, 97, 100, 102,
  150, 209n82, 210n95
Swaziland, 150, 160
Symons, Arthur, 28

Table Mountain, 2, 158
Tchaka, 142, 149, 207n71, 209n84,
  210n88, 212n106, 226n33
Tess of the D'Urbervilles (Hardy), 53
"There Is Nothing of Any Importance"
  (Page), 123. See also *Far from the
  Limelight* (Page)
Thoughts on South Africa (Schreiner),
  191n72, 193n93
Thirty-Nine Steps, The (Buchan), 155–
  60, 162–63, 182–83n97
Three Hostages, The (Buchan), 157–63,
  182–83n97
Times, 7, 66, 114, 138, 177n32,
  186n19, 215n15, 217n29
Traffics and Discoveries (Kipling), 12
Transvaal, 3, 16–19, 24, 29–31,
  35, 54, 66, 74–78, 137–40,
  146, 174n7, 194n100, 197n131,
  197n133, 210n95, 228n51, 232n14.
  See also South African Republic
Treaty of Vereeniging, 146
Trollope, Anthony, 7
Trooper Peter Halket of Mashonaland
  (Schreiner), 39–40, 191n71
Trotter, David, 224n9

Undine (Schreiner), 27–29, 185n11,
  190n65, 190n69
Union of South Africa, 3, 10, 40,
  66, 104, 114, 135, 144, 153, 167,
  174n7, 178n37, 229n54, 235n56
Union of South Africa Act, 136
Union of South Africa Treaty, 147,
  223n4

United Kingdom, 1, 6, 10, 27, 30–31, 64, 67, 139, 148, 163–65

Valente, Joseph, 220n67
van den Heever, C. M., 10
van Wyk Smith, Malvern, 10
Veldt Trail, The (Page), 134
Victoria, Queen, 3, 111, 191n72
Victoria Cross, 160
Victorian era, 8, 15, 41, 59, 63, 70, 131, 153, 196n116
Victorian femininity, 32, 36, 53. *See also* femininity
Victorian Narratives of Failed Emigration (Wagner), 9
Victorian Settler Narratives (Wagner), 9
Virginia of the Rhodesians (Stockley), 213n2, 219n61, 221n76
Voice of Missions, 228n51
voortrekkers, 90, 164–65, 169, 207n66, 234n36
Vril. See *Coming Race, The* (Bulwer-Lytton)

Wagner, Tamara S., 9
Wakefield, Edward Gibbon, 64–65
Walkowitz, Judith, 134
War in South Africa, The (Doyle), 11
Webb, Lillian Julia. *See* Stockley, Cynthia
Weenen Massacre, 90
Where the Strange Roads Go Down (Page), 117–19, 121, 124–25, 127, 220n63, 220n70, 222n79
whiteness, 13–15, 24, 38, 66, 84–85, 92–95, 111, 117, 142, 176n20, 179n53. *See also* race
White Writing (Coetzee), 9–10
Wild Honey (Stockley), 7
Willan, Brian, 235n48

womanhood, 28, 33, 59, 72–74, 77–81, 101, 110, 126–32, 188n39, 206n64. *See also* gender; women
women: and agency, 25, 67, 81–83, 104–105; and emigration, 64–67, 110; and equality, 39, 58, 72; exclusion of, 61–62, 73, 95, 227n48; and female civilizing mission, 65, 116; influence of, 15, 54, 63, 81–83, 87; and men, 118; and misogyny, 20, 185n11, 199n9; opportunities for, 37, 41, 59, 65, 69, 115; and political power, 4, 53–54, 58, 64, 69, 71, 114–15, 169; recognition of, 118, 170; as surplus, 64–69, 104, 115; as symbol of Africa, 78. *See also* femininity; gender; men; womanhood
Women's Christian Temperance Union, 205n50
Women's Franchise Ordinance, 113–14
Women's Land Army, 130, 221nn74–75
World War I, 6, 17–18, 66, 70, 104, 114–15, 131, 136–38, 155–57, 162, 164, 188n32
World War I novels, 128, 157

Year's Housekeeping in South Africa, A (Barker), 219n60

Zambesia, 111–13
Zambesia (Mathers), 173–74n3
Zambia, 216n24
Zimbabwe, 181n75. *See also* Rhodesia
Zululand, 76, 84–86, 211n100
Zulus, 29, 165, 168; depictions of, 43, 76, 82–103, 139, 141–43, 148–53, 168, 180n63, 208n74, 211n98, 211n100, 212n109. *See also* Bambatha Rebellion

www.ingramcontent.com/pod-product-compliance
Lightning Source LLC
Chambersburg PA
CBHW020641230426
43665CB00008B/264